Introduction to

COMPUTING AND ALGORITHMS

CUSTOM EDITION

Introduction to

COMPUTING AND ALGORITHMS

CUSTOM EDITION

RUSSELL L. SHACKELFORD

Georgia Institute of Technology

ADDISON-WESLEY

An Imprint of Addison Wesley Longman, Inc.

*Reading, Massachusetts • Menlo Park, California • New York • Harlow, England
Don Mills, Ontario • Sydney • Mexico City • Madrid • Amsterdam*

Sponsoring Editor: Susan Hartman
Production Editor: Amy Willcutt
Assistant Editor: Julie Dunn
Compositor: Michael and Sigrid Wile
Copyeditors: Roberta Lewis/Nancy Young/Stephanie Magean
Proofreader: Sarah Corey
Text Designer: Melinda Grosser for *silk*
Art Source: PC & F, Inc.
Cover Designer: Diana Coe

Manager of Addison Wesley Longman Custom Publishing: Lynn Colgin
Production Administrator: Cynthia Cody

Introduction to Computing and Algorithms, Custom Edition consists of materials from *Introduction to Computing and Algorithms* by Russell Shackelford (0-201-31451-7).

Access the latest information about Addison-Wesley titles from our World Wide Web site: http://www.awl.com/cseng

ISBN: 0-201-63613-1

00 01 9 8 7 6 5 4

Preface

Overview

This book, and the introductory course that it represents, are results of our efforts at Georgia Tech's College of Computing to simultaneously achieve two goals:

1. Correct some of the well-known problems of CS introductory courses.
2. Respond to a diverse audience of students who need a computing foundation.

Our efforts have gained widespread acceptance locally: Enrollments skyrocketed from 100 annual enrollments to 1400 in only two years. The course is now part of the university's core curriculum, serving more than 2600 students per year.

Thus, we have been gaining experience with both a new approach to introductory computing education and new class management techniques required by the rapid increase in enrollments. Along the way, we have instituted processes that allow us to track both student performance and student opinion. As a result, we know more about the effects of our efforts than would otherwise have been the case. This process has allowed us to have some insight about the consequences of some of the risks we took in designing the new course and to have confidence in the results, which are indeed positive.

Progress, Revision and Opportunity

Since the publication of the first edition, the pedagogical approach reflected in this book has been adopted at some twenty colleges and universities. Various other institutions are "waiting in the wings" for the publication of our associated CS-2 book, as they wish to adopt Georgia Tech's approach to the freshman year all at once. The broader population of faculty now involved in using this approach is itself a valuable asset which we hope to use wisely. Sadly, it proved to be much more difficult than originally thought to obtain the identities of the various faculty using the book. As a consequence, the electronic discussion group, which we intended to begin shortly after publication, is only now getting started. As the saying goes, "Better late than never."

Fortunately, our students are rather adept at identifying our mistakes and shortcomings. This revised edition features a host of corrections to errors identified by students and undergraduate TAs. It also features a major revision to the treatment of the object-oriented paradigm provided in Chapter 7. As it happened, that chapter

v

was a relatively recent addition to the course agenda at the time of initial publication (replacing a chapter on state machines, including Turing machines and other automata) and thus had been class-tested far less than had the other chapters. It now has been significantly revised based on the experiences of myself and others in teaching that material over the last few years. I am particularly indebted to both David Smith and Jon Preston for their input and pointed advice regarding the revision to this material.

At present, those of us involved in teaching this material at Georgia Tech are embarking on a wonderful new adventure. Faculty at several institutions within the University System of Georgia (of which Georgia Tech is one component) have expressed interest in working closely with us in an effort to evolve a viable and substantive approach to distance education. With significant support from the Georgia Tech Foundation, we are now moving rapidly to begin offering alternative means of access throughout the State of Georgia.

Faculty at some colleges want to import our lectures into their classrooms, others want to distribute our materials to their students on CD-ROM, and still other faculty wish to deliver it themselves but want to exploit our material-development resources, student-support newsgroups, etc. The common thread is that we are searching for ways to make more effective use of faculty time, which is in such short supply. Our approach is based on three principles: (1) we must use technology to support and strengthen (not replace) a strong human element in the instructional process; (2) we must provide meaningful choices at the local level, providing faculty and students with a variety of ways to access and use course materials; (3) we must establish cooperative, shared ownership of the evolving shared course. Faculty at other schools will be invited to do more than be consumers of what we develop; they will be invited to help us produce new and better materials and approaches.

As we begin the initial three-year project within Georgia, we are now also pursuing support that will allow us to work with those at schools outside of Georgia as well. We believe that this is a very important opportunity, and we are interested in hearing from any and all who might wish to participate with us.

Target Audience and Prerequisites

The target audience for this book is a broad population of college and university students. The teaching and learning agenda and supporting materials have been field tested for seven years with a student population that includes those majoring in computer science, the engineering disciplines, the natural sciences, the social sciences, mathematics, management, and architecture. We lack experience with those majoring in the humanities and the health sciences only because Georgia Tech does not offer degree programs in those disciplines.

There are no college-level prerequisites. It is assumed that students have a high school–level foundation in algebra and in reading, writing, and thinking skills.

Explanation of Approach

Several key points concerning the approach we have taken are provided in Chapter 1. The following sections of Chapter 1 are particularly relevant:

1.3 Eight Challenges to Computing Education

1.4 Seven Reasons Why Pseudocode Should Be Your First Language

1.7 Four Goals of This Book

1.1 One Key Concept

Scope of Coverage and Coverage Options

This book supports the following three-part agenda with various coverage options.

Part 1. The Computing Perspective

The agenda of this part of the text is to provide a non-technical context for the reader. Chapter 1 is new. It provides students with some perspective on both computing and computing education. Its purpose is to give students a smattering of "factoids" about various aspects of both the changing world of computing and the world that computing is changing. It is broad enough to strike one or more of the interests of most any instructor. We hope that any teacher will find something in Chapter 1 that will allow him or her to focus on whatever perspectives or developments they think are worthy of note as a student begins the study of computing. (The old Chapter 1 proved to be too controversial for some faculty and, in this edition, has become the Supplemental Chapter found at the end of the book. The Supplemental Chapter situates computing in the context of Western history and science. The goal is provide students with a perspective on computing that is about humankind's timeless search for knowledge and understanding of our world. We want this chapter to trigger questions and curiosity about issues that are a great deal broader than the usual technical context.) The purpose of both the new and old Chapters 1 is the same: to support the traditional collegiate goal of stimulating students to ponder and question "big issues." Chapter 2 follows with a high-level overview of what algorithms are, what their components are, and what it means to think in terms of algorithms.

COVERAGE OPTIONS

Subsequent chapters do not require Chapter 1 material. Thus, it can be ignored or assigned as optional reading. Chapter 2 material is basic to subsequent material and thus is not optional.

Part 2. The Algorithm Toolkit

These chapters make up the bulk of the text. In Part 2, we rapidly cover the entire range of algorithmic constructs and components in the context of a pseudocode. Chapter 3 covers basic data and operations. Chapter 4 covers procedural abstraction, including procedures, functions, parameters, and recursion. Chapter 5 covers the complete range of data structures, including records, arrays, linked lists, trees, and graphs. Chapter 6 introduces frequently applied algorithmic methods such as searches, traversals, sorting, and optimization algorithms. Chapter 7 introduces the object-oriented paradigm with associated constructs. Chapter 8 addresses issues of correctness and verification. Chapter 9 provides students with the means for understanding and estimating the cost and complexity of algorithms, and distinguishes between reasonable and unreasonable performance. As a result of mastering the work in these chapters, students will be well prepared to adapt to virtually any programming language, and will have been introduced to basic tenets of both software engineering and computer science theory.

COVERAGE OPTIONS

Chapters 3, 4, 5, and 6 are necessary, with the later chapters being dependent upon earlier ones. Chapter 7, which introduces the object-oriented paradigm, may be skipped altogether by those who do not yet teach this paradigm. For those who do, Chapter 7 may be taught directly after Chapter 6 or it may be delayed until after Chapter 9. We have experimented with teaching this material at various points in the course and currently do so following Chapter 6. Our experience indicates that introducing it earlier (immediately after Chapter 5) is not viable. However, it works if positioned between Chapters 9 and 10. The main advantage to moving it up to its current position is that this ordering provides greater opportunity for homework experience, thus helping students assimilate the material.

Part 3. The Limits of Computing

The goal here is to help students understand what computing can and cannot do. Chapter 10 distinguishes between concurrency and parallelism, then shows students how to identify the logical relationships that limit the performance gains possible via parallel processing. Chapter 11 extends Chapter 9's coverage of performance from algorithms to problems, and introduces students to the concepts of tractable, intractable, and NP-complete problems. It closes with a summary of the practical versus theoretical view of what kinds of problems computing can solve. Finally, Chapter 12 returns to the historical theme of Chapter 1 and draws parallels between the development of the various paradigms of Western history and the development of the various programming paradigms of the last 50 years.

COVERAGE OPTIONS

For a course that seeks to give students perspective on what computing can and cannot do, this section is necessary. For a course that seeks only to give students a pre-programming foundation in algorithms and related constructs, this section can be considered optional. Obviously, we favor the approach of giving students the broader perspective from the beginning of study and thus treat this material as mandatory. At the same time, we recognize that reasonable people can and do disagree about course goals and priorities, and others may wish to devote an entire term to the first two sections, leaving no room for the third.

Notes to Faculty

This text differs from the usual introductory computer science text in the following important ways:

- It acknowledges that teaching modern programming languages has become "too much" for an introductory course.

When the generic introduction to programming course first evolved in the mid–1960s, such a course was a reasonable endeavor. At that time, computer science as we know it today did not yet exist. Computing meant programming, and the programming languages themselves were quite simple. Such a course had to teach only a few things (i.e., assignment, numerical operations, atomic data types, arrays, if-then-else statements, procedures with parameters, file operations, and simple text I/O formatting). Could we teach all that in a term? We most certainly could.

In the intervening 30 years in computing, nearly everything has changed several times. Now, when we look at the agenda for introductory programming, we find not only the eight items from the original agenda, but many more besides. The agenda now includes pointers, linked lists, trees, recursion, structured design, interactive debuggers, interactive programs, human-computer interface, on-screen graphics, larger programs, software engineering, algorithmic complexity, multiple languages, application software applications, and now, object-oriented design and portable applets. The list has grown by a factor of three. Furthermore, as we go down the list we find that the complexity of each item is greater than that of earlier ones. In effect, the teaching-and-learning challenge has grown by a factor significantly greater than three.

We decided that it had become too much for our students. We had seen seniors who had developed bad habits, who did not have an adequate sense of design, and who evidenced poor software development practices. The fault was not that of the students nor the teachers. Rather, it was a flaw in the design of the instruction. With respect to foundational introductory material, there was simply too much to teach in too little time. As a result, much of it was not taught and learned effectively. Students did learn the details. They could point their pointers and traverse their data structures. But they somehow never "got" what we wanted them to "get"—an integrated view of abstraction, design, implementation, and evaluation. We observed that we never taught those things together and found it to be a small surprise that the students didn't put them together. And in large part we didn't teach those things together because there was not enough time.

- To gain time, we have chosen to bypass the many annoying details inherent in real programming languages and real programs.

Modern programming languages have several annoying aspects. Chief among them is their absolute rigidity with respect to syntax and semantics. Making programs actually work in this context can be an exercise in frustration, especially for novices. In fact, coping with the extremely rigid requirements for successful compilation and execution appears to be the single largest factor that distracts students from the key principles we want them to master. Therefore, we bypass this set of distractions by using a pseudo language that does not support compilation or execution except by a human processor. The fact that students cannot spend untold hours wrestling with a compiler saves everybody involved an immense amount of wasted time and energy.

In addition, we save considerable time by confining ourselves to essential constructs (more or less) and by ignoring the various permutations that come with real languages. For example, we save at least a week and a half by ignoring complex I/O commands in favor of simple read and print statements, a week by having a single loop construct in lieu of three or four, a half-week by having a single decision statement, and so on. In effect, we eliminate a great deal of unessential language minutiae while keeping just enough to make student algorithms understandable and unambiguous. The minimalist syntax, combined with the absence of compilation and execution annoyances, means that we can focus on important principles and their application. We know that students get distracted by the little stuff, so we eliminate a lot of it without sacrificing capabilities that support abstraction.

■ It gives students the "big picture."

Computing education is relevant to nearly everyone, and this fact means that we can no longer withhold important topics until upper-division courses. Doing so means that non-CS majors never get exposed to the material. Reducing syntax and compilation worries means that we can introduce key principles of computer science at the earliest level. Because we can truly emphasize basic software engineering principles (rather than just pay lip service to them) at the introductory level, students don't learn bad habits that later must be unlearned. Because we introduce the down-to-earth principles and application of complexity theory early, students never get a chance to become "afraid" of theory; instead, they see estimates of algorithmic performance as a natural and normal consideration.

The coupling of the algorithm-oriented lecture-and-homework agenda with the lab emphasis on using powerful software applications (such as spreadsheets and equation solvers) means that students learn to use these applications guided by the algorithmic principles of abstraction and modular design that wise use of these complex applications requires. And because students can conceptually master the complete range of algorithmic constructs in the first course, they enter the subsequent "Introduction to Programming" course knowing the big picture of what they are trying to do and why. They then progress through the programming course at a much more rapid pace, completing programs of greater size and complexity than was possible before.

■ It bridges the gap between the structured programming and object-oriented programming paradigms.

It appears that the object-oriented programming (OOP) paradigm is in the process of replacing the time-honored structured programming paradigm as the methodology of choice for many programmed solutions. The OOP paradigm is a great deal more than a set of language features. It implies a fundamentally different mindset with respect to algorithm design. At the same time, much of the world is, and will continue to be, embedded in the structured paradigm. Thus we face a dilemma. Shall we continue with the structured paradigm that is of known capability and usefulness, or shall we convert to the emerging OOP paradigm and ignore the practical disadvantages of its use for many of our students and their future employers?

We believe that, for the moment, neither option is sufficient. On the one hand, we cannot ignore the movement to OOP (in general) or to hardware-independent OOP via Java (in particular). We believe that Java-like languages, in synergy with the World Wide Web, will dramatically shape the foreseeable future. At the same time, we are skeptical of approaches that discount the structured approach, especially since it serves as the basis on which the dominant OOP languages are built and since the structured approach does indeed have its own place in the legitimate needs of many students and employers.

For the present, we opt to grow students through the structured paradigm to the OOP one. Thus, the chapters on procedural and data abstraction and on algorithmic methods establish the basics of the structured paradigm. These are followed by an introduction to the fundamentals of the OOP approach via a minimalist set of additional constructs. Thus, students are prepared for work in languages such as Pascal, Ada, C, and FORTRAN. They are also primed to "hit the ground running" and quickly get up to speed in the OOP world of Java and C++. To those who might argue that we should move more fully to an OOP orientation, we say, "Yes, but not just yet." We expect that future editions of this text may well feature a more clearly OOP orientation, but we believe that the time for ignoring the structured paradigm has not yet come. This is a time of transition in the world of software, and this edition is intentionally a transitional text.

Supplements

This text is supplemented by five resources:

1. Complete guided laboratory materials for a range of applications as described in Chapter 1 (see section 1.7.3). Links to all of the supplements can be found on the book's official Web site at http://www.awl.com/cseng/titles/ 0–201–31451–7/.
2. A complete set of lecture notes in the form of presentation quality Powerpoint slides. A set of more than 500 slides is available in both portrait and landscape orientation. These too are accessible via the publsher's web page.
3. A complete set of assignments, including quizzes, homeworks and final exam, all with detailed grading criteria. These are also available via the publishers web site.
4. The aforementioned discussion group. Adopters who wish to participate should contact the author directly at russ@cc.gatech.edu
5. The author's research and that of his colleagues. This research includes various activities concerning methods for tracking and optimization of teaching-and-learning effectiveness. Those interested in working in partnership on related projects may contact us via e-mail at curriculum.support

Acknowledgments

Within the space of only five years, at Georgia Tech we have evolved a new approach to introductory computing education and have seen it accepted as part of the university's core curriculum. From the perspective of five years ago, each of these two changes seemed unlikely, if not impossible. My friends and colleagues Peter Freeman and Richard LeBlanc have been extremely supportive and encouraging throughout the troublesome process of changing the local status quo. Indeed, they are the people who enabled these changes. In addition, Richard LeBlanc also played an active role in critiquing both the course and this text, which represents it.

The heart and soul of this project are the many, many undergraduate students who have worked as teaching assistants. It is these undergraduate students who played key roles in making the course evolve from an idea into a working process that smoothly serves more than a thousand students per term. Most have worked long hours for low pay in order to make their university a better place. There are far too many to name. Of particular note are the very special contributions of (in alphabetical order) John Brewster, Mark Canup, Charlie Carson, Becky Carvin, Dameon Kindall, Bill Leahy, Brian McNamera, Ben Parrott, Jon Preston, Roy Rodenstein, Enda Sullivan, and Brian Toothman, each of whom put their mark on one or more aspects of the course and/or this book. Each of them saw something significant that needed doing and took the trouble and the initiative to step forward and do it. Others, including Jason Bennett, Stu Bernstein, Mike Brogdon, Theresa Browne, Paul Griswold, Jim Hudson, Steven Knickerbocker, Danny Lentz, Geoff Menegay, Kristen Schaffer, Emily Stretch, and Adrian Yang also made important contributions. It has been instructive to me to find that undergraduate students have produced more constructive, valuable innovations in the introductory curriculum than have the combined populations of graduate students and faculty. Personally, I have found working with undergraduates to be a delightful and wonderful thing, and I recommend it highly.

Our approach is based on a vision that was heavily influenced by the work of David Harel. We consider his book Algorithmics: The Spirit of Computing, to be a seminal work in articulating the fundamental ideas of computer science. It was intended for "the sophisticated layperson and computer expert" alike. We have tried to adapt his agenda to the needs of the modern college student. Irrespective of whether we have succeeded or failed, it is Harel's work that prodded us to try. We are indebted to him for the ways that he reminded us of what we already knew, taught us a few things we didn't, and opened our eyes to a new realm of exciting possibilities.

Transforming a course and its agenda into a textbook is a complex and exhausting undertaking. While I had field tested a draft of the text at Georgia Tech, prior to my association with AWL it had not benefited from any focused, high-quality review. In the process of preparing this text, I received immense and invaluable assistance from the following people who reviewed and critiqued the original draft: Roger M. Smith, Yale University; Charles Marshall, SUNY at Potsdam; Stephen Fenner, University of Southern Maine; R. Phillip Bording, University of Texas at Austin; Peter B. Henderson, SUNY at Stony Brook; John Dickinson, University of Idaho; Niels da Vitoria Lobo, University of Central Florida; Ralph Bravaco, Stonehill College; and Ray Hawkins, North Carolina A&T State University. The text is significantly improved because of their effort. I am particularly indebted to them for several downright wonderful suggestions, some of which I was able to incorporate. As mentioned earlier, the important changes made to this revised edition were made possible by David Smith and Jon Preston, as well as numerous students and TAs.

Of the many fine people at Addison Wesley Longman who have done an admirable job of helping me through this process, and of putting up with me throughout it, those in the forefront include Dorothy Moore, Susan Hartman, Amy Rose, Julie Dunn, Tom Ziolkowski, and (most recently) Lynn Colgin and Cindy Cody. In addition, I owe particular debts to text editors Stephanie Magean and Bobbie Lewis who have helped me overcome some of my many stylistic writing sins. Finally, prior to my association with AWL, I was fortunate enough to receive valuable support and advice from Debbie Berridge who worked with a competing company.

Russell Shackelford
Atlanta, Georgia
July, 1999

Contents

P A R T

II

The Algorithm Toolkit   53

CHAPTER

3

Basic Data and Operations   55

CHAPTER

4

Tools for Procedural Abstraction   87

CHAPTER

5

Tools for Data Abstraction   141

CHAPTER

6

Algorithmic Methods   221

CHAPTER

7

Tools for Modeling Real-World Objects   253

CHAPTER

8

Tools for Verifying Correctness   297

CHAPTER

9

Tools for Estimating Cost and Complexity   317

PART III

The Limits of Computing 351

CHAPTER 10

Concurrency and Parallelism 353

CHAPTER

11   The Hierarchy of Problem Complexity   377

CHAPTER

12   Epilogue: A History of Computing and Algorithms   393

Supplemental Chapter: A History of Technology and Culture   S-1

The Computing Perspective

PART 1

CHAPTER 1

Computing by the Numbers: A List of Lists

What do you need to know about computing? That is an important question about which various people will have various opinions. Our opinions evolved over several years of teaching introductory courses to thousands of students from many academic disciplines. What we have learned is reflected in this book. In it, we aim to do something important: we try to give you a foundation in computing that will help you adapt and adjust to any programming language, any programming paradigm, and any set of changes that come down the road. One of the few things that we know for sure is that computing is about change, and we want to prepare you for whatever changes come your way.

We begin in this chapter with a list of lists. In it, we touch on a smattering of important things you should know about computing, about what it means to get a good education in computing, and about how we try to help you do that in this book.

1.1 Ten Facts About Computing and Change

Computing is changing the world. This much will be obvious to anyone who's been paying the slightest bit of attention. However, there are many things about this change that may not be obvious. To help everyone get up to speed, here's a list of ten facts about computing and change.

1. COMPUTING IS STILL VERY YOUNG

Computing itself is a very new discipline. A few decades ago, terms such as "computing," "information processing," and "high tech" would have made no sense, even to a very well-educated person. In the early 1960's, most colleges had no such thing as a "computer science" course. Only a couple of years ago, phrases such as "web surfing" and "e-commerce" would have been nonsense terms that had no meaning.

2. COMPUTING IS NOW A CORE DISCIPLINE

Despite its youth, computing is already emerging as a mainstream discipline, taking its place with the other sciences and arts as a field that everyone needs to know something about in order to be a well-educated citizen and to have a fair chance at success in the real world.

3. COMPUTING TECHNOLOGY IS SHRINKING THE WORLD

Just a few short years ago, time and distance were significant obstacles that kept different parts of the world isolated from one another. Computer-enabled electronic media now informs us of events around the world within seconds of their occurrence. Computer networks allow people on different continents to communicate more easily and cheaply than people only a couple miles apart could have done just a few decades ago. For many years, people have had idealistic visions of the human race as a single harmonious family rather than as groups of warring opponents. While modern communications do not make ideals real, they do allow people around the world to be more in touch than was ever thought possible.

4. COMPUTING IS CHANGING HOW HUMAN ENTERPRISE OCCURS

In only a few years, computers and networks have become the fastest-rising medium for commerce, creativity, and interaction that the world has ever seen. Regardless of whether one is buying books or ice cream, selling stock or used cars, creating educational materials or rock-n-roll music, working as a writer or as a technician, the effect is the same: one has many powerful new tools and options. What was once empty cyber-hype is now daily reality. Computing is actually transforming how people work and play, learn and teach, plan and decide, buy and sell, order and deliver, and so on.

5. COMPUTING TECHNOLOGY IS PROGRESSING AT AN EXPONENTIAL RATE

Over the last few decades, one pattern has held constant: Every couple of years, the power of our computing technology doubles. This means that the cheapest, least powerful PC that one can buy at Wal-Mart is more powerful than the pioneers who built the first computers could have imagined. The constraints of computing used to be the limits of what our devices could handle. Now, the limit is our ability of think of creative new ways to use the incredible computing power at our disposal.

6. AS COMPUTING TECHNOLOGY GETS CHEAPER, COMPUTING EXPERTISE GETS MORE EXPENSIVE

It used to be that computers were expensive and programmers and other computer-technicians were comparatively cheap. In the last twenty years, this balance has been reversed. While cheap home computers rival the power of yesterday's supercomputers, the freedom and salary requirements of people with desirable technical skills are greater than ever. People with the right set of skills can make six-figure salaries while working from their home.

7. Computing-related professionals are in short supply

As computers get faster, better and cheaper, and as our computer software gets more and more powerful, some expect that our technology will become so sophisticated that there will be a reduced need for people with computing-related skills. While this may prove one day to be true, such a day is a very long way into the future. For your generation and the generation after yours, there is and will be a need for people with a wide range of computing expertise. Recent national studies have documented the existence of a critical shortage of people with such skills, and the shortage is expected to worsen.

8. Computing technology is being built in to everything that does anything

One reason why there is (and will be) a shortage of people with needed technical skills is that the range of computing-related applications is growing by the day. It is already the case that computers have become critical components of virtually every device that does much of anything. From cars to wrist watches, household appliances to children's toys, computers have become "basic parts." Before long, computers may reside even in those things that we do not think of as devices, e.g., our clothing.

9. Computing allows us to solve problems that would otherwise be impossible

In the 1970s, automakers claimed that it was impossible to design cars that could meet emerging standards for clean air and fuel economy while satisfying consumer demand for reliability and performance. And they were correct: In the early 1970's it *was* impossible. The only reason it's possible now is that key automotive functions are under computer control. Computer-enabled discovery and problem solving is affecting nearly all realms of human activity. Regardless of whether the domain is basic science, health research, environmental engineering, global finance, or mass production, computing has changed the rules about what we are able to do.

10. The ideas of Computing are transforming how we know what we know.

In computing, we get things done via algorithms. An algorthim is the logic, the plan of attack, the recipe of action, that underlies a computer program. To get computers to do anything at all requires that we specify very precisely what it is that we want them to do. This requires a way of thinking, a mode of problem-solving, which is changing how we do research across the board. Working with computers forces us to think in certain ways, and we are discovering that those ways of thinking enable us to discover many things that we didn't know before.

1.2   Nine Advantages of the Digital World

Whenever you do computing, you are manipulating digital representations of some artifact (financial or scientific data, recorded sounds or movies, or whatever.). "Digital" refers to the representation of those artifacts in the form of binary numbers (i.e., in the "base 2" number system, in which the only numerals are 1s and 0s), so that a computer can process them. This is necessary, because processing binary data is the only thing that computers can do. Through software, we translate between forms that people understand (e.g., these words you are reading) and the form that computers understand (e.g., the digital data files in which my word processor stored them). Thus, computerization means that we represent our thoughts and creations in digital form. This simple fact provides many advantages. Here are nine of them:

1. SPACE

Processors have gotten to be tiny enough that their space requirements are negligible. Every modern digital watch or hearing aid contains a computer. Cellular phones have become quite tiny, but they could become quite smaller still if only people didn't have such a distance between our ears and mouth or need so much room for our fingers. Not only are digital devices small, but the digital data they process takes up virtually no space. An entire 20-volume encyclopedia set can be recorded on a single CD-ROM, and our ability to encode more data in less space is getting better all the time. In the digital world, size and space just isn't much of a problem.

2. TIME

Computer chips get faster and faster all the time. Every couple of years, processing power doubles. The cheapest desktop computer that you can buy would have been a supercomputer twenty years ago. Today, our computers spend most of their processing time doing nothing, sitting around waiting for us to hit a key or move the mouse. Computers are everywhere, doing things faster than we can. For example, every new car now contains several computers to manage the engine, the brakes, the exhaust, and other aspects of its operation. A car with antilock brakes, for example, has computers that monitor the rate of spin for each wheel 30 times per second or more. It constantly compares the speed of each wheel with the speed at which the car is moving. If it detects that one wheel is slowing faster than the car is slowing, then it knows that the wheel is about to lock up, so it releases the brakes on just that wheel for a split second. This goes on whenever you brake, with a computer monitoring your braking about 20,000 times per minute. You can't monitor your own braking near that well, but digital devices can do it quite easily.

3. PRECISION

Computers not only work faster than we do, they also work much more precisely than we (or our earlier mechanical devices) can. For example, one auto manufacturer achieved sufficiently clean emissions via computer control that the car satisfied aspects of California's standards for "zero emission vehicles." Of course, the car's engine was burning gasoline, so we know it was polluting at least a tiny amount, but the pollution was so small that equipment couldn't detect it. So the regulators had a new computer-based testing device invented that could measure emissions to an additional three decimal places of precision. This new device was able to recognize that some emissions were indeed being produced, nomatter that the amount was so small as to have been previously unmeasurable. The regulators then changed the standards to take advantage of this additional degree of precision. And so, we see a loop, a circle of achievement in which computers allow us to control pollution so precisely that they can't be measured, then computers allow us to measure the tiny amount of pollution, at which point we can insist on even cleaner air, and so on. Without the precision which computers provide, neither the reduced pollution, nor the increased sensitivity of pollution measuring devices, nor the tighter standards for clean air would have been possible.

4. RELIABILITY

Computers do nothing but execute algorithms expressed in computer programs. As long as a computer is executing the same program on the same data, it will behave in exactly the same way, again and again and again. This reliability, coupled with the other advantages we've mentioned, is why computers are increasingly being built into anything that does anything. Cars, coffee makers, watches, cameras, telephones, stereos, TVs, electric razors, heart pacemakers, the list is endless. Reliability is why we deploy computers to monitor safety conditions at nuclear power plants, to inform and assist combat aircraft pilots as they fly into harm's way, and to monitor the vital signs of critical care patients who are at immediate risk of death. Put quite simply, if both the computer and the software are engineered properly, they are most reliable machines ever invented by the human race.

5. CONNECTIVITY

Digital artifacts are portable, in that they can be transferred around the world in seconds with perfect accuracy. I am writing these words on a weekend in Gulf Shores, Alabama. So far today, I have received electronic reports on various aspects of computing curricula from colleagues located in Spain, South Africa, Atlanta, New York City, Scotland, Chicago, Washington, California, Korea, and Indiana. Tomorrow, I will send copies of the text of this chapter to my Publishing Manager in North Carolina, to the publishing company near Boston, to the typesetter who works from another location in Massachusetts, and to two of my colleagues in Atlanta. They will have their copies in minutes. During the coming week I will work on this chapter further, but from Atlanta. Next weekend, I will be in Richmond for a curriculum meeting, and will work on it some more from there as well. Where I am doesn't make any difference whatsoever. Of course, for certain kinds of tasks (playing baseball, for example), having people in the same place still matters. But for many kinds of tasks, location no longer matters at all. As long as I have my notebook computer and access to a telephone, I can do this from anywhere and can communicate with others no matter where they are.

6. PERSISTENCE

Not only can digital artifacts travel across space, they can also travel across time. Digital data can be recorded on media such that it will never degrade, weaken, or become unreadable. This is unlike tape recordings that are based on magnetic signals which weaken and fade over time. Each time you view or hear a digital representation, you will see it or hear it with the same degree of clarity and detail that was there the very first time. Copies of digital artifacts can be truly perfect, unlike other media. If you begin with a recording (of, say, music or a film) and then make an analog copy of it, the copy will be inferior to the original. If you then make a copy of that copy, it will be worse still. This is called "generational loss" because each generation is worse than the prior one. If you begin with a digital recording and make digital copies, each copy can be an exact duplicate of the original, with no generational loss of any kind. All that's being copied is a collection of 1s and 0s, which are easy to "get right".

7. MALLEABILITY

Digital artifacts are malleable. This means that we can alter them, modify them, manipulate them however we wish. For example, you could begin with a photo of yourself, use a scanner to digitize it so that it can be stored in a computer. Once the photo is in that form, software tools will allow you to change it in any way you desire. If the photo was taken in your dorm room, you could remove that as background and instead make it appear that you were in Paris. You can adjust the lighting effects of the picture to adjust for different times of day and angles of the sun. You can create a perfectly realistic illusion that you and someone you've never met had your photo taken together. You can have an image of yourself gradually morph into an image of your dog. You can create entire realities that never were, such as the kind of special effects that we routinely see in films and television shows. The good news is that we can shape digital images in any way at all, limited only by our imagination. The bad news is that we'll never again be able to assume that a picture is really proof of anything.

8. EXPERIMENTATION WITH IDEAS

Computers do exactly what we tell them. In general, they are flawless at doing what we tell them to do, and problems in their behavior are likely rooted in the instructions we give them. Computers thus can show us the ways in which our ideas are adequate and the ways they are inadequate. Pretend that you are an economist and have an idea about how to better manage the economy. Or that you are a social scientist and have ideas about how to design social programs to help the needy without encouraging undesirable dependence. Or that you are a mechanical engineer who has new ideas about protecting passengers in a car crash. How will you know if your ideas are good ones? With the ready availability of computers and software, you can test out your ideas in a simulation, provided that you can specify the phenomena to be simulated well enough. In a car crash, passenger safety is essentially a matter of physical forces and their impact on the human body. Since we know a lot about the Natural Sciences, we can (and car companies already have) constructed computer simulations that tell them how a car will crumple up in a crash, and how that will effect the body of a passenger, before that model of car has even been built. However, our state of knowledge in the Human Sciences isn't nearly so complete as it is in the Natural Sciences. Therefore, we don't know enough to be able to simulations that would tell us about the actual effects of economic policies or social programs. To the degree that we know how to specify those aspects of the world that matter for a given problem, we can simulate those aspects of the world and see how our ideas perform before we actually try them in the real world. To the degree that we don't know how to specify relevant aspects, then our inability to construct adequate simulations tells us exactly where our knowledge needs to grow. So, either way, we can learn something.

9. Resistance To Centralized Control

Computers and computer networks make it difficult for those in authority to control the flow of ideas. Before computers, the power over information resided in those who owned the media (newspapers, radio, TV). While the owners of the media still have tremendous power and influence (and use it to maximize their ratings), they can no longer determine which ideas and stories people can access. If a society allows its people to participate in the Internet, then those people can share ideas with others around the globe. Censorship is virtually impossible if Internet connectivity is permitted. Thus, the only way for the governmental "powers that be" to limit the ideas to which its people have access is by closing down access to the Internet itself, which would imply all manner of economic hardship for the entire society.

1.3   Eight Challenges to Computing Education

Computing has already changed the world a great deal. In fact, it has done so to the point where computing education itself must change, just to keep up. Already, we are faced with several challenges about how to best help students learn about computing. What was an adequate approach to teaching-and-learning just a few years ago is already obsolete. Here's a list of eight things that have already changed about computing education.

1. Computing Isn't Just for Computer Nerds Anymore

Only a few years ago, most college students didn't study computing. Of the few who did, many were technically oriented people who loved computers and programming. Increasingly, however, people from all academic disciplines are studying computing. Because computing now affects everybody, everybody needs to understand computing. Thus, introductory computing courses can no longer be aimed only at "techno-nerds." They now must be suitable for everybody.

2. We Don't Have Four Years To Get Important Ideas Across

As computing becomes a mainstream discipline, those students who graduate with degrees in CS are a minority of CS students. The majority of students major in other disciplines, and they study computing for only a course or two. Traditionally, however, computer science curricula have featured two years of programming courses prior to the junior and senior courses where computing's important ideas were introduced. To do that now means denying most students access to the important conceptual and intellectual contributions that computing makes to virtually all disciplines. This simple fact means that the basics of computing's important ideas must be introduced in the first courses (as we do in this book).

3. Computer Programming Is Different Than It Used To Be

When the traditional introductory computer science courses evolved in the late 60's, learning about computing usually meant learning to program in a relatively simple programming language, such as early versions of Fortran (for science and engineering problems) or COBOL (for business and accounting problems). This involved mastering the use of only eight or nine constructs. By the late 70's, such languages had been replaced by Pascal, a language that required mastery of about twice as many constructs, but which was designed for the purpose of teaching-and-learning. By the late 80's, Pascal was no longer adequate for the increasingly complicated needs of modern software. By the late 90's many introductory programming courses used "industrial strength" languages such as C++ and Java. Such languages are extremely complex and require coverage of about thirty constructs, not eight or nine, and many of the newer constructs are quite complicated. Because of this increase in the complexity of programming languages, students have a harder time learning the essentials. Thus, an introductory course should emphasize basic, universal concepts and skills, rather than focus on programming in complicated languages which overload students and interfere with their ability to tell what's important. That's one role for this book: as a primer to make sure you master the basic constructs before you move on to programming in a complex production-quality language.

4. APPLICATION PROGRAMS ARE NOW COMPLEX AND POWERFUL

Off-the-shelf computer programs (such as word processors, spreadsheets, databases, and web browsers), are called "application programs." Traditionally, such programs were not used in computer science courses because they were thought to be not worthy of attention. Instead, people were expected to learn them on their own. In recent years, however, such programs have become very powerful and very complex. In fact, for many kinds of problems, using an application program is the smart solution. The boundary between "programming" and "using software packages" has become blurred, such that the same principles that underlie effective program design (such as modularity, abstraction, reusability and other topics covered in this book) also underlie the effective use of application programs. Thus, the proper use of such software tools requires an adequate foundation in good principles. While students may indeed learn how to *operate* such programs on their own, learning to use them wisely is another matter. Ignoring powerful applications deprives students of guidance in their effective use and misses opportunities teaching important computing principles. That's why the labs associated with this book focuses on using software applications.

5. KEY PRINCIPLES MATTER MORE

As computer hardware has become cheaper and cheaper, we ask computers to do more things for more people. One big effect of this is that computer software has become more and more complicated. In fact, the complexity of software, and the associated difficulties of designing and building software to work properly, has lead to the creation of an entire discipline, called Software Engineering. In general, software programs have become so large, so complicated, and so interdependent on one another that the key principles of Software Engineering are more important than ever. That's one reason why this book focuses on the algorithmic principles that are the foundation of Software Engineering: We want students to understand those principles early.

6. We Can't Rely On Small Projects To Encourage Good Habits

The academic calendar makes it difficult to teach computing properly. In college, student work is divided into courses that last for only small chunks of time (usually 15 weeks for semesters or 10 weeks for quarters). This means that the course projects you do must be small enough to complete in that time. Moreover, in the early computing courses, it's important that you get practice with each concept or construct as you encounter it. As a result, there are usually several projects over the term. This means that each project must be small enough to be completed in a week or two. This simple fact causes problems. Many of the crucial things involved in doing computing properly come from the fact that real projects are large and complicated. Because academia doesn't give you much of a chance to work on large projects, it naturally happens that students develop habits based on their experience with small projects. Unfortunately, the effect of this is that students often learn bad habits (i.e., "small project" habits). We cannot change this; it is built in to the structure of academia. But we can try to minimize it by focusing on those things that are important for large projects. That's why this book spends more time discussing how to use constructs properly than how to "debug" a program. You'll learn debugging in subsequent programming courses. We think it's more important to get key principles across first, principles about how to use the various algorithmic constructs properly. That way, you'll know how to use them wisely when you get to a programming course.

7. Limitations Are Important

One of the nice things about the discipline of computing is that computer scientists know a good deal about the limits of computing. There are certain kinds of problems for which computing is very useful, but there are other kinds of problems (including those that would seem to be "number-crunching" problems) for which computing is of no use at all. At a time when computing is being hyped as a solution to all manner of problems, it's important for citizens to know about the limitations of computing. We should teach basic material about this in the introductory courses, which is why the third section of this book is about the limits of computing.

8. Programming Languages Aren't Necessarily The Best Way

In programming courses, student grades are based largely on programs which students submit throughout the term. Regardless of how much we emphasize principles (such as abstraction and design), as the deadline for a program nears, students naturally tend to forget all that and instead focus on getting their programs to somehow work. As a result, we find that students in programming courses spend their time manipulating an increasingly complex set of language constructs and features without adequate attention to the principles that govern their effective use. While faculty may *intend* that students obtain a foundation in important algorithmic principles, students often focus on the *manipulation* of the constructs and environments while ignoring as much as possible the principles of design and abstraction which underlie their effective use. The result is that many students leave such courses complaining that they managed to get their programs to work but that they aren't sure what they learned, i.e., they don't have the "big picture" of *what* they were doing or *why* they were doing it. Which leads us to the topic of our next list: Pseudocode.

1.4 Seven Reasons Why Pseudocode Should Be Your First Language

In this book, we don't use a real programming language. Instead, we use a "pseudocode." The prefix "pseudo-" means "pretend." Thus, "pseudocode" means "pretend code" or "fake language." Of course, you might wonder, "Why in the world should I go to the trouble of learning a fake language when I could be learning a real one?" That's a very good question. There are several good answers.

1. The "Baby Duck" Problem

Perhaps you've heard about the phenomena of "imprinting." The classic example concerns baby ducks. It seems that baby ducks of a certain age become imprinted on whoever or whatever plays the role of mother. In experiments when a person or a doll (rather than the "mother duck") played the role of the mother, the baby ducks developed the habit of following after that particular person or doll as if it were their mother. Later, when their mother was returned to them, they never accepted her in the mother role. The term "imprinting" refers to this phenomenon wherein the baby ducks were "programmed" to accept only the first example of the "mother role," regardless of who or what it was. It appears that a similar thing happens with students and programming languages. Students tend to get "imprinted" on whatever language they first learn and think that first language is somehow "best." The problem with this is that no programming language is "best." Every programming language was invented for a particular purpose and is usually more useful for that purpose than for other purposes. Furthermore, every programming language has weaknesses (such as poorly implemented features, or awkward syntax, or missing features, or features that encourage bad design). Thus, when students favor their first language, they accidentally favor the poor aspects of that language.

We want students to be able to tell the difference between good features and bad, to know what is good and bad about a given programming language, and to pick the best language for the job at hand. When we surveyed advanced students about this, most all reported that they had had to learn their third or fourth programming language before could do this and began to realize that their first language wasn't best. This is unfortunate, especially since many students never have reason to learn three or four different languages. Therefore, pseudocode is good as a first language precisely because it isn't real. Each student knows that it is a language for learning basic principles. Because it's not a real language, we've been able to include many desirable language features in it. In subsequent courses, where students use a real language, they can compare that language to pseudocode and evaluate the real language for both good and bad features. The purpose of pseudocode is to imprint you on good features and practices so that you'll take good habits with you when you later work with real languages.

2. The Big Picture In A Single Course

We've already mentioned how complicated programming languages have become. Modern languages have three to four times as many constructs as did earlier languages, and using all of them properly requires both discipline and an understanding of basic principles. Because of the explosion of language features, it has been many years since a single programming course could cover all of them. As a result, many colleges introduce programming over a span of two courses. One problem with this approach is that students in the first course can't really get the "big picture" of algorithmic constructs, as many are withheld for the second course. By using pseudocode, we can introduce the full range of algorithmic constructs in a single course. We can do this because we eliminate many unessential details of real languages, and because students don't have to worry about the many complications of debugging. As a result, students can enter a subsequent programming course already understanding algorithmic constructs and their proper use, and are then free to focus on issues of program implementation, testing, debugging, etc. In colleges where students can choose among programming courses that use different programming languages, this allows all students to get a common set of foundational principles in a shared first course. Then, students can branch off and apply that foundation to whatever programming language is appropriate to their needs.

3. MINIMIZING ANNOYING DETAILS

In virtually every real programming language, there are many details that must be dealt with simply to satisfy some requirement of making that language work on a computer. This is especially true in modern production quality languages. For example, C++ and Java each have many complicated and annoying details that must be dealt with. For most students, such things are distractions that interfere with their mastery of the essentials. Because pseudocode isn't a real language, we can dispense with most of these annoying details and instead give students simplified constructs that make the important ideas clearer. In addition, most programming languages are quite similar and have many constructs in common. But how is a student to know this? How can a student who is just learning about such things be expected to tell the difference between an important construct and an annoying detail? Most students cannot. We use pseudocode to show students the important and universal algorithmic constructs without causing students to confuse those constructs with annoying, unimportant language details. The fact that pseudocode can express important universal constructs without too much detail is why most computer scientists use pseudocode, and not a real language, when they develop solutions.

4. DESIGNED FOR TEACHING

As we said earlier, each programming language is designed in a particular context for a particular purpose. Fortran was designed for science and engineering applications, COBOL for business and accounting use. Among more modern languages, Java is used for the development of much of the software you might find on the World Wide Web. However, it wasn't originally designed for that purpose. Originally, it was intended as a language for programming new generations of household appliances that are expected to talk to one another. Both Java and C++ inherit much of their terse syntax from the C language. It is well known that this kind of syntax often confuses students and makes programs quite difficult to understand. Why was C designed to have such with such a troublesome syntax? Because it was designed at a time when computer programs were typically printed on teletype machines that were quite noisy. Thus, the terse syntax isn't there to help with programming but rather to reduce the amount of mechanical clatter that a teletype machine makes when printing a program! Unfortunately, the fact that we don't have to use noisy teletypes anymore doesn't make understanding C programs any easier. Pseudocode was designed explicitly for teaching. In some ways it is similar to the old teaching language, Pascal. In many ways it is simpler than Pascal. Yet it has more modern features. It evolved over a period of years of active use with thousands of students. We tried to invent the most minimal language that would still support desirable features, such as strong data typing, structured and object-oriented paradigms, an appropriate mix of high- and low-level constructs, and so on.

5. Don't Just React. Think!

Anyone who has ever written computer programs knows that it can be frustrating. Computers, by their very nature, do exactly what you tell them to do. This is often quite different from what you *meant* to tell them to do. Furthermore, most programming languages have many, many small details that must be perfectly mastered or else the program won't run. When students first try to program they often spend a great deal more time and energy debugging their programs than they do writing them. Many students report that debugging drives them nuts, requiring countless hours reacting to the various error messages that their programs cause. We think this is a bad way to learn the basics. We don't want you spending most of your time reacting to whatever bad things your program might do. Instead, we want you thinking about what your program should be doing and how it should be doing it. By their very nature, real languages tend to distract your attention to your flaws and errors. We want you to learn about good solutions first, then learn how to master errors later, after you know what a good solution looks like.

6. Evaluating Your Own Code "By Hand And Mind"

Using a real programming language means that you can run your program on a computer to see if it really works. At first glance, this seems to be a good thing. If you are going to learn how to program, you will indeed need to execute your program to insure it works, discover how it doesn't, repair your errors, and so on. This is proper and necessary. However, there is a downside to learning about algorithms this way. Students quite naturally focus their attention so much on making their programs "get the right answer" or "produce the correct behavior" that they forget about principles of good design and implementation. The very fact that you cannot run a program written in pseudocode means that you will not be distracted by running your program to see what happens. Instead, the only way that you can evaluate the correctness of your algorithm is to check it "by hand and mind." Research tells us that programmers who pay close attention to their programs by checking them before running them actually spend significantly less time producing successful programs. In contrast, those programmers who simply write a program and then run it "to see what it does" spend more time. We want you to develop the good habit of evaluating your own code, not just for correctness but also for good design as well. While students could check their programs first, in our experience they don't (especially with a deadline looming). The best way we know get you to check your own code properly is to use a language like pseudocode that you "must" check yourself rather than relying on program execution to reveal errors to you.

7. Getting Someone Else To Look At Your Code

One of the "dirty little secrets" of computer science education is that many student programs are graded without a teacher actually looking at them. The student's program can be run to see if produces the correct answer or behavior, and can be graded on that basis without any evaluation of design or implementation quality. This does not happen to everyone, of course. Many instructors go through each student's program in detail, making annotations about the ways it is good and the ways that it requires improvement. Unfortunately, even the best instructors are sometimes pressed for time. When this happens, programs written in a real language can be run on a computer to see if they behave properly, then given a cursory examination of design and implementation style. This takes less time than is required to sit down and really look at a program thoroughly. I know several instructors who I fully respect as good people committed to doing a good job, yet they often do this simply because other matters are pressing on them and they don't have enough time. I have done the same thing myself. One of the good things about pseudocode is that this sort of "quick and dirty" grading is not an option. In the same way that pseudocode means that you must evaluate your own code "by hand and mind," it also forces whoever grades your work to do the same. In fact, some instructors have told me that they think this is one of the best things about pseudocode: it forces them to actually examine student code. While this takes more time, they feel that it is well worth it, as they are better able to see exactly where students are strong and exactly where they need to get stronger.

1.5 Six Stages of Effective Problem Solving

When using a computer to solve any kind of complex problem, regardless of whether that means writing a program or using an off-the-shelf application program, one does not just "sit down and type." While such an approach can indeed produce a quick and dirty solution, it is unlikely to produce a good solution that will work reliably in various circumstances. To arrive at good solutions to complex problems, one must progress through six stages to develop a good and thorough solution.

1. Analysis

This is the part of the job where one clarifies the nature of the problem and the requirements of the solution. For example, imagine that your job is to construct a solution that will keep track of where a shipping company's trucks are when they're out on their various routes. There are many different things this might mean. Before going any further, one must clarify exactly what everyone needs, wants, and expects. As the saying goes, "the devil is in the details," and failing to get a firm agreement about what all those details might be is a formula for sure disaster. This stage of activity is beyond the scope of this course. Instead, problems will be provided to you that are already rather well-specified. Should any assignment be unclear in any way, you should be sure to clarify exactly what is expected. If you don't, then you are risking the same kind of result that one can get from poor problem analysis: you might create a perfect solution to a problem that is somewhat different from what the customer (or instructor) requires.

2. ABSTRACTION

Abstraction is a crucial concept in computing. It means "separating the essential idea from a particular embodiment of it." For example, the idea of a triangle goes beyond the particular details of any one triangular shape we might draw, just as the idea of a shoe is broader than whatever particular shoes you might be wearing. In computing, we want to create solutions that are broadly applicable. For example, if we were to create a program to add up a list of numbers for us and produce their sum, we'd want our program to work if the list became longer or shorter. To do this, we must be careful to design our solution so that we "abstract out" the essential task of "summing a list of numbers" from the particular details of how many numbers are in a particular list. Throughout this book we emphasize abstraction and remind you to use algorithmic constructs to achieve good abstraction.

3. DESIGN

Design refers to the plan for a given software solution. Just as one would not begin to build a modern house without a set of blueprints, so too must we have a design for software solutions before we start to build them. Students often overlook this need. There are three main reasons for this. First, students are generally not very experienced with building software solutions, so they haven't experienced all the things that go wrong when trying to build something without a good design. Second, college courses generally give students small "toy problems" to solve, and many of these "toy problems" can indeed be solved without much of a plan, just as a small shed or shack can be built without blueprints. Thirdly, in college, solutions constructed by students are of interest only until they are completed and submitted for a grade. Once a student submits his or her program, it's usually time to forget about that one and move on to the next one. In the real world, once a solution is built, it is used by others, its flaws are revealed, repairs are performed, and the true costs of "bad design" become evident. In the real world, creating the solution is the cheap part. As much as 80% of the cost of software lies in "living with it" after it is built. College students generally don't realize this. In this book, we emphasize good design by making sure you know both when to use the various algorithmic construct and how to use them properly.

4. IMPLEMENTATION

Implementation refers to the actual construction of a solution. If the job is creating a computer program, then the implementation stage is when the programmer actually writes the code. Many students tend to treat this as if it were the first phase. Notice that it is really the fourth step. In this book, we emphasize proper implementation at a high level, which means that we care primarily that you can implement pseudocode algorithms that feature good abstraction and design.

5. EXPERIMENTATION

Once the code is written, does it work as intended? It is not enough to assume or hope that it does. Rather, the solution must be systematically tested against various sets of test data to provide convincing evidence that it does indeed function as intended. This aspect is part of our lab agenda vis-à-vis application programs, and it should be a central component of any subsequent courses in programming.

6. EVALUATION

Once we know that a solution works, we must still ask "is it a good solution for the problem?" For example, a program might reliably produce correct results, but might take too long to do so, or feature a user interface that makes it hard for people to use, or require more memory than the target machines might have, etc. This is another aspect that should be a central component of a subsequent course in computer programming.

1.6   Five Concerns Of Growing Importance

Computing is changing in many ways. There are many ways in which the old "rules of the game" no longer apply in the ways that they once did. While some of these concerns are beyond the scope of this course, they are good things for you to keep in mind as you see the changes in the world of computing unfold around you. We've picked five of them, just to get you thinking.

1. A NEW VIEW OF "EFFICIENCY"

Until rather recently, one of the major priorities of computer programmers was something they called "efficiency." By efficiency, they meant the degree to which a computer program required the use of computer hardware resources to solve a problem. The main resources that programmers worried about were time and space. Time means "how long will this program tie up the computer's main processor?" Space means "how much computer memory does this program require?" These concerns were once quite important, as computer hardware was very expensive and in short supply. Programmers became quite adept at using various tricks and techniques to create programs that were efficient, i.e., that didn't require more processor time or memory than was absolutely necessary. In recent years, however, the economics of computing have changed as hardware has become quite cheap. As a result, we are using computers to do things that are more complicated and the programs we create are much larger and more complex. With the increase in the complexity of our software, a new problem emerged: we discovered that creating large and complex software is quite difficult and expensive. The new economics of computing mean that we care less about how much processor time or memory a program uses. Instead, we care that a piece of software can be easily *maintained*, so that we can easily find and fix errors. We also care that software can be *reused*, so programmers can write new programs by using program components that have already been written and tested (instead of creating all parts of a new program from scratch). In most circumstances, we are willing to sacrifice time and space in return for reuse and maintainability. This change means that programmers must go about their business quite differently than before, with a different set of priorities. The tricks and techniques that were useful for making programs run fast in small memory also make programs hard to maintain and reuse. Thus, many assumptions that you might find in programming books are not only obsolete but also counterproductive. In this book, we try to emphasize ways to construct algorithms that support the modern concerns, not the old ones. For those of you who have a programming background, this might mean that you have to break old habits to develop new ones.

2. THE DIFFERENCE BETWEEN DATA AND INFORMATION

For most of the brief history of computing, people used computers to process data. In most organizations, the computing department used to be called the "Data Processing Center" or something similar. Of late, we see a change in terminology. In many organizations, the computing department is now called the "Office of Information Technology" or the like. This change, from "data processing" to "information technology" is indicative of a change in what we want from computing. Our needs and expectations have risen to the point where we are no longer content with data; what we want now is information. What is the difference? "Data" refers to some set of facts. "Information" is useful knowledge based on some data. Consider the problem of evaluating whether or not a given baseball player is a good a hitter. We can easily track certain data about a hitter's performance, e.g. batting average, runs batted in, slugging percentage, and so on. But do they really tell us how good a hitter someone is? No, because the context and its implications must also be considered. If someone hits for a high average, bats in many runs and hits numerous home-runs, is that person a good hitter? It depends. If those data reflect the performance of a 25-year-old man playing in the major leagues, then they would indicate one thing. But if those data reflect his performance in neighborhood games against 12-year-old boys, then we would conclude something quite different. Processing data is rather straightforward; generating useful information is much more complex. With each passing year, the need for finding ways to use our computing technology to help us obtain useful information grows. Corporations are no longer content to use computers to process payroll or track inventory. They want information technology to help them recognize their problems and solve them, identify their challenges and meet them. People who have expertise in such things will be in great demand for many years to come.

3. THE SHIFT TO DISTRIBUTED SYSTEMS

Until recently, each computer did its own work and each program ran on a single computer. That is now changing. Through the combination of the World Wide Web (which allows computers from around the globe to communicate with each other) and modern object-oriented programming languages (such as Java), we can now create computer programs that don't reside on any one computer. Instead, you might find some program on the web and tell it to run. That program may consist of several program components that cooperatively do whatever the program's job is. One part of the program might be on a computer in Chicago while another part of the program is on a machine in Atlanta. A third part might be on a machine in Tokyo, with another part in London, and so on. If we think of a computer as something that runs a computer program, where is the computer that runs this one? In fact, it's distributed all over the globe. There is no single computer running the program. Instead, there is a network of computers that are cooperating with one another to do the job. This is what is known as *distributed computing*. You take advantage of it every time you use a bank's ATM machine to get cash from your bank account. And we are seeing more and more examples of it everyday. Making distributed computing work requires object oriented programming. After teaching you the basics of conventional (or "structured") programming in the early chapters, we introduce you to the basic ideas of object-oriented paradigm in Chapter 7.

4. Interfaces for Interaction

Most people who use computers now do so via a Graphical User Interface (or GUI, pronounced "gooey") as provided by Windows or Apple MacIntosh software. Before GUIs, computer users had to interact with the computer by typing commands on the keyboard. For any given computer program, a user might have to remember hundreds of cryptic commands. A good GUI allows people to learn to use it without study or memorization. The current crop of GUIs are better than they old ones, but we have not solved all the problems of user interface. Now that computers (and thus their owners) communicate with one another via the WWW, there is a whole new set of interface issues to be solved. How can we create group-oriented software (or "groupware") that allows people at different physical locations to cooperatively solve problems or create useful things without working face to face? How can we create software that will show the user those web pages or e-mail messages that he or she wants to see, but not clutter up the screen (and the user's life) with those that are of no interest? How can we create software that will allow a programmer to know which existing program components might be useful for whatever that programmer is trying to do? How can we create software that will help a user interact with data in a way that helps that user discover information? These are problems that have less to do with technology and more to do with people. And it will take professionals who understand both the technology and human nature to solve them.

5. Effects on Society

Computing has already changed many things about how the world works, and is changing more things all the time. History teaches us that change usually has both good and bad aspects. The industrial revolution allowed us to produce better and better goods, but it also caused workers to work indoors in conditions that were often unhealthy. The automobile has given us great freedom about where we go and where we live, but it has also threatened the environment and contributed to the breakdown of both communities and families as people routinely move hundreds or thousands of miles away from home. In what ways will we see the same kind of tradeoffs in the ways that computing changes things? If people can do their work from anywhere in the world, might it be a bad thing to no longer really know one's coworkers? If people communicate more and more by e-mail, might we lose a good feel for who each other really is? If computing helps us interact with people around the globe, might it also cause us to interact less with the people next door? These are large, fuzzy questions that have no easy, clear-cut answers. Will we be able to learn from the history of the good and bad changes that earlier technology brought and thus minimize the bad changes that computing might bring? Or are we destined to follow the technology blindly to where ever it might take us? Who will be the ones to study such things and keep us informed? What kind of education will best enable people to ask the right questions and obtain sound answers?

1.7 Four Goals of this Book

This book is different from other introductory computing textbooks. This is because we're trying to do certain things. What are those things? We have four goals, summarized below.

1. PROVIDE A TRUE INTRODUCTION TO THE FIELD

Unlike introductory courses in other disciplines, traditional introductory CS courses have failed to provide substantive coverage of the conceptual and intellectual foundations of the discipline. Instead, we have always had students "do programming" from the very beginning of study without providing them with a foundation. What subject matter is relevant for an introductory course in computing? The approach we have taken is to acknowledge that the central concept that underlies computer science is the algorithm and thus we make algorithms the central object of study. This approach calls for the introduction of basic ideas, including both essential algorithm constructs and certain foundational aspects of theory, tailored to students at the freshman level.

2. PROVIDE CONCEPTUAL CONTENT

The immense impact of computing has made it necessary for all college students to possess basic computer-use skills. At many colleges, there has been rising demand for basic instruction in the use of computers and of standard software applications. Often, this has resulted in the creation of pre-programming courses focused on the computer as a tool, i.e., teaching students to use software applications. We emphatically agree that an introductory computing course should include this focus, but we do not agree that such a focus is sufficient. In our view, "application use" is primarily a skills issue and thus is properly the focus of a lab agenda. It is lacking in substantive content, and one can therefore question whether it is inappropriate as the basis for a college-level course. To us, offering college credit for learning how to use a spreadsheet is uncomfortably analogous to an Electrical Engineering department offering college credit for learning how to solder, or a Mechanical Engineering school giving academic credit for a course in welding. Thus, we have developed a two-pronged approach. The first prong is the lecture-and-homework component reflected in this book. It focuses on conceptual tools for constructing and analyzing algorithms. We believe that this lecture-and-homework agenda should be similar at various colleges regardless of institutional specifics.

3. SUPPORT THE DEVELOMENT OF SOFTWARE SKILLS

The second prong of our approach is the lab-and-project component that focuses on a variety of standard software applications. In contrast to the lecture-and-homework agenda, the lab agenda will naturally vary somewhat from school to school, based on institutional mission and on local computing resources. Our lab agenda is implemented in an environment of generic PCs and PC-based software, with telnet access to centralized UNIX resources. In principle, it can be implemented in a range of local environments. Our lab agenda consists of four modular components: *Communications Tools and Facilities,* a four-week module that introduces e-mail and newsgroups, text and graphics editing, desktop publishing, and HTML home page creation. *Data Processing Tools and Facilities,* a four-week module that introduces databases, spreadsheets, and equation solvers. *A Taste of Programming,* a six-week module that prefaces the second course, "Introduction to Programming," by introducing the basics of Matlab and Java, including component construction and rapid prototyping, in a way that is intended to be stimulating and fun. *Lab Skills Evaluation,* a "show me you can do it" lab-based final exam that occurs during the last week of class. Further information about our lab agenda and supporting materials may be obtained by your instructor or other faculty who adopt the book for use in their classes.

4. PREPARE YOU FOR PROGRAMMING

The complaints of faculty who teach traditional "Introduction to Programming" courses are remarkably similar. Students in such courses can be counted upon to ignore good practices of design and implementation, to doubt the value of documentation, to evidence poor abstraction in their programs, to show a tendency to "hack" solutions, all the while largely ignoring faculty's words of wisdom about how to "engineer" a good program that will do the job properly. These and similar teaching-and-learning problems are remarkably widespread. In our view, each of them is a natural consequence of the traditional introductory approach to programming that (a) blurs together design and implementation issues, (b) presents students with program implementation tasks too early, and (c) focuses lecture on the language-specific implementation of generally applicable constructs. We believe that the traditional approach errs by giving students experience in a narrow language-specific context (thus defeating effective abstraction). At the same time, it puts students into programming situations in which they must satisfy algorithm-execution requirements (thus implicitly focusing student attention on implementation, not design). The results are predictable: Students quickly lose all sense of design and abstraction as they "wrestle with a compiler at 2 a.m." Any trace of an engineering attitude is quickly replaced by desperate prayers such as, "let's try putting a semicolon here and, oh please, let it work!" We believe that overcoming such problems requires that we separate the treatment of (a) effective design and abstraction from (b) implementation and testing. Our experience tells us that if we fail to separate these two aspects, students' desperation concerning the latter is guaranteed to overwhelm and distract their attention from the former. Thus, we use this book to focus your attention on logical abstraction and design in the first course so that you may enter a subsequent programming course knowing what you are trying to do. Essential algorithmic concepts and techniques are introduced in this book. This in turn liberates the second course to focus on effective implementation, testing, and debugging skills and strategies. In short, we think that the secret to preparing you for programming is to simply give you some good preparation. We believe that to do otherwise (especially at a time when complex languages such as C++ and Java are used in introductory courses) is unwise and actually hurts the learning process.

1.8 Three Aspects of Computing

There are three aspects of computing. In this course, we want you to become familiar with the first, get stronger at the second, and become explicitly aware of the third. We describe each below.

1. TECHNOLOGY

By technology, we refer to the actual physical devices: the computers, screens, modems, keyboards, etc., that you buy and use. We also refer to the software that you buy, download for free, or create: the programs that you run on the computer to do things. The technology is a collection of products that you can acquire and use. You may or may not choose a career in which you help create this technology. Regardless, you will be acquiring and using new technology throughout your life.

2. SKILLS

By skills, we refer to those things that you learn how to use a computer to do: using the technology to complete tasks and solve problems. Depending on the lab agenda that your instructor chooses for this course, you might gain basic proficiency with spreadsheets, databases, communications software, web browsers, and equation solvers. In addition, you will become familiar with one or more computer operating systems (UNIX, Windows, MacOS, etc.). You may also learn how to construct your own web pages, establish links to others, and so on. All these things are skills that can support you immediately by qualifying you for any number of part- or full-time jobs. They can also support you by enabling you to utilize them in ways that support work in your chosen major. More important than any of these particular skills, however, is the generic ability to learn to use software. For this reason, we recommend that you gain experience in learning to as many software packages as you might be curious about. Learning to use a given piece of software isn't nearly as important as is "learning how to learn" new software. This is something that one can learn only through experience, so the more practice you get, the stronger your ability will be.

3. WAYS OF THINKING

Using computers well requires certain ways of thinking. These are similar to the kind of thinking that you will acquire by creating algorithms in a programming language and/or in the pseudocode we use in this book. The homework problems you will solve, the projects you will do, all these will help you get better at subdividing problems into smaller, more manageable parts, specifying detailed "recipes of action" by which solutions can be constructed, and so on. This kind of thinking can help you become stronger at problem solving in general, either within or beyond the discipline of computing.

1.9 Two Ways that Computing Teaches Us About the World

The term **computing perspective** refers to a way of looking at the world, and at phenomena in it, as if reality were governed by a computer program. This does not mean that reality is governed by a computer. It only means that it is useful to think of phenomena as if they were. This perspective is useful in two important ways.

1. AN ALGORITHMIC CONCEPTION OF PHENOMENA

The computing perspective allows us to see problems as a different kind of puzzle, to understand them in terms of information and communication. For many kinds of problems, this is more useful. For example, consider medical researchers who have been trying to solve the puzzle of treating and preventing cancer. Until recently, they viewed the cancerous tumor itself as the problem. In the last two decades, however, the thrust of cancer research has evidenced the algorithmic approach. Researchers now believe that the cancer itself is not the problem but rather a symptom. Evidently, we all get cancer routinely and, for those of us who remain healthy, cancer is routinely destroyed by our immune system. Researchers study the immune system to learn how to strengthen or augment its ability to prevent cancer from prospering in the body. The computing perspective enables them to ask crucial questions: What process enables a person's immune system to recognize the presence of cancerous cells? What "information" is the immune system picking up? How is this process different than the process that causes another person's immune system to ignore those same kinds of cells? If an immune system recognizes the presence of cancer, how does one part of this system "send instructions" to another part in order to destroy the cancer? How is this process different in a system in which cancer is recognized but not effectively killed? What interferes with one part of the immune system "communicating with" another part, thus allowing the cancer to survive? In asking these kinds of questions, the researcher is thinking of the human body as if it were a computer governed by a computer program. In some people, the "program" (the immune system) processes "information" (biochemical "signals") about cancer more effectively than does the "program" of other people. In effect, researchers are trying to figure out how to "debug" the immune system, much like computer programmers seek to find and correct errors in a computer program. Of course, this is not to say that the immune system *is* a computer program (it's not), nor that the cells *are* computers (they aren't). Instead, it means that it is useful to think of them "as if" they were. Nor does it mean that medical researchers are particularly knowledgeable about computing. The medical researcher may not be *aware* that he is applying a computing model, and may not even know what the word "algorithm" means. But he is thinking that way nonetheless.

2. A MEANS OF SIMULATION AND EXPERIMENTATION

The computing perspective also allows us to use computers to simulate and experiment with phenomena that we otherwise could not study. For example, when doctors are concerned about the state of a patient's brain or other critical organ, they cannot simply cut the patient open just to have a look. However, technicians can use computers that process ultrasound or magnetic resonance signals to create accurate visual images of what doctors cannot see. When engineers want to analyze the safety aspects of automobile design, they cannot strap people into car, then crash them into a wall at 50 miles per hour just to see what happens to them. However, they can and do crash cars occupied by inanimate dummies connected to computer sensors that gather data on the various forces and shocks. When economists seek to study the complexities of economic phenomena, they cannot arbitrarily implement a series of experimental economic policies just to see what happens. Doing so could wreck the economy, ruin businesses, and put millions out of work. However, by constructing algorithmic models of economic behavior, they can simulate the economy and use real-life scenarios to improve the adequacy of their model. Experimentation is crucial to science and discovery, and computing allows us to experiment with new things in new ways.

1.10 One Key Concept

1. THE ALGORITHM

As we shall see in later chapters, algorithms are the "logical recipes" that underlie computer programs. To put it another way, a given computer program expresses an algorithm in some particular programming language. The goal of an algorithm is to externalize some capability that has heretofore required a human mind so that we can have an electronic box perform tasks that *used to require* a person's mental work. Researchers on the cutting edge of virtually every discipline rely on some form of algorithmic model. From economics to medical research, from social theory to financial analysis, from basic science to city planning, from weapons development to human psychology, virtually all cutting edge research relies on algorithmic models in fundamental ways. The algorithm is providing both the foundation for scientific development and the conceptual framework in which we understand a broad range of phenomena. In fact, in virtually all aspects of science, business, and industry, the "way of thinking" that is implied by computing is changing not only what we do, but how we think. If you want to be at the leading edge of your profession, *whatever that profession might be,* you will be using computers and you will be influenced by algorithmic models of whatever phenomena your work focuses upon. This does not mean that you will have to *program* computers in the traditional sense. It does mean that it is advisable for you to have a solid foundation in understanding computation and how "computer people" think and solve problems. Irrespective of your career goals, you should understand that computing is increasingly providing the conceptual framework in our society. In order to be a well-educated citizen of the twenty-first century, you will have to understand the basic foundations of computing, to view the world from the "computing perspective." To do so means, quite simply, that you learn to think in terms of algorithms, and learn what algorithms can and cannot accomplish. In the rest of this book, we will provide you with a firm foundation and a good, solid beginning.

CHAPTER 2

The Algorithmic Model

We use the term *computing perspective* to refer to a way of looking at the world as it would be seen through the eyes of a computer scientist. You do not have to be a computer scientist to do this, but you do need to know a handful of the fundamental concepts that help computer scientists see things in a certain way.

Computers are devices that do only one kind of thing: They carry out *algorithms* to process information. To computer scientists, the algorithm is the central unifying concept of computing, the mode of thought that is at the core of the computing perspective. Thus, to see things from the computing perspective, you need to understand algorithms.

In this chapter we introduce algorithms, show simple examples of them, explain their relationship to computers, and discuss the keys to seeing things from the computing perspective.

2.1   What Is an Algorithm?

Any precise set of instructions that adequately specifies behavior and is not ambiguous, can be considered to be an algorithm.

Definition: An algorithm is a specification of a behavioral process. It consists of a finite set of instructions that govern behavior step-by-step.

Although algorithms are central to computing, they need not have anything at all to do with computers. Years before computers were invented, your great-grandmother carried out an algorithm every time she followed a recipe to make an apple pie. Other everyday examples of algorithms abound.

EXAMPLE 2.1   When I assembled the office chair in which I am now sitting, I executed the following algorithm that was provided by the manufacturer:

```
algorithm "Assembly Instructions for Office Chair"
1. Place the chair seat upside down on a table or other flat work surface.
2. Attach the mounting plate to the underside of the chair seat using
   4 bolts.
3. Attach the chair arms to the underside of the chair seat using 2 bolts
   per arm.
4. Place the chair base with castors on the floor.
5. Insert the large end of the pneumatic cylinder into the center of the
   chair base.
6. Slide the plastic cover over the pneumatic cylinder.
7. Place the chair seat (with attached mounting plate and arms) over
   the small end of the pneumatic cylinder. Guide the top end of the
   cylinder into the hole in the mounting plate. Press down firmly on
   the chair seat.
8. Install the backrest by sliding its metal prong into the slot at the
   rear of the mounting plate.
9. Adjust the backrest to a comfortable height, then tighten the knob at
   the rear of the mounting plate.
end algorithm
```

Algorithms for tasks such as baking pies or assembling office chairs specify behavioral steps that involve the physical manipulation of physical matter (e.g., cooking ingredients or assembling chair components). In contrast, using algorithms and computers to perform tasks involves the manipulation of *data*, simply because data processing is what computers do. We will discuss the relationship of algorithms to computers later in this chapter.

Any algorithm receives input, processes that input according to its specification of behavior, and produces output. In the case of the algorithm for assembling an office chair, the input is the set of unassembled chair parts, the algorithm is the list of assembly instructions, and the output is the assembled chair. For algorithms that process data, the same model applies:

Before we examine the requirements of algorithms, let's look at an algorithm that solves a data-processing problem.

EXAMPLE 2.2   *Problem specification:* Process a list of the baseball players in a league and their performance at the end of the season to determine the league's batting champion for that year. A player must have a minimum number of "at bats" (i.e., attempts) in order to be eligible. The player with highest batting average (number of hits divided by number of at bats) is the batting champion.

Context: The processor of this list should be a person using pencil and paper, not a computer. When we say "create a space" or "record some number," the task should be done on paper.

Attempted solution:

```
algorithm "Batting Champion"
1. Create labeled space for a number called "MIN AB."
2. Obtain the minimum number of at bats required.
3. Record that number as "MIN AB."
4. Obtain a master list of baseball players that includes the needed per-
   formance data: player's name (Name), number of hits (Hits), and number
   of at bats (AB).
5. Create labeled space for a name called "BA Leader."
6. Create labeled space for a number called "Best BA."
7. Begin with a zero average: record 0 as "Best BA."
8. Consider the data for the first player in the master list.
9. If (this player's AB is greater than MIN AB) then
     9.1. Create labeled space for a number called "This BA".
     9.2. Divide this player's Hits by his AB, record the result as
          "This BA."
     9.3. If ("This BA" is greater than "Best BA") then
            9.3.1. Record "This BA" as "Best BA."
            9.3.2. Record this player's Name as "BA Leader."
10. Cross this player off the master list and consider the data for the
    next player in the list.
11. Repeat steps 9 and 10 until every player in the master list has been
    considered.
12. Create labeled space for a name called "Batting Champion."
13. Record the name in "BA Leader" as "Batting Champion."
end algorithm.
```

Notice how indentation is used to show that steps 9.1 through 9.3 are executed only if the condition in line 9 is true. If the condition in line 9 is not true, then 9.1, 9.2, and 9.3 are not executed. Similarly, lines 9.3.1 and 9.3.2 are indented under line 9.3, indicating that they will be executed only if the condition in line 9.3 is true.

The attempted solution is indeed an algorithm, in that it consists of a finite set of instructions that governs behavior step-by-step. But is it correct? At first glance, it might appear to be. In fact, in *most* circumstances, it will correctly perform the task. Unfortunately, it will not *necessarily* produce correct results. There are two circumstances in which the solution will fail to produce correct results:

- In line 9 the algorithm checks to see if each player's number of at bats is *greater than* the minimum required for the batting champion. If a given player's number of at bats is *equal to* the minimum, that player should qualify, but this algorithm misses him.
- In line 9.3 the algorithm checks to see if each player's performance is *greater than* the best batting average so far. If several players have the highest, they should share the championship for that category. This algorithm recognizes only the one who appeared first in the list.

These two errors are of the same nature: *The algorithm tests for the wrong condition*. It tests for "greater than" when it should test for "greater than or equal to." Notice, however, that these two errors have different consequences:

- The first error will produce results that are *wrong*.
- The second error will produce results that are *incomplete*.

In both cases, the errors occur because the algorithm failed to adequately consider all the possible cases that the data might be expected to present.

Warning: Successful algorithms must consider all possible cases presented by acceptable data.

From these examples of errors, we can specify another requirement of algorithms:

Definition: To be correct, an algorithm must produce results that are *correct* and *complete* given *any and all* sets of appropriate data.

EXAMPLE 2.3 Let's now try to repair the Batting Champion algorithm:

```
algorithm "Batting Champion"
1. Create labeled space for a number called "MIN AB."
2. Obtain the minimum number of at bats required.
3. Record that number as "MIN AB."
4. Obtain a master list of baseball players that includes the needed per-
   formance data: player's name (Name), number of hits (Hits), and number
   of at bats (AB).
5. Create labeled space for a list of names called "BA Leader."
6. Create labeled space for a number called "Best BA."
7. Begin with a zero average: record 0 as "Best BA."
8. Consider the data for the first player in the master list.
9. If (this player's AB is greater than or equal to MIN AB) then
      9.1. Create labeled space for a number called "This BA."
      9.2. Divide this player's Hits by his number of AB, record the result
           as "This BA."
      9.3. If ("This BA" is greater than "Best BA") then
           9.3.1. Record "This BA" as "Best BA."
           9.3.2. Erase the list of "BA Leader."
           9.3.3. Add this player's name to the list "BA Leader."
      9.4. If ("This BA" is equal to "Best BA") then
           9.4.1. Add this player's name to the list "BA Leader."
10. Cross this player's name off the master list of players and consider
    the data for the next player in the list.
11. Repeat steps 9 and 10 until every player in the master list has been
    considered.
12. Create labeled space for a list of names called "Batting Champion."
13. Record the list of names "BA Leader" as "Batting Champion."
end algorithm.
```

The repairs to our original version involved several changes:

- Because multiple players might tie for leader status, we changed lines 5 and 12 so they instruct the processor to create space for "a list of names" rather than just "a name."
- For the same reason, instructions 9.3.2, 9.3.3, 9.4.1, and 13 all refer to "list of names" rather than "a name."
- We changed the test in line 9, from "greater than" to "greater than or equal to," to recognize players who have exactly met, as well as those who exceeded, the minimum number of at bats.
- The test in our original 9.3 was an error because it failed to recognize a player whose batting average tied the current leader. However, simply changing this test from "greater than" to "greater than or equal to" would not have been adequate. Why? Because we need to take different actions depending on whether the current player ties the current leader or betters him. If he *exceeds* the best performance so far, we must record the current player's batting average as the new standard and erase the former leaders in that category (9.3.1 and 9.3.2). If the current player *equaled* the best performance so far but did not exceed it, we do not do those things. In either case, we add his name to the list of leaders (9.3.3 and 9.4.1). Again, we use indentation to indicate which instructions are executed *only if* the conditions in previous instructions are satisfied.

Our repairs made the totality of step 9 more complex. We had to do more logic to handle not only the normal case (when there is only a single leader) but also the exceptional case (when multiple players might be tied for the leadership).

The kind of evolution we have seen here in developing our Batting Champion algorithm is typical. Often, people who are new to the challenge of constructing algorithms will originally consider only the most obvious case and then will have to wrestle with making repairs.

Warning: You will succeed more quickly at constructing algorithms if you make it a habit to think first about the problem and its data, and then to enumerate all the special cases that the algorithm must handle.

2.2 Properties of Good Algorithms

After repairs, our Batting Champion algorithm is a correct data-processing algorithm. It is in "plain English" and therefore suitable to be executed by a "human processor" who understands English and who has access to the appropriate data.

There are many real-world circumstances in which such "natural language algorithms" are critically important. For example, any nurse who works in a critical care environment (e.g., in a shock-trauma, intensive care, or cardiac care unit) *must* be able at times to function primarily as a processor who executes algorithms. The same is true of combat aircraft pilots. Such work demands life-and-death decisions that must be made rapidly, often when there is no warning and no time to think. Indeed, individuals holding these jobs are extensively trained and tested to be able to function "without thinking." We want such people to behave with the efficiency of a computer and much of their training involves the rote memorization of algorithms.

Regardless of whether the processor is a cardiac care nurse saving a life or a computer controlling the safety systems of a nuclear power plant, it is imperative that the algorithms they execute are good ones. In addition to correctness, there are other properties that we demand for an algorithm to be considered "good."

Definition: Well-designed algorithms have three key properties: (1) precision, (2) simplicity, and (3) levels of abstraction.

2.2.1 Precision

Algorithms need to be *precise*. This is because no matter who carries out an algorithm, the result should always be the same if given identical input. In line 11 of our Batting Champion example, it would not have been appropriate to say "Repeat steps 9 and 10 until we're *about finished* with the list of players," because that lends itself to various interpretations. One person might think that it means looking at the performance of every player, while another might decide that looking at 90 percent of them is close enough. And, as we shall soon see, a computer would not be able to interpret such an ambiguous instruction because a computer only understands definite, precise instructions. Thus we took care to be precise and unambiguous:

```
Repeat steps 9 and 10 until every player in the list has been
considered.
```

2.2.2 Simplicity

Each step of an algorithm must also be *simple*. A good general rule is that each step should carry out one logical step. For example, in the Batting Champion algorithm, the entire task is broken down into several elementary steps, none of which takes long to complete or involves complex instructions. When we did run into something complex (e.g., line 9), we broke that step down into its appropriate subtasks in order to keep each instruction simple.

Of course, "simplicity" itself is not a very precise term. What is simple to one processor may not be simple to another. And, even if we could agree on exactly what simplicity means, it is not always clear how to make things simple. Because of our need for simplicity, and because of the ways that simplicity is a "fuzzy" term, we require the third property: levels of abstraction.

2.2.3 Levels of Abstraction

Although each element of an algorithm must be simple, "simple" is a relative term. Many things that are elementary to a college student may not be so a first grader. Hence, we have *levels of abstraction*. For creating algorithms, levels of abstraction are important in two ways.

First, every algorithm must be based on the knowledge appropriate to the processor. For example, my grandmother cooked all her life. If someone gave her a recipe involving a pie crust, she would know how to create the crust without further instruction. My brother has not cooked much and, if he were given the same recipe, he would require detailed instructions about what to do. Thus, depending on the person, two different levels of abstraction are called for.

Levels of abstraction are important, both in creating new algorithms and in understanding algorithms that already exist. They allow us to hide the details of a given activity and refer to just a name for those details. Thus a pie recipe might say:

```
Prepare blueberry filling
Prepare crust
Fill crust
Top pie with lattice crust
Bake at 350 for 45 minutes
Cool and serve
```

Such a recipe would be clear to an experienced baker, yet someone who didn't understand those six steps would have to consult more detailed instructions for each step. My grandmother might need to consult only the algorithm for "prepare blueberry filling," while my brother might need to consult the detailed algorithm for all six steps. In writing any algorithm, care must be taken to choose the correct level of abstraction for the intended processor.

The second way in which levels of abstraction are important involves the challenge of organizing things effectively. Algorithms are created by people. Once created, they must be read, understood, checked, and repaired by people. People have certain cognitive limits: they can only keep so many thoughts in mind at one time. Studies have shown that, for most people, the limit is about six (actually, seven plus or minus two). If an algorithm involves too many ideas, people get confused. Therefore, levels of abstraction must be used to organize the ideas expressed in algorithms.

Well-designed algorithms will be organized in terms of levels of abstraction. This means that we can refer to each of the major logical steps without being distracted by the details that make up each one. The simple instructions that make up each logical step are hidden inside *modules*.[1] These modules allow us to function at a higher level, to hide the details of each step inside a module, and then to refer to that module by name whenever we need it.

In addition to clarity, modules have other advantages:

- Each module can be built and tested by people working independently.
- Equivalent modules (those that perform the same task by different methods) can be interchanged with one another.
- The same module can be reused multiple times.

[1]We employ the generic definition of module used in electronics—that is, an interchangeable unit that may be readily plugged in or detached from a system. In certain programming languages, module has a more specific technical meaning, but we are not concerned with particular programming languages here.

EXAMPLE 2.4 We can restructure the Batting Champion algorithm to reflect more levels of abstraction. We do so by hiding the many details inside modules that we then "invoke" (or "use" or "call") whenever they are needed.

```
algorithm "Batting Champion"
1. Invoke "Define MIN Num of At Bats"
2. Obtain a master list of baseball players that includes the needed per-
   formance data: player's name (Name), number of hits (Hits), and number
   of at bats (AB).
3. Invoke "Set Up Needed Data Space."
4. Consider the data for the first player in the master list.
5. If (this player's AB is greater than or equal to MIN AB) then
      5.1. Invoke "Calculate Batting Average."
      5.2. Invoke "Consider Batting Average for the Championship."
6. Cross this player's name off the master list of players and consider
   the data for the next player in the list.
7. Repeat steps 5 and 6 until every player in the master list has been
   considered.
8. Invoke "Output Findings Re: Batting Champion."
end algorithm.
```

This results in an algorithm that is easier to read and understand.

By hiding the details inside appropriate modules, we can understand the main ideas without being distracted. This is a key goal of using levels of abstraction:

- Each module represents an abstraction. The name of the module describes the idea that the module implements. The instructions hidden within the module specify how that abstraction is implemented.
- We can see *what* is being done (the *idea*) by reading the descriptive name of the module without having to pay attention to *how* it is being done.
- If we want to understand *how* it is being done, we can look inside the module to find out.

For example, if we want to know exactly how "Consider Batting Average for the Championship" is specified, we can consult that module. Here's what it might look like:

```
module Consider Batting Average for the Championship
1. If ("This BA" is greater than "Best BA") then
      1.1. Record "This BA" as "Best BA."
      1.2. Erase the list "BA Leader."
      1.3. Add this player's Name to the list "BA Leader."
2. If ("This BA" is equal to "Best Average") then
      2.1. Add this player's Name to the list "BA Leader."
end module
```

This is the same logic that had been cluttering up the "main" algorithm. We haven't changed it; we've just relocated it to get it out of the way. To do so, we've created a module that represents an abstraction—that is, "what it means to consider a player's average for the Batting Championship."

Definition: To make use of levels of abstraction, you can create an abstraction for each idea by doing the following:

- Create a module for the idea.
- Place the group of instructions that implement that idea inside the module.
- Invoke that module whenever the instructions for that idea need to be carried out.

Doing things this way gives us an algorithm that features a certain structure. We have a main algorithm that is not cluttered up with details. Instead, it describes the high-level logic of the algorithm. It coordinates the work of the modules and decides when each module is needed. It does not do the detailed work of the algorithm: the modules do that. Thus the main algorithm is analogous to a manager or coordinator, and each module to a skilled worker who knows how to do a specific job.

There may be any number of levels of abstraction in an algorithm, depending on the problem at hand. Higher and lower levels of abstraction are relative terms. The highest level is the level of algorithm purpose—for example, "identifying the leading hitters." The next highest level contains the logical steps involved in carrying out that purpose. Below that level are the particular instructions, typically hidden inside modules, which specify *how* to carry out each of those higher-level logical steps. One module may invoke another module, and so on, for as many levels of depth as are necessitated by the problem. *Remember:* It is the problem that guides the development of the algorithm; some algorithms may thus have few levels of abstraction, while others will have many, depending on the problem.

Warning: *All* algorithms must be constructed to feature levels of abstraction.

The crucial benefits of levels of abstraction become increasingly clear:

- Levels of abstraction are the means by which we can create algorithms that instruct processors to do complex things. Without them, algorithms would be so cluttered up with details that it would be practically impossible to understand them.
- Levels of abstraction allow us to easily substitute one set of particulars for another—that is, we can plug in modules that are equivalent in their effect but achieve that effect in different ways. By isolating details in a modular design, we can readily make selective improvements without having to undertake a major redesign.

Levels of abstraction thus make the complex jobs of creating, correcting, and updating algorithms manageable.

2.3 Algorithms and Computers

Algorithms give us a way to specify behavior via instructions. Computers are devices that can carry out instructions to manipulate data. They are machines that transform data, not physical matter. Computer science creates the means by which we can externalize the human ability to manipulate data into the things we make.

By using algorithms with computers, we seek to mechanize mental behavior, to incorporate ideas and abstractions into the computer so that the computer can carry out ideas for us by doing the behavior we specify.

2.3.1　What Computers Do

When we construct algorithms for a computer, we face a frustrating irony: *the computer is a remarkably stupid device*. It has no common sense whatsoever, it cannot resolve ambiguity, it requires every step to be very precise, and it will always do *exactly* what you tell it to do even if you have (accidentally) told it to do the wrong thing.

Definition:　A computer is an electronic device that manipulates two levels of electric current: high and low. It treats the high level as a "one," the low level as a "zero." The *only* thing a computer can do is manipulate numbers consisting of ones and zeros: it can store them in memory, retrieve them from memory, do arithmetic operations on them, and compare their values.

Any time a computer appears to do something smart, it is an illusion. All it can do is manipulate ones and zeros *very rapidly*. The illusion of smartness comes from the algorithm that the computer is executing. It is the algorithm that makes the computer appear smart.

2.3.2　Computers and Binary Data

Because computers only understand ones and zeros, they require the use of the $base_2$ notation, which represents numbers using only those two numerals. The numbering system used by people is $base_{10}$, which represents numbers using the numerals "0" through "9." Numbers represented in $base_2$ notation are called binary numbers. Numbers represented in $base_{10}$ notation are called decimal numbers.

Different numbering systems follow the same pattern. For any given number, each digit represents the base raised to some power. The rightmost column represents the "ones" column or $(base)^0$. Then, moving leftward, the next column represents $(base)^1$ or the base itself. The third digit represents $(base)^2$, the fourth digit represents $(base)^3$, and so on, with each column representing the (base number)*(the meaning of the column to its right). Table 2.1 shows the meaning of the first eight digits for decimal numbers and binary numbers.

To read a number in either system, we simply sum the digits according to what each one represents. Thus, the meaning of "2041" in $base_{10}$ is determined by adding two thousands, zero hundreds, four tens, and one one. The meaning of "1101" in $base_2$ is determined by adding one eight, one four, zero twos, and one one, which is

TABLE 2.1

	Digit 8	Digit 7	Digit 6	Digit 5	Digit 4	Digit 3	Digit 2	Digit 1
base$_N$	$(N)^7$	$(N)^6$	$(N)^5$	$(N)^4$	$(N)^3$	$(N)^2$	$(N)^1$	$(N)^0$
base$_{10}$ (decimal)	10^7 10,000,000	10^6 1,000,000	10^5 100,000	10^4 10,000	10^3 1,000	10^2 100	10^1 10	10^0 1
base$_2$ (binary)	2^7 128	2^6 64	2^5 32	2^4 16	2^3 8	2^2 4	2^1 2	2^0 1

thirteen. The number eleven is represented in base$_{10}$ as "11" because eleven consists of one ten and one one. In base$_2$, eleven is represented as "1011" because it consists of one eight, zero fours, one two, and one one.

As you know, to make multi-digit decimal numbers easier for people to read, the digits are grouped in chunks of three, with each chunk separated by a comma, for example, 207,625. To make binary numbers easier to read, the digits are grouped in chunks of four, with chunks separated by blank space, for example, 1001 0111 (the binary representation of the decimal number 151).

2.3.3 Levels of Abstraction in Computers

If we want a computer to be able to carry out an algorithm, the algorithm must be expressed in ones and zeros—the only form the computer can understand. This simple requirement presents a difficulty because people do not think in terms of ones and zeros. They think in terms of ideas and meanings. If a computer can understand only ones and zeros, we require some way to bridge the gap between the level at which people think and the level at which computers function.

When digital computers were first invented in the 1940s, there was no way to bridge that gap. Therefore computer programmers had to translate their ideas into ones and zeros. Because this method is so difficult, tedious, and error prone, later generations of computer researchers have developed a better approach. For a computer system to execute an algorithm for a human user of that system, four logical levels of abstraction now come into play:

1. *The Human User Level:* The user interacts with a piece of *application software* (a computer program such as a spreadsheet, word processor, web navigator, or operating system) in order to complete some task. The user must only understand how to use the program; he or she does not need to understand the algorithm that makes it work.

2. *The Algorithm Level:* The program being used is an implementation of an algorithm that was developed by another person or group. Generally, algorithms are expressed in some algorithm language or code that is more precise, less ambiguous, and more compact than a "natural language" such as English.

   A language for writing algorithms may be conceptual (such as the one to be used here) or it may be a specific programming language (such as Fortran, Pascal, C++, Java, etc.). The advantage of using a programming language is that the algorithm can then be executed on a computer (see "The Translation Level" below). The disadvantage of programming languages is that they are created for specific purposes—that is, there is no single one that is best. In addition, programming languages usually involve a large number of annoying technical details that can make writing good algorithms more difficult.

3. *The Translation Level:* For an algorithm to be executed by a computer, the algorithm must be expressed in the particular code of some programming language. Every programming language comes with special translation software—either a *compiler* or an *interpreter*,[2] which translates the code from its human-understandable form (as written by a person in a programming language) to a computer-understandable form (a list of ones and zeros).[3] Thus, to have a usable computer program, one must (1) write the algorithm in a programming language and (2) have that program translated by a compiler or interpreter into a form that the computer can understand.

4. *The Hardware Level:* The hardware manipulates the ones and zeros it is given to produce output based on the input. The result may be text or graphics written to a computer screen, the sending of a document to a printer, the recording of data on a disk for later use, etc.

At each level some algorithmic process is at work. The least precise level is the top one: people often define a task in imprecise ways. At each of the lower levels, the algorithmic process is explicit, precise, and unambiguous. Table 2.2 summarizes the activity at each level.

The ones and zeros we see at the hardware level are also used to store computer programs and data. These are called *files* on a computer disk (or another storage medium such as a CD-ROM or magnetic tape). The contents of every file is a list of ones and zeros, which means that the computer cannot tell whether a file is a data file or a program file; it simply does whatever it is told. When we run a program on some data, the computer is simply acting on one set of 1s and 0s (the program), which tells

---

[2]Compilers and interpreters do equivalent jobs. They take as input the *source code* (written in some programming language) and output *object code* that the computer understands. Compilers perform the translation all at once, producing an entire body of code in ones and zeros. Interpreters do it by translating a single line, telling the computer to execute it, then translating the next line, and so on.

[3]There is sometimes an intermediate level between the programming language and the binary code (assembly language), in which case an extra layer of translation is involved. Don't worry about this. This is a purely technical matter that has nothing to do with the logic of the algorithm and is of no importance here.

TABLE 2.2

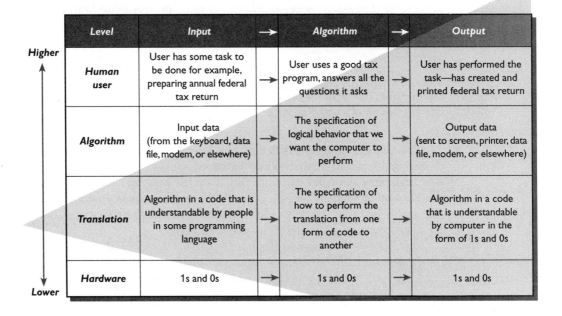

Level	Input	→	Algorithm	→	Output
Higher					
Human user	User has some task to be done for example, preparing annual federal tax return	→	User uses a good tax program, answers all the questions it asks	→	User has performed the task—has created and printed federal tax return
Algorithm	Input data (from the keyboard, data file, modem, or elsewhere)	→	The specification of logical behavior that we want the computer to perform	→	Output data (sent to screen, printer, data file, modem, or elsewhere)
Translation	Algorithm in a code that is understandable by people in some programming language	→	The specification of how to perform the translation from one form of code to another	→	Algorithm in a code that is understandable by computer in the form of 1s and 0s
Hardware	1s and 0s	→	1s and 0s	→	1s and 0s
Lower					

it how to manipulate some other set of 1s and 0s (the input data) to produce yet another set of 1s and 0s (the output data).

The representation of algorithms and data by binary numbers is the process that transformed computers into useful tools.

Fortunately, we do not have to concern ourselves with the ones and zeros, or with the details of how we get from our high-level ideas down to low-level machine instructions. (For those who are curious, there are other computer science courses that cover the entire range of these issues.) Thanks to the accomplishments of earlier computer scientists who built the software tools that give us the benefits of these levels of abstraction, we can ignore the low-level complexities and focus on the crucial level: *the specification of behavior and how to articulate such specifications as algorithms.*

Henceforth, we shall be concerned with the top two levels: the human level and the algorithm level. Except on occasion, we will not pay attention to the levels below these two. For now, it is important that you obtain a foundation in algorithms. With such a foundation, specific programming languages will be easier to learn.

2.3.4 Algorithms vs. Computer Programs

What is the difference between a computer program and an algorithm? An *algorithm* is the set of logical steps, apart from their expression in any programming language. A *computer program* is an expression of some algorithm in some particular programming language.

Definition: An algorithm is the specification of behavior, and a computer program is one expression of an algorithm.

There might be several different computer programs, each written in a different programming language, that follow the same logical steps. They all would express the same algorithm, but they would not be the same program. Similarly, there might be three assembly manuals for one office chair, one written in English, one in French, and one in Japanese. These would be different assembly manuals but they would all express the same series of steps, the same algorithm.

Fortunately, the various programming languages are far more similar to one another than are different natural languages. Once you know how to think in algorithmic terms, you will have an easier time learning the various programming languages.

2.3.5 Data vs. Information

While there is nothing about the idea of algorithms that requires data (witness the baking of apple pies), *using* algorithms and computers to simulate and model phenomena does require data, simply because data processing is what computers do.

Since we are concerned with algorithms and their power when combined with computers, we will be concerned with both algorithms and data. From the computing perspective, algorithms *always* act upon data, and there is no practical way to consider one without the other.

Thus, whenever we make use of a computer model of whatever phenomena we might be studying, we must represent these phenomena in terms of data that the computer can manipulate. If we are analyzing a baseball season, we collect data describing a player's performance at bat and in the field. Similarly, if you go to Home Depot to buy kitchen cabinets, an employee will input the dimension of your kitchen into the computer, will use a mouse to indicate whatever arrangement of cabinets and appliances you are considering, and will then show you on-screen pictures of how your kitchen will look from various angles. Obviously, the computer does not have itty-bitty pictures of refrigerators and ovens inside it; instead, numerical representations based on your kitchen and its layout are used to generate visual representations for you. Within a computer, *all* information is represented as some form of data.

Definition: Data are not the same thing as information. Note the following use of these terms:

- *Information* means knowledge about something.
- *Data* means a specific representation of some information.
- An algorithm manipulates data, not information.

Sometimes data and information are essentially the same, as in the case of determining the batting champion. Often, however, things are not so simple. For example, imagine that we want an algorithm to determine the following:

- Is a baseball player a "good hitter"? At first, we might assume that we can equate "being a good hitter" with the picture painted by various data (e.g., batting average, number of runs batted in, number of home runs, etc.). But do such data really give us the information we're after? Imagine that we see good performance numbers for a player, only to learn that they were earned by a 20-year-old who was playing with a group of seven-year-olds. If we looked only at his performance data, we would conclude he was a good hitter. If we looked at the *context* in which he generated that data, we might conclude something quite different.
- Is a student a "smart person"? What data would we use? If we use SAT scores or IQ test results to evaluate this question, we may not be using appropriate data. We know that intelligence is a very complex thing, that there are many kinds of intelligence, and that certain individuals who are very intelligent do poorly when taking tests. So, what do such data really tell us? Does an SAT score tell us about intelligence or about more specific "going to school" skills?
- Is a person "healthy"? Again, data can be misleading. For example, someone writing an algorithm might equate "an absence of high blood pressure" with "being in good health." Yet a patient who has good blood pressure numbers might have a serious disease that does not affect blood pressure in any way.

Data are nothing more than a representation of *some kind* of information. A given piece of data may be quite poor at representing the information with which we are concerned. Translating between "meaningful information" and "data" can be easy or it can be complicated, requiring complex transformations from one to the other. Only people can do this sort of thing; computers cannot.

Warning: A computer will act on whatever data it is given. That data may or may not adequately represent the information that we want to process. Human judgment is required to ensure that the data represent the appropriate information.

2.4 Algorithm Components

As you develop algorithms, you will experience working with, at most, five kinds of components: (1) *data structures,* (2) *data manipulation instructions,* (3) *conditional expressions,* (4) *control structures,* and (5) *modules.*[4]

---

[4]From a theoretical viewpoint, data structures and modules are matters of convenience and are not required. We can indeed create correct algorithms without them. However, doing so is a bad idea because the resulting algorithms are difficult to create, understand, and repair. To create "good" algorithms for practical application, all five components are indeed required.

2.4.1 Data Structures

Data are the representations of information used by an algorithm. This includes input and output data as well as any interim data generated by the algorithm for its own internal use. Data structures are "containers" for data values. In most circumstances, we want a data structure to be variable—that is, a given data structure's contents can and will change as the algorithm acts upon it. In the Batting Champion algorithm, "Best BA" is a variable whose contents may change as the algorithm executes. In some circumstances we want the contents of a data structure to be fixed—for example, we don't want an algorithm to be able to change the value of *pi*. In the Batting Champion algorithm, "MIN AB" was a constant: We recorded its value once and thereafter did not change it. Thus we have "variables" and "constants." Inside a computer, each data structure (variable or constant) will occupy some location in the computer's memory.

To use data, we must have a way of distinguishing one piece of data from another, and a way of referring to certain data over and over again. This is easy: we simply give each data structure a name. While we can choose whatever names we like, the names should be *descriptive* of the data. Thus, if we are using a data structure to hold the sum of several other values, it would be better to call that variable "Sum" than "Fred." In the Batting Champion algorithm, we called one of the variables "Best BA," not "Ethel." In computer jargon, the descriptive names we make up for data structures (and for other purposes) are called *identifiers*.

In addition to naming data, we also need to organize data in a manner that will help us solve the problem at hand. Before we repaired our original, flawed version of the Batting Champion algorithm, "BA Leader" was a single variable. After repair, it became a *list* of variables. As we shall see, how we organize our data can go a long way toward making an algorithm simple—or needlessly complicated.

Creating complex data structures that we can easily reference and manipulate is one of the key ways to create useful abstractions. We shall discuss this in Chapter 5.

2.4.2 Data Manipulation Instructions

An algorithm requires instructions that allow it to do the following:

- Obtain data values from the "world" and store them in data structures.
- Manipulate those data values—that is, modify the value of a data structure via arithmetic operations, copy the contents of one data structure to another, etc.
- Output the resulting data values "back to the world."

Thus in the Batting Championship algorithm we used instructions to obtain and manipulate data in various ways and to generate results based on those manipulations. The basic instructions we require are discussed in Chapter 3.

2.4.3 Conditional Expressions

Algorithms also feature "decision points." The ability of an algorithm to make decisions and act on them is what makes algorithms (and computers) powerful. If a computer could do no more than simply follow a rote list of operations, then it would be nothing more than an automated calculator.

 This is the crucial difference: A computer can make decisions and act on them, while a simple calculator cannot.

All such decisions are based on *conditional expressions* that are either true or false (e.g., "X = 17"). In the Batting Champion algorithm, we used conditionals to tell us whether each player qualified for the batting championship ("this player's AB is greater than or equal to MIN AB") and whether the performance of each player who qualified should be considered for the championship ("This BA" is greater than "Best BA" and "This BA" is equal to "Best BA").

If the condition is true, the algorithm executes certain instructions; if it is not, then it doesn't. However, simple decisions can be used to decide extremely complicated things; as we shall see in later chapters, this is achieved via abstraction.

2.4.4 Control Structures

The elements of algorithms that govern what happens *after* an algorithm makes a decision are called *control structures*. Without control structures, decisions are of no value. What good is a decision if you cannot act on it? Without control structures, the algorithm is just a rote list of instructions that are executed sequentially, and a computer executing such an algorithm is still nothing but a glorified calculator. Control structures allow an algorithm to *act* on the decisions it makes—that is, they allow us to specify that certain instructions will be executed if one decision is reached and that other instructions will be executed if a different decision is reached.

In the Batting Champion algorithm, we used "If" statements to determine which instructions were executed based on the results of conditionals. For example:

```
2. If ("This BA" is equal to "Best BA") then
     2.1. Add this player's name to the list "BA Leader."
```

According to the above, instruction 2.1 is executed only if the condition is met.

2.4.5 Modules

Algorithms can become very complex. Simply placing all the various components of such algorithms together will produce algorithms that are hard to understand, hard to repair, and hard to extend. Instead, *modules* (or *subalgorithms* or *routines*) are used to group together those instructions and data that are required by a given logical task. For example, in the last version of the Batting Champion algorithm, we used modules to hide the details of various logical steps, such as "Consider Batting Average for the Championship."

Using modules in this way raises the level of abstraction and thus allows clearer thinking, faster repairs, and easier modifications. Modules enable us to find practical ways to use algorithms to solve complex problems. They make algorithms, and the abstractions that constitute them, manageable.

2.5 Seeing Things from the Computing Perspective

To view the world from the computing perspective, it is necessary that you be able to do five things:

1. Conceive of behavior as expressions of algorithms.
2. Conceive of things or beings that exhibit behavior as "processes."
3. Conceive of algorithms as levels of abstraction.
4. Realize that an algorithm's usefulness can be limited by its complexity.
5. Put aside (temporarily) other perspectives and view the world in terms of algorithms and data.

2.5.1 Conceiving Behavior as Expressions of Algorithms

Conceive of behavior? What kind of behavior? *Any* kind: the behavior of objects, plants, birds, chemical reactions, devices, people, parts of people (e.g., the immune system or a muscle), corporate or governmental organizations, cockroaches, planets, baseball teams, the weather, *anything* at all.

Conceiving of some behavior as an expression of an algorithm means that you must try to imagine what set of instructions is being carried out by the thing or being that is doing the behavior.

The algorithm you imagine that describes the behavior may be correct or it may be completely wrong or even ridiculous. However, for our purposes, the *correctness* of your guess about the algorithm is less important than your ability to imagine it. A wrong first attempt is often a good starting point for refinement and repair because it can help you see the kind of errors you may have made.

If you develop an algorithm that is not the actual algorithm being carried out in the behavior but does effectively specify instructions which would reproduce that same behavior, then your imagined algorithm can still be very valuable because it *simulates* whatever the real algorithm might be. Such algorithms can be valuable in science, engineering, business, and other fields.

2.5.2 Conceiving of Things That Exhibit Behavior as Processes

In computer science jargon, a *process* is like a noun that is doing something. Thus a given car and driver in a traffic jam is a "process," and the behavior of that car-and-driver is an expression of some "algorithm." Since we are interested in all kinds of behavior, we do not want to get lost trying to categorize all the kinds of things that might be *doing* behavior. So, we simply call them all *processes*.

Definition: A process is anything that is carrying out behavior specified by an algorithm. Thus a computer, together with a computer program that it is executing, is a process; a computer that is turned off is not. Your grandmother cooking at the stove is a process, while an unused stove is not. Some computers can execute multiple programs at the same time; in such a case, that one computer and the several programs it is executing constitute several processes.

As you engage in studying, or in goofing off instead of studying, you are a process. What algorithm do you carry out when you are a "study process"—that is, what are the specific steps in your "behavior recipe"? What algorithm do you carry out when you are a "goofing-off process"? What steps do those two algorithms have in common? At what point to they diverge into different steps?

2.5.3 Conceiving of Algorithms as Having Levels of Abstraction

As we have already discussed, the idea of levels of abstraction is crucial to imagining, creating, understanding, and improving algorithms.

 Warning: We do not want an algorithm to be a giant sequential list of steps.

From the human point of view, such a large list of instructions proves to be hard to create, understand, analyze, verify, and repair. Thus levels of abstraction allow the algorithm designer to do a better job of thinking.

 We want a hierarchy of abstraction in which the top level lists the main ideas without cluttering things up with a detailed list of what they mean. The details of each of those main steps are described in their own separate module.

2.5.4 Understanding How an Algorithm's Usefulness Is Limited by Its Complexity

Any algorithm consists of a series of steps that must be followed to achieve the intended behavior. One person might carry out these steps faster than another, just as a fast computer would execute a given program in less time than would a slower computer. However, the speed of the processor has nothing to do with the amount of work that an algorithm requires. Regardless of the speed of the processor, the algorithm itself implies that a certain number of steps will be carried out.

 Definition: There is a certain amount of work that is called for by every algorithm, irrespective of the speed at which a given processor can do that work. The speed of the processor determines how long it takes to get the work done, but the algorithm, together with its input, determines the amount of work to be done.

When we talk about the complexity of an algorithm, we generally refer to the *rate* at which the work grows for a given input into that algorithm, *not* to the actual number of steps.

For example, imagine two different algorithms for baking an apple pie. For both, the input is the number of pies that we wish to have baked. Let's say that one recipe calls for 15 specific steps while the other calls for 30 steps. Furthermore, for simplicity, let's imagine that each step takes the same amount of time and effort, and that there is no improvement in efficiency if you choose to bake 10 pies rather than one pie. What can we say about these algorithms? Well, at first glance, we see that the first algorithm is twice as efficient as the second. We can also see that for an input of 10, the first algorithm will mean executing 150 steps, while using the second algorithm will mean executing 300 steps. Intuitively, we can easily judge that the first recipe is to be preferred over the second one, if they both produce tasty apple pies.

However, the *rate* at which the work grows for each algorithm is the same. In both cases, increasing the size of the input increases the number of steps in a *linear* fashion. Thus the second recipe requires exactly twice as many steps as does the first, regardless of how many pies are to be baked.

Unfortunately, algorithmic complexity is not always so simple. For certain kinds of problems, algorithmic complexity is a major problem. For some kinds of algorithms, the rate of work grows by the square of input size—that is, baking 10 pies would increase the work by a factor of 100 compared to baking only one pie and baking 1000 pies would increase the work by a factor of a million!

Worse yet, for certain other problems, the rate of work grows by a exponential factor (i.e., 2 to the Nth power where N is the size of the input). With such an algorithm, baking 10 pies instead of one would increase the amount of work by a factor of 2 raised to the tenth power, or about 1000, and baking only 20 pies would increase the amount of work by a factor of 2 raised to the twentieth power, or about a million! (What if the input was 1000?). Table 2.3 shows the approximate amount of work required for different input for algorithms of different complexity.

Clearly, linear algorithms are better than quadratic ones, and exponential algorithms are generally infeasible for practical problem solving. Unfortunately, exponential algorithms are the best we can do with many kinds of real-world problems, such as routing a sales force, or packing trucks, or scheduling classrooms in an optimal fashion. And, lest you think that raw computer power can compensate for such complex algorithms, there are certain kinds of algorithms that could not be executed by

TABLE 2.3

Size of Input (N)	Linear (growth at rate N)	Quadratic (growth at rate of N^2)	Exponential (growth at rate of 2^N)
16	16	256	65,536 (64K)
64	64	4,096 (4K)	A number with 19 zeros
256	256	65,536 (64K)	A number with 77 zeros

TABLE 2.4

Algorithm attributes	Correct	Incorrect
Reasonable complexity	Useful	Need repair to be useful
Unreasonable complexity	Useful in theory, not in practice	Not good for anything

the fastest computer built, or even by the fastest computer anyone might imagine, and produce a result within your lifetime!

 Warning: There are many perfectly correct algorithms that are of no practical value simply because they require too much work *regardless of the speed of the computer.*

For example, our current understanding of the science of weather is such that we believe that a reliably correct weather forecast for tomorrow might require *several years* of computation.

Furthermore, for many of these problems, we believe that there can be no substantial improvement in the solution algorithm. Thus, as we try to understand the algorithms implied by various behaviors, we also try to estimate their complexity. Algorithms that are sufficiently complex to be unreasonable to run may have theoretical value but no practical value whatsoever. It is important to know what those are before trying to solve problems with them. As Table 2.4 shows, an algorithm must be both correct and of reasonable complexity if it is to have any practical use.

We shall discuss the performance properties of algorithms in Chapter 9 and of the kinds of problems that we try to solve with algorithms in Chapter 11.

2.5.5 Putting Aside Other Perspectives

The computing perspective provides a new way of looking at the world and understanding reality. It does not necessarily provide the right answers, nor is it necessarily the most useful way to look at any given phenomenon. However, it does give us a way to perceive, model, simulate, and understand many phenomena that have not previously been well understood. It has also contributed to important breakthroughs in fields ranging from medicine and psychology to engineering and industrial production. Furthermore, it provides the intellectual framework that underlies advanced research in virtually every field of modern science. As a result, it is crucial to learn to see things from the computing perspective.

 This does *not* mean that you have to throw away other perspectives or beliefs. It *does* mean that you should *add* the computing perspective to your repertoire of ways of seeing the world.

Why? The computing perspective is shaping the world today and will likely continue to do so throughout your lifetime. The coupling of *algorithmic thinking* with the *algorithm execution abilities of computers* has lead to a historically unprecedented tight coupling of the following:

- *Abstraction:* What is the idea you want to investigate or the problem you want to solve?
- *Design:* How are you going to execute it?
- *Implementation:* What algorithms and resources are needed to make your idea or your solution work?
- *Experimentation:* What is going to happen when you try out your idea?
- *Evaluation:* How well did your idea perform? How does it need to be refined?

In a large and growing body of disciplines, the state of the art is to conceive of phenomena in algorithmic terms, implement computer-based models of that phenomena, and use the resulting simulated world for experimentation and exploration. This approach is revolutionizing what can be known, predicted, designed, built, and governed.

Regardless of what you choose as a career, the computing perspective will be a powerful force in shaping the world you live in. For this reason, it is important that you come to understand it.

FOOD FOR THOUGHT

Confusing Models with Reality

Our models of reality represent our *best guesses* about the truth. As such, they are crucial to the development of science and knowledge. We develop a model that appears to be adequate for the purpose of helping us explain or understand something. We then not only test that model but also use it as a basis for expanding our knowledge. Eventually, we reach the limits of a model by learning enough about reality that we can see that our model is flawed, incomplete, or inadequate. Then, over time, we develop new models that improve on the old, and so on.

For the last few hundred years, the dominant model has been the mechanical model. It views reality as if it were a large, complex machine and seeks to understand the laws governing that machine. This model has been the basis for much of the dramatic evolution of industry and science since the Middle Ages. It enabled our ancestors to make great strides in the natural sciences (physics, chemistry, biology, geology, astronomy, etc.), and to overpower the limits imposed on us by the forces of nature (witness the railroads, the automobile, the airplane, etc.).

The mechanical model appears to have been more valuable with respect to natural phenomena (the material world of objects and matter) than with human phenomena (the invisible world of processes and experiences). Thus, while the mechanical model has been adequate—for example, in helping understand much about the *material aspects* of medicine (surgery, setting broken bones, removal of diseased organs)—it is not adequate for other, more complex aspects of human health and well-being (infections, immune disorders, psychiatric problems, etc.).

Unfortunately, because we have not developed models that can explain the complexities of life, it is unavoidable that we apply our models to phenomena for which they are not adequate. Thus, despite the inadequacies of the mechanical model for certain kinds of health phenomena, it was nonetheless deployed as the basis for certain treatments. For example, hysterectomies were performed on women who were judged to be overly emotional, lobotomies were performed on people judged to be crazy, and so on. In retrospect, things were attempted that would never be allowed today. At the time they were attempted, however, they were viewed as the "best shot."

An unavoidable difficulty is that most people who apply models don't realize that they are filtering reality through their model. They confuse their best guesses with the truth. Thus, for some of the early pioneers in psychosurgery, what they were doing was clearly the "right thing," was the "wave of the future," and so on. Only in retrospect can we clearly see them as having advocated an improper course of action and recognize the error (and human costs).

Today, the same sort of issues apply. With the emergence of the computational model, we can expect all manner of individuals who are visionary, who see the application of the new model to all manner of phenomena. Some such visionaries will be correct, and the future will judge them to be "ahead of their time." Others will be incorrect, and history will either ignore them or judge them to be misguided crackpots or worse. The problem is that we do not know what the future will tell us about who's a genius and who's a crackpot. Thus we should proceed with care.

You can expect to see all manner of developments that apply the computational model to human phenomena. Much of it will imply that people are like computers, and that the best way to solve human problems is to develop informational programs, to enhance people's ability to process information, and so on. There is much about this approach that is very sensible. And there is much that is not. Whatever problems arise, they will mostly have the same flaw: They will ignore the ways that people are *not* like computers, ignore the ways that people are *not* just "processors of information," ignore the things about people that a computational model *cannot even see,* much less adequately explain.

Thus we urge you to do two things. First, become familiar with the idea of the computational model and try it on for size. Why? Because it *is* the wave of the future and it *is* at the foundation of the huge strides in knowledge that are being made today. But we also urge you to *think critically* about what you see and hear and to be your own judge about what makes sense and what does not. After all, a model is only a model.

SUMMARY

Algorithms are precise and finite specifications of behavior. They are the central unifying concept of computing and have proved to be extremely powerful at extending the range of our knowledge and capabilities.

Algorithms consist of simple and precise instructions. Well-designed algorithms are organized by levels of abstraction that allow us to combine the detailed, simple instructions for each logical step into modules. This allows us to see the high-level logic of the algorithm and thus solve complex problems, without getting lost in the various details of each step. Levels of abstraction also allow us to modify the algorithm with minimal work. There are only five kinds of algorithm components:

1. *Data structures,* which hold data values.
2. *Data manipulation instructions,* which allow the algorithm to obtain data values from the real world and store them in its data structures, manipulate those data values, and output the resulting data values back to users.
3. *Conditional expressions,* which allow algorithms to make true/false decisions.
4. *Control structures,* which allow an algorithm to act on its decisions.
5. *Modules,* which allow effective abstraction for solving complex problems.

In Part 2 (Chapters 3 through 9, "The Algorithm Toolkit"), we will discuss the full range of algorithm-building constructs, including all of the conceptual tools that are available for constructing algorithms and for designing the data structures on which they operate. By the end of that section, we will have described and discussed *all* the elements that are necessary to design and construct algorithms and associated data.

No matter how far you go in the study of computing, no matter how many programs you write, no matter what degree of technical expertise you will achieve, virtually all the programming you ever do will boil down to manipulating the constructs discussed here. Of course, we do not expect you to be an expert immediately. In the weeks to come, you will rapidly gain experience at mastering all of the constructs and the ideas behind them. For the moment, it is important that you understand the basic ideas, for they are the foundation of everything that computers and computing can do.

EXERCISES

In the following exercises, your algorithms should be written in plain English for a human processor to execute with paper and pencil. For Exercises 2.1 through 2.4, first specify the cases that the algorithm must handle, then construct an algorithm that correctly performs the specified task.

2.1 You are given a list that contains the names of millionaires and the amount of money each one paid in income taxes last year. Construct an algorithm that will produce a list of the names of millionaires who paid less in taxes than you did.

2.2 Construct an algorithm that creates a simple index for a dictionary that has no table of contents or index. The simple index shall specify, for each letter in the alphabet, the page number on which definitions for words beginning with that letter first appear.

2.3 Construct an algorithm for sorting the paper money in your wallet. (Assume that you have no bills larger than a fifty.) All the ones should be grouped together, then the fives, tens, and so on. There are several ways to do this. Think of at least two and then think of a reason to choose one of them over the other. What is your rationale? Why is one approach better than the other?

2.4 You are given a class roll for your computer science class. The roll consists of student names (last name, first name, then middle initial) sorted in alphabetical order. Construct an algorithm that will insert the names of some additional students who registered late. Their names must be inserted into the roll so that it remains in alphabetical order.

For Exercises 2.5 through 2.12, consider the following algorithm. Its purpose is to specify behavior for students registering for college classes. Assume that you must take at least 15 credit hours to be a full-time student.

```
algorithm Class Registration
1. Make a list of courses for which you want to register.
2. Label the courses with a priority, giving priority 1 to your highest
   priority course and priority 10 to your lowest priority course.
3. Create labeled space for a number called "Hours Scheduled."
4. Begin with an empty schedule: Record 0 as "Hours Scheduled."
5. Choose the highest priority class on the list.
6. If (the chosen class is not full) and (its class time does not conflict
   with classes already scheduled) then register for class:
   6a. Add the class to your schedule.
   6b. Add the class hours to the "Hours Scheduled."
7. Cross the class off of your list.
8. Repeat steps 5 through 7 until ("Hours Scheduled" is greater than or
   equal to 15) or (all classes have been crossed out).
end algorithm.
```

2.5 Does this algorithm work in the normal case? What *is* the normal case?

2.6 Walk through this algorithm using pencil and paper and your current class schedule. Does it work in your case?

2.7 In what ways does this algorithm place restrictions on the student that were not given in the statement of the algorithm's purpose?

2.8 Repair the algorithm to correct the problem identified in 2.7.

2.9 Under what circumstances will this algorithm fail by preventing you from taking a full load when it shouldn't?

2.10 Repair the algorithm to correct the problem(s) identified in 2.9.

2.11 Identify those instructions that are at a high level of abstraction—that is, that call for behavior without specifying the details of how to do it. For two of them, create a module that specifies the details that a first-term freshman might need.

2.12 The algorithm *Class Registration* specifies behavior for registering for classes but does not specify important things about the context. When are you allowed to register? Where do you go to do it? Do you pay tuition before or after you register for specific classes? Create the "big picture" algorithm of the larger process, the algorithm that might invoke *Class Registration* as one of its modules.

2.13 Define *abstraction*.

2.14 How do we create algorithms so that they feature abstraction?

2.15 All algorithmic decisions are made on the basis of true/false questions. Are there any kinds of real-life questions that cannot be resolved in this way? If so, give examples. If not, how might complex, "fuzzy" questions be resolved in this binary (true/false) paradigm?

2.16 What do you think will be the limits of what can be accomplished using algorithms? Where, if anywhere, will algorithms prove to be useless?

2.17 In what kinds of circumstances might correct algorithms be harmful or dangerous? Give examples.

The Algorithm Toolkit

PART II

CHAPTER 3

Basic Data and Operations

Just as writing a document in a natural language requires that you first master both the language and the set of characters in its alphabet, so too does creating algorithms require a foundation in basic data and operations and the means of writing down those ideas. This chapter will introduce the following foundational material:

- Basic operators, including those for assignment, arithmetic, comparison, and communication with the world outside the algorithm;
- Basic data, including the types of data that are built into the language;
- The meaning and use of variables, constants, and literal data; and
- The basics for making decisions and selectively acting on their results.

3.1 A Language for Algorithms

Experience has shown that it is necessary to express algorithmic ideas in a form that is more precise and compact than a "natural language" such as English. Thus, throughout this chapter and those that follow, we will be introducing not only the important ideas of algorithms but also a written language in which to express these ideas.

There are many languages we might use for this purpose, including any number of programming languages that allow algorithms to be translated into a form that computers can execute. The advantage of using a programming language is that students can actually "run" their algorithms on a computer and see the effects. Unfortunately, for the purpose of introducing algorithmic concepts, this approach has three serious drawbacks:

- Programming languages are created with some specific purpose in mind and thus emphasize some features at the expense of others. There is no single programming language that is "best." The use of any one would result in compromises that obscure the difference between important properties of algorithms and the properties of certain kinds of programs.
- Programming languages include numerous annoying details that are related to technical issues. Such features introduce extra complications unrelated to the logical aspects of algorithmic problem solving, and they tend to clutter up both our algorithms and our minds to no obvious benefit.
- Students at the introductory level are likely to become so involved in the mechanics of making their programs work that they lose sight of the importance of good design and logical correctness. For this reason, there is a benefit in using a language that *cannot* be readily translated for execution, thus keeping the student's attention focused on the algorithm itself without being distracted by the various minutiae involved in "making a program work." The significant hassles that one learns to conquer and avoid in the technical discipline of programming are in our view best left for a subsequent course.

For these reasons, we use a pseudocode,[1] which is similar to many current programming languages in its expressive power but minimizes the annoying technical details. It features the important ideas embodied in various languages such as Java, C++, Pascal, and Fortran, without including all the specific details that are peculiar to each one. Thus, pseudocode allows students to focus on algorithms without program-related distractions. Students who master this "algorithms first" approach can thus succeed more rapidly with "real" programming languages in subsequent courses.

In this chapter, we introduce you to the basic concepts and constructs, and to the language (or *code*) in which we express them. In subsequent chapters, we focus on more complex concepts and constructs that will provide more abstraction power, based on an understanding of the foundational ideas presented in this chapter.

---

1. Pseudocode is not a real programming language. It is, however, a real full-featured algorithmic language. We could develop translation software to allow its use in programming, but we do not want such a capability at the introductory level. The language itself has been called "RUSCAL" by thousands of students over the years at Georgia Tech, the name coming from a combination of the author's first name (Russell) and the name of the popular programming language (Pascal). It has since been suggested that RUSCAL should honor those people who *really* developed and refined it: the many undergraduate teaching assistants in the course for which this book was developed, which means that RUSCAL actually stands for "Really Underpaid Students Created A Language."

3.2 Creating Simple Variables

Some algorithms involve only simple pieces of data, like a few numbers or characters. We do not need to organize such data because the situation is simple. We merely need a way to refer to the data unambiguously throughout an algorithm. For this we use atomic (or simple) variables.

Definition: A **variable** can be thought of as a named box, or cell, in which one or more data values are stored and may be changed by the algorithm.

Definition: An **atomic variable** is a variable that can hold only one individual piece of data, such as a number or a character.

In a computer, each variable will be associated with some location in the computer's memory. For the algorithms created in pseudocode, each variable may be associated with a box created with pencil on paper.

The act of creating a variable is known as *declaring the variable*. For each of the variables we require, we must explicitly declare each one of them to be of some data type.

EXAMPLE 3.1   Let's first consider a simple example: declaring the variables needed in an algorithm for calculating the area of a rectangle. Two pieces of information (*length, width*) are required in order to calculate a third *(area)*. Thus, we must create three variables in which we can store whatever those particular values might be. We can do so by writing

```
length isoftype Num
width isoftype Num
area isoftype Num
```

Observe the general format. Each of the three variable declarations conforms to the format:

```
<identifier> isoftype <data type>
```

Notice that we use the symbols < and > as "place holders" to indicate a slot for something specific to be filled in, for example `<identifier>` means "the name we give to the variable goes here," and `<data type>` means "the data type of the variable goes here." We shall use this place holder notation throughout this book.

Let's consider the components of a variable declaration more closely.

Definition: Identifier is simply algorithm terminology for a name we make up. We must give a *unique identifier* to each piece of data so that there will be no ambiguity. To support abstraction, all identifiers should be descriptive.

Definition: Following the identifier, we use the keyword `isoftype`. A **keyword** is any word having a specific meaning in a computer language.

Definition: Each variable must be declared to be of some data type. To specify the type of the data, we use the keyword is `isoftype`, which is obtained by *concatenating* (or hooking together) the English words *is, of,* and *type*.

Definition: A keyword cannot be used as an identifier. This is because each word in an algorithm must have an unambiguous meaning. Thus, a keyword such as `isoftype` is "taken" and is not available for any other purpose.

Definition: Each variable must be declared to be of some **data type.** In this case, we required variables to store numeric values. In such circumstances, we create variables to be of type `Num`. We shall discuss other data types shortly.

3.2.1   Variable Identifiers

Each programming language has its own set of rules about identifiers for variables. There is no convention with which everyone agrees. In order to read and understand the algorithms in this book we shall use the following conventions:

- Variable identifiers are all lowercase characters. They may contain any characters including numerals and punctuation symbols but may not include blanks or spaces.
- The first character of each word in the variable name must be a letter.
- If the variable name consists of multiple words, they must be concatenated using underscores:

  ```
  this_is_a_legal_variable_name
  thisIsNota Legalone
  ```

- The initial letters of data types are capitalized—for example, we declared our three numeric variables to be of type `Num`, not `num`.

3.3   Operators

We declare variables in order to create space for them (in a computer's memory or on a piece of paper). Once we create variables, various kinds of *operators* allow us to establish and manipulate the values stored in the variables. There are three basic categories: (1) assignment, (2) arithmetic, and (3) input/output operators.

3.3.1   Assignment Operators

Definition: Assigning or copying a value into a variable is called **assignment.** We use the *assignment operator* (`<-`) as a symbol for this operation.[2]

---

2. Notice that the symbol for the assignment operator is typed with two keys: the < (less than) and the - (hyphen). Despite the fact that it is two keystrokes, think of it as a single symbol: a left-pointing arrow.

EXAMPLE 3.2   Let's specify the data for a rectangle that has a length of 4 and a width of 7. We might write the following:

```
length isoftype Num
length <- 4

width isoftype Num
width <- 7
```

Definition: An **assignment statement** is any statement that includes an *assignment operation.* When an assignment statement is executed, the value on the right side of the assignment operator is copied into the variable on the left side. It is of the form

```
<variable_identifier> <- <expression>
```

where **expression** can be any symbol or combination of symbols that resolves to a value.

The first assignment statement in Example 3.2 means "place the value 4 into the variable named `length`." The second assignment means "place the value 7 into the variable named `width`."

Whenever a variable identifier is used on the right side of an assignment operator, it represents the value currently stored in that variable. When the assignment statement is executed, the value stored in that variable is substituted for the variable's identifier.

EXAMPLE 3.3   Using the variables and values from the previous example, we can calculate the area of the rectangle as follows:

```
area isoftype Num
area <- length * width
```

Since we have already assigned the value 4 to `length` and the value 7 to `width`, the expression `length * width` evaluates to 4 * 7 or 28. When the assignment is performed, the result (28) is assigned to the variable on the left side of the assignment operator, in this case `area`.

EXAMPLE 3.4   An assignment statement can be confusing to the untrained eye when the same identifier appears on both the right and left sides of the assignment operator. Consider the following code segment:

```
current_balance isoftype Num
current_balance <- 1000

deposit isoftype Num
deposit <- 250

current_balance <- current_balance + deposit
```

Our definition of an assignment statement included the following: "the value on the right side of the assignment operator is copied into the variable on the left side of the assignment operator." This implies that the value to the right of the assignment operator must first be determined before it can be assigned as the value to the variable on the left.

In this example, it means "take the value of current_balance as it exists before we change it" and "add it to the value of deposit," then "store the new result in the variable current_balance." Thus, based on the values we initially assigned to the two variables, current_balance will hold the value 1250 after the last statement is executed.

3.3.2   Arithmetic Operators

Basic operations include the four basic arithmetic operations as denoted by the operator symbols shown in parentheses:

- *Addition* (+)
- *Subtraction* (–)
- *Multiplication* (*)
- *Division* (/)

We also have two additional arithmetic operations that are related to division:

- *Integer division,* denoted by DIV (returns a whole number quotient, ignoring any remainder, for example, 11 DIV 3 returns 3)
- *Modulo,* denoted by MOD (returns only the remainder, ignoring any whole-number quotient, for example, 11 MOD 3 returns 2)

PRECEDENCE RULES FOR ARITHMETIC OPERATORS

As with standard arithmetic, parentheses are used to govern the order of operations. Unless parentheses indicate otherwise, *precedence rules* govern the order of arithmetic operations as: Multiplication and/or division operations are performed first, as they are encountered in a left-to-right sequence, then addition and/or subtraction operations are performed as they are encountered in a left-to-right sequence.

EXAMPLE 3.5   Consider the following code segment:

```
a isoftype Num
a <- 2

b isoftype Num
b <- 3

c isoftype Num
c <- 4

x isoftype Num
x <- a + b * c
```

This code would store the value 14 in variable x. The statement that assigns to x is equivalent to

```
x <- a + (b * c)
```

In contrast, the statement

```
x <- (a + b) * c
```

would store the value 20 in variable x. Similarly, the following code segment

```
y isoftype Num
y <- a - b + c
```

would store the value 3 in variable y, as would the statement

```
y <- (a - b) + c
```

In contrast, the statement

```
y <- a - (b + c)
```

would assign −5 in variable y.

3.3.3   Input/Output Operators

For any algorithm, we require some means of getting data from the world to the algorithm (*input*) and some means of returning the results of the algorithm back to the world (*output*). For our purposes, there are two input/output operations: (1) read and (2) print.

Definition: In our pseudocode, **read** is a keyword. It signifies a read operation that is used to obtain input values from the world outside of the algorithm—that is, from a data file on a diskette, from a person typing at a keyboard, or from a radar receiver in an F-16 fighter plane. We obtain data from outside the algorithm via the read operator using the syntax

```
read(<list of variable identifiers>)
```

where list of variable identifiers is one or more variable identifiers. If there are two or more variable identifiers in the list, they are separated by commas.

In effect, the read operator does three things: (1) it obtains the data value, (2) it *assigns* it to the specified variable, and (3) it *moves on* to be ready for the subsequent input value.

EXAMPLE 3.6   In the code segment

```
x isoftype Num
read(x)
```

the read statement means "read in the next input value and store it in variable x."

EXAMPLE 3.7   To read the next two input values and store them in variables length and width, we could write

```
read(length)
read(width)
```

We can achieve the same effect by using a single read operation with those two identifiers separated by a comma:

```
read(length, width)
```

Warning: Each read operation obtains the *next* data value and *consumes* it. That is to say, we need not do anything to move on to the next one. The act of reading in a value uses up that input value and automatically gets ready for the next one.

Thus in the example above we do *not* read the same value into both variables. Instead, the first input value is stored in `length`, and so is "used up," and the second value is stored in `width` and is similarly "consumed."

Definition: In our pseudocode, `print` is a keyword. It signifies a print operation that is used to send values back to the world outside of the algorithm—that is, to a printer, to a data file, to a computer monitor (screen), or to the weapons control system in an F-16. We send data to the world outside the algorithm via the `print` operator using the syntax

```
print(<list of data>)
```

where a `list of data` may is one or more variable identifiers or values. If there are two or more data values in the list, they are separated by commas.

If we are printing out the values of variables, the `print` operator does two things: (1) it *retrieves* the data value currently stored in the variable, and (2) it *communicates* it to the outside world.

EXAMPLE 3.8 We would like to output the two values obtained in the previous example's code segment. We could write:

```
print(length)
print(width)
```

or

```
print (length, width)
```

In addition to printing out the values stored in data structures, we can also print values that are explicitly given in the print statement.

Definition: Literals (or *literal values*) are values that are explicitly stated in a statement. Such values are called literals because they are not symbolically represented by an identifier and are instead to be taken "literally."

EXAMPLE 3.9 We can print out literal values without storing them in a variable. The instruction

```
print(17)
```

will print out the value 17, while the instruction

```
print("This is a textual message.")
```

will print out the sentence, This is a textual message. (This literal is an example of a *string of characters*, which we will discuss shortly.)

Given a few simple atomic variables and these simple operations, we can create algorithms that do simple things.

EXAMPLE 3.10   Find the area of any rectangle via the following algorithm:

```
algorithm Rectangle_Area
   length isoftype Num
   width isoftype Num
   read(length, width)

   area isoftype Num
   area <- (length * width)

   print ("A rectangle that has a length of ", length)
   print ("and a width of ", width, "has an area of ", area)

endalgorithm
```

Note that we use only two I/O constructs read and print regardless of where we get the data or where we are sending it.[3] For our purposes, we do not need to worry about the details of exactly where the data come from (perhaps keyboard or data file or modem), or about where they go (perhaps screen, printer, etc.), or about how this is done (let's assume "technical magic"). Similarly, we need not worry about the details of formatting the data. We will pretend that technical magic allows the print construct to insert spaces and lines wherever necessary to separate one piece of data from the next.

Warning: If an algorithm is supposed to be used by a person sitting at a computer, we will explicitly state that. You thus may be asked to print messages to the user such as the following:

```
user's_age isoftype Num
print("Please enter you age.")
read(user's_age)
```

If this is not *explicitly* stated as part of a problem, do *not* worry about giving instructions to the user of the algorithm. Doing so will create needless clutter and complication.

3.4   Atomic Data Types

So far, we have declared each of our variables to be of type Num (for *number*). This is only one of our four atomic data types: (1) numbers, (2) characters, (3) booleans, and (4) pointers.

---

3. Some students want to know why we do not deal with the "real-world" details of managing I/O from various sources. We do this for two reasons: (1) we are concerned with algorithmic concepts, not annoying technical details, and (2) in the real world, proper program design will ensure that such details are so well encapsulated that they will be hidden from most programmers anyway. Interested students will have ample opportunity to program such "low-level" tasks in subsequent systems programming courses.

3.4.1 Numbers

Numbers include both integers and real numbers. For our purposes, a single number can be of any magnitude. Thus the values 3, 5.127198 and 2,319,384,732 are each single numbers.

Most programming languages distinguish between *integers* and *real numbers* and treat each as a different type. They do so for obscure technical reasons concerning how numeric values are represented in binary form inside the computer. While you must be concerned with such details when dealing with a real programming language, there is no reason for us now to treat integers and reals as different types. Thus we consider all numbers to be of the same type, called *number* or Num.

3.4.2 Characters

Characters are alphanumeric and special symbols (such as punctuation) written between single quotation marks (or apostrophes) to distinguish them from variable names and numbers. Examples might include 'q,' 'x,' '4,' and '&'. Unlike numbers, which can be of any magnitude, a simple character variable can hold only a single symbol. For brevity, we often refer to the type character as Char (pronounced either "care" or "char").

To store a multiletter word would require multiple character variables. As you can imagine, requiring a separate variable for each character in a word would be very annoying. We'll see how to overcome this problem soon when we discuss *strings*.

Note that the character '4' (in single quotation marks) is treated differently in an algorithm than the number 4. The *character* '4' is a *numeral*, a character, just like the letter 'a.' It has no numeric value and cannot be part of an arithmetic expression. The *number* 4 has numeric value and can be part of an arithmetic expression. Similarly, the character '+' is just a character while the symbol + is an arithmetic operator.

By the same token, the character 'x' is different than x. The character 'x' is a character of the alphabet. In contrast, x looks like an identifier for a variable that we might have declared via:

```
x isoftype Char
```

 EXAMPLE 3.11   Given the declaration,

```
this_char_variable isoftype Char
```

the statement

```
this_char_variable <- 'x'
```

will store the character value *x* in the variable this_char_variable, while the statement

```
this_char_variable <- x
```

will attempt to locate another character variable whose identifier is x, retrieve its value and assign it to this_char_variable. If there is no such character variable, then an error has occurred.

3.4.3 Booleans

Booleans are variables that have only a *binary* capability—that is, they can store only two possible values: TRUE or FALSE. (Inside a computer, a boolean variable might take the form of a *single binary digit*, with the value *1* representing TRUE and the value *0* representing FALSE.) As with other atomic variables, a boolean variable can hold only one value at any given moment. With boolean variables, TRUE is a single value (not "a word of 4 characters") and so is FALSE.

We shall see the usefulness of boolean variables in Section 3.9.

3.4.4 Pointers

Pointers store the memory addresses of other variables. We say that a pointer variable "points" to another variable because the address stored in it reveals where another variable "lives" in memory. If you are not familiar with pointers, you will discover that they are very powerful tools. We mention them only because they are one of our four atomic data types, but don't worry about them now. We will discuss pointers and the details about how they are used in Chapter 5.

3.5 Complex Data Types

Complex data types are those that can store more than a single atomic data value. Because they store more than one atomic value, variables that are declared to be of some complex type require multiple memory cells. Complex data types are constructed of atomic variables in various combinations.

3.5.1 Strings

A *string* is a complex data type that is a single list of characters, such as a normal English word, name, or sentence. Thus it consists of multiple characters. Since each character requires its own memory cell, a string variable will require as many character cells as there are characters in the string. Whereas we represent characters using single quotation marks (or apostrophes), we indicate a string by using double quotation marks. A string may be assigned, read, compared, and printed. It is also able to size itself "by magic"—that is, it can grow or shrink to the exact size needed.

In Chapters 5 and 7, we shall see how strings really work and how we might select specific characters within a string. For now, assume that string variables work by magic, and that all we can do is *assign* them, *read* them, *compare* them (we'll see how soon), and *print* them.

EXAMPLE 3.12 The following code segment shows how we might use a string variable:

```
chapter_num isoftype Num
chapter_num <- 3

chapter_title isoftype String
chapter_title <- "Basic Data and Operations"
```

```
print("This chapter is Chapter ", chapter_num)
print("and it is called ", chapter_title)
```

Later, we shall see how to manipulate individual characters within a string. For now, think of strings as being indivisible—that is, although they consist of a number of characters we cannot (just yet) break them down into individual characters. We introduce them now because they will help us solve simple data processing problems.

3.5.2   Other Complex Data Types

The concepts and constructs for constructing other complex data types of our own design are covered in Chapter 5.

3.6   Declaring and Initializing Variables

3.6.1   Location of Data Declarations

When writing an algorithm, you may use many different types of variables. As explained earlier, you must explicitly declare each variable *before* using it. You need only create a given variable once. You may declare variables anywhere in an algorithm. As a general rule, it is best to declare a variable shortly before it is first used.

Some programming languages require that you group together all such declarations in a special variable section at the beginning of the algorithm. Others allow you to declare variables anywhere in your code, just as we do. Both approaches have their advantages and disadvantages. The first approach makes it easier to see at a glance exactly what data are required, but it means that the algorithm creator must jump back and forth between the data declaration section at the top of the algorithm and the instruction section below. While there are various opinions about this, there is no clear "right" decision. Our choice here will be the second approach.

3.6.2   Choosing Identifier Names

Recall that we want an algorithm to feature *abstraction*: the consideration of an essence apart from its specific embodiment. Applying this idea to data, we want our data identifiers to represent the ideas or roles that the data play in the algorithm apart from whatever their specific values might be. Therefore, when creating data to hold values, we give them identifiers that represent the *idea* of what those data cells will hold. Choosing identifiers for variables and constants gives us our most basic tool for abstraction.

For simple algorithms, you might not see the need for appropriate names and instead prefer to use cute or humorous ones. However, as soon as algorithms become complex or useful enough to be read by someone else, clever names become a bad idea. Descriptive, informative names are far better.

Warning: Identifiers should describe the data they hold. Thus algorithms with identifiers such as "lucy," "ricky," "fred," and "ethel" should be avoided (unless you have a good reason!)

3.6.3   Initializing Variables

The declaration of a variable only creates the variable; it does not assign any value to the variable, and there is no value to which a new variable is automatically set. In order for a new variable to have a certain initial value, it must be explicitly *initialized* to hold the desired value. As we have seen, this may be done via an *assignment* operation or a *read* operation.

Initializing a new variable is the process of assigning a specific value to it through an assignment operation, a read operation, or some other means. Prior to initialization, a variable is considered to be *undefined*. This does not mean that it is empty; rather it means that the variable is somehow unpredictable.

BAD EXAMPLE 3.13   Consider the following code segment:

```
this_new_variable isoftype Num
print(this_new_variable)
```

While we don't know what value might result, we do know that the value will be *unpredictable*.

Warning: All variables must be explicitly initialized before we can know what value they hold. Unless a value has been assigned to a variable, the variable is *undefined*—that is, the variable has some garbage value, but we have no way to predict what that value might be. Thus, all variables must be initialized before their value is retrieved.

Once it is declared, there are three ways to initialize a variable. Given the declaration

```
this_num_var isoftype Num
```

we can

- Assign it a value via the assignment operator, for example,

```
this_num_var <- 4
```

- Read in a value from the outside world, for example,

```
read(this_num_var)
```

- Use parameter passing. (Don't worry about that now. Parameter passing will be discussed in Chapter 4.)

3.7   Fixed Data

Variables allow the algorithm to store and modify data values. Sometimes we have need for data values that the algorithm may not change. There are two ways that we might represent fixed data: by using (1) constants or (2) literals.

3.7.1   Constants

A constant does just what its name suggests: It stores a value that is *not* variable, a value that remains the same throughout the algorithm. Like variables, constants must be declared before they are used. Whereas variables are declared to be of some data type, constants are declared to represent some fixed value. Because the value of a constant will, by definition, not change, there is no need to specify the type of data, only its fixed value. Thus we use the form

```
<identifier> is <some value>
```

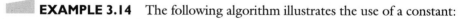 **EXAMPLE 3.14**   The following algorithm illustrates the use of a constant:

```
algorithm CircleFacts
    PI is 3.14159

    radius isoftype type Num
    read(radius)

    area isoftype Num
    area <- PI * radius * radius

    circumference isoftype Num
    circumference <- 2 * PI * radius

    print ("A circle with a radius of ", radius)
    print ("has an area of", area,  )
    print ("and a circumference of ", circumference)
endalgorithm
```

3.7.2   Literal Values

Most algorithms are made up of variables and constants. In most circumstances, it is preferable to use those constructs than it is to "hardwire" information into a program.

 Definition: We use **hardwire** as a metaphor to describe the practice of building data values into an algorithm by placing literal values in code statements rather than using symbolic identifiers.

Hardwiring specific values into an algorithm should be avoided. This is because we want an algorithm to be at a high level of abstraction to work on any set of appropriate data, not just the particular values we hardwire into it. When we do have need for a nonchangeable value, the best approach is to declare a constant. Using a constant makes it easier to find such values, should we ever need to change the algorithm by modifying them. It also raises the level of abstraction by allowing us to refer to a descriptive name, rather than some out-of-context value.

However, there are occasions where it might be reasonable to build values into an algorithm.

EXAMPLE 3.15   Messages sometimes need to be written to the screen, prompting the user or supplying the user with information. If we do not need to reuse the same textual message in various places, we might use *literal strings*:

```
algorithm Week's_Pay
    hours_worked isoftype Num
    print ("Enter the number of hours you worked this week.")
    read (hours_worked)

    hourly_rate isoftype Num
    print ("Enter how much you make per hour.")
    read(hourly_rate)

    pay isoftype Num
    pay <- hourly_rate * hours_worked
    print ("You earned ", pay, " this week.")
endalgorithm
```

In this example, all the textual messages are strings but are they are neither variables nor constants. They have no identifier to symbolize them. They are *literal string values*.

We could have created string constants for these messages, and we would have done so if we needed to use a certain message repeatedly in various locations throughout an algorithm. However, since we required them only once, we didn't bother.

BAD EXAMPLE 3.16   In the code, below, the number .05 is a literal.

```
gross_sales isoftype num
read(gross_sales)

net_commission isoftype num
net_commission <- gross_sales * .05
```

This is an example of an inappropriate use of a literal. Why? Because we know that the value .05 represents something but the algorithm does not tell us *what* it represents. Because the identifiers for the two variables tell us something about the situation, we might guess that .05 represents the commission rate for a sales representative, but we do not really know. We should *never* have to guess.

GOOD EXAMPLE 3.17   It would have been far better to have written the following:

```
COMMISSION_RATE is .05

gross_sales isoftype num
read(gross_sales)

net_commission isoftype num
net_commission <- gross_sales * COMMISSION_RATE
```

3.8   General Rules

3.8.1   General Structure of an Algorithm

Now that we have seen some simple examples, we can identify certain features of the general structure of an algorithm that will be found in all our algorithms:

■ The *header line,* which is the first line of the algorithm, contains the keyword `algorithm`, followed by the algorithm identifier—that is, the name we choose for the algorithm. We capitalize each word in the algorithm identifier and concatenate multiple words using underscores.

- The *end line,* which is the last line of the algorithm, contains the keyword `endalgorithm` to specify where the algorithm stops.
- The algorithmic steps are specified by indenting the various statements between the *header line* and *end line.* The indentation visually frames the body of the algorithm for the human eye and removes any confusion about where the algorithm starts and stops.
- Within the body of the algorithm, variables are declared then used to store data; `read` and `print` statements are used to communicate values between variables and the outside world.
- Also within the body of the algorithm, *white space* (i.e., one or more blank lines) is used to break the algorithm into logical chunks. In Example 3.10, there are three logical activities (*obtaining the data, doing the calculation,* and *printing the results*). Two blank lines are used to visually subdivide the algorithm into its logical parts, making it visually obvious that there are three logical steps involved. Used properly, white space provides information to the reader. In Example 3.10, the reader knows at a glance that there are three logical steps *before* he reads the various instructions.

3.8.2 Formats for Identifiers

As mentioned earlier, there are certain conventions that we want you to follow concerning identifiers. You may find them annoying at first, but we will insist that you follow them simply because they will make it easier to read your algorithms. With respect to identifiers, the rules are as follows:

- Each identifier may consist only of alphanumeric symbols: alphabetic characters, numbers, and punctuation symbols. No blank spaces are allowed.
- The first character of an identifier must be a letter.
- Variable identifiers should *not* be capitalized. You may abbreviate words and connect multiple words together. If a variable identifier consists of two or more words, connect them with an underscore symbol—for example, `num_credit_hrs` for "number of credit hours."
- Type identifiers should have their first letter capitalized—for example, `Num`.
- Constant identifiers should have *all* letters capitalized. This makes it easy to distinguish at a glance which identifiers refer to variables and which refer to constants. Thus, within a class registration algorithm, we might declare

```
MIN_NUM_CREDIT_HRS is 15
my_credit_hours isoftype Num
```

- Algorithm identifiers, like type identifiers should have the first letter of each word capitalized:

```
algorithm Register_For_Class
algorithm Calc_Federal_Taxes
```

3.8.3 Type Matching

A *variable* is always declared to be of a given type. A *constant* is implicitly a type as indicated by the constant value that it is defined to represent. A *literal* value is also implicitly of a type. Thus every data value that appears anywhere in an algorithm is of some data type, either explicitly or implicitly.

Each data operation must involve only a single data type. Any operation involving values of more than one data type is illegal. It is considered to be a *type mismatch error*. You must assume that any type mismatch is an error that will cause your algorithm to fail.[4]

BAD EXAMPLE 3.18   The constant declaration and the variable declarations shown below are legal. Each of the assignment statements feature a type mismatch and are therefore errors.

```
PI is 3.14159
this_variable isoftype Num
this_variable <- 'a'
this_variable <- TRUE
this_variable <- "A textual message"

that_variable isoftype Char
that_variable <- 7
that_variable <- PI
that_variable <- FALSE
that_variable <- "A textual message"

another_variable isoftype Boolean
another_variable <- 1
another_variable <- PI
another_variable <- 'D'
another_variable <- "A textual message"

yonder_variable isoftype String
yonder_variable <- 12
yonder_variable <- 'q'
yonder_variable <- TRUE
yonder_variable <- PI
```

3.9   Algorithmic Decisions

As we said in Chapter 2, the power of computing comes from the ability of algorithms to make decisions and act on them.

---

4. Type mismatch errors have their origins in the kind of obscure technical details that we generally wish to avoid. However, they can be useful and we thus keep them as a concept for reasons of disciplined thinking, not for program implementation.

3.9.1   The Basis of Decisions

All algorithmic decisions result in TRUE/FALSE answers. They are based on the evaluation of conditional expressions, such as

```
"is the number of hours for which I've registered so far greater than or
equal to 15?"
```

which might be expressed in an algorithm as

```
my_credit_hours >= 15
```

A conditional expression always evaluates to a boolean value—that is, it is either TRUE or FALSE. This is crucial, as there can never be any ambiguity: either the number of hours is "greater than or equal to 15" or it is not. The general syntax of a conditional expression is

```
<operand> <relational operator> <operand>
```

Two values are compared according to the *relational operator*. There are six relational operators:

1. Greater than (>)
2. Greater than or equal to (>=)
3. Equal to (=)
4. Less than or equal to (<=)
5. Less than (<)
6. Not equal to (<>)

To make a comparison, we need two operand values, one on either side of the relational operator. Each operand can be as follows:

1. An *identifier* which has some value associated with it:

   ```
   this_variable < that_variable
   ```

   or

   ```
   that_variable >= THIS_CONSTANT
   ```

2. *A literal value:*

   ```
   this_variable >= 15
   ```

3. An *expression*:

   ```
   (x + y) <> (a * b)
   ```

   where x, y, a, and b are each either an identifier, a literal, or another expression.

3.9.2   Decisions and Data Types

We make decisions by comparing two values. To do so, it is necessary that both values be of the same data type. You may compare any two values of the same type. Comparing two values that are not of the same type will result in type mismatch errors.

Thus you may compare one *character* to another, one *number* to another, one *string* to another, and one *boolean* to another. The comparisons are performed as follows:

- Comparisons of numbers are done in the obvious way: if two numbers are not identical, then one is greater than the other. In the case of real numbers, we assume an infinite number of significant digits.[5]
- Comparisons of *characters* are based on alphabetic order—for example, 'a' is considered less than 'b.'
- Comparisons of *strings* are based on character-by-character, position-by-position comparisons until a difference is found. Thus, the string "snork" is greater than "snark": the two strings are equal until the third character, then the 'a' (the first letter of the alphabet) is less than the 'o' (the fifteenth). You may assume that this kind of comparison happens "by magic," such that the condition ("snork" <= "snark") will resolve to FALSE.
- Comparison of booleans are based on the assumption that a TRUE is a one and FALSE is a zero. However, the situation where we want to see if one boolean result is greater than another rarely, if ever, arises.

3.9.3 Acting on Decisions

Once the conditional expression has been evaluated—that is, reduced to either a TRUE or FALSE value—a control structure is needed to govern what happens next. The simplest control structure is the if-then-else construct. Its general form is shown below:

```
if <conditional expression> then
    statement_A
    statement_B
else
    statement_C
    statement_D
    statement_E
endif
statement_F
statement_G
```

If the conditional expression is TRUE, statements A and B will be executed and statements C, D, and E will be skipped. If the conditional expression is FALSE, statements A and B will be skipped and statements C, D, and E will be executed. Thus either statements A and B will be executed or statements C, D, and E will be. There is *no way* for all five statements to be executed in a simple sequence.

Also, notice how important the endif is. The decision statement begins with if and continues through endif. Regardless of the decision, statements F and G will be executed because they follow the if-then-else and are not a part of it.

---

5. A computer will have some finite number of digits, but we don't care about that now.

EXAMPLE 3.19   A simple code segment will illustrate the *if-then-else* construct:

```
algorithm Pass_Fail
   PASSING is 60

   average isoftype Num
      read(average)

   did_pass isoftype Boolean
   if (average < PASSING) then
      did_pass <- FALSE
   else
      did_pass <- TRUE
   endif

   if (did_pass) then
      print("At least you passed.")
   else
      print("Geez, how could you fail?")
   endif
end algorithm
```

EXAMPLE 3.20   The `else` part of the `if-then-else` construct is optional. The follow...g code segment shows the use of `if` without an `else`:

```
if (cash >= .60) then
   buy a Coke
endif
attend class
```

Because there is no `else` clause, the result of the decision statement will either be that you have enough money, so you buy a Coke, or you don't have enough money, so you don't buy one. Regardless of the result, the next instruction is executed so, whether you buy a Coke or not, you still go to class.

EXAMPLE 3.21   Sometimes two choices are not enough. In such cases, we can make use of one or more `elseif` clauses. The following example illustrates the use of the `elseif` option:

```
algorithm Assign_Letter_Grades
   numerical_average isoftype Num
   read(numerical_average)

   letter_grade isoftype Char
   if (numerical_average >= 90) then
      letter_grade <- 'A'
   elseif (numerical_average >= 80) then
      letter_grade <- 'B'
   elseif (numerical_average >= 70) then
      letter_grade <- 'C'
   elseif (numerical_average >= 60) then
      letter_grade <- 'D'
   else
      letter_grade <- 'F'
   endif

   print("The grade for the course is ", letter_grade)
endalgorithm
```

Observe that there is an initial `if` and a final `else`. For each condition in between, we use an `elseif`.

An `if-elseif-else` statement tests its conditions only until it finds a condition that resolves to TRUE. As soon as it finds a TRUE condition, it executes the statements indicated for that condition and stops looking any further. The next statement executed is the statement located immediately after the `endif`.

Warning: When using the `elseif` clause, make sure that you are testing conditions in a sequence that gives the results you intend.

Bad Example 3.22 will show you how important the ordering of the conditions are. If we had tested the conditions in reverse order, we would have had a problem!

BAD EXAMPLE 3.22 Having conditions in the wrong order can lead to errors:

```
if (numerical_average < 60) then
    letter_grade <- 'F'
elseif (numerical_average >= 60) then
    letter_grade <- 'D'
elseif (numerical_average >= 70) then
    letter_grade <- 'C'
elseif (numerical_average >= 80) then
    letter_grade <- 'B'
else
    letter_grade <- 'A'
endif
```

What is happening here? We would assign a grade of F to anybody with an average less than 60, which is correct. However, we would assign a grade of D to anybody with an average greater than 60 *regardless* of what his or her passing average was! Someone with a 97 average would receive a letter grade of D.

Warning: The final `else` is usually very important. If we do not use a final `else`, then we do not specify an action for any possible data state for which we have not explicitly tested. In the examples above, we trusted our `if-elseif-else` to initialize the value of `letter_grade`. Failure to have an `else` clause could create a situation in which `letter_grade` is never assigned a value. In a computer program, this could cause the program to "blow up" or "crash." Therefore, always use an `else` clause when using one or more `elseif`s unless you are *absolutely sure* that any possibility of data for which you have not tested does indeed require "no action." Doing this can keep an algorithm from failing.

EXAMPLE 3.23 Let's consider a "plain English" example where we do not use a final `else` because the `if` and `elseif` conditions call for all the needed actions. We therefore do not want to take any action if neither of those conditions are met:

```
if (gas gauge shows "Empty") then
    get to a gas station pronto
elseif (gas gauge shows less than a quarter-tank) then
    get to a gas station pretty soon
endif
```

In this example, the absence of a final `else` clause is appropriate. If our gas tank is neither empty nor nearly empty, we have no need to go to a gas station to fill up.

EXAMPLE 3.24 Here's another example where the final `else` is critical. It is supposed to decide what to do at the gas station when you need gasoline. But does it?

```
if (<you have enough money for a full tank>) then
    <fill it up>
    <pay with cash>
elseif (<you have a credit card that you can use>) then
    <fill it up>
    <pay with your credit card>
endif
```

In this example, we have not specified any action at all if you need gas and have neither enough cash for a full tank nor a useable credit card. Should you not get any gas? Or should you buy as much gas as you can pay for with whatever cash you have? Or what? We haven't specified any action at all. According to this condition, unless you have some way to pay for a full tank, you would drive around until you ran out of gas. It might not cause you to run out of gas every time, but sooner or later it probably will.

There is only one known way to make sure that you don't have errors in your algorithm: *trace it.* Tracing is the single most important thing you can do to discover accidental errors and repair them.[6] To trace your algorithm, create space on paper to record the value of each variable and constant, update variable values whenever the algorithm calls for it, and do *only* what the algorithm tells you to do. Novices will often assume that they are smart enough to know what they wrote. Well, being smart isn't the problem. Algorithms must work for a processor that doesn't know what you think. Thus to trace an algorithm properly, you must try to be as stupid as a computer: You must make no assumptions, forget what you know about the problem, and simply process data just as a computer would, step by step, with zero common sense.

---

6. Current research into the programming process shows that experienced professionals, not just novices, benefit from systematic "code reviews" (in which they trace their code before trying to translate it.) This activity is the biggest single contributor to increased programmer productivity. This finding runs contrary to the widespread but unfounded assumption that using "debuggers" is the fastest way to produce a correct computer program.

3.9.4 Complex Decisions via Boolean Operators

Sometimes a condition may contain many small decisions that join together to make one complex condition.

Definition: Decisions are combined via the **boolean operators:** AND, OR, XOR, NOT. These are called boolean operators because they are used to produce boolean decisions from complex decision statements. The AND operator takes two conditions and compares them. The result is TRUE only if both of the conditions are TRUE.

EXAMPLE 3.25 The following code segment illustrates the use of the AND operator.

```
if ((you want to eat out) AND (you have enough money)) then
    go out to dinner
else
    eat at home
endif
```

This conditional expression contains two parts joined by the logical AND operator. Each part is itself a condition. This means that the condition is TRUE *only if both parts are* TRUE. If one or both parts are FALSE, then the condition is FALSE and the else clause is executed.

Definition: The OR operator takes two conditions and compares them. The result is TRUE if *at least one* of the conditions is TRUE.

EXAMPLE 3.26 The following code segment illustrates the use of the OR operator.

```
if ((you want to eat out) OR (you have enough money)) then
    go out to dinner
else
    eat at home
endif
```

According to this decision statement, you go out to eat if you want to, or if you can afford it, or both. According to this decision statement, if you can afford to go out, you do so even if you don't want to, and vice versa.

Definition: The XOR ("*exclusive or*") takes two conditions and compares them. It resolves to TRUE if exactly one of its operands is TRUE. It resolves to FALSE if both operands are TRUE or both are FALSE.

EXAMPLE 3.27 The following code segment illustrates the use of the XOR operator. Pretend that $2 bills do not exist.

```
if (<you have a Five Dollar bill>) XOR (<you have five Ones>) then
    print ("You have exactly $5 in paper money.")
```

```
else
   print ("You've got either more or less.")
endif
```

Definition: The NOT operator acts on a single expression instead of joining two expressions. When placed in front of an expression, it reverses the result of the logical test.

EXAMPLE 3.28 The following code segments illustrate the use of the XOR operator.

```
is_raining isoftype Boolean
read(is_raining)
if NOT(is_raining) then
   walk to the park
else
   stay indoors
endif
```

Without the NOT, walk to the park would be executed if the value of the boolean variable is_raining were TRUE. The NOT reverses this, so that you walk to the park only if it is NOT raining, that is, if the value of the variable is_raining is FALSE. We might have achieved the same results with the logic

```
is_raining isoftype Boolean
read(is_raining)
if (is_raining) then
   stay indoors
else
   walk to the park
endif
```

The NOT operator is useful if you find yourself thinking that you need a statement that "does nothing."

BAD EXAMPLE 3.29 Let's look at a code segment that requires a "do nothing" statement:

```
if (<conditional expression>)
   don't do anything
else
   take some action
endif
```

In such circumstances, you can achieve the effect you want by using the boolean NOT operator and eliminating the else clause:

GOOD EXAMPLE 3.30 Using the NOT operator can eliminate the need for a "do nothing" statement:

```
if NOT(<condition>) then
   take some action
endif
```

Warning: You may run into a stumbling block when trying to figure out the correct logical test to make the algorithm do what you want it to do. In many cases you can use just one of the boolean operators (AND, OR, XOR, NOT), but a combination of them may be needed to make complex decisions. In such cases, it is easy to make mistakes and those mistakes can be tricky to detect. It is imperative to be careful. This means *tracing* your code!

EXAMPLE 3.31 An example of a complex decision. A couple wants to buy a house satisfying the following criteria: It must be in either Atlanta or Miami, cost no more than $120,000, and be in good shape. Construct a decision statement for them.

```
if (((location = Atlanta) OR (location = Miami)) AND (NOT(cost >
   $120,000)) AND (condition = good))then
   buy the house
else
   keep looking
endif
```

Notice how important the parentheses are. Parentheses indicate the order in which the expressions are evaluated, just as in mathematics. The innermost expressions are always evaluated first. In this example, we first evaluate the expression ((location = Atlanta) OR (location = Miami)), and replace the expression with its value (TRUE or FALSE). Because of the parentheses, we then evaluate the last two expressions and replace them with their boolean value. The final result is obtained by ANDing the two boolean values. Only if both results are TRUE will the entire condition be TRUE. We need to be careful with parentheses to make it work.

Boolean decisions are binary. Among other things, this means each decision test can compare *only two values at a time*. In cases having more than two values that must be compared, we use parentheses to group them so that we compare only two values at any one time.

BAD EXAMPLE 3.32 The following example does not work because it compares more than two values at once:

```
if ((you want a new car) AND (you like this model) AND (you can
   afford it)) then
   buy the car
else
   fix your old one
endif
```

GOOD EXAMPLE 3.33 We could revise the code to obtain the correct result:

```
if (((you want a new car) AND (you like this model)) AND (you can
   afford it)) then
   buy the car
else
   fix your old one
endif
```

The parentheses order the conditions so that we first do an AND test on the first two conditions, which results in a TRUE or FALSE value. We then AND that result with the result of the third condition, giving us the final result.

3.9.5 Nested Decisions

If-then-else decision statements can also be *nested*. This means they can be placed inside of one another.

EXAMPLE 3.34 The following algorithm uses a nested decision. It can help you decide what to do with your time:

```
if (you have a week off) then
    if ((you want to go somewhere) AND (you can afford it)) then
        go on a vacation
    else
        stay at home
    endif
else
    do what you have to do
endif
```

By combining boolean operators with nested decisions, we can decide complex things. To do so, it is necessary to break down decisions into simple TRUE/FALSE questions.

FOOD FOR THOUGHT

A Tale of Two Henrys

Henry Ford not only revolutionized the automobile industry, he created it as an industry. Prior to Ford, cars were built individually, much like artisans produce handcrafted goods. When Ford invented the assembly line, he bridged a gap between the mechanical model and the computational model. His assembly line reflected a maturation of the mechanical model: he developed a process that was itself a machine. Each worker on the assembly line was, in effect, a cog in that machine, performing a specific function again and again. His assembly line also showed attributes of the computational model. He abstracted out and made explicit the behavioral procedures necessary to efficiently accomplish the task. In short, he saw the production process *as a process*.

But perhaps the real hero here is a different Henry: *Henry Leland.* Without him, Ford could not have developed the assembly line. Most people have never heard of Leland, but they are probably familiar with some of his accomplishments. Leland founded both the Cadillac and Lincoln automobile companies (Cadillac made great cars, but lost money. Facing bankruptcy, it was acquired by General Motors. Leland later founded Lincoln with similar results. Henry Ford bought Lincoln.). However, Leland's most significant contribution was much more basic than founding luxury car makers. Here's his story.

In the late 1800s, Leland worked at Colt, the famous gun maker, where he witnessed pioneering efforts to standardize the parts of the guns being produced there. At the time, a part from one gun was unlikely to work properly on another seemingly identical gun. Despite the fact that all guns each had certain parts, no two parts were truly interchangeable, a situation that Colt was trying to change. Leland left Colt for a job at a company that made precision tools, such as micrometers. While there, he observed the process by which metal products could be made to reliable, precise dimensions. He saw that precision was indeed possible in handmade tools.

Leland absorbed details from both jobs and put the two lessons together. The result led to something that may seem obvious now, but was radical at the time: the precision manufacture of standardized parts. The initial success of his Cadillacs was largely due to this: It was the only car that featured truly *interchangeable* parts. Prior to Cadillac, when a car part broke, the replacement part had to be hand-fashioned by the local "machinist" (often the local blacksmith), or a factory mechanic had to travel to the car, or the car had to be returned to the factory. For the first time, a Cadillac customer could simply "order a part" that would fit.

At Cadillac, Leland proved that using standardized parts was viable. However, while standardization *allows* an assembly line, it does not require one. Cadillacs were built the old way, one at a time. After he left Cadillac and before he founded Lincoln, Leland worked for Ford. He faced a difficult battle trying to convince Henry Ford to adopt standardization. At first the idea was considered "crazy" and "too much trouble," but Leland stayed at Ford until he convinced the "other Henry." Leland's contribution allowed Ford to mechanize how we make machines.

Leland looked at the *processes* of making a machine and took things to a higher level of abstraction. Before him, while a machine might produce identical results, the process of *making* machines was analogous to the process of creating documents *before* the printing press: each one was unique. After Leland, industry became "a machine for making machines." His breakthrough was recognizing the importance of interchangeable parts.

While particular problems had to be overcome, there is no reason why someone could not have done this earlier.

Pit Stops in France

Throughout the twentieth century we can see numerous examples of algorithmic approaches that *could* have occurred earlier but did not. One example comes from stock car racing, which grew out of the illegal racing that occurred during Prohibition between moonshine runners and government agents. Many early stock car drivers learned to race on Appalachian mountain roads, escaping from federal "revenuers" who were in hot pursuit. By the 1950s, legal stock car racing had become established in the American South and was soon to begin gaining in popularity elsewhere.

In the early 1960s, Henry Ford II tried to purchase the Italian car maker Ferrari, but his offer was turned down. Outraged, he decreed that Ford should invade European racing, where Ferrari was king, and beat Enzo Ferrari at his own game. The result was the famous Ford GT40 race cars that dominated the Ferrari team and the rest of the automotive world at LeMans. The Fords won four years in a row, then retired from competition.

Ford's strategy included a particular strength that the American teams brought with them from stock car racing: the perfected "pit stop." The race at LeMans is a 24-hour endurance race and involves numerous stops for fuel, tires, rested drivers, and repairs. While the European racers were not casual about their pit stops, they had never witnessed what they saw from the American teams. As a GT40 entered the pits, it was literally attacked by a swarm of mechanics and support personnel, each with his own particular job, each climbing over and around the car in a well choreographed frenetic ballet. While European cars would receive the same service, it might take minutes. The GT40s were in and out of the pits in a matter of *seconds*.

Again, we see algorithmic thinking applied to what is, on the surface, a mechanical phenomena. True, the car itself is mechanical, but its efficient servicing is a human process. The Americans had "abstracted out" each element: each procedure was isolated from the others, assigned to specific agents, then collectively choreographed to maximize efficiency. As with the assembly line, the *process* had received careful analysis, decomposition, and abstraction: exactly those things that are essential to algorithmic solutions. And, again, there is nothing about this approach that is dependent on any particular technology. There is no reason why the Europeans could not have developed such solutions decades earlier. But they didn't. Why? Simply because it *did not occur to them*.

Algorithms for Home Runs and Stolen Bases

In the mid-1970s Earl Weaver, manager of the Baltimore Orioles, brought a computer into the dugout. His great teams of the late 1960s and early 1970s were things of the past, and he was looking for every edge he could find to try to help his Orioles get back to the World Series. He carefully tracked each batter's performance against each pitcher. He kept track of where in the field each ball was hit, how well each batter did for each kind of pitch, what kind of pitches each opposing pitcher threw in each kind of situation, and so on. He did all this in the belief that these data could help him know how and when to best deploy his players. Evidently, by 1979 he had figured out how.

He took an old idea, and he took it to a new level. For the 1978 season, he had acquired Gary Roenicke, a .236 hitter who had averaged less than three home runs per season. For the 1979 season, he also acquired John Lowenstein, a career .238 hitter who had averaged only four home runs per year. Their records were remarkably similar in their mediocrity. Yet in 1979, he combined them into a "virtual left fielder" who hit 36 homers and 98 RBI. How? By decomposing each player's performance into component situational attributes then recombining them as necessary to optimize the result. In short, he developed a data-based algorithm for deciding when to play each of them. The resulting decisions often confounded the experts by going against conventional wisdom. But the results speak for themselves. In 1982 his virtual left fielder hit .292 with 45 home runs and 140 RBI, leading the league in the latter two categories, and the teams Weaver assembled (or should we say "programmed"?) made it back to the World Series in 1979 and 1983 despite having few great players. His methods for tracking performance data are now routine throughout major league baseball. However, we don't know if he ever told anybody what his algorithm was.

There's been a similar transformation in the "art" of base stealing. Only a few decades ago, a base stealer was a special talent, somebody who had both speed and "the knack." In recent years, base stealing has become demystified. How? By decomposing the activity into its component parts. Clock the time it takes each opposing pitcher to go from his wind-up to getting the ball to the catcher. Clock the time it takes each opposing catcher to throw to second base. Add the two: that's how much time you've got. Clock the time it takes each of your base runners to run from their lead at first base to their slide into second. Compare. The decision to steal or not falls out of the equation. In the past, a catcher with a pretty good arm could throw out most runners. As a result of the new approach, even the best catchers today are usually able to throw out runners in less than half of the attempts to steal. Why didn't teams take this approach to base stealing in the 1950s, or the 1930s, or the 1890s? All you need is a stopwatch. Well, actually, you need more: you need the right "way of thinking."

Look Around

The fact is that each of these developments, and many more, *could* have occurred years before they actually did. They were dependent upon a given mental approach, a certain way of thinking: "process thinking" or "algorithmic thinking." Of course, none of the people we've mentioned here necessarily *knew* that they were thinking algorithmically (just as there is no reason to think that Copernicus realized that he was "thinking mechanistically"). In all probability, they never heard the word "algorithm." But they *were* thinking algorithmically nonetheless, bringing new ideas into daily practice. Examples of this are everywhere, if you only look for them. As a result, history may judge the twentieth century to be the time when algorithmic thinking arrived in everyday life.

SUMMARY

The elemental building blocks of algorithms include data, operations, and decisions.
The elementary building blocks of data include:

- Atomic data types—that is, numbers, characters, booleans, and pointers
- Complex data types, such as strings
- Constants, which allow us to establish and refer to fixed data values by meaningful names.
- Literals, which allow us to hardwire textual messages or other values into an algorithm.

The basic operations that may be performed on data include:

- Arithmetic operators (+, -, *, /, DIV, MOD), which operate numerical data

- Relational operators (>, >=, =, <=, <, <>), which may operate on numerical, character, boolean, or string data
- Boolean operators (AND, OR, XOR, NOT), which allow us to combine simple conditional expressions into complex ones.

Decisions are always based on the evaluation of conditional expressions that allow algorithms to make TRUE/FALSE decisions. Control structures, such as the if-then-else construct, allow algorithms to act on their decisions.

These are the basic low-level tools. In subsequent chapters, we will discuss how to use these tools to create effective higher-level abstractions.

EXERCISES

3.1 Explain the difference between *data types* and *variables*.

For Exercises 3.2 through 3.6, write the appropriate variable declarations:

3.2 For keeping track of how many students are registered for a class.
3.3 For storing whether or not a class is a senior level class.
3.4 For storing someone's name.
3.5 For storing someone's social security number.
3.6 For storing someone's address: one for street address, another for city/state/ zip code.

For Exercises 3.7 through 3.12, you may assume the variables of the appropriate type.

3.7 What happens as a result of

```
x <- 5 * 4 - 8 / 2
```

3.8 What happens as a result of

```
x <- 5 * (4 - 8) / 2
```

3.9 What happens as a result of

```
y <- (5 * 4) - 8 / 2
```

3.10 What value(s) of *j* cause the message to be printed?

```
if ((3 + 7) * (20 - 4) > 5 + 20 * j) then
    print("Snork")
endif
```

3.11 What value(s) of *j* cause the message to be printed?

```
if ((3 + (7 * 20) - 4) > (5 + 20) * j) then
    print("Snork")
endif
```

3.12 What values of *x* and *y* cause the message to be printed?

```
if (x <= y) then
```

```
        if (x * x > y * y) then
            print("Frazz")
        endif
    endif
endif
```

For Exercises 3.13 through 3.17, you have been given the following code segment:

```
x isoftype Num
read(x)
y isoftype Num
read(y)

if ((12 - 7 > y) AND (13 - x >= 27) then
    if (x * y > 0) then
        print("Snazzly")
    else
        print("Glibberama")
    endif
else
    if (x * y > 0) then
        print("Grontzes")
    else
        print("Where's my fish?")
    endif
endif
```

What will happen given the following conditions:

3.13 The first input value is 5 and the second is 14.

3.14 The first input value is −5 and the second is 14.

3.15 The first input value is 5 and the second is −14.

3.16 The first input value is −5 and the second is −14.

3.17 The first input value is 14 and the second is −5.

3.18 Write an algorithm that will prompt the user to type in three numbers, then read in those three numbers from the user, calculate the largest of the three, and print out the result.

3.19 Write an algorithm that will read in two boolean values and then determine if they are both TRUE or both FALSE.

3.20 Write an algorithm that will read in two boolean values and then print true if only one of them is TRUE or false otherwise.

3.21 Let's look again at Example 3.23 but now assume that $2 bills do exist. (Thomas Jefferson is pictured on them; if you visit his home, Monticello and buy an admission ticket with a bill of $10 or more, you will receive change in $2 bills.) Rewrite the algorithm so that it will work with $2 bills as well as $1 and $5 bills.

3.22 Write an algorithm (in plain English) to describe the process of making a peanut-butter and jelly sandwich. Assume that you are writing this algorithm for someone who can follow directions in the kitchen but who has no common sense and who has never eaten a sandwich before. Be sure to go into enough detail and to maintain a low enough level of abstraction (i.e., don't just say, "put jelly on bread"—this could mean put the jar of jelly on top of the loaf of bread!).

3.23 Write an algorithm that reads in the gross sales in dollars for each of two companies as well as their total expenses. Based on this information, calculate which company has the greatest profit. Also calculate which company has the highest ratio of profit to expenses. Print out the results with appropriate textual messages.

3.24 Using data in Exercise 3.20, calculate the profit for three companies instead of two.

3.25 Using data in Exercise 3.20, calculate the profit for four companies instead of two.

CHAPTER 4

Tools for Procedural Abstraction

The algorithms we have looked at so far have been quite simple, illustrating only basic features. However, most algorithms solve complicated problems that can be broken down into subtasks. As discussed in Chapter 2, if an algorithm involves a complicated subtask or subtasks that are performed in various places in the algorithm, it is best to write an individual algorithm for each subtask. The main algorithm will then call the minialgorithm, or *module*,[1] to execute the subtask. The module then "does its thing" and returns control to the main algorithm. Each module is a component that is used to construct the larger algorithm.

By doing this properly, we create *procedural abstraction,* a topic introduced in this chapter. We will also focus on the two basic kinds of modules used to achieve it, the use of parameters to create well-defined interfaces between modules and the important benefits this provides. We also show how procedural abstractions can be used to achieve recursive solutions. Finally, we introduce the concept of a stack and show how it can be used to trace the execution of a recursive algorithm.

---

[1]As mentioned in Chapter 2, we use the word *module* in the generic sense of the term (i.e., meaning an interchangeable component). In certain programming languages the word has a more specific meaning, but here we use the broader definition. The word *call* has a particular meaning in algorithms and programming. It means to "invoke a module" (i.e., to trigger the execution of a given module simply by using its name in an instruction).

4.1 The Basic Idea

Algorithms that feature good *procedural abstraction* will evidence a high degree of modularity. This means there will be a number of relatively independent modules that together solve the task at hand.

The main algorithm organizes and coordinates the various modules, while each module takes care of exactly one logical task. Thus there will be one main algorithm and as many modules as required, one for each subtask.

Such a modular design creates a hierarchy of abstraction, represented graphically in Fig. 4.1. At the top level is the main algorithm that coordinates the overriding logic, the main subtasks, or logical "chunks," of the algorithm. Below it are the various modules, each of which is responsible for of one of the logical chunks. Depending upon the complexity of each subtask, those modules may themselves call other modules, and so on.

Judging from this figure, we would expect that `Main` will primarily consists of instructions that call those modules in the level immediately below it, and will contain relatively few instructions that directly manipulate data. Its work is delegated to the modules at the level below, and its job is to control and coordinate them. According to the diagram, we would expect that `Get_Data`, `Task_One`, and `Output_Data` are all relatively simple and straightforward tasks since they evidently require no lower-level modules. `Task_Two` appears to be more complex since it has two subordinate modules.

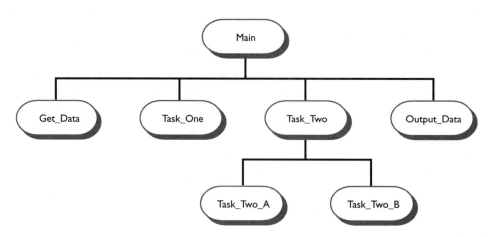

FIGURE 4.1   A hierarchy of abstraction

4.2   Why Modularity?

Good modularity in an algorithm accomplishes five things:

1. *It makes algorithms easier to write.* It lets us focus on simple subtasks rather than forcing us to cope with all the details of a complicated problem all at once. In effect, we chip away at a problem, solving little bits and pieces at a time, until we've solved the whole thing.

2. *It makes algorithms easier to read.* Breaking the algorithm into simpler, more understandable chunks allows someone other than the algorithm author to quickly understand what is going on. This is crucial to the software industry, where algorithms need be read and worked upon by many different people over time.

3. *It raises the level of abstraction.* Annoying details are *encapsulated* inside modules. By hiding the specific little details of a given logical step in a module, we can consider the larger, more fundamental steps of the algorithm without getting lost in the details. If we are concerned about how the details are handled, we know exactly where to look.

4. *It saves time, space, and effort.* Often, we need the same task in multiple places in an algorithm. Once a module is written, it can be called from many different places in an algorithm. For example, imagine you have a data processing algorithm that needs to compute the minimum of two numbers and that there are several places in the algorithm where this is needed. You could insert the instructions into the algorithm wherever needed, but this approach would be tedious, time consuming, and error prone. It would be much more efficient to write one module, `Min_2_Nums`, and call it whenever you need it.

5. *It extends language.* It allows us to *invent new capabilities* that are not provided by the language. Once a module is created, calling it by name is logically no different from using some built-in language feature such as `read` or `print`. Thus, if we wish that the language has some capability that it does not, perhaps we can write a module that will "do" that capability. Thereafter we may call that module whenever we want the capability, as if we had added it to our personal version of the language.

In effect, we can use procedural abstraction to create new *primitives* for the language. Used in this way, it is a very powerful tool. It not only helps with the algorithm on which we are now working, but it also helps later when we can reuse that same module in future algorithms.

If done properly, it means that we create the "recipe of action" for a given task only once, which provides us with many advantages:

- We minimize the number of error possibilities.
- We save ourselves the effort of duplicating groups of instructions needlessly.
- We keep our algorithm small.
- We give ourselves a module that we can use in future algorithms.

 Algorithms should be modular and feature a high degree of procedural abstraction. If your algorithm proves to be perfectly correct but you have put all the small details together into a large collection of steps, it will be considered far *less* valuable than a highly modular one that contained major errors.

4.3 The Need for Module Interfaces

Procedural abstraction gives us the same kind of benefit that Henry Leland contributed to Henry Ford: *interchangeable parts*.[2] If a module is well designed, we can use it in any number of algorithms, just as a car manufacturer can use an appropriately designed oil pump in building different engines for various models of cars. To obtain the benefit of interchangeable parts, an *interface* is required to allow a given part to be connected to whatever algorithm might be using it.

Definition: According to its standard definition, **interface** means the surface regarded as the common boundary between between two bodies or spaces. In algorithms, each module *is* its own body and *has* its own memory space.

In the case of an automobile oil pump, each engine that uses it must be designed to have the proper number of attachment points in the appropriate pattern so that the oil pump may be properly attached to the engine. The same is true for algorithmic modules. We require some means of specifying how the module is to be connected to the rest of the algorithm. In algorithms, this is accomplished by means of parameters.

4.3.1 Parameters

The interface between mechanical components is defined in terms of physical properties such as the arrangement of bolts or the shape of flanges. The interface between algorithmic modules is defined in terms of *parameters*.

Definition: A **parameter** is a special kind of variable that allows a data value to be passed between a module and whatever algorithm might use it.

Parameters are similar to other named variables, with one key difference: They specify the interface to modules. Parameters are used *only* when it is necessary to pass information between modules. We shall see examples soon.

4.3.2 Three Types of Parameters

Logically, there are three kinds of parameters:

1. *Input* (or `in`) parameters, which allow values to be passed *to* a module by the calling algorithm.
2. *Output* (or `out`) parameters, which allow values to be passed *from* the called module back to the calling algorithm.
3. *Input/output* (or `in/out`) parameters, which allow both *in* and *out* communication.

---

[2]Discussed in the Food for Thought section at the end of the previous chapter.

When we create a module, we specify the number and kinds of parameters that it requires. This determines the interface for that module. Any algorithm that uses a module must use the parameters that are specified as that module's interface. We shall see examples of parameters as we learn to create and use modules.

4.4 Modules: Their Creation and Use

There are two kinds of modules: *functions* and *procedures*. Each module must be of one of these two kinds as determined by the kind of task it performs.

Definition: A **function** is an expression of a single value (like a mathematical function). A function is not allowed to produce multiple values, and it may not read input or print output.[3] Like mathematical functions, algorithmic functions *resolve to a single value* i.e., each function call *becomes* whatever value is produced by the function.

Definition: A **procedure** is a kind of module that is used for varied tasks. It may produce any number of values, and it is permitted to have effects on the world outside of itself (such as modifying variables of other modules and reading and printing).

The differences between the definitions of procedures and functions allow us to determine whether a module for a given task should be implemented as a function or a procedure before we write it. For example, if we want a module that will calculate the minimum of two numbers, we can see that it should be a function because it produces a single value. In contrast, a module that determines both the minimum and maximum values found in a list of numbers would have to be a procedure because it produces multiple values. Similarly, Get_Data and Output_Data modules would have to be procedures because they communicate with the world outside the algorithm.

4.4.1 Creating Procedures and Functions

To illustrate how we create and use modules appropriately, let's consider a simple set of algorithmic tasks. The algorithm's purpose is to obtain a number from the user, calculate the cube of that number, and output the result back to the user. Thus, the algorithm is a three-step process:

1. Obtain a value.
2. Cube the value.
3. Output the result.

---

[3]In some programming languages, functions may be used to read input and print output. For our purposes, this is not allowed because the *idea* of a function is that it will resolve to a single value without having *any other effects*. Since reading input consumes the next available input value, allowing a function to read input would mean that the function would be doing two things, not one: It would resolve to a value *and* it would change the state of the input. Similarly, using a function to print output would be "changing the world" (e.g., it would change what is printed on a screen or printer). For our purposes, functions may do only one thing: resolve to a data value.

Because the purpose of the algorithm is so simple, each modular component will itself be very simple. We shall create modules for each of these three tasks in turn.

EXAMPLE 4.1   First, we want to create a module that obtains a number from the user. Because the task involves obtaining a value from the real world, we know that we require a procedure, not a function. We declare the procedure as follows:

```
procedure Get_A_Number (input_value isoftype out Num)
// Purpose: prompt the user to type in a value, obtain that
// value and return it to the calling algorithm.

    print("Enter a number: ")
    read(input_value)

endprocedure //Get_A_Number
```

The header line of a procedure defines its interface. There are two parts to a procedure's interface:

1. *The procedure identifier.* In this example, the identifier is `Get_A_Number`. This tells an algorithm how to call the procedure. Whenever an algorithm wishes to invoke this procedure, it does so by simply using the procedure identifier as a line of code.
2. *The specification of the parameters that the function requires.* In this case there is only a single parameter, `input_value` of type `Num`. Procedure `Get_A_Number` does not require any data from the algorithm; instead, its job is to obtain data from the user and provide it to the algorithm. Therefore, the parameter is specified to be an *output* parameter, indicating that communication through this parameter is one way: *from* the module *to* the algorithm.

Following the header line, there are three parts to the procedure:

1. The purpose comment.
2. The body of the procedure.
3. The end line.

The *purpose comment* describes the purpose of the procedure. It provides information to help a human reader understand what the procedure is supposed to do. It is not an executable statement. If an algorithm is written for execution on a computer, the computer ignores such comments. We use double slash marks before all comments. Any text following double slash marks is a comment, not an instruction.

Definition: Documentation is a comment to the human reader. Documentation explains what the algorithm is supposed to do. Without documentation, a reader must figure out the module's purpose. Thus documentation is a required part of algorithms.

Experience shows that documentation is useful for the algorithm writer as well. Novices typically create their algorithms and then document them. Research has shown that algorithms are written *faster* when the documentation occurs first. It helps you stay focused on the purpose at hand:

- At the level of the main algorithm, it allows you to keep the big picture in mind and to see what role each logical chunk plays.
- At the module level, it helps you to focus on the immediate subproblem.

Following the purpose comments, we write the *body* of the procedure, which includes the instructions and any variable declarations needed for the procedure to do its job. There are as many instructions as required to carry out the procedure's purpose. Because our Get_A_Number procedure does such a simple task, its body contains only two instructions.

The *end line* demarcates the end of the procedure. It contains the keyword end-procedure followed by comments identifying the name of the procedure (which means that we will never be confused about which procedure is being referred to).

Let's look again at Example 4.1, and review the general form of a procedure declaration:

```
procedure <procedure identifier> ( <parameter list> )
// <purpose comments>

   <list of executable instructions and variable declarations>

endprocedure //<procedure identifier>
```

The specification of a parameter in the header line of a module *serves as the declaration of that parameter*. No other declaration is needed or permitted for that identifier. Once we declare a parameter to have a given identifier, we *need not* and *cannot* use that identifier to declare another variable in the module.

Warning: Declaring multiple uses of an identifier *within the same module* is illegal due to the resulting ambiguity about the meaning of the identifier.

EXAMPLE 4.2   Next, we want to create a module that receives a numeric value from the algorithm, computes the cube of that value, and provides the calling algorithm with the result. Because the task involves computing a single value and does not require communication with the world outside the algorithm, we know that we require a function, not a procedure. We declare the function as follows:

```
function Cube returnsa Num (in_value isoftype in Num)
// Purpose: returns the value of in_value raised to
// the 3rd power

   Cube returns (in_value * in_value * in_value)

endfunction //Cube
```

The header line of a function determines its interface. There are three parts to a function's interface:

1. *The function identifier*. In this case, the function identifier is Cube.
2. The *specification of the type of data value that the function returns*. In this case, the function returns a result of type Num. Functions differ from procedures in that

functions *resolve* to a value (i.e., the function call itself *becomes* the value that the function produces). This is the means by which a function sends data back to the calling algorithm. Thus, we need to specify what type of data the calling algorithm must expect it to become.

3. *The specification of the parameters that the function requires.* In this case there is only a single parameter, in_value of type Num. Because functions send values back to the calling algorithm only by resolving to the value they compute, all function parameters are specified to be input parameters, indicating that communication through the parameters is one way, *from* the algorithm *to* the module.

Following the header line, there are three parts to a function:

1. A *purpose comment*. This is equivalent to the purpose comments found in procedures.
2. *The body of the function.* This body is similar to that of procedures in that it includes the instructions that constitute the way that the function does its job. In addition, functions require an executable instruction of the form

```
<function identifier> returns <expression>
```

Such an instruction is where the final value of the function is specified. In our simple example, this is the only instruction required. A function may have as many instructions as required to perform its task, but one of them must be of this form in order to establish the function's value.

3. The *end line*. This demarcates the end of the function and contains the keyword endfunction. Except for the keyword, the end line of a function is equivalent to that of a procedure.

The following illustrates the format for a function:

```
function <function identifier> returnsa <data type> (<list of input
    parameters>)
// <purpose comments>

    < instructions required to produce the function's value >

    <function identifier> returns <data value or expression of the data
        type specified in the header line>

endfunction  //< function identifier >
```

EXAMPLE 4.3   Our next task is to create a module that outputs result data to the user. Because the task involves sending a value to the world outside the algorithm, we know that we require a procedure, not a function:

```
procedure Output_A_Number (value_to_be_printed isoftype in Num)
// Purpose: prints out the value of value_to_be_printed
// along with a textual message.

    print ("The resulting value is", value_to_be_printed)

endprocedure //Output_A_Number
```

In this case, the interface specifies a single *input* parameter of type Num. It is an *input* parameter because the procedure requires that the calling algorithm provide the value that is to be output; thus the data comes *in* to the procedure from the calling algorithm.

Sometimes students get confused about `in` versus `out` parameters. They might ask, "Shouldn't an `Output_A_Number` procedure use an `out` parameter since it is sending data "out" to the user?" Well, no, it shouldn't.

`In` and `out` refer to the direction of communication between the module and the algorithm that calls it. They do not refer to communication between the algorithm and the real world (we use `read` and `print` statements for that).

We can see the difference between `in` and `out` parameters in Example 4.3. Since `Output_A_Num` must receive data from the algorithm in order to know what value to output, data are coming *in* to the procedure from the calling algorithm. Similarly, while the `Get_A_Num` procedure is reading data in from the world, it sends that data to the calling algorithm. Thus the data value goes *out* from the module to the calling algorithm and needs to be an `out` parameter.

4.4.2 Calling Procedures and Functions

Not only are functions and procedures somewhat different in how they are declared, they are also different with respect to how they are used by the calling algorithm.

A function is used as a *value* or an *expression*. A procedure is used as a *stand-alone instruction*.

To illustrate how procedures and functions are called and used by an algorithm, let's create the algorithm that will use the modules we've just created to perform the tasks specified in Section 4.4.1.

EXAMPLE 4.4   This example creates an algorithm that uses the modules from Examples 4.1 through 4.3 to obtain a number from the user, calculate the cube of that number, and output the result back to the user:

```
algorithm Cube_A_Number
// Purpose: obtain a number from the user, calculate the
// cube of that number, and output the result back to the
// user.

    this_num isoftype Num
    Get_A_Number (this_num)

    this_num <- Cube(this_num)

    Output_A_Num (this_num)

endalgorithm  //Cube_A_Number
```

Notice the different usage. The *function call* is used as an expression in a place where we might have used a particular value. The *procedure calls* are used as stand-alone instructions. This difference in usage follows logically from the differences in what the two kinds of modules are allowed to do.

Warning: Often, students who have no experience with algorithms make the mistake of calling a *function* as if it were a *procedure*.

The following example illustrates improper use of a function call:

```
algorithm Cube_A_Number
// Purpose: obtain a number from the user, calculate the
// cube of that number, and output the result back to the
// user.

   this_num isoftype Num
   Get_A_Number (this_num)

   Cube(this_num)

   Output_A_Num (this_num)

endalgorithm  //Cube_A_Number
```

The function `Cube` has been called here as if it were a procedure. What is the consequence of this? Imagine that the number obtained by `Get_A_Number` is 3. We know, then, that function `Cube` will resolve to the value 27. Calling `Cube` as shown above is thus equivalent to using the value 27 as a line of code. `Cube` has produced the correct value, but the calling algorithm has not done anything with it. Instead, it has tried to use the value produced by `Cube` as if it were an instruction. This is an error that would bring execution of the algorithm to a halt.

Furthermore, observe that because we have never assigned the value returned by `Cube` to the variable `this_num`, `this_num` still holds the original value obtained from the user. Thus, even if execution were to somehow continue past the point of the error, procedure `Output_A_Num` would be sent the value 3, not the value 27, and thus would produce *another* error by generating the wrong output.

 To use functions correctly, it is necessary to use them as if they are a particular value (i.e., as if they are an expression). This is because a function *resolves* to a particular value. Each function call *becomes* the value that the function calculates. Thus, function calls must be used as if they were values. They may appear anywhere in an algorithm that you could use a variable identifier or literal value.

4.4.3   Using Multiple Parameters

In this section we will use a series of examples to illustrate procedures and functions that require multiple parameters. So far, we have seen procedures and functions that make use of only a single parameter. Often, the purpose of a module will require multiple parameters. Let's consider an algorithm in which this is the case.

EXAMPLE 4.5   First, we will create a module that obtains from the user the diameter of a circle, expressed in centimeters, and that calculates and outputs the area and circumference of such a circle, expressed in inches. We can outline the high-level logic of the algorithm as follows:

1. Obtain the diameter, expressed in centimeters, from the user.
2. Convert the diameter from centimeter to inches.

3. Calculate the attributes of the circle.
   a. Calculate the circumference.
   b. Calculate the area.
4. Output the results.

Notice that the high-level structure of the algorithmic task happens to fit the structure represented in Fig. 4.1. The algorithm has four main logical chunks, one of which (calculating the attributes of the circle) involves two ideas and so can be decomposed into two subtasks. Since we have the high-level structure of the algorithm, we can declare the modules that are required.

EXAMPLE 4.6   Here we want to create a module that obtains a number from the user that represents the diameter of a circle in centimeters. We could use `Get_A_Number` for this purpose, but it may not be adequate because we need the user to know what we expect: the diameter of a circle expressed in centimeters. Thus we declare a procedure that communicates this. It requires only a single `out` parameter.

```
procedure Get_Diam_In_Centimeters (input_value isoftype out Num)
// Purpose: prompt the user to type in a value which represents
// the diameter of a circle expressed in centimeters, obtain
// that value, and return it to the calling algorithm.

    print("Enter the diameter of a circle in centimeters: ")
    read(input_value)

endprocedure //Get_Diam_In_Centimeters
```

EXAMPLE 4.7   Next we want to convert centimeters to inches. Since this requires that we produce a single value without any I/O, we know that a function is required.

```
function Centimeters_To_Inches returnsa Num (centimeters isoftype in Num)
// Purpose: convert a number representing a distance in
// centimeters to the appropriate value in inches.

    CM_PER_INCH is 2.54 //Conversion factor
    Centimeters_To_Inches returns (centimeters / CM_PER_INCH)

endfunction //Centimeters_To_Inches
```

EXAMPLE 4.8   In this example, given the diameter of a circle, we will calculate its circumference and area. This module produces more than one result value and thus must be a procedure.

```
procedure Calc_Circle_Attributes (diameter isoftype in Num, area,
    circumference isoftype out Num)
// Purpose: given the diameter of a circle, calculate its
// circumference and area.

    area <- Circle_Area(diameter)
    circumference <- Circle_Circumference(diameter)

endprocedure  //Calc_Circle_Attributes
```

This procedure requires multiple parameters. It requires one piece of data from the calling algorithm to use in its calculations, and it must return two values to the calling algorithm. Thus, it needs a total of three parameters: one in parameter and two out parameters.

The parameter list in the module's header line *defines the interface* that the calling algorithm must use. In this case, it specifies that the first parameter will send the diameter to the procedure, the second parameter will be used to send the circle's area back to the calling algorithm, and the third will be used to send back the circle's circumference.

This procedure does not do any calculation itself. Instead, it calls two functions that do the work for it. This is because the procedure is required to do two different tasks. Good abstraction means that each module does only one task. Therefore, this procedure will coordinate the appropriate function calls (which in this case is trivial), and the two functions will each do their specialized task.

Notice that we can articulate the appropriate function calls despite the fact that they haven't been written yet. This is because we know enough about circles to know what information those functions require and, since they each require only a single parameter, there's no ambiguity about their interface. If this procedure were calling modules that required multiple parameters, we could not articulate the calls to them until we knew how their interface was defined.

Observe that the procedure of Example 4.8 will work for dimensions expressed in inches, centimeters, or any units of measurement. The issue of conversion is handled elsewhere in the algorithm. This procedure doesn't care what the units of measurement are, and neither do the functions it calls. Let's write those functions now.

EXAMPLE 4.9   Here we compute the area of a circle based on its diameter. Since this requires that we produce a single value without any I/O, we know that a function is required.

```
function Circle_Area returnsa Num (diameter isoftype in Num)
// Purpose: compute the area of a circle as determined by
// its diameter.

   PI is 3.14159
   radius isoftype Num
   radius returnsa diameter / 2
   Circle_Area <- PI * radius * radius

endfunction  //Circle_Area
```

EXAMPLE 4.10   Next we compute the circumference of a circle based on its diameter. This requires that we produce a single value without any I/O, so we know that a function is required.

```
function Circle_Circumference returnsa Num (diameter isoftype in Num)
// Purpose: compute the circumference of a circle as
// determined by its diameter.

   radius isoftype Num
   radius <- diameter / 2
```

```
Circle_Circumference returnsa 2 * PI * radius

endfunction  //Circle_Circumference
```

EXAMPLE 4.11   This example creates a module that outputs the original metric data and the two resulting circle attributes to the user. Because the task involves sending a value to the world outside the algorithm, we know that we require a procedure, not a function. Because it outputs three values, we know that three parameters are required.

```
procedure Output_Circle_Attributes (diam_centimeters, area_inches,
    circumference_inches isoftype in Num)
// Purpose: prints out values to the user reporting the
// original diameter in centimeters, the area of the circle in
// square inches, and the circumference of the circle in inches.

    print ("A circle with a diameter of ", diam_centimeters)
    print ("centimeters has ", area_inches," sq.in. of area")
    print ("and ", circumference_inches,"in. of circumference ")

endprocedure  //Output_Circle_Attributes
```

EXAMPLE 4.12   This example creates an algorithm that uses the modules from Examples 4.6 through 4.11 to obtain from the user the diameter of a circle expressed in centimeters, calculate the area and circumference expressed in inches, and output the original value and the results back to the user.

```
algorithm Calc_Circle_Facts
// Purpose: an algorithm that obtains from the user the
// diameter of a circle expressed in centimeters, calculates
// the area and circumference expressed in inches, and outputs
// the original value and the results back to the user.

    cm_diam isoftype Num
    Get_Diam_in_Centimeters(cm_diam)

    inches_diam isoftype Num
    inches_diam <- Centimeters_To_Inches(cm_diam)

    inches_area isoftype Num
    inches_circumference isoftype Num
    Calc_Circle_Attributes (inches_diam, inches_area, inches_circumference)

    Output_Circle_Attributes (cm_diam, inches_area, inches_circumference)

endalgorithm //Calc_Circle_Facts
```

In Example 4.12 we see the main algorithm for the task. Observe that the last two lines consist of calls to procedures that require multiple parameters. Because of this, the calls cannot be articulated until *after* those modules are defined. Without consulting the header lines for those modules, there is no way to know what interface they each require. While we could guess as to the data needed, we have to consult the header lines of those modules to know the order in which the parameters must be specified.

4.5 Parameter Lists

Now that we have seen the use of multiple parameters, and the parameter lists which they require, there are a few particular features of parameter lists that must be noted. We have seen two types of parameter lists: (1) the formal parameter list and (2) the actual parameter list.

Definition: The **formal parameter list** specifies the parameters in the declaration of the module. This is where the type of each parameter (in, out, or in/out) and the data type of each one (Char, Num, etc.) are defined. Thus the formal parameter list is what defines the interface to the module.

Definition: The **actual parameter list** specifies the values passed to the module whenever the module is called. This is where the variables or values to be passed to the module are specified by the calling algorithm. The actual parameter list must conform to the interface defined in the formal parameter list.

Four rules govern this relationship between *actual* and *formal* parameter lists:

1. The number of parameters in the actual and formal parameter lists must be consistent. The actual list must provide the same number of parameters as does the formal parameter list.
2. Actual parameters are associated with formal parameters based on their position in the the parameter list.
3. The corresponding actual and formal parameters must be of the same type.
4. The only time that an actual parameter can be a literal or constant (rather than a variable) is if it is associated with a formal *input* parameter. This is because output (and, as we shall soon see, input/output) parameters require a variable to which they can write results. When literal values are passed as parameters, there *are* no variables in which to store results.

Listing the correct actual parameters in the wrong order leads to error. In Example 4.12, the names chosen as variable identifiers in the calling algorithm indicate the intended use of the variables (e.g., that variable inches_area is intended to store data representing the area of the circle expressed in inches). This is what does in fact occur, because it is specified as the second parameter in the actual parameter list and thus will be associated with procedure Calc_Circle_Attributes' second formal parameter, area. However, if the calling algorithm had reversed the last two actual parameters (by reversing the positions of inches_area and inches_circumference in the actual parameter list), the data intended for inches_area would have wound up in inches_circumference and vice versa. Pay careful attention to the correct ordering of actual parameters; consult the formal parameter list of the module being called to be sure of the appropriate ordering.

In the formal parameter list each parameter is declared to be of a given data type. The corresponding actual parameter must be of the same type. In our example, all formal parameters were of type Num, so all actual parameters must be of type Num as well. If not, a type mismatch error will occur.

The Scope of Data

Like the main algorithm, each module may contain its own variables. For example, the functions Circle_Area (in Example 4.9) and Circle_Circumference (in Example 4.10) each declared a variable radius. This fact suggests certain questions. Can variables declared in one module be shared with another module or with the main algorithm? If a variable is declared in the main algorithm, can that data be accessed by the various modules that that algorithm calls? All such questions concern the scope of data.

Definition: The **scope of data** refers to the part or parts of an algorithm that can access a declared data identifier.

4.6.1 Three Philosophies of Scope

There are three different philosophies for defining the scope of data: (1) unlimited scope, (2) partially restricted scope, and (3) completely restricted scope.

UNLIMITED SCOPE

According to this idea, everybody knows about and can access everybody else's variables. Experience has shown that *unlimited scope* causes many problems. One of them is the problem of data integrity: How can we be sure exactly what information is represented by the value of a variable? Data integrity problems arise when variables are written to by different modules in an unpredictable way. The problem of data integrity is just another way of saying "we're not sure what a given data value really represents." In algorithms, we must always know what each value represents. This means that as a practical matter unlimited scope just does not work.

PARTIALLY RESTRICTED SCOPE

There are many possible schemes for partially restricting the scope of data. Indeed, programming languages created over the last 20 years are similar in many ways but vary tremendously in their numerous schemes for partially restricting the scope of data. Some schemes are simple and others are complex. Each scheme involves a set of rules and mechanisms that govern who is allowed to see whose data and under what circumstances. For our purposes, this involves needless complication.

COMPLETELY RESTRICTED SCOPE

According to this rule, nobody can see anybody else's data. This means that any named variable can be accessed *only* by instructions in the section of the algorithm in which it was declared. Thus variables declared in the main algorithm cannot be directly accessed by any of the modules, and variables declared in a given module cannot be directly accessed by either the main algorithm or by other modules. In effect, it is as if each module is its own separate algorithm: It uses its own variables, but not those from any other module. This limitation provides several benefits. Chief among them is that if we become puzzled about how a particular value might have been assigned to a variable, we know where to look: The statements inside its scope are the only ones that have access to it. For our purposes, this rule has no significant disadvantages. As we shall later see, it does not limit our ability to create algorithms that feature a high level of abstraction.

4.6.2   The Scope of Variables

In our language the scope of variable data is completely restricted. The scope of each named variable is limited to the part of the algorithm in which it is declared. Outside of the algorithm or module in which a variable is declared, the identifier for that variable *has no meaning* and *its data cannot be accessed*.

Of course, if we restrict the scope of variables in this way, we require some way for the various modules to communicate with one another. As we have already seen, this is what parameters are for. They provide a mechanism for selectively transferring data values between variables in different modules within an algorithm.

4.6.3   The Scope of Constants

So far, our discussion of scope has been limited to named variables. But what about named constants? For example, the functions Circle_Area (in Example 4.9) and Circle_Circumference (in Example 4.10) each used the constant PI. But PI was declared only in the former.

Constants do not present us with the same kind of data integrity risks that variables do, simply because a constant *is* constant (i.e., once its value is set by the algorithm's author, no instruction within the algorithm can change it). However, constants might well present data integrity problems if we have different values for the same idea coexisting in an algorithm. We want PI to be the *same* PI everywhere. If there are different values of PI floating around, the value of PI isn't constant, is it? We thus need to have only a single declaration for each constant, one that everyone can see and use. Therefore we want constants to have unlimited scope.

In our language, constant definitions have unlimited scope. Any constant declared anywhere in the algorithm can be seen by everybody. No constant can be declared more than once.

When a constant is required by various modules, declare the constant when you first require it. After it is declared, assume that all other portions of the algorithm can make use of it.

This policy would be very troublesome in a programming language for several reasons. Among them is the impact it would have on the interchangeability of modules. Since we do not wish to construct a great many technical rules about these things, and since the algorithms we will be working on are reasonably small, we can get away with applying common sense on this point. The potential problems are not likely to arise in what we do here. For your work in this course, make sure each constant is declared at the point of its first use, and make sure that it is not redeclared elsewhere.

4.7 The Kinds of Parameters

We have said that parameters are an interface, and that they are somehow shared between the called module and the calling algorithm. We have also said that the actual parameter list specifies the variables that the calling algorithm *sends* to the module it is calling. But what does it mean to say that a parameter is sent? To understand what is going on requires that we consider where these parameters really are and what it means to pass a parameter.

To illustrate, let's consider two nonsense algorithms called `Your_Algorithm` and `My_Module`. We use nonsense modules here because we are not concerned with what these modules do, only with how they communicate.

Let's say that the header line of `My_Module` is declared such that it has three Num parameters but that we have not as yet specified the kind of parameter for each one (`in`, `out`, or `in/out`). Thus, its header line might look like this:

```
procedure My_Module (apple isoftype _____ Num, orange
          isoftype _____ Num, banana isoftype _____ Num)
```

Let's also say that `Your_Module` is declared as follows:

```
procedure Your_Algorithm
// Purpose: algorithm to use in illustrating parameter passing.

   larry,
   moe,
   curley isoftype Num
   read(larry, moe, curley)

   My_Module(larry, moe, curley)

endalgorithm //Your_Algorithm
```

Thus, when `Your_Algorithm` calls `My_Module`, it will pass `larry`, `moe`, and `curley` as actual parameters. They will be received by `My_Module` according to its formal parameter list. Thus, within `My_Module`, `larry` will be associated with `apple`, `moe` with `orange`, and `curley` with `banana`. The identifiers `larry`, `moe`, and `curley` are meaningless within `My_Module`, but instructions within `My_Module` can still have access to those variables via the parameters `apple`, `orange`, and `banana`, respectively.

In all cases, *regardless of the kind of parameter*, the original data values "belong" to the variables declared in `Your_Algorithm`. That is where the data values "live." By passing these variables as parameters to `My_Module`, `Your_Algorithm` is allowing `My_Module` to have access to `Your_Algorithm`'s variables. The only difference between `in`, `out`, and `in/out` parameters is the *kind of access* that `My_Module` is granted. We will discuss each of the three types of parameters in turn.

4.7.1 Input Parameters

Input parameters are used to provide data from the calling algorithm to the module. An in parameter provides a *copy* of the value of the actual parameter but does not allow access to the original. Thus, if My_Module's three formal parameters were all in parameters, then My_Module would have its own variable apple which contains a copy of the value stored in larry, its own variable orange which contains a copy of the value stored in moe, and its own variable banana which contains a copy of the value of curley. My_Module can manipulate its own copies as it wishes but does not have any access to the actual parameter variables. For example, the instruction

```
apple <- orange + banana
```

will inspect the values of orange and banana (provided by moe and curley, respectively), compute their sum, then write the result to apple. My_Module thus changes the value of apple, which was originally copied from larry, but does not change the value of larry. After this instruction, larry still stores its original value, while apple no longer does. Because these are in parameters, they provide no way to *write* to the variables passed by Your_Algorithm.

Definition: A **formal *input* parameter** provides a *copy* of the value stored in the corresponding actual parameter. The called module can then *read* from and *write* to its copy, but it does not have access to the original actual parameter variable itself.

(In discussing parameters, we refer to three kinds of access: (1) *read*, (2) *write*, and (3) *read/write*. As we use the term "read" in this context, we mean it in the "plain English" sense of the word i.e., being able to "look at" the contents of a variable. We do not mean the *I/O* operation read, which refers to communication with the world. Similarly, when we say "write," we mean the ability to assign a value to a variable. We do not mean the *I/O* operation print.)

An important feature of in parameters is that they allow a module to obtain data values that "belong" to another part of the algorithm without any risk of that data being contaminated.

Because in parameters provide only a copy of the actual parameter, the module that receives an in parameter cannot manipulate the value of the corresponding actual parameter in any way. The called module may manipulate the passed in value without risk that it will modify the original. It can modify only its local copy, not the original.

This security advantage of in parameters helps protect data integrity. Thus in parameters are inherently safer and therefore should be used whenever they are sufficient. In other words, it is best to make *all* parameters in parameters unless there is a good reason *requiring* a parameter to be out or in/out.

These points are best understood by looking at several brief examples.

EXAMPLE 4.13[4]

```
function Is_Even returnsa Boolean (the_num isoftype in Num)
// Purpose: returns TRUE if the_num is EVEN, else False.

    if ((the_num MOD 2) = 0) then
        IsEven returns TRUE
    else
        IsEven returns FALSE
    endif

endfunction //Is_Even
```

EXAMPLE 4.14

```
function Is_Odd returnsa boolean (the_num isoftype in Num)
// Purpose: returns TRUE if the_num is ODD, else False

    IsOdd returns (NOT(IsEven(the_num))
endfunction //Is_Odd
```

EXAMPLE 4.15

```
function Sales_Commission returnsa Num (sale_price, commission_rate
        isoftype in Num)
    // Purpose: calculates the sales commission for a given sale.

    Sales_Commission returns (sale_price * commission_rate)

endfunction //Sales_Commission
```

EXAMPLE 4.16[5]

```
function Is_Vowel returnsa boolean (this_char isoftype in Char)
// Purpose: returns True IFF this_char is a vowel.

    if ((this_char = 'A') OR
        ((this_char = 'E') OR
        ((this_char = 'I') OR
        ((this_char = 'O') OR
        (this_char = 'U'))))) then
            Is_Vowel returns TRUE
    else
            Is_Vowel returns FALSE
    endif

endfunction //Is_Vowel
```

---

[4]Sometimes there are situations in which someone might blur together two different levels of abstraction. For example, in the case of function IsEven, "clever" programmers might write it so that it contains only the instruction IsEven returns (the_num MOD 2). Notice what they are doing: They know that (the_num MOD 2) will produce either a 1 or a 0. Furthermore, they are assuming that, because the value TRUE may be represented as the number 1 and FALSE may be represented by the number 0, they can be clever and exploit this to make IsEven more compact. But in doing so, they are confusing *the logic of the algorithm* with *the specific representation* that a computer uses for certain logical values.

[5]We use IFF to mean "if and only if."

EXAMPLE 4.17

```
function Calc_Water_Bill (gallons_used, cost_per_gallon
                              isoftype in Num)
// Purpose: calculates the amount of a customer's water bill;
// the customer is to pay the larger of the calculated amount
// or the minimum amount.

    MIN_H2O_BILL is 20     // minimum monthly water bill is $20

    calc'd_amt isoftype Num

    calc'd_amt <- gallons_used * cost_per_gallon
    Calc_Water_Bill returns Max_2_Nums(calc'd_amt, MIN_H2O_BILL)

endfunction  //Calc_Water_Bill
```

In comparing Examples 4.13 through 4.17 you can see that a module's formal parameter list provides a clear specification of the in parameters required by the module.

4.7.2   Output Parameters

Output parameters grant access to *write* to the actual parameter itself, but not to *read* its original value. If My_Module's three formal parameters were all out parameters, then My_Module would be able to use apple to store a value in larry, orange to store a value in moe, and banana to store a value in curley. Once My_Module used that capability to write to those variables, it could then retrieve those values for other use. However, My_Module has no way to discover what values were originally stored in any of these variables. For example,

```
apple <- orange + banana
```

would be an illegal instruction *unless* My_Module had first assigned values to orange and banana. The attempt to assign a value to apple is fine because, as an out parameter, apple has the authority to change the value stored in the actual parameter larry. The problem here is that My_Module is attempting to retrieve the values of orange and banana. Because orange and banana are out parameters, My_Module has no way to read the values stored in them *unless* it has first assigned values to them. If it has not yet done so, then their values are undefined.

Definition: A **formal *output* parameter** is allowed to *write to* the corresponding actual parameter, but cannot *read* the actual parameter's original value. After an *output* parameter is used to modify the original value of the actual parameter, it may then see what it has written there.

Output parameters provide the called module with *write-only* access to the calling algorithm's original data. They are used only to pass "result data" from the called procedure to the calling algorithm in circumstance where the called procedure has no reason to know or care about the original values stored there.

EXAMPLE 4.18 Let's look at a simple example of a procedure using an out parameter:

```
procedure Get_Mailing_Address (name, street, city isoftype out String)
// Purpose: obtains mailing from the user in a 3-line format.

   print ("Please type in your Name:")
   read (name)

   print ("Please type in your Street Address, including")
   print ("any P.O. Box or Apartment Number:")
   read (street)

   print ("Please type in your City, State and Zipcode:")
   read (city)

endprocedure //Get_Mailing_Address
```

EXAMPLE 4.19 Let's look at another example requiring out parameters. It works, but it features a low level of abstraction. We'll see how to improve upon it in Examples 4.21 and 4.22.

```
procedure Min_Max (a, b, c isoftype in Num,
                   min, max isoftype out Num)
// Purpose: accepts three num values, identifies and
// returns the smallest and largest of those three

   if ((a >= b) AND (a >= c)) then
      max <- a
   elseif ((b >= a) AND (b >= c)) then
      max <- b
   else
      max <- c
   endif

   if ((a <= b) AND (a <= c)) then
      min <- a
   elseif ((b <= a) AND (b <= c)) then
      min <- b
   else
      min <- c
   endif

endprocedure //Min_Max
```

This procedure receives three numbers and determines which of those three is the largest and which is the smallest. The module itself is declared to have a total of five parameters, all of which are of type Num: a, b, and c are *input* parameters, and min and max are *output* parameters. The procedure is able to obtain the three data values it requires via its three *input* parameters, do its calculation, and send its results back via two *output* parameters.

EXAMPLE 4.20 Procedure Min_Max from Example 4.19 might be called via:

```
algorithm Example_4.20
// An example of passing parameters to a procedure
```

```
x,
y,
z isoftype Num
read(x, y, z)

little,
big isoftype Num
Min_Max(x, y, z, little, big)
```

endalgorithm //Example 4.20

In Example 4.20, copies of the values of x, y, and z are provided to the Min_Max module via the three parameters, a, b, and c, respectively. When the module finishes, the value assigned to min will be stored in little, and the value assigned to max will be stored in big.

The original values of x, y, and z are important since they provide the original values that Min_Max will use in its calculation. In contrast, the original values of little and big do not matter at all. They correspond to the *output parameters* of the module and thus do not communicate any data values to the module; their initial values are irrelevant. With an output parameter, the called module cannot see what the value is, but whenever it assigns a value to an output parameter variable, it is really replacing the value stored in the original. Here, the calling algorithm did not initialize the variables little and big before sending them as parameters. If they had been initialized, those original values would be written over (i.e., they would be replaced by procedure Min_Max's results).

EXAMPLE 4.21 The version of procedure Min_Max given in Example 4.19 is correct in that it will produce correct results. However, it features *poor abstraction*. Notice that all the details specifying how to calculate the min and max values are mixed together in the procedure. Because min and max each represent an idea, it would be better to create abstractions for each of them, and then use those abstractions in Min_Max, as shown below. The following shows a better solution to the min_max procedure than the one we saw in Example 4.19.

```
function Min_2_Nums returnsa Num (first, second isoftype in Num)
// Accepts two num parameters and returns the smallest value

   if (first <= second) then
      Min_2_Nums returns first
   else
      Min_2_Nums returns second
   endif

endfunction //Min_2_Nums
```

```
function Max_2_Nums returnsa Num (first, second isoftype in Num)
// Accepts two num parameters and returns the largest value

   if (first >= second) then
      Max_2_Nums returns first
   else
      Max_2_Nums returns second

   endif
endfunction //Max_2_Nums
```

```
procedure Min_Max (a, b, c isoftype in Num,
                   min, max isoftype out Num)
// Purpose: accepts three num values, identifies and
// returns the smallest and largest of those three.

   partial_max isoftype Num
   partial_max <- Max_2_Nums(b, c)
   max <- Max_2_Nums (a, partial_max)

   partial_min isoftype Num
   partial_min <- Min_2_Nums(b, c)
   min <- Min_2_Nums(a, partial_min)

endprocedure //Min_Max
```

This version of procedure `Min_Max` features higher abstraction than does the original from Example 4.19. It does not worry about the details of how to find the minimum and maximum of two values. Instead, it makes calls to functions that do that work for it. We accomplished this by creating two general-purpose modules: the functions `Min_2_Nums` and `Max_2_Nums`, which might be reused in other algorithms.

In this version of procedure `Min_Max`, two local variables, `partial_min` and `partial_max`, are used to hold the results of comparing two of the three values. In the third and sixth instructions, these temporary results are then compared with the remaining value. Recall, however, that we can use a function wherever we might use a value. Thus, while there is nothing wrong with using the local variables `partial_min` and `partial_max`, we really do not need them. Instead, we can use function calls in their place, as shown in Example 4.22.

EXAMPLE 4.22   This example shows the best solution to the `min_max` procedure. This uses function calls in lieu of local variables:

```
procedure Min_Max (a, b, c isoftype in Num,
                   min, max isoftype out Num)
// Purpose: accepts three num values, identifies and
// returns the smallest and largest of those three.

   max <- Max_Of_2(a, Max_Of_2(b, c))
   min <- Min_Of_2(a, Min_Of_2(b, c))

endprocedure //Min_Max
```

This version of procedure `Min_Max` requires no local variables. The roles that were played by the local variables in the previous version (i.e., as temporary holding cells for intermediate results) become unnecessary because of the way we use function calls. In the first instruction of Example 4.22, the `out` parameter `max` is to be assigned the results of a call to `Max_2_Nums`. But what are the parameters sent to `Max_2_Nums`? The first parameter is `a`, but the second parameter is itself *another* function call: `Max_2_Nums (b, c)`. This call must be resolved first so that the value it returns can be plugged in as the second parameter of the call `Max_2_Nums(a, Max_2_Nums (b, c))`.

While this sort of thing may look funny to you at first, it really is the cleanest solution. We've gone from 14 lines of code in our first version to only 2 lines in our final version. More importantly, we've cleaned it up so that it is easier to see what is being done.

4.7.3   Input/Output Parameters

Input/output parameters grant access both to *see* the value of the actual parameter and to *modify* it. The phrase "anything goes" comes to mind. Thus, if `My_Module`'s three formal parameters were all `in/out` parameters, `My_Module` would be able to use `apple` to find out what value is stored in `larry` and to change that value, `orange` would be able to retrieve and change the value stored in `moe`, and `banana` would be authorized to learn the value of `curley` and to modify it. Thus it would be perfectly legal for my `My_Module` to contain the instruction

```
apple <- orange + banana
```

because `in/out` parameters have both *read* and *write* access to the original values.

Warning: Anytime a variable is passed by the calling algorithm as an `in/out` parameter, the calling algorithm is giving the called module *complete access* to one of its variables. For this reason, you should not use `in/out` parameters indiscriminately. Use them *only as needed* by the particular requirements of the algorithmic task at hand.

EXAMPLE 4.23   This example uses low abstraction. Imagine that a calling algorithm wants two numbers to be sorted so that the smaller number is first. This might be done via the following algorithm. First, we'll show a version that features poor abstraction, then a version, in Example 4.24, that raises the level of abstraction.

```
procedure Sort_2_Nums (smaller, larger isoftype in/out Num,
                       is_a_tie isoftype out Boolean)
// Receive two values, returns them in sorted order;
// IFF the values are equal, then is_a_tie is True.

   if (smaller = larger) then
      is_a_tie <- True
   else
      is_a_tie <- False
      if (smaller > larger) then
         temp isoftype Num
         temp <- smaller
         smaller <- larger
         larger <- temp
      endif
   endif

endprocedure  //Sort_2_Nums
```

This module will see if the two numbers are out of order. If so, it will swap them. If they are already in order, they will not be swapped. The end result is that `larger` will be assigned the larger value and `smaller` will be assigned the smaller value. If they are equal, the boolean parameter `is_a_tie` will return `TRUE`; if they are not, it will return `FALSE`.

Consider the formal parameter list of Sort_2_Nums. If this procedure was called via the instruction

```
Sort_2_Nums(x, y, are_equal)
```

then read/write access to the variables x and y would be sent to the Sort_2_Nums procedure, along with write-only access to the boolean variable are_equal. Regardless of whether or not they were originally in order, after Sort_2_Nums is executed, the larger value will be stored in x, the smaller value will be stored in y, and the are_equal boolean variable will indicate if the two values are equal.

EXAMPLE 4.24 This example uses high abstraction. The version of Sort_2_Nums given in Example 4.23 is correct, but it has the same weakness we've seen before: It features poor abstraction. In this case, it is cluttered up with the details of comparing and swapping. Below is a different version of Sort_2_Nums that features higher abstraction.

```
procedure Swap (number_1, number_2 isoftype in/out Num)
// Receives 2 nums and swaps them.

    temp isoftype Num
    temp <- number_1
    number_1 <- number_2
    number_2 <- temp

endprocedure //Swap


procedure Sort_2_Nums (smaller, larger isoftype in/out Num
                       is_a_tie isoftype out Boolean)
// Receive two values, returns them in sorted order;
// IFF the values are equal, then is_a_tie is True.

    is_a_tie <- (smaller = larger)
    if (smaller > larger) then
        Swap(smaller, larger)
    endif

endprocedure //Sort_2_Nums
```

Here, we created a general-purpose procedure for swapping two values and hid within it the details of how a swap is performed. This made Sort_2_Nums even more trivial.

We also replaced

```
if (smaller = larger) then
    is_a_tie <- TRUE
else
    is_a_tie <- FALSE
    ...
```

with the equivalent but cleaner instruction:

```
is_a_tie <- (smaller = larger)
```

The condition (smaller = larger) may or may not be true. Regardless, the result will be assigned to is_a_tie.

With practice, you will naturally get better at quickly recognizing the high-abstraction ways to do things. For now, just be sure to notice the kinds of differences you see between low- and high-abstraction solutions.

4.8 A Larger Example

Consider the algorithm `Grade_Calc` in Example 4.25. Its purpose is simple: Based on a student's various numerical scores (exam, quiz, project, and lab) and on the weights assigned to each by the professor, it calculates a letter grade for the course.

EXAMPLE 4.25 We could write this algorithm without any procedural abstraction, as follows:

```
algorithm Grade_Calc
// Purpose: calculates course grade based on student's
// average for projects, quizzes and lab, and on
// student's exam score.

    // grade factor constants:
    PROJ_FAC is .35 //weight of project average
    QUIZ_FAC is .30 //weight of quiz average
    LAB_FAC is .10 //weight of lab tasks
    EXAM_FAC is .25 //weight of exam

    // letter grade threshold constants:
    A_CUTOFF is 90 //min score for A
    B_CUTOFF is 80 //min score for B
    C_CUTOFF is 70 //min score for C
    D_CUTOFF is 60 //min score for D

    // obtain student data:
    student_name isoftype String
    print ("Enter your name: ")
    read(student_name)

    proj_avg isoftype Num
    print("Enter your project average: ")
    read(proj_avg)

    quiz_avg isoftype Num
    print("Enter your quiz average: ")
    read(quiz_avg)

    lab_avg isoftype Num
    print("Enter your lab average: ")
    read(lab_avg)

    exam_score isoftype Num
    print("Enter your exam score: ")
    read(exam_score)

    //calculate student's course average.
    course_avg isoftype Num
    course_avg <- (proj_avg * PROJ_FAC) + (quiz_avg * QUIZ_FAC)
        + (lab_avg * LAB_FAC) + (exam_score * EXAM_FAC)
```

```
// determine student's letter grade.
ltr_grd isoftype Char
if (course_avg >= A_CUTOFF) then
    ltr_grade <- 'A'
elseif (course_avg >= B_CUTOFF) then
    ltr_grade <- 'B'
elseif (course_avg >= C_CUTOFF) then
    ltr_grade <- 'C'
elseif (course_avg >= D_CUTOFF) then
    ltr_grade <- 'D'
else //course_avg <D_CUTOFF
    ltr_grade <- 'F'
endif

// output final results.
print("The course grade for", student_name)
print("is: ", ltr_grade,".")

endalgorithm //Grade_Calc
```

All the algorithmic steps are provided in a single chunk. There is no procedural abstraction, and understanding what this algorithm does requires that you read and understand the whole thing at once.

Since the problem it solves is so simple, this should not present any difficulties. However, remember that this algorithm solves a trivial problem. No single part of it would tax the ability of a bright 11-year-old child. Thus, like all our examples, it is used to simply illustrate concepts. If we had a reasonably complex example, you would find it much more difficult to grasp the "sense" of the algorithm if it were all mixed together in a single list of instructions.

EXAMPLE 4.26 Let's express the same Grade_Calc algorithm in an appropriately modular way. We must first identify the logical subtasks that are required to solve the problem.

```
algorithm Grade_Calc
//Purpose: calculates course grade based on student's average
//for projects, quizzes and lab, and student's exam score

    // obtain student data
    student_name isoftype String //student's name
    proj_avg,                    //student's project average
    quiz_avg,                    //student's quiz average
    lab_avg,                     //student's lab average
    exam_score isoftype Num      //student's exam score
    Get_Data(student_name, proj_avg, quiz_avg, lab_avg, exam_score)

    // calculate numerical average
    num_grade isoftype Num //student's numerical Course grade
    num_grade <- Calc_Avg(proj_avg, quiz_avg, lab_avg, exam_score)

    // determine letter grade
    ltr_grade isoftype Char //student's letter Course grade
    ltr_grade <- Calc_Ltr_Grade(num_grade)

    // output results
    Output_Grade(student_name, ltr_grade)

endalgorithm //Grade_Calc
```

Without knowing the details of how any particular logical step is performed, we can see the high-level logic of what is being done. To learn about each logical step, we need only consult the referenced module. Each module is declared in the four examples that follow.

EXAMPLE 4.27

```
procedure Get_Data (student_in_name isoftype out String,
                    proj_in_data, quiz_in_data, lab_in_data,exam_in_data
                    isoftype out Num)
//Purpose: obtains name and grade components from student.

    print("Enter your name: ")
    read(student_in_name)

    print("Enter your project average: ")
    read(proj_in_data)

    print("Enter your quiz average: ")
    read(quiz_in_data)

    print("Enter your lab average: ")
    read(lab_in_data)

    print("Enter your exam score: ")
    read(exam_in_data)

endprocedure //Get_Data
```

EXAMPLE 4.28

```
function Calc_Avg returnsa Num (proj, quiz, lab, exam
    isoftype in Num)
// Purpose: calculates overall course average based on exam
// and averages for projects, quizzes, and labs.

    // grade factor constants:
    PROJ_FAC is .35 //weight of project average
    QUIZ_FAC is .30 //weight of quiz average
    LAB_FAC is .10 //weight of lab tasks
    EXAM_FAC is .25 //weight of exam

    Calc_Avg returns ((proj * PROJ_FAC) + (quiz * QUIZ_FAC) +
                (lab * LAB_FAC) + (exam * EXAM_FAC))

endfunction //Calc_Avg
```

EXAMPLE 4.29

```
function Calc_Ltr_Grade returnsa Char (course_grd isoftype in Num)
//Purpose: converts numerical course grade to a letter grade.

    // letter grade threshold constants:
    A_CUTOFF is 90
    B_CUTOFF is 80
    C_CUTOFF is 70
    D_CUTOFF is 60

    letter isoftype Char        //student's final course grade
    if (course_grd >= A_CUTOFF) then
```

```
        letter <- 'A'
    elseif (course_grd >= B_CUTOFF) then
        letter <- 'B'
    elseif (course_grd >= C_CUTOFF then
        letter <- 'C'
    elseif (course_grd >= D_CUTOFF) then
        letter <- 'D'
    else //course_grd < D_CUTOFF
        letter <- 'F'
    endif

    Calc_Ltr_Grade returns letter

endfunction //Calc_Ltr_Grade
```

EXAMPLE 4.30

```
procedure Output_Grade(out_name isoftype in String,
    out_grd isoftype in Char)
//Purpose: output the final letter grade.

    print("The course grade for ", out_name)
    print("is: ", out_grade,".")

endprocedure //Output_Grade
```

Note that in the four examples above we have not significantly changed the instructions of the algorithm, only the organization of it. The changes to the instructions concerned only parameters and identifiers. All in all, we did little more than partition the program into one high-level main algorithm and a few lower-level modules. Let's now look at the impact of these changes.

4.9 The Importance of Procedural Abstraction

4.9.1 Writing Algorithms

Procedural abstraction allows us to effectively distribute the work of creating an algorithm among different people. Each individual module might thus be assigned to a different person. This kind of division of labor utilizing teams of programmers is standard practice in the software industry.

Because each module communicates with the rest of the algorithm only via a clearly defined *interface* of parameters, none of the algorithm writers need to be concerned about the specific code written by others. Instead, all they need to coordinate is the parameters by which the various modules communicate.

In addition, they do not need to waste time trying to agree on identifier names for each piece of shared data. They can instead concentrate on the type of data they are sharing and the number of parameters that are required for the various modules. Once the number and kind of parameters are known, the algorithm writers are free to go off and create their own code as best suits their tasks. Without procedural abstraction, they would be faced with a nightmare of arguments about identifier names, who gets to access which variables and who does not, and so on. This approach dramatically increase the opportunity for bad teamwork, wasted time, and errors. The use of distinct modules that communicate only via parameters reduces the number of problem areas and allows everyone to be clear about the interaction of the various subalgorithms.

Even when an algorithm is written by single person, these same advantages are important. Over the hours (or days or weeks) it might take to develop an algorithm, the algorithm writer will forget many details and waste a great deal of time recovering forgotten information. Modular design allows writers to focus attention on individual modules and to forget the details of the other modules when they are not working on them.

As a practical matter, students tend to want to spend no more time on homework (such as algorithm and programming projects) than is necessary. This is quite reasonable. However, many students accidentally arrange to spend far more time on their work than is necessary by failing to take the few minutes required to do a high-level design that specifies what modules they need for the solution to a problem. Instead, they jump right into writing code.

Warning: Both daily experience and formal experiments have shown that you actually *save* significant time by investing a bit of it up front in high-level design work. This means that you will save significant time by doing what is called a top-down design.

Definition: **Top-down design** is jargon for a very basic idea: organizing your solution.

Before writing any code, be sure to follow a logical sequence of steps:

- *Map out the modular structure of your algorithm.* What modules do you need? What is the relationship among them? Draw a picture similar to Fig. 4.1 showing the structure of how the modules relate.
- *Refine your modular design.* For each module, give it a descriptive identifier. Write the *purpose comment* for each module. Does each module do *only one* logical task? Any module that does not should be further subdivided so that the higher module will be a manager and decision maker that controls the lower-level modules that actually carry out its work. Continue this process as many times as necessary until each module is a simple "one-trick pony." At this point, each module will be doing something simple enough that it can be more easily written.
- *Define the interface of each module before writing any code.* For each module, what data does it require in order to do its job? What results must it produce? How will those results be communicated? Specify the formal parameter list for each module.
- *After specifying each module's task and interface, begin the bottom-up work of constructing each module, one by one.* In short, start writing code. On any significant problem, coding will go *much* faster if you've done a thorough job of doing the previous design and specification. If you don't do this, you'll probably waste much time looking for a solution.

4.9.2 Testing Code

The use of parameters to define the interface between modules is particularly valuable when testing algorithms implemented in software. Testing and validation is an important undertaking that is often poorly understood and inadequately performed. The goal is to demonstrate that the software being tested does what it is supposed to do and that it does so reliably. *This is not a trivial task.* It tends to be complicated and expensive, and it is a problem that plagues the software industry. Novices tend to think that the time it takes to write an algorithm or a program is where most of the time is spent. This is not so. Much more time is spent on testing and debugging a program than on writing it. For this reason, anything that can make testing and debugging go faster is well worth the trouble.

 Using parameters to define an interface between modules allows each module to be tested for errors individually without being hooked up to the rest of the algorithm. This is particularly valuable because it is extremely difficult (sometimes impossible) to determine what part of a large program is producing a given error.

Module-by-module testing requires temporary algorithms, or *drivers*, which send appropriate input test data to a module, and *stubs*, which are temporary modules that receive data output by the tested module. Thus programmers might have a "fake" Get_Data procedure that they use to send various combinations of data to a module, and a fake Output_Results module that will indicate what values the module is producing. By using drivers and stubs to test each module individually, problems can be isolated before the modules are combined into a large program. By testing the parts of the algorithm individually, the task of determining the exact causes of an error is made a great deal easier. Determining the cause of an error is the hard part of debugging. Once the cause of an error is known, the needed repair is usually straightforward.

Thus, the extra work of testing with stubs and drivers actually can save an immense amount of time. Unfortunately, novice programmers often do not want to bother with it because they naively (and incorrectly) assume that this "extra" work *costs* time. Such misperceptions often result in programmers spending 3 or 4 times as many hours working on a program than is necessary. Remember this when enrolled in any programming course.

4.9.3 Maintaining Code

When algorithms are implemented as computer programs, those programs must be *maintained*. This includes fixing bugs that may show up over time (if testing has not been thoroughly done), refining existing features, and adding new features. It may also include adapting a program to run on a different kind of computer or with a different *operating system*.[6] Maintenance is very expensive. In fact, writing a program is

---

[6]An operating system is a special breed of computer program. It manages the computer's hardware resources such as primary memory (RAM), secondary memory (disk space), and its various communication ports. In effect, it is a program that *allows* the user to run other programs.

cheap when compared to the costs of maintaining it. In the software industry, as much as 90 percent of the cost of software is due to maintenance.

Algorithms that feature procedural abstraction make the programs that implement them a great deal cheaper to maintain. The programmers who maintain them can more readily identify the parts of the code where changes are required and what the consequences of those changes will be.

Without the use of parameters and the interface specification they provide, the *unintended* consequences of a single change to an algorithm can be nearly impossible to determine. With good modular design, the consequences of changing code in one module can be anticipated by examining the various interfaces and identifying other modules that might be affected.

4.9.4 Reusing Logic

Frequently, a given task must be performed multiple times within an algorithm.

Procedural abstraction allows us to write the algorithm for a given task once and then use it (and reuse it) whenever it is required. This is, quite obviously, far preferable to "reinventing the wheel" each time a given task is called for.

The next example illustrates how procedural abstraction can help reuse logic within an algorithm.

EXAMPLE 4.31 Two friends have made a bet about who will do better in the class. Their algorithm, called `Compare_Grades`, is similar to algorithm `Grade_Calc`, which appeared earlier in this chapter.

```
algorithm Compare_Grades
// Purpose: accepts data as input from Student1, then
// from Student2; determines who wins the bet based on
// the higher course grade.

   s_1_name isoftype String //student1 name from input
   proj_data,  //project average from input
   quiz_data,  //quiz average from input
   lab_data,   //lab average from input
   exam_data isoftype Num //exam score from input

   Get_Data(s_1_name, proj_data, quiz_data, lab_data, exam_data)
   s_1_grade isoftype Num //Course grade for Student 1
   s_1_grade <- Calc_Avg(proj_data, quiz_data, lab_data, exam_data)

   s_2_name isoftype String //student2 name from input
   Get_Data(s_2_name, proj_data, quiz_data, lab_data, exam_data)
   s_2_grade isoftype Num //Course grade for Student 2
   s_2_grade <- Calc_Avg(proj_data, quiz_data, lab_data, exam_data)
```

```
        OutputResults(s_1_name, s_2_name, s_1_grade, s_2_grade)
endalgorithm//Compare_Grades
//————————————————————

//insert algorithm Grade_Calc's procedure Get_Data here.
//————————————————————

//insert algorithm Grade_Calc's function Calc_Avg here.
//————————————————————


procedure Output_Results (student1_name, student2_name isoftype
                            in String, student1_grd, student2_grd isoftype
                            in Num)
//accepts two scores, decides which output message should be generated,
//then prints that message.

   if (student1_grd > student2_grd) then
      print(student1_name, " wins,", student2_name, " pay up.")
   elseif (student1_grd < student_2grd) then
      print(student2_name, " wins,", student1_name, " pay up.")
   else // must have two equal grades
      print("It's a tie. Pay the prof.")
   endif

endprocedure //Output_Results

//————————————————————
```

Notice that the main algorithm calls both Get_Data and Calc_Avg twice.

Be aware of the life span of data. Modules do *not* remember data from one invocation to the next. Whenever a module is called, it manipulates data according to its instructions. When it finishes, its variables "die." Thus all data that are not returned to the calling algorithm are lost. If that module is called again, it has no recollection of the data values it calculated before. In other words, each time a module is called, it begins "fresh."

In the example above, the first call to Get_Data obtains data for Student1, and the first call to Calc_Avg calculates the course grade for Student1. The course grade for Student1 is stored in s_1_grade, since this is where the result of function Calc_Avg is assigned.

After the data for Student1 are processed, the algorithm then processes the data for Student2. The second call to Get_Data obtains data for Student2 and, via Get_Data's output parameters, writes over the various scores earned by Student1. The fact that we are writing over of data (i.e., losing the various scores belonging to Student1) is of no consequence since the algorithm has already determined the course grade for Student1, has returned that value to the main algorithm's s_1_grade, and has no further use for other scores for that student. Note that we use different variables for each student's name since we require both students' names for purposes of generating output.

After obtaining data for Student2, the algorithm makes its second call to Calc_Avg. Observe that the actual parameter list used to call Calc_Avg is no different from the first call. However, the first call to Calc_Avg returns a value to s_1_grade, while the second call to Calc_Avg returns a value to s_2_grade.

By changing the variable to which the value of the function is assigned, we instruct procedure Calc_Avg to return its result to a different location. Observe that this occurs without changing function Calc_Avg in any way. Calc_Avg is the same; only the variable to which its result is assigned is different. This same effect can be achieved with procedures by altering the actual parameter list.

EXAMPLE 4.32 Recall that we have already created procedures Sort_2_Nums and Swap. Now, imagine that we wanted to have a procedure Sort_3_Nums. By reusing our existing modules, we can solve it quite simply:

```
procedure Sort_3_Nums (small, medium, large isoftype in/out Num)
// Purpose: receives 3 numbers, sorts them in ascending order.
// No special action is taken if multiple values are identical.

    is_a_tie isoftype Boolean
    Sort_2_Nums(small, medium, is_a_tie)
    Sort_2_Nums(medium, large, is_a_tie)
    Sort_2_Nums(small, medium, is_a_tie)

endprocedure //Sort_3_Nums
```

Here we have exploited the decoupling between the name and the data that parameters allow. Using parameters allowed us to have Sort_2_Nums operate on various combinations of three values as needed to ensure that the three are in sorted order. (If you're not certain that Sort_3_Nums really works, trace it.) This is a simple example of a *very powerful* principle.

By using parameters to decouple the name of the data from the data itself, we can use the same code in various situations within an algorithm, simply by changing the actual parameter list. This is far preferable to rewriting code to suit the various demands of each particular situation.

Had we not used parameters, we would not have been able to do this, and we would have had to rewrite the code that calculates whatever is done within Sort_2_Nums. Perhaps this would have meant redundant code (i.e., two versions of it, one version for each call). Or, perhaps it would have meant unnecessary and convoluted code (i.e., assorted variables and if statements to make Sort_2_Nums send its results to whichever variables should have received it). Both of these alternatives are very messy and are bad practice. By simply using parameters appropriately, we did not have to alter Sort_2_Nums in any way.

4.9.5 Reusing Code in Different Algorithms

In our Compare_Grades algorithm, we also have an example of how procedural abstraction and the interface specification it provides allow us to reuse code among different algorithms.

Observe that `Compare_Grades` contains three modules. Observe further that two of these three (`Get_Data` and `Calc_Avg`) were lifted directly from algorithm `Grade_Calc` without being changed in any way. The code was stolen from `Grade_Calc`, plain and simple. And it works.

This is very good. We want to reuse code whenever it is reasonable to do so. Reusing code is far better than rewriting code in every algorithm. There is no good reason to reinvent the wheel again and again.

Observe also that the variables declared in algorithm `Compare_Grades` are different from those used in `Grade_Calc`. Thus the actual parameters sent to `Get_Data` and `Calc_Avg` in algorithm `Compare_Grades` included identifiers unknown in algorithm `Grade_Calc`.

Notice further that this did not interfere in any way with reusing the `Get_Data` and `Calc_Avg` modules. Again, we exploited the *decoupling* of the data and the names of data that parameters allow. It does not matter which identifiers are used within the reused modules, nor does it matter which identifiers are used in the new algorithm. The names do not have to correspond, and we do not have to go back and edit our code to make them correspond. Instead, we exploit the relationship between the *actual* and *formal* parameter lists to make the old code work in the new algorithm. This is a simple example of a powerful principle.

Procedural abstraction allows us to make different pieces of code (perhaps written at different times by different people) work in harmony without rewriting the algorithm. ▪

4.10 Recursive Control

Many tasks are inherently repetitive, including most tasks in which lists of data are processed, from tracking inventory and computing salaries to processing experiment data and calculating grades. When faced with a repetitive task, we not only want to trigger some modular capability but also to trigger it *as many times as necessary*. Procedural abstraction allows us to manage repetition via recursion.

Definition: Recursion is a process in which a module achieves a repetition of algorithmic steps by calling a clone of itself. It does this via a *recursive call*: a call from within a procedure or function in which *its own identifier* is used. ▪

4.10.1 Two Forms for Recursion

Generally, recursive modules conform to one of two forms. Form 1 is as follows:

```
if (terminating condition) then
   do final actions
else
   take one step closer to terminating condition
   call "clone" of module
endif
```

This is Form 2:

```
if (NOT(terminating condition)) then
    take a step closer to terminating condition
    call "clone" of module
endif
```

Definition: The **terminating condition** in a recursive algorithm is the condition that stops the module from calling itself again.[7]

Every recursive module must have a terminating condition. Furthermore, it is necessary to eventually reach the terminating condition; otherwise, the repetition will go on forever. If, at any given step, the terminating condition is not true, we must do something that will move us closer to it and then call the module again. If we keep getting closer to the terminating condition and eventually reach it, the recursion will stop, and we will have our solution.

Both forms of recursion given above contain a test for the terminating condition and the recursive call. The difference between them is that in Form 2 nothing more is done once the terminating condition is reached; the module is finished. When the terminating condition is reached in Form 1, there are still some instructions to carry out, but there is no more recursion.

A recursive function will always use Form 1 since a function must always resolve to some value and thus must execute a *return* statement regardless of the path of execution through the function.

A recursive procedure may use either form, depending on the particulars of the problem.

EXAMPLE 4.33   Let's write a recursive algorithm that will print the integers from 1 through 10. To write such an algorithm, we need to extract the steps that are repeated over and over again during the solution process. One step we know will be repeated is the `print` instruction, which needs to be executed exactly 10 times. This gives us a hint about our terminating condition: It should be satisfied after the number 10 has been printed. Because we want to stop after this has occurred and have no other tasks to do once that condition is reached, we shall use recursive Form 2 for this module:

```
procedure Print_Ten (counter isoftype in Num)
// Purpose: repeatedly print out value of counter and
// increment it by 1 until the value exceeds 10.

    if (NOT(counter > 10)) then
        print(counter)
        Print_Ten(counter + 1)
```

---

[7]Others may call the terminating condition the *base case*. It doesn't matter which name you use so long as you understand the idea.

```
        endif

    endprocedure //Print_Ten
```

This module is a *procedure* because it has effects on the outside world (i.e., it prints data to some output device). The identifier of the procedure is `Print_Ten`. It accepts one parameter, which indicates where we are in the process of climbing from 1 to 10. The first call to this module must come from outside of the module and it must initialize `counter` to the value 1. For example, the main algorithm might feature the instruction:

```
    Print_Ten(1)
```

Subsequent calls are done recursively, increasing `counter` by 1 each time until its value finally equals 11 and satisfies the terminating condition, thus finishing the recursion.

4.10.2   Tracing Execution of a Recursive Module

Table 4.1 traces the execution of the procedure from Example 4.33. Note that this procedure will work for a variety of initial values, but what will it do? If the initial call passes the value 3, it will print out the integers 3 through 10. If the initial parameter value is 1.4, it will print out the values 1.4, 2.4, 3.4, . . . , 8.4, 9.4. In fact, it will print out the series of all the values from the initial value, incremented by 1, up to but not exceeding 10. It will behave appropriately if passed a negative number, and it will behave appropriately if passed a number greater than 10. Thus it seems that we've written a procedure that is more general than it had to be: It will *repeatedly print and increment by 1 from any initial value up through 10.*

EXAMPLE 4.34   Let's make this algorithm more general by using a second parameter in place of the literal value 10. In this way, we can have the algorithm print out numbers to whatever value is specified by the additional parameter.

```
    procedure Print_Increments (counter isoftype in Num, ceiling isoftype in
                                Num)
    // Purpose: repeatedly prints out the value of counter and
    // increments it by 1 until the value exceeds ceiling

        if (NOT(counter > ceiling)) then
            print(counter)
            Print_Increments(counter + 1, ceiling)
        endif

    endprocedure //Print_Increments
```

To print out the numbers 1 though 10, the initial call would be

```
    Print_Increments(1, 10)
```

Print the values 7 through 23 would require the call

```
    Print_Increments(7, 23)
```

So far, we've achieved an algorithm that is general with respect to both starting and stopping values; the only rigid component is the fixed rate of increment, 1. We might

TABLE 4.1 Trace of recursive execution

Module call	Parameter received	Test: "Continue recursion if . . ."	Test Outcome	Value printed	Parameter passed
First	1	(NOT (1>10))	Continue	1	2
Second	2	(NOT (2>10))	Continue	2	3
Third	3	(NOT (3>10))	Continue	3	4
Fourth	4	(NOT (4>10))	Continue	4	5
Fifth	5	(NOT (5>10))	Continue	5	6
Sixth	6	(NOT (6>10))	Continue	6	7
Seventh	7	(NOT (7>10))	Continue	7	8
Eighth	8	(NOT (8>10))	Continue	8	9
Ninth	9	(NOT (9>10))	Continue	9	10
Tenth	10	(NOT (10>10))	Continue	10	11
Eleventh	11	(NOT (11>10))	Terminate	N/A	N/A

make the algorithm more flexible such that it can work with any size increment by adding a third parameter by which the step interval can be passed. For example,

```
procedure Print_Increments (counter isoftype in Num, ceiling
                            isoftype in Num, step is in Num)
// Purpose: repeatedly prints out Counter and increments it by
// Step until the value exceeds Ceiling.

   if (NOT(counter > ceiling)) then
      print(counter)
      Print_Increments(counter + step, ceiling, step)
   endif

endprocedure //Print_Increments
```

Here, all we've done is add a third parameter, Step, which governs the size of the increment. If we want to examine the values from 3 to 100 in increments of 1.5, we would make the initial call

```
Print_Increments(3, 100, 1.5)
```

which would result in printing

```
3, 4.5, 6, 7.5, 9, ... , 96, 97.5, 99
```

4.10.3   Problem Solving with Recursion

Recursion is a very powerful tool for problem solving. At allows us to solve complex problems simply and cleanly by breaking a complex solution down into three simple steps of a fuzzy algorithm:[8]

1. Reduce the problem to a simple subtask that gets you one step closer to a solution with each step.
2. Once you have decomposed the solution into subtasks, express the solution for the subtask in the form of a recursive instruction.
3. Use the recursive subtask solution to build a solution to the original problem.

EXAMPLE 4.35   Let's use recursion to create a module, Power, that is an abstraction of exponentiation (i.e., raising some *base* value to *exponent*). Our Power function will take two parameters as input data: base is the base number and exp is the exponent to which base will be raised. Since Power is a function, it reduces to the appropriate value each time it is called, and only *input* parameters are used.

1. In the context of our example, we do not want to try solve for x^y all at once. Instead, we want to find a way to conceive of the problem in terms of smaller, easier steps. A useful insight is that we may not know what value x^y produces but we do know that $x^y = x * x^{(y-1)}$. In the same way, we know that $x^{(y-1)} = x * x^{(y-2)}$, and so on. If we keep transforming each value x^y into $x * x^{(y-1)}$, we reduce the exponent each time. Eventually, y will reduce to 0, at which point we know what x^y is: for any x, x^0 is 1.
2. Now that we know that we're trying to solve for each (x^y) by transforming it into $(x * x^{y-1})$, we can compose the recursive call that will get us one step closer:

   ```
   Power returns (x * Power(x,y-1))
   ```

3. Now that we have the basic recursive mechanism, we can refer to the appropriate recursive form for functions:

   ```
   if (terminating condition) then
      take final steps
   else
      take one step closer, make recursive call
   endif
   ```

[8]We say it's a "fuzzy algorithm" because the steps are neither precise nor unambiguous. If they were, we wouldn't need people to write algorithms; we could have computers do it.

The terminating condition is achieved when the exponent y is reduced to 0. At that point, we know that (x^y) is 1. Thus we know what our terminating condition is, what our final action is, and what our recursive "one step closer" instruction is. Given these things, we can create our function:

```
function Power returnsa Num (base, exp isoftype in Num)
// Purpose: computes the value of base raised to the exp
// power. Requires a non-negative integer for exp.

   if (exp = 0) then
      Power returns 1
   else
      Power returns base * (Power(base, exp-1))
   endif

endfunction  //Power
```

Note how compact and neat this function is. It has a simple terminating condition ("is exp equal to 0?"), executes a single instruction if the condition is met (`Power returns 1`) or a single instruction if the condition is not met (`Power returns (base * Power(base, exp-1))`). Yet it will compute the result of *any* base value raised to *any* positive exponent.

Note also that we never directly solve for x^y. Instead, we repeatedly solve for x^{y-1}, reducing the exponent each time, until the exponent is 0. When the exponent is reduced to 0, the solution is trivial: $x^0 \leftarrow 1$.

Many people find this confusing to understand and follow at first. In the next section we shall "walk through" an example in order to demonstrate a method to help you keep track of execution.

4.10.4 Using a Stack to Trace Your Code

In order to trace the execution of a recursive module, we will use a construct called a *stack*.

Definition: A **stack** is very simple to define: It is a pile upon which you can place things and from which you can only remove whatever is at the top. There are two stack operations: (1) push, which adds a new item to the top of the stack, and (2) pop, which removes the topmost item from the stack. An item that is on the stack but not at the top may be accessed only after first removing (popping) each item on top of it, thus making the desired items the topmost one.

An example of a stack is the cafeteria mechanism for storing clean plates: A number of plates are placed on a springlike device, and the first person through the line takes the topmost plate. The plate that was immediately below the top plate then itself becomes the top plate and is taken by the next person through, and so on. The key notion here is that plates can be added and removed *only* from the top.

A *stack* is based on the idea of a *last in, first out* (LIFO) list of items. This means just what it says: The last item placed in the list (*pushed* onto the stack) is the first one that may be retrieved from the list (*popped* off the stack).

This complements another idea for managing lists: *first in, first out* (FIFO). We shall discuss mechanisms for implementing both LIFO and FIFO lists later in Chapter 6. For now, don't worry about how to create the algorithm for a stack; just make sure that you understand the idea of a stack and of its push and pop operations.

A stack is a useful abstraction for tracing the behavior of algorithms as they execute. In fact, it is the means by which computers keep track of programs as they execute. As you learn how to trace with a stack, you will also be learning how a computer really goes about executing an algorithm. However, we do not use stacks here because computers do. Instead, we use them for three other reasons:

1. Stacks provide a useful, visual way to keep track of what an algorithm is doing.
2. Stacks are a foolproof method for tracing *if* you can make yourself behave as "stupidly" as a computer behaves. This means that when you are tracing your algorithm, you should not make assumptions or show any hint of common sense; you should instead simply follow the algorithmic instructions as they happen.
3. Stacks can be done anywhere since they require nothing more than paper and pencil or chalkboard and chalk.

To keep track of recursion (or any modular algorithm) we *push* a new *frame* on the stack each time a module is called. The frame contains the data values for the module. The first frame on the stack will be the algorithm that initiated the recursive call.

Imagine that our recursive `Power` function is called from the main algorithm via

```
total <- Power(7,3)
```

We place a frame for the calling algorithm on an empty stack. Since the assignment to `total`, above, cannot be done until the `Power` function returns a value, this instruction above is unfinished business, and so we label it. Thus the stack might look like this:

```
Main algorithm: Unfinished: "total <- Power(7,3)"
```

As `Power(7,3)` begins to execute, we give it its own frame by pushing a new frame onto the top of stack.

```
Power(1st): base=7     exp=3
Main algorithm: Unfinished: "total <- Power(7,3)"
```

As the initial call to `Power` executes, the terminating condition is not met since the current exponent value is 3, not 0. Thus the `else` clause is executed:

```
Power returns base * Power(base, exp-1)
```

Given the current data values (base=7, exp=3), this is equivalent to

```
Power returns 7 * Power(7,3-1)
```

which is the same as

```
Power returns 7 * Power(7,2)
```

Thus we have encountered a *recursive call:* The first clone of Power makes a second call to Power. Until that second call to Power completes, the first call also has unfinished business: It cannot complete its work until the second call provides it with a value. We record the unfinished business of the calling module in its frame on the stack and then draw (or push) a new frame for the newly called clone of Power.

Power(2nd): base=7,exp=2
Power(1st): base=7, exp=3, Unfinished: "Power returns 7*(7,2)"
Main algorithm: Unfinished: "total <- Power(7,3)"

As the second call to Power executes, the same thing happens all over again: The terminating condition is not satisfied and the else clause is executed. The second call to Power makes a third call to Power and is left waiting for the resulting value so it can complete its business. Thus we update the top frame and push yet another frame on the stack, which now looks like this:

Power(3rd): base=7, exp=1
Power(2nd): base=7, exp=2, Unfinished: "Power returns 7*Power(7,1)"
Power(1st): base=7, exp=3, Unfinished: "Power returns 7*Power(7,2)"
Main algorithm: Unfinished: "total <- Power(7,3)"

As the third call executes and the same thing occurs, we add the appropriate notation to the top of the stack and then draw a new frame for the recursive call.

Power(4th): base=7,exp=0
Power(3rd): base=7,exp=1 Unfinished: "Power returns 7*Power(7,0)"
Power(2nd): base=7,exp=2 Unfinished: "Power returns 7*Power(7,1)"
Power(1st):base=7, exp=3, Unfinished: "Power returns 7*Power(7,2)"
Main algorithm: Unfinished: "total <- Power(7,3)"

When the fourth call is made, the value of exp that is passed to the fourth clone of Power is 0. Because exp is 0, as the fourth call to Power executes, the terminating condition is satisfied. This triggers the if clause, not the else, and for the first time we do *not* have a recursive call. The fourth call to Power simply returns the value 1 and then terminates.

Let's take a careful look at the stack at this point in execution:

- There is a stack frame for each instance of a call to the recursive module. Each stack frame stores its own data values. Yet no "answer" has been computed.
- What has occurred, however, is that all the data needed for a solution is now on the stack. Except for the final frame, which achieved the terminating condition, each of the other "partial solutions" is spelled out on the stack as unfinished business. Each frame is also waiting for some value to be passed back down the stack from the frame above it so that it can terminate.
- Thus we are poised for a chain reaction as the partial answers cascade down the stack. The cascade begins with the final call that resolved to the value 1.

With the fourth call finished, the unfinished business of the third call can be completed: We now know that Power(7,0) has reduced to the value 1. Thus we can substitute the value 1 for Power(7,0) in the frame for the third call. After making that substitution in the third frame, we have no further use for the fourth call's frame. We therefore erase (or pop) it from the stack. The stack now looks like this:

```
Power(3rd): base=7,exp=1 Unfinished: "Power returns 7*1"

Power(2nd): base=7,exp=2 Unfinished: "Power returns 7*Power(7,1)"

Power(1st): base=7, exp=3, Unfinished: "Power returns 7*Power(7,2)"

Main algorithm: Unfinished: "total <- Power(7,3)"
```

The third call now has the information it requires to finish its business:

```
Power returns 7 * Power(7,0)
```

This has now resolved to

```
Power returns 7 * 1, or 7
```

This completes the work of the third call to Power: It has resolved to the value 7. Since its work is done, we can substitute its value, 7, for the unfinished business of the second call. After doing the substitution, we pop the frame for the third call off the stack. Its value, 7, is now available to the second call to Power.

```
Power(2nd): base=3, exp=3 Unfinished: "Power returns 7*7"

Power(1st): base=3, exp=4, Unfinished: "Power returns 7*Power(7,3)"

Main algorithm: Unfinished: "total <- Power(7,3)"
```

```
Power returns 7 * Power(7,1)
```

has resolved to

```
Power returns 7 * 7, or 49
```

This completes the work of the second call to Power: It has resolved to the value 49. Since its work is done, we *pop* it off the stack and forget about it. Its value, 49, can now be substituted in the unfinished business of the first call to Power.

```
Power(1st): base=7, exp=3, Unfinished: "Power returns 7*49"

Main algorithm: Unfinished: "total <- Power(7,3)"
```

```
Power returns 7 * Power(7,2)
```

has now resolved to

```
Power returns 7 * 49, or 343
```

This completes the work of the first call to Power: It has resolved to the value 343. Since its work is done, we pop it off the stack and are done with it. Its value, 343, can now be substituted for the original call in the main algorithm. At this point, all evidence of the Power function is gone from memory except for the final value it produced, 343.

```
Main algorithm: Unfinished: "total <- 343"
```

Now, finally,

```
total <- Power(7,3)
```

has resolved to

```
total <- 343
```

With the assignment of 343 to total, the job is complete. The stack frame for the main algorithm will stay on the stack until the algorithm itself ends, at which point its frame is erased and all trace of the algorithm is gone from memory.

Notice what has just happened. Our recursive function has constructed a solution from a series of partial solutions. In effect, it cloned itself as many times as required to build a chain of partial solutions up the stack. Once the terminating condition was reached, what happened?

- The recursion stopped (i.e., no more frames were placed on the stack).
- The recursion stopped because the final call resolved to a known value, not unfinished business. Thus, for the first time, one of our function calls completed the job of finding its partial answer.

- As soon as one partial answer was produced, the solution started building, cascading one step at a time from the top to the bottom. Each function call received the data for which it was waiting from the stack frame above, produced its own partial answer, and then returned its partial answer to the frame below, which had been waiting for it.
- This chain reaction continued until the final answer was constructed. At that point, the recursive procedure had finished its job and vanished from the stack.

 This set of actions explains the essence of how recursion helps in solving problems. Recursion supports the systematic construction of solutions by a chain of partial solutions. Although recursion is useful in many circumstances, it is especially so in situations where it can take advantage of a stack to store the intermediate solutions in their unfinished state until such time as needed values are computed.

Despite the compact nature of the function, notice all the work that was accomplished. Remember, the entire function consisted of only a single recursive if-then-else statement:

```
if (exp = 0) then
   Power returns 1
else
   Power returns (base * Power(base, exp-1))
endif
```

This exact logic would have worked the same way, regardless of the base number and the positive exponent integer passed to it even had we asked it to compute the value of 119 raised to two-hundred-thirty-eighth power. Simply by passing it different parameters, an immense amount of work can be done.

4.10.5 The Role of Recursion

Recursion is one of two means of achieving repetition. The other means is *iteration* (which is defined and discussed in Chapter 5). In the past, programmers did not use recursion very much. Instead, they relied almost exclusively on iteration. Such a bias was largely due to a single factor: In some circumstances, recursion can require a great deal of memory. As we have seen, each recursive call requires memory for its own frame on the stack. For a recursive solution that involves many, many recursive calls, a computer might run out of memory before it can complete the job.

Just a few years ago, memory was expensive, so computers did not have much of it. In those times, there were good economic reasons to shy away from recursion. Today, even the least expensive new computer has *at least* a thousand times as much memory as did the expensive minicomputers of 1980. We thus don't worry as much as we used to about running out of memory.

Nonetheless, even if we had a billion times as much memory, a recursive solution to certain kinds of problems can still exhaust memory. (We'll discuss such algorithms in Chapter 9.) But even this potential difficulty does not mean that we should be skeptical of recursion. If we expect that memory consumption might be a problem, it is usually a straightforward matter to convert recursion to iteration if need be, *once we know what the recursive solution is.*

For these reasons and others, the historical programmer bias against recursion has become obsolete. Recursion is extremely powerful, and there is currently no good reason not to use it. As computing is used to solve increasingly complex problems, recursion becomes more and more important. It is a very powerful tool for algorithmic problem solving. It is therefore important to master recursion early and well. We have found that students do much better if they study recursion first, before iteration. Thus the next chapter will introduce iteration, after which we will compare the two and discuss the advantages and limitations of each approach.

Recursion and the Afrika Corps

In the early years of World War II, the German army dominated the British and French forces. Yet the most famous German general, one who was most respected by his Allied opponents, is the one who suffered the first German defeat. It was against him that the tide turned in favor of the Allies, yet he is regarded highly in military lore. He was Field Marshal Erwin Rommel, known to his British enemies as the Desert Fox.

By 1940, the Germans had been victorious throughout Europe and had established continental Europe as a fortress. The British elected to attempt their resurgence at a point where the Germans were furthest from their supply sources and weakest in numbers. The site was North Africa.

Rommel was the commander of the German Afrika Corps and was thus responsible for holding off the first British offensive of the war. The German army occupied virtually all of Europe, and Hitler was considering plans for invading both England and Russia. With troops committed elsewhere and ambitious plans afoot, Hitler left Rommel to "make do" with inadequate support in terms of both men and material. Rommel rose to the occasion by deploying innovative tactics by which he held off superior numbers of British (and later, American) forces for an extended period.

He accomplished this in large part by deploying a *recursive algorithm* to organize and coordinate his troops in battle. Ordinarily, any commander would keep a healthy segment of his forces in reserve. This was deemed necessary because an enemy attack would threaten some portion of his line, and he needed to have reserve troops available to move up from the rear to support his front line troops at the point where they were attacked. Because his forces were so outnumbered, Rommel did not have enough troops to do this. He required that all his forces be committed to battle to have any hope of taking the day.

This, of course, left him with the serious problem of: how to respond to points of threat when he had no extra troops to deploy?

Rommel's recursive solution was to decentralize control of his forces, giving each local commander the authority to deploy without approval from above, and to specify for those local commanders the recursive algorithm they were to execute. (Because battle is ongoing, there is no terminating condition in it. Rommel *wanted* infinite repetition.) Here's the logic of that algorithm:

```
procedure Rules_Of_Engagement

    look (to your left and to your right)
    if (you see your comrade in trouble) then
       go help him
    endif
    RulesOfEngagement

end //procedure Rules_Of_Engagement
```

In battle, this algorithm was deployed throughout Rommel's army. Commanders of small units in a skirmish would use it to manage their local troop deployment in that skirmish, just as commanders of large battalions would use it to manage the fighting in large battles. Regardless of the scale of fighting, the effect was the same: Rommel's troops would converge automatically on the point of attack.

This convergence of troops to the point where they were most needed did not occur because of a series of orders from the top command down to soldiers in the field. Instead, it happened as a result of a distributed, organic, recursive process: If a given unit was in trouble, its neighbor units would come to its aid. And, in turn, *their* neighbor units would see their movement and slide over to help them, and so on. In short, it was a self-managed, chain reaction with a powerful result: *Wherever* the Allies attacked, they would soon be facing the brunt of the German forces in the area.

Rommel eventually lost but not because he was "out-generaled." He lost because he was finally overwhelmed by superior forces and a lack of reinforcements and supplies. Despite his eventual defeat, he went home a hero.

Later in the war, he was implicated in a failed plot to kill Adolf Hitler. Because of Rommel's popularity, Hitler didn't want this to be known to the German people. He threatened to have Rommel's family killed unless Rommel agreed to quietly commit suicide. Unable to protect Germany from destruction, Rommel chose to kill himself in order to save those he could protect, his family.

SUMMARY

The goal of *procedural abstraction* is to subdivide complex problems into manageable "chunks." This is accomplished by creating modules that each serve a particular logical purpose and hide the details involved. Thus, each module represents a single abstraction, or idea, and the implementation details are *encapsulated* within the module.

Doing this allows us to solve complex problems by thinking at a higher level of abstraction than would otherwise be possible. Procedural abstraction leads to greater convenience and efficiency by allowing us to distribute algorithm writing among different people and by allowing us to reuse modules in various contexts.

There are two types of modules: *procedures* and *functions*.

- *Procedures* can accomplish a wide variety of tasks, may have effects on the data of other modules, and may affect the real world outside the algorithm.
- *Functions* are like mathematical functions (i.e., they resolve to a single value and are not permitted to have any other effects).

Procedural abstraction requires that we define *interfaces* through which modules communicate. *Parameters* are the means of establishing communication interfaces between modules. There are three kinds of parameters: *input, output*, and *input/output*. For any given situation, one of these three types of parameters is called for, depending on the particulars of the problem at hand.

Modular organization of data and instructions provides a powerful tool for controlling repetition: *recursion*. Recursion is a means of managing repetition by having a given module call a clone of itself. Recursive modules generally consist of a single, simple, and clean decision statement that achieves powerful repetitive effects. Recursive modules generally approximate one of two forms. Regardless of which form is used, a recursive module must have both of two attributes:

- It must have a *terminating condition*.
- The terminating condition must eventually be satisfied.

A *stack* is a mechanism for implementing a LIFO list. There are two primary stack operations:

- *Push*, which adds a new item at the top of the stack.
- *Pop*, which removes an existing item from the top of the stack.

We can use the idea of a stack to help us *trace the execution* of a modular algorithm. Whenever a module is called, we push a frame onto the stack for it. Each frame contains the space for the module's data and for noting any unfinished business the module has if it should call another module. When a module completes, we pop its frame from the stack, and all trace of its variables vanishes. A stack is particularly helpful in tracing the execution of a recursive module.

In the past, there were practical, economic reasons why recursion was rarely used by programmers. As economics change, and as computing is used to solve increasingly complex problems, recursion becomes more and more important as a powerful, practical problem-solving tool.

EXERCISES

For Exercises 4.1 through 4.12, specify whether the module appropriate for the described task should be a *function* or a *procedure*.

4.1 Reading in four pieces of data from the user.

4.2 Reading in one piece of data from the user.

4.3 Determining the smallest of several values.

4.4 Determining the average of several values.

4.5 Determining whether or not two values are equal.

4.6 Returning two values such that they are sorted in ascending order.

4.7 Returning the largest two of several values.

4.8 Deciding whether the value of a given `Char` variable is a vowel or a consonant.

4.9 Determining the winner in a contest

4.10 Determining the winner and the runner up in a contest.

4.11 Printing the results of a contest.

4.12 Deciding whether to quit or try again.

For Exercises 4.13 through 4.23, write a module to carry out the indicated task. Each module must be either a procedure or a function as implied by the problem. All parameters should be in, out, or in/out *as appropriate to the task.*

4.13 Reading in four pieces of numerical data from the user to be used elsewhere in the algorithm.

4.14 Reading in one piece of numerical data from the user to be used elsewhere in the algorithm.

4.15 Determining the smallest of four numerical values and returning that value.

4.16 Determining the average of four numerical values and returning that value.

4.17 Determining if two character values are identical and returning the answer.

4.18 Returning four numerical values such that they are sorted in ascending order.

4.19 Returning the largest two of three character values.

4.20 Deciding whether the value of a given character variable is a consonant and returning the results of that decision.

4.21 Determining and returning the winning (high) numerical score of a contest with five contestants.

4.22 Determining and returning both the winner and the runner-up scores in such a contest.

4.23 Printing the results of that contest showing all five scores.

4.24 Describe each of the following parameters: in, in/out, and out and when each should be used.

4.25 What is the difference between *actual* and *formal* parameters?

4.26 In the following algorithm, which variables are *actual* parameters and which are *formal* parameters?

```
algorithm Calculate_Product

    height1 isoftype num
    height1 <- 45

    height2 isoftype num
    height2 <- 60

    height3 isoftype num
    height3 <- 49

    height_product isoftype num
    height_product <- Multiply_Three(height1, height2, height3)
```

```
    print(height_product)

endalgorithm //Calculate_Product

    //*****************************************

function Multiply_Three returnsa Num (num1, num2, num3
    isoftype in Num)
// Purpose: takes in three parameters and returns
// their product.

    Multiply_Three returns (num1 * num2 * num3)

endfunction // Multiply_Three

    //*****************************************
```

For Exercises 4.27, 4.28, and 4.29, specify whether each parameter should be in, in/out, or out.

4.27 procedure GetInput (num1 isoftype ___ Num,
                    num2 isoftype ___Num)
// Purpose: reads in the two numbers for use
// by other modules.

4.28 function Equal returnsa Boolean (num1 isoftype _____
                        Num,num2 isoftype _____ Num)
// Purpose: returns TRUE if two numbers are equal.

4.29 procedure Increment (number isoftype _____ Num,
            increment_size isoftype _____ Num)
// Purpose: increments the value of the first
// parameter by the value of the second one.

4.30 Implement the contents (declarations, if any, and instructions) for the procedure of Exercise 4.27.

4.31 Implement the contents (declarations, if any, and instructions) for the function of Exercise 4.28.

4.32 Implement the contents (declarations, if any, and instructions) for the procedure of Exercise 4.29.

4.33 Using the modules from Exercises 4.27 through 4.29, write an algorithm that will do the following: obtain four numeric values from input, determine how many *different* numeric values you have obtained, and then print out your findings. Your algorithm should consist of whatever variable declarations are needed, along with assignment statements and calls to the relevant modules. Your algorithm should *not* perform any task that the modules can do for it.

4.34 What is wrong with the use of data in the following nonsense algorithm? (Assume that the modules that are referenced but not provided do exist and are correct.) Look for multiple problem areas.

```
algorithm Doo_Wop
    this_var isoftype Num
    that_var isoftype Boolean
    other_var isoftype Num

    Get_Data(this_var, that_var, other_var)
    Shoobie_Doo(this_var, that_var, other_var)
```

```
      Output_Data(this_var, that_var, other_var)
   endalgorithm //Doo_Wop

   procedure Shoobie_Doo (a, b, c isoftype in/out Num)
      this_var <- that_var + other_var
   endprocedure //Shoobie_Doo
```

For Exercises 4.35 and 4.36, perform a top-down design for the specified tasks. Show the main algorithm in detail and show the header lines (including formal parameters) and purpose comments for each module that the main algorithm uses. Implement the details of the main algorithm only, not the modules. Apply the concept of abstraction (i.e., decompose the problem into distinct logical subtasks).

4.35 Read in an employee's salary, calculate the appropriate state and federal Income taxes, social security, medicare withholding, and net salary, and then print the resulting information. (Details concerning how to calculate each withholding amount can be ignored since they should be hidden inside modules).

4.36 Read in data concerning the number of miles driven, number of gallons of gasoline consumed, and total gasoline expenditures. Now calculate both *miles per gallon* and *cost of fuel per mile* and print out the all the information. (Details concerning how to calculate each item can be ignored, since they should be hidden inside modules).

4.37 When should you use procedures in your programs? What kind of parameters can be used in the declaration of procedures?

4.38 What makes functions different from procedures? When should you use functions in your programs? What is the only kind of parameter that can be used with functions and why?

For Exercises 4.39, 4.40, and 4.41, design and implement procedures and functions to handle the class information of a university. Use good modularity and documentation in all of your answers.

4.39 Write a module (either a procedure or function) named `Get_Student_Info` that will ask the users for the following information and return their responses to the calling module:

```
social_security_number
age
grade_level (should be "F," "S," "J," or "R" for
        Freshman, Sophomore, etc.)
gpa
good_standing (should be true if their GPA is >= 2.0,
          otherwise false)
```

4.40 Write a module (either a procedure or a function) that will take in a `grade_level` (as defined above) and print out "Freshman," "Sophomore," "Junior," or "Senior" depending on the class rank.

4.41 Write a module named `Print_Student_Info` that will print out the following information: social security number, age, grade level, GPA, good standing. If called with the following:

```
   Print_Student_Info(1234567890, 21, "J", 3.2, true)
```

your output should look something like this:

```
Student 1234567890 is 21 years old.
Class rank: Junior
GPA = 3.2
Student is in GOOD STANDING
```

4.42 You have been given the following function:

```
function Unknown returnsa Num (in_num isoftype in Num)

    if (in_num = 0) then
        Unknown returns 0
    else
        Unknown returns Unknown ((in_num - 1) + in_num)
    endif

endfunction   //Unknown
```

Use a stack to trace the execution of this function and report the number to which it resolves when called via

```
Unknown(4)
```

4.43 Consider the following algorithm and report the exact output that is printed.

```
algorithm Magic

    a isoftype Num
    a <- 3

    b isoftype Num
    b <- 3

    c isoftype Num
    c <- Operation (a,b)
    print ("The values are: ",a,b,c)

    Mystify (a,b,c)
    print ("The values are: ",a,b,c)

    Mystify (c,b,a)
    print ("The values are: ",a,b,c)

endalgorithm // Magic

function Operation returnsa Num (num1, num2 isoftype in Num)

    if (num1 > num2) then
        Operation returns (num1 * num2)
    else
        Operation returns (num1 + num2)
    endif

endfunction // Operation

procedure Mystify (num1, num2 isoftype in/out Num,
                   num3 isoftype in Num)

    num3 <- num3 - 1
    num1 <- num1 + num3
    num2 <- num1 + num2
```

```
    print ("My numbers are: ", num1, num2, num3)

end //procedure Mystify
```

4.44 What is the output from the following program? Trace the execution of this program using a stack.

```
algorithm Follow_Me

    a isoftype num
    a <- 1

    b isoftype num
    b <- a * 2

    c isoftype num
    c <- Min_2_Nums(b, a)
    print (c, b, a)

    Normalize(a, b, c)
    c <- Min_2_Nums(a, b)
    print (a, b, c)

    Normalize (b, c, a)
    a <- c / b
    Normalize (c, a, b)

endalgorithm Follow_Me

procedure Normalize (i, j, k isoftype in/out Num)
// this procedure takes in three parameters and modifies them

    i <- j * k
    j <- k * i
    k <- i * j
    print (i, j, k)

end //procedure Normalize

function Min_2_Nums (as given in Example 4.12)
```

4.45 Write a recursive module that will do the following: read in a number; if that number is negative, halt; otherwise, print the number and make a recursive call to itself. Explain your choice of either a function or a procedure.

4.46 Fibonacci numbers are a sequence of numbers defined as follows: For 1 or 2, the Fibonacci number is 1. For a larger number n, the Fibonacci number is equal to the sum of the Fibonacci numbers for n−2 and n−1. For example, for $x >= 3$, $Fib(x) = Fib(x-1) + Fib(x-2)$.

This definition gives us

```
Number:          1 2 3 4 5 6  7  8  9
Fibonacci number: 1 1 2 3 5 8 13 21 34
```

Thus the Fibonacci number for 5 is the sum of the Fibonacci numbers for 3 and 4, which means: 2 + 3, or 5. Write a recursive function that computes the Fibonacci number for a given a positive number parameter (which you may name n).

4.47 Write the recursive procedure `Find_GPA` that will find a student's grade point average (GPA). It will require two parameters to keep track of the total number of credit hours and quality points for the student. The procedure will ask the user if he or she wants to enter another class. If the user enters y, the procedure will read in the grade and credit hours for a course, calculate the quality points for the class, update the necessary variables, and then repeat. If the user enters n, the procedure will print out the student's GPA and terminate.

4.48 Write the recursive function `Factorial`. This function will receive an integer value that is 0 or greater and will return the factorial of that number. For example, 4! = 4 * 3 * 2 * 1. *Factorial* is defined recursively as

```
N! (i.e., n factorial) = N * (N-1)! for N >= 1
0! (i.e., "0 factorial") = 1
```

Show the stack trace as it exists at its tallest point when it is called by `Factorial(5)`.

4.49 Write the recursive function GCD (for greatest common divisor). The function will receive two integer values and will return the largest integer that can be divided evenly into both numbers. GCD is defined recursively as:

```
GCD of two integers (x, y) is x if y = 0.
GCD of two integers (x, y) is GCD(y, x MOD y) if y <> 0
```

Show the stack as it exists at its tallest point when GCD is called by `GCD(35, 149)`.

CHAPTER 5

Tools for Data Abstraction

Manipulating data is what computers do. We often want computers to process large amounts of data, so we need ways to manipulate lists and other groupings of large amounts of data. To satisfy these needs, we require more than just the few basic data types that are built into our language. We require constructs and methods that allow us to not only manipulate data but to also create *data abstractions*.

We use data abstractions to encapsulate the data details of information ideas. In creating data abstractions, we build data groupings that reflect the relationships among various data and allow us to conveniently manipulate large amounts of data.

In this chapter, we introduce the means of solving two kinds of data abstraction problems:

- Grouping logically related data items together.
- Creating collections (lists or otherwise) of large amounts of similar data.

In addition, we introduce *iteration,* which is another means of implementing repetition.

5.1   The Meaning of Data

In Chapter 2, we drew a distinction between information and data. As we said then,

- Information means knowledge about something.
- Data means a specific representation of some information.

The distinction between information and data presents one of our primary opportunities to use abstraction. This is why we insist on data identifiers that are descriptive and meaningful:

- A variable's *identifier* describes the information that we wish to represent as data.
- A variable's *data type* specifies how we will represent that information as data.

For example, consider the following variable declaration:

```
employee_age isoftype Num
```

The role of the identifier (i.e., `employee_age`) is to describe the information to be represented, while the role of the data type (i.e., `Num`) is to specify the data representation itself.

Thus, the identifier's job is to inform the reader about the information being represented by the data. Based on the information so provided, a reader can make reasonable judgments. For example, if the value stored in `employee_age` is 462, we would suspect an error because, while 462 is a valid number, it is not a reasonable value to represent a person's age. What does it mean when we encounter such a value for a person's age? Has bad data been entered? Is there an error in the algorithm? If so, what kind of error is it? Is the algorithm reporting a person's age in months, not years, or is there some other kind of error? We discuss issues concerning errors and correctness in Chapter 8, but already we can see that a descriptive identifier provides useful information that is not provided by information-poor identifiers such as `x` or `fred`.

As with other uses of abstraction, our goal is to distinguish between the *essence* (the idea, in this case a person's age) and the *specific embodiment* (the low-level details, in this case a numerical data representation). The appropriate choice of data identifiers gives us our most basic tool for data abstraction.

5.2 Organizing Multiple Pieces of Data

So far, we have only considered variables of the atomic data types (`Num`, `Char`, `Boolean`), which can hold only one piece of data at a time, and `Strings`, which allow us to store textual words, phrases, etc. Because it often happens that various pieces of data logically belong together, these structures are not sufficient for many of our needs. Thus, we require ways to construct more complex data structures from the atomic and `String` data types that are built into the language.

When we have many pieces of data that are closely related in some way, it is both logically correct and efficient to organize the data into one single structure instead of having a different variable name for each piece of data. The data structures formed in this way are *composite,* or *complex structures,* containing several, perhaps many, cells. You can think of them as a group of individual data structures that are all united under one name.

If we organize data properly, we achieve data abstraction. Just as procedural abstraction means that we isolate the details of a given set of logical steps and then refer to them by a meaningful name, data abstraction means that we do the same thing with data: We hide the details of how we organize data and then refer to complex logical chunks of data by a single meaningful name. Thus, we can refer to a complex group of data by single name without getting lost in the details of how it is organized.

Suppose we wish to keep track of all the students at a university, but we do not want to fool around with declaring many little variables for each one of many thousand students. If the university had 12,000 students, and we wished to store only five pieces of information about each student, we would be faced with a task of declaring and manipulating some 60,000 different variables. Common sense tells us that dealing with 60,000 variables individually involves far too many annoying details. Instead, we want to organize the data such that

- The data pertaining to a given student are located in one data structure, not in five unrelated variables.
- The data pertaining to each of the 12,000 students are collected into a single structure for the entire student body as a whole, not in 12,000 unrelated structures.

This means that we can quickly access particular pieces of data for each and every student without undue amounts of searching. This kind of organization is something that people figured out how to do hundreds of years before computers were invented. In many cases, we continue to use those methods today. For example, in a college using paper-based information, each student's file might be placed in a folder that is kept in a file cabinet. This provides an example of hierarchical data structures:

- The highest level contains a collection of data for all students (i.e., the filing cabinets).
- The next lowest level contains the collection of data for a given student (i.e., a specific folder located somewhere in the filing cabinets).
- The next lowest level contains the specific information items stored for each student (i.e., whatever is stored within the student's folder).

To obtain the benefits that computing provides, we must at minimum adapt this kind of data organization for use in our algorithms. At best, we can create other data organization schemes that perform better than those that are typically used with paper-based data.

As we shall soon see, there are just a few basic constructs that allow us to group data together. Each has its benefits and its costs, and none is best for all circumstances. However, we shall also see that these few tools can be used to construct data structures of infinite variety. Thus, they allow us to design and use whatever data structures are best suited to the problem at hand.

5.3 Records

We often wish to group data that are of different types (e.g., numeric, textual, or boolean). To accomplish this, we can use a record. A record is a data structure that groups together data of different types, or perhaps of the same type.

FIGURE 5.1

Employee Record	
Employee name:	George P. Burdell
Employee soc. sec. number:	987-65-4321
Employee rate of pay ($/hour):	$20
Full time status (Yes/No):	Yes
Benefits status (Full/Partial/None):	Partial

Suppose we are creating an algorithm to keep track of employees for a given company. For example, we might want to store the following data for each employee:

- Employee's name.
- Employee's social security number.
- Employee's rate of pay.
- Whether or not the employee is full time.
- Whether or not the employee receives full, partial, or zero benefits.

To store this information, we would use the record shown in Fig. 5.1. This structure unites five different data items, or *fields*, within a single data record.

Definition: A data **record** is a composite structure composed of some number of fields. It is a structure for grouping related data items.

Definition: A data **field** is an individual data item within a record.

5.3.1 Creating New Record Data Types

Records give us the ability to group various kinds of data together, but notice that we have little use for creating only a single complex variable of a given record structure. A group of 137 employees would require 137 such record variables. We certainly would not want to declare 137 different variables, specifying the particular details of our five-field structure each time. Instead, we want to create the appropriate *type* of record just once and then declare 137 different *instances* of it. To be able to do this, we must be able to create new data types.

By creating new data types of our own specification, we add to the *type definitions* that we can use in an algorithm. Once we have created a new data type, we can then create variables of that new data type, just as we can create variables of the built-in types (such as Num, Char, and String).

We create new data types by defining them. This is similar to the way that we create variables by declaring them. Our syntax is similar to that of a variable declaration. Instead of using *is of type*, or isoftype, we use *defines a* or definesa.

EXAMPLE 5.1 To create a new data type for the structure shown in Fig. 5.1, we might declare

```
Employee_Record_Type definesa record
    employee_name isoftype String
    soc_sec_num isoftype Num
```

```
        pay_rate isoftype Num
        full_time isoftype Boolean
        benefits isoftype Char
endrecord  //Employee_Record_Type
```

5.3.2   Accessing the Fields of a Record

Once a new data type has been defined, we can use it as the basis for declaring as many variables of that type as we require:

```
employee1,
employee2,
employee3 isoftype Employee_Record_Type
```

Following the declaration of these three variables, we have three distinct occurrences of `Employee_Record_Type`. Each one is a variable with five data fields.

To access the particular fields within each record variable, we concatenate the identifier of the record variable (the variable identifier) with the identifier of the data field (the field identifier), separated by a period as follows:

```
employee1.soc_sec_num <- 123456789
```

or

```
employee3.pay_rate <- 12.50
```

or

```
employee1.employee_name <- "Burdell, George P."
```

When accessing a given data field within a record variable, we must identify both the record variable and the appropriate field within the record.

The record identifier is unique since each declared record variable has its own identifier. The field identifier is generic to the data type, and each variable of the data type will share the same field identifiers. Novices sometime err by using the record type identifier in lieu of the variable identifier as follows:

```
Employee_Record_Type.pay_rate <- 12.50
```

This instruction doesn't specify which employee's record is to be updated and thus is imprecise and ambiguous.

Because the identifier of a given record variable refers collectively to all the fields in its structure, we can assign the entire contents of one record variable to another variable of the same type in a single operation as follows:

```
employee1 <- employee2
```

Similarly, we can pass an entire record variable via a single parameter of the appropriate type. For example, the header line of a procedure might look like the following:

```
procedure Print_Employee_Data (this_employee isoftype
                        in Employee_Record_Type)
```

5.4 Distinction Between Types and Variables

The following is a fundamental difference between a type definition and a variable declaration:

- Defining a new variable gives us specific space in memory to store data. Each variable must be declared to be of some data type.
- Defining a new (i.e., user-defined) data type expands our repertoire of available data types and thus allows us to declare variables of the new type.

5.4.1 Data Types Expand the Language

The ability to create new data types allows us to expand our language.

We can invent new data types to fit the data representation needs of a given problem. We are not confined to simple atomic types and Strings. Instead, we can construct whatever structure suits the task at hand.

By itself, however, defining a new data type does *not* create any variables of the new type. As with built-in data types, we must explicitly declare any variables we require. With new data types, we must define the data type first, before we declare any variables to be of the new data type.

5.4.2 The Scope of Data Types

Because data types are just definitions that can be used to create variables, but are not themselves variables, the scoping rule is different from that of variables. Recall that variables can be "seen" only within the module in which they are declared (i.e., they are all "local"). This scope rule is important because we are concerned about the data integrity of variables and thus wish to control *who* can change the value of *what*.

Data types do not present us with this problem. Unlike the value stored in a variable, the algorithm itself cannot modify the definition of a data type. In this respect, data types are similar to constants: The meaning of a new data type is defined by the algorithm author, and the algorithm cannot change it. Thus, we apply the same *unlimited scope* rule to data types that we have already applied to constants: The scope of a type definition is unlimited within an algorithm. That is to say, if you define a new data type anywhere within an algorithm, that type definition can be seen and used for declaring variables anywhere (i.e., in the main algorithm or in any of the modules).

You should declare each new data type prior to its first use, and you may not redefine it anywhere else. If both the main algorithm and a module require the same new data type, define the data type in the higher-level location (i.e., the main algorithm).

5.4.3   The Abstraction Power of User-Defined Data Types

By making the distinction between the definition of new user-defined data types and the declaration of variables such that each is done separately, we obtain great convenience when it is necessary to modify the definition of a data type.

EXAMPLE 5.2   Let's extend the data stored in a record. Consider the following record type definition to allow us to keep track of parties on or near campus:

```
Party_Record definesa record
    location isoftype String
    hour_started isoftype Num
endrecord //Party_Record
```

Once defined, we can declare a variable of this type as follows to keep track of as many parties as we wish:

```
halloween,
new_year's,
beginning_of_term,
middle_of_term,
end_of_term isoftype Party_Record
```

If we wished to store additional data about such parties and thus needed to expand the number of data fields, we could ask the algorithm author to redefine the type definition as follows:

```
Party_Record definesa record
    location isoftype String
    hour_started isoftype Num
    police_came isoftype Boolean
endrecord //Party_Record
```

Because the details of a type definition are localized in one place, we need only modify that definition. Upon executing the algorithm thereafter, all variables declared of type `Party_Record` will automatically have the additional field. The changes are made only once and cascade to all variables of that type.

5.4.4   Anonymous Data Types

Certain programming languages require explicit type definitions, while others do not. Even if a given language does not require that you distinguish between types and variables, you should do so anyway. If you do not take advantage of this ability to abstract out the details of data structure design from the actual declaration of variables, you will be creating inferior data structures, which are called *anonymous data types*. This name comes from the fact that such poor designs combine the declaration of a complex variable with the definition of a new data type such that the data type itself has no identifier and thus is anonymous.

The declaration below illustrates the blurring together of type and variable declarations. Because the type definition is embedded in the declaration of variable `this_employee_record`, the type itself has no identifier, and as a result, we cannot declare other variables or parameters to be of this type.

```
this_employee_record isoftype record
    employee_name isoftype String
    soc_sec_num isoftype Num
    pay_rate isoftype Num
    full_time isoftype Boolean
    benefits isoftype Char
endrecord //this_employee_record
```

 WARNING: Do NOT use the above type of declaration. It shows a poor abstraction featuring an anonymous data type. ◼

The following is an example of good abstraction with distinct *type* and *variable* declarations.

EXAMPLE 5.3

```
Employee_Record_Type definesa record
    employee_name isoftype String
    soc_sec_num isoftype Num
    pay_rate isoftype Num
    full_time isoftype Boolean
    benefits isoftype Char
endrecord //Employee_Record_Type

this_employee_record isoftype Employee_Record_Type
```
◼

Anonymous data types are bad since they hardwire too many details into too many places in your algorithm. Whenever you declare a complex variable that *includes* a data type declaration, you are guilty of anonymous data typing. We consider this a significant shortcoming and therefore make it illegal. Many programming languages permit such design errors, but this fact does not mean that anonymous data typing is permissible. After all, the design of automobiles permits you to drive into a wall at high speed, but this fact does not recommend that you actually do so.

5.5 Pointers

In Chapter 3, we mentioned pointers only briefly. Pointers are somewhat analogous to telephone call forwarding, which allows us to change the location to which a phone call is directed. With call forwarding, we can call one phone number and our call can be redirected to another one. In effect, we can reach someone without knowing his or her current location. This is what pointers do: They allow our algorithm to change the location to which an identifier refers.

The need for such a data structure may not be obvious when writing algorithms to be executed on paper. This is understandable because the concept of pointers was developed as a tool for computer programming. Hence, the concept of pointers requires some explanation.

Computer memory is made up of many locations (generally millions), each of which can hold a piece of data. These locations are very similar to the cells to which we have referred, with one difference: In writing algorithms, we create our cells out of thin air by merely giving them a name, whereas the memory cells in a computer physically exist in the computer.

These memory cells are numbered sequentially. When the computer processor needs to access a memory cell, it refers to it by its number, or *address*. When an algorithm is written in a programming language for use on a computer, each variable identifier used in the algorithm is associated with the address of the memory cell that has been allocated for that variable. In modern programming languages, the programmer does not have to worry about any of this.[1] Facilities of the programming language environment keep track of the identifiers used by the programmer and automatically associate these with corresponding memory cell addresses.

A pointer is a cell that holds the address of another data cell. By looking at the value of the pointer, the computer finds out where in its memory to look for the data value pointed to by the pointer.

To begin to understand the basics of pointers, consider Fig. 5.2. In Fig. 5.2a, we show two variables, `this_ptr` and `that_ptr`, both of which are *pointer* variables (abbreviated `ptr`) and both of which point to a `Num` variable holding the value 4. Thus, the algorithm can access the numeric value 4 by referring to the value pointed to by `this_ptr` or by referring to the value pointed to by `that_ptr`.

Figure 5.2b shows what would happen if we were to then assign the value 9 to the variable pointed to by `that_ptr`: We would also be changing the value to which `this_ptr` points.

Figure 5.2c shows what the result would be if we were to then reassign the pointer variable `that_ptr` to point to the `Num` variable pointed to by `other_ptr`. The algorithm could obtain the value stored in it by referring to either `other_ptr` or `that_ptr`.

The pointer variable itself holds an address. To change the value of a pointer we assign a new address to it. For example, when we changed the value of `that_ptr` to make it point to the same cell that `other_ptr` points to (Fig. 5.2c), we would have used the statement

```
that_ptr <- other_ptr
```

This statement means "we change the value of `that_ptr` so that it points to the memory address to which `other_ptr` points." This is the same thing as saying "go to the pointer variable `other_ptr` and copy the address stored there into `that_ptr`."

---

1. This saves the programmer from worrying about low-level details such as addresses and thus moves programming to a higher level of abstraction. Modern programming languages that provide this kind of benefit are called *high-level languages:* They allow programmers to (among other things) use the abstraction of identifiers without worrying about the actual memory address at which they are stored.

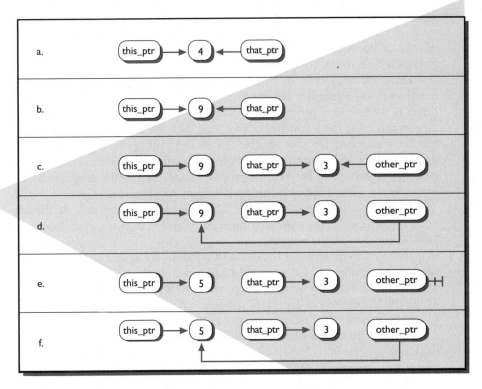

FIGURE 5.2

If we now wanted `other_ptr` to point to the location to which `this_ptr` points, we would use the statement

```
other_ptr <- this_ptr
```

this would give us the state shown in Fig. 5.2d.

Notice that at various times `that_ptr` has not only referred to different *values* but has also referred to different *memory cells*.

If a pointer is not currently pointing to another cell, we say that its value is `NIL`. The value `NIL` is not the same thing as no value. Instead, it is a particular value that means "this pointer does not currently point to anything."

We assign the value `NIL` to pointer variable `other_ptr` via the following instruction:

```
other_ptr <- NIL
```

Figure 5.2e shows how we draw a `NIL` pointer as a blunted line.

So far, we have seen how to refer to the *location* to which a pointer points. We also require some way to refer the *value* to which a pointer points (i.e., the value to be found at the location to which a pointer points). To do so, we dereference the pointer, which means "follow the pointer and see where it points."

Before we can dereference a pointer, it must be pointing at something. Let's first reassign `other_ptr` so that it once again points to the same location to which `this_ptr` points:

```
other_ptr <- this_ptr
```

We can now dereference it via an instruction such as:

```
other_ptr^ <- 5
```

This produces the state shown in Fig. 5.2f. Notice that we did not assign the value 5 to `other_ptr`; we assigned it to `other_ptr^`. We use the *carat* symbol to indicate that we are dereferencing a pointer variable. Observe the crucial difference:

- If we wish to change the location to which a pointer points, we refer to the pointer identifier (e.g., we might use the instruction `other_ptr <- this_ptr`).
- If we wish to change the value stored at that location, we refer to the pointer identifier followed by the dereferencing symbol (e.g., we might use the instruction `other_ptr^ <- 3`).

The important idea here is that pointers do not themselves hold data values. Instead, they hold addresses of other locations where data values may be found (i.e., they allow our efforts to access data values to be "forwarded" to other locations). Pointers are the only kind of variable that can do this.

An algorithm can change the *value* stored in variables that are not pointers but cannot change the *location* to which they refer. *Pointers* allow us to create variables that can refer to *various locations*.

We shall see how to declare and use pointers in the upcoming sections of this chapter when we discuss structures that require the use of pointers.

5.6 Dynamic Data Structures

We have seen how to unite dissimilar data within a single structure by defining record data types and then declaring record variables of those types. Such structures are *heterogeneous* since they collect data of various types within a single record.

This leaves us with the problem of how to group together many occurrences of data of the *same* type. For example, we know how to create records that store various kinds of employee data, but how do we create a structure that will contain the data for all the various employees of a company? Or, more simply, we know how to create a variable to store a number, but how can we create a structure in which we can store a *list* of such numbers?

To store lists of values, we have two choices: *static* or *dynamic* structures. Static structures are, by definition, fixed in size, while dynamic structures grow and shrink as needed. For pedagogical reasons, we shall cover dynamic structures first and will wait until later in the chapter to cover static list structures.

We do not have to specify the size of dynamic structures. They grow and shrink dynamically so that they always fit the list data exactly. Our built-in type `String` is one example of a dynamic structure; a `String` variable can grow and shrink to store a character string of any length.

Dynamic structures are also known as *linked* structures because their elements are linked together by *pointers*. Pointers are useful primarily for allowing us to create and use dynamic structures, and thus, there has been little to say about them until now when we deal with dynamic data. There are three kind of dynamic data structures: *linked lists, trees,* and *graphs.* We shall discuss each in turn.

5.7   Linked Lists

A linked lists is the simplest form of linked structure. It consists of a chain of data locations, called *nodes*. This idea is shown in Fig. 5.3. In this case, each node hold only one piece of data.

Definition: A **linked list** consists of any number of linked nodes such that each node has at most one predecessor and at most one successor. Thus, it is a linear structure.

The nodes of a linked list may hold multiple different data items in any combination we require. The only stipulation is that all nodes in a given list must have the *same* structure (i.e., they must have room for the same data types). Thus, we say that a linked list is also a *homogeneous* structure.

5.7.1   The Structure of a Linked List

In addition to storing a data value, each node must also tell us how to locate the subsequent node in the list. Thus, each node must contain at least two pieces of information: a data field that stores some data value and a pointer field that stores the location of the next node in the list. Thus, we can see that each linked list node is actually a record variable with at least two fields: a `data` field and a `next` location field. The `data` field may be of whatever data type we wish to store in the list. In this example, we have a data field that stores a number. The `next` location field will always be a pointer. Thus, a lower-level drawing that better indicates the actual implementation of the list from Fig. 5.3 is shown in Fig. 5.4. The last pointer in the list is `NIL`, signi-

FIGURE 5.3

FIGURE 5.4

fying that this pointer does not point to anything. A NIL pointer is always used to mark the end of the list.

In Fig. 5.4, each node consists of two fields: a number and a pointer. Thus, each node itself must be a record since it contains dissimilar data types. You might expect that nodes are defined in a type definition such as is shown in the following incomplete definition of a simple list node:

```
List_Node definesa record
    data isoftype Num
    next isoftype Ptr
endrecord
```

The above type definition is wrong because a pointer declaration must include a specification of the type of data to which it can point. This is because a given pointer can only point to one type of data.

Example 5.4 shows a complete definition of a simple list node.

EXAMPLE 5.4

```
List_Node definesa record
    data isoftype Num
    next isoftype Ptr toa List_Node
endrecord //List_Node
```

In Fig. 5.4, we have a linked list consisting of four record variables, each being of type List_Node and each one thus having both a data field and a next field.

As shown, the linked list is not good for anything because we cannot "get at it" (i.e., there is no identifier for the linked list, and without an identifier, we have no way to refer to it). Thus, we need some means of naming the linked list. To name a linked list, we use an atomic pointer variable of the same type that we used for defining the next field as follows:

```
list_head isoftype Ptr toa List_Node
```

With list_head pointing to first node in the list (we'll discuss how to arrange this shortly), our list would look like the drawing shown in Fig. 5.5.

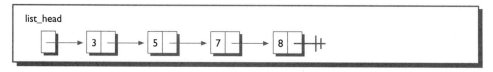

FIGURE 5.5

Observe that `list_head` is *not* a node. It contains no data value, only the address of the first node in the list. Strictly speaking, it is not part of the linked list. Instead, it is a named pointer variable that gives us a way to access the list.

This is the second time we have declared a pointer to point to a `List_Node`. We first used one in defining the `next` field within each `List_Node`, and now we declare one as a named variable that points to the beginning of the list. We use a pointer to a `List_Node` in these two situations for one reason: Both the named `list_head` variable and the `next` field within each unnamed node must be able to point to record variables of type `List_Node`.

5.7.2 Using Pointers to Access Nodes

To illustrate how to use pointers, we shall begin by using the linked list shown in Fig. 5.6 as an example. It implies the declarations:

```
List_Node definesa record
    data isoftype Num
    next isoftype Ptr toa List_Node
endrecord //List_Node

list_head isoftype Ptr toa List_Node
current isoftype Ptr toa List_Node
```

Ignore how we created the list and how we arranged to have `list_head` point to the list of four nodes. (We'll see how to do these things soon.) For now, observe that `list_head` points to the first node in the list, while `current` is pointing to a question mark. The question mark implies that the value of `current` is *undefined* (i.e., we have declared it as a variable but have not assigned any value to it). Pointers, like any other variable, should always have some value assigned to them. Thus, if `current` is not pointing to anything, we should assign it the value `NIL`, via

```
current <- NIL
```

We would pictorially represent the result of this as shown in Fig. 5.7.

We might also assign `current` to point to the first node in the list via the instruction

```
current <- list_head
```

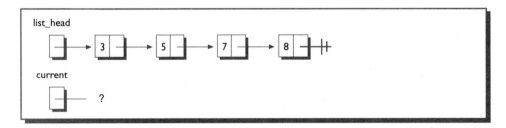

FIGURE 5.6

FIGURE 5.7

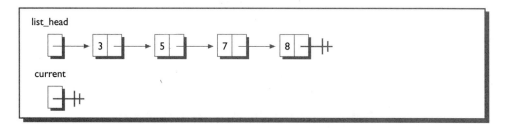

The variable list_head points to the first node in the list because it knows where that first node is (i.e., list_head contains the address of that node). By assigning the *value* of list_head to current, we obtain the address from list_head and store a copy of that address in current. Thus list_head and current both hold the same value: not a data value per se, but an *address* (i.e., they both now know where the first node is to be found and thus we say that each one points to the first node in the list). We show the result in Fig. 5.8.

To access the contents of the nodes themselves, we must follow a pointer that points to them. To follow a pointer, we use the carat symbol (^), which means "follow the pointer and go where it leads." Thus, to retrieve the value stored in the data field of the first node and store it in Num variable some_num_var, we would write

```
some_num_var <- list_head^.data
```

This statement is read as "follow list_head to wherever it points; once there, inspect the value stored in the data field and copy that value into some_num_var."

We've seen how to dereference a pointer to retrieve a value from a node. Now, let's look at how we can dereference a pointer to store a value in a node.

EXAMPLE 5.5   To store the value 4 in the data field of the first node of Fig. 5.8, we would write

```
list_head^.data <- 4
```

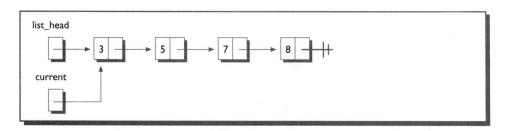

FIGURE 5.8

FIGURE 5.9

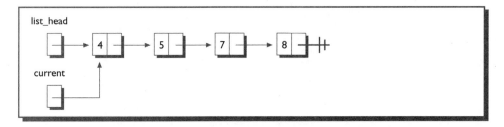

This statement is read as "follow `list_head` to wherever it points; once there, access the `data` field and store 4 in it." As a result of this instruction, the list would look like the drawing in Fig. 5.9. Note that, because `list_head` and `current` each point to the same node, the same effect could have been achieved via the following instruction:

```
current^.data <- 4
```

If we were to now use the instruction

```
some_num_var <- current^.data
```

it would result in 4 being assigned to `some_num_var`. Because the two named pointers both point to the first node, we could accomplish the exact same thing with

```
some_num_var <- list_head^.data
```

To access the second node in the list, we can simply chain together a list of references that point to it. For example, we could assign to `some_num_var` the value stored in the second node (i.e., 5) with the instruction

```
some_num_var <- list_head^.next^.data
```

which means "begin with the `list_head` pointer and follow it to wherever it points; once there, access the `next` field; then, follow that pointer to wherever it goes; once there, access the `data` field, and copy whatever value you find there into `some_num_var`."

 We can chain together references to pointers and data fields in whatever fashion is necessary to get to where we want to go, regardless of the length of the chain of reference. The key trick is to grasp what is meant by the two symbols ^ . (people often say "up dot" or "hat dot" to refer to the carat followed by the period). Up dot means, quite simply, "follow the pointer to the node to which it points and then look in the field..." .

The up and the dot each mean something quite specific:

- The up means dereference the pointer, which is programmer jargon for "follow the pointer and see where it goes."

■ The dot means look inside the field that is specified next.

Note that the dot has the same meaning regardless of whether we're using pointers or not (e.g., `this_employee.pay_rate` where `this_employee` is a record variable of type `Employee_Record_Type`, which has `pay_rate` is one of its fields).

Thus, to assign to `some_num_var` the `data` value of the third node (in this case, 7), we could write

```
some_num_var <- list_head^.next^.next^.data
```

This instruction means, "follow `list_head` to wherever it goes and once there, look in the `next` field; follow that pointer to wherever it points; once there, look in the `next` field that you find there; follow that pointer to whatever node it references and then look in the `data` field. Take the data value you find there and copy it into `some_num_var`."

As you can see, chaining together pointer references can become confusing and tedious. Fortunately, there is a better way. We can achieve the same effect by changing the location to which a pointer refers. Thus, to easily access the second node in the list, we would first use the instruction

```
current <- current^.next
```

This means that we assign to `current` whatever value is stored in `current^.next`. Since `current` points to the first node in the list, we know that `current^.next` points to the second node in the list. Thus, assigning current^.next to current results in `current` pointing wherever `current^.next` points (i.e., to the second node). After making this assignment, the list would look like the drawing of Fig. 5.10. Now both current and `list_head^.next` have the same value: Both of them have a copy of the address of the second node in the list.

Similarly, we can move `current` to point to the third node in the list by using exactly the same instruction again. Because `current` now points to the second node, we know that `current^.next` points to the third node. Thus, applying the instruction

```
current <- current^.next
```

to the list shown in Fig. 5.10 produces the state of the list shown in Fig. 5.11.

This mode of reference (moving a pointer) allows us to walk through a linked list step by step. For example, if we wished to sum the values stored in a linked list such as

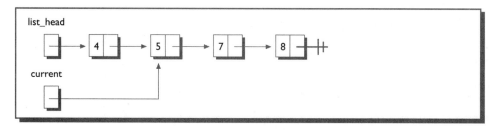

FIGURE 5.10

FIGURE 5.11

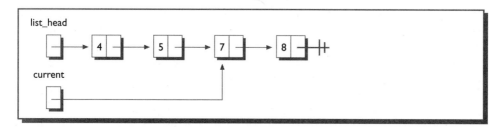

the one above, we might do so with a repetitive module that begins with `current` pointing to the first node in the list and then on each of its several repetitions

- Adds `current^.data` to a variable that is used to store the sum.
- Advances `current` to `current^.next`.

It repeats the above two steps until it reached a state where the value of `current` is NIL.

When manipulating pointers in a linked list, note that it is necessary to be careful about the implications of which pointer we adjust. Observe that, in our examples, we declare and manipulate temporary pointers (such as `current` or `temp`). We do so because of the danger in moving `list_head` itself. We want `list_head` to *always* point to the first node in the list and must be careful that we do not move it away accidentally. If we executed

```
list_head <- list_head^.next
```

the pointer `list_head` would now point to the second node, while `current` would still point to the third node, as shown in Fig. 5.12. By moving `list_head` down the list we have lost our access to the first node. Even though the first node points to the second node, *nothing points to the first node*. This means that we have effectively lost the first node in the list. (We will discuss what happens to lost nodes shortly.) Thus, be sure to move `list_head` (or whatever you call your primary list-access pointer) only when you intend to change what you mean by "head of the list."

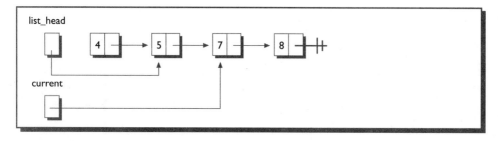

FIGURE 5.12

5.7.3   Using Pointers to Add Nodes

A big advantage of linked lists lies in the fact that we do not have to know in advance how many elements there will be in a linked list. This is because we can dynamically create more elements and add them as we go along. We can add a node to our list by creating a new one and inserting it into the list at the end, at the beginning, or at any point in between.

For example, consider the linked list shown in Fig. 5.13a. To create a new node, store the value 9 in it, and add that node to the end of the list, we would use the instructions

```
temp <- new(List_Node)
temp^.data <- 9
temp^.next <- NIL
current^.next <- temp
```

Let's consider what each of these four instructions does.

- The first instruction,

```
temp <- new(List_Node)
```

creates a new variable of type `List_Node` and stores its location in `temp`. After this instruction executes, we have a new node, and the pointer `temp` points to it. Thus, the situation looks like that shown in Fig. 5.13b.

The question marks indicate that the values of both of the new node's fields (`data` and `next`) are undefined.
- The second instruction,

```
temp^.data <- 9
```

assigns the value 9 to the `data` field of the node that is pointed to by `temp`, resulting in the state shown in Fig. 5.13c.
- The third instruction,

```
temp^.next <- NIL
```

sets the value of the new node's next pointer to `NIL`, giving us the state shown in Fig. 5.13d. Now, the new node has been created, and the values of its two fields have been initialized.
- What remains is to connect the new node to the rest of the list. This is accomplished by the fourth instruction,

```
current^.next <- temp
```

The value of `current^.next` had been `NIL` but is assigned to point to *whatever* is pointed to by `temp`, resulting in the state shown in Fig. 5.13e. This drawing is accurate, but it shows the new last node as visually separated from the rest of the list. To show the same list more visually connected, we redraw it as shown in Fig. 5.13f. Note that Fig. 5.13e and f shows different drawings of the same exact list. Pause and examine the two figures until this becomes apparent to you.

FIGURE 5.13

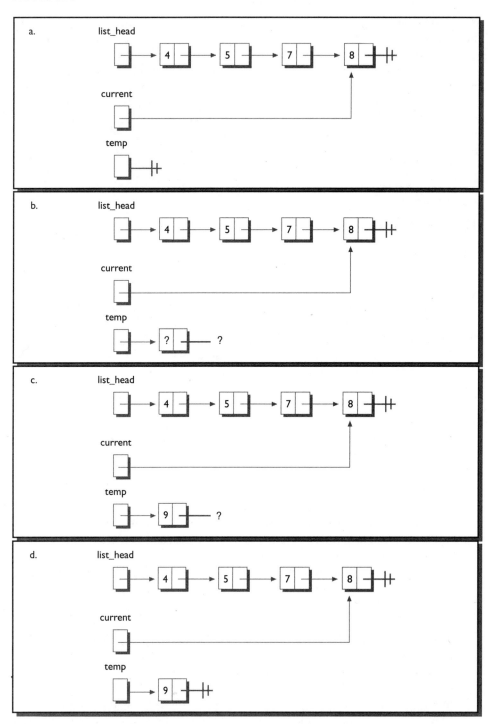

FIGURE 5.13 *(continued)*

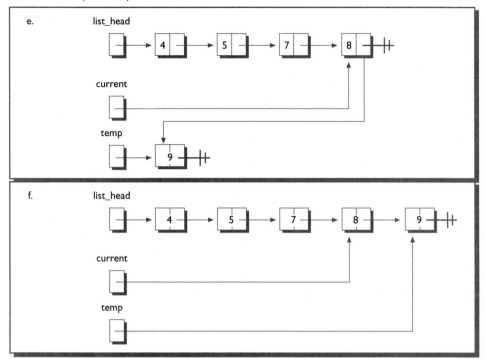

5.7.4   Using Pointers to Delete Nodes

We can also *delete* nodes from a linked list as needed. Doing so means that no space is wasted by variables that are no longer required.

> To delete a node, we simply arrange that there is no pointer pointing to it.

In some programming languages, an automatic process gathers such nodes and returns their space to available memory. This is known as *garbage collection*. In other languages, explicit actions must be taken to free the space used by such nodes. For simplicity, we'll adopt the former convention.

EXAMPLE 5.6   Imagine that we want to obtain the value from the first node in the list shown in Fig. 5.14 and then delete the first node from the list. We could do this with the following instructions:

```
some_num_var isoftype Num
some_num_var <- list_head^.data
list_head <- list_head^.next
```

FIGURE 5.14

- The first instruction declares the variable `some_num_var`.
- The second instruction obtains the data value from the first node and stores it in `some_num_var`.
- The third instruction adjusts the `list_head` pointer by replacing its contents (i.e., the address of the first node) with whatever address is stored in the first node's `next` pointer (i.e., the address of the second node).

When applied to the linked list shown in Fig. 5.14, these instructions produce the list shown in Fig. 5.15.

5.7.5   Navigating Through a Linked List

We can use the logic we have just seen to selectively add nodes to an existing linked list and to selectively delete certain nodes that are no longer required by a list. To do these things, however, we must be able to find the specific locations at which the list changes are to be made. Thus, we shall first discuss how to *traverse* and *search* an existing linked list. Then we will explore how to use these capabilities to make linked lists grow and shrink as needed.

5.7.6   Traversing a Linked List

Definition: Traversing a linked list means stepping through the list, node by node, to access each node, one by one, in turn.

A linked list traversal algorithm starts with a pointer pointing to the beginning of the list, allowing us to print or process the data in the first node. It then moves to each successive node in turn. The traversal ends after we arrive at the last node in the list.

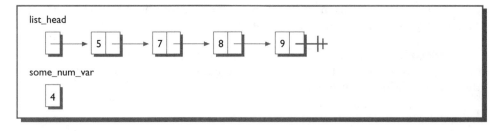

FIGURE 5.15

We can recognize the last node of any linked list because it is the only node in the list whose `next` pointer has the value `NIL`.

Any traversal algorithm is inherently repetitive (i.e., it must execute an appropriate series of instructions some number of times). As with all repetitive algorithms, this may be accomplished with a recursive routine.

5.7.7   A Recursive Linked List Traversal

The purpose of this recursive linked list traversal is to start at the beginning of the list and continuously print and move until we encounter the list's end. Once we reach the end, we simply stop (i.e., there are no terminating steps). Therefore, we use the second recursive form:

```
if NOT (terminating condition) then
    move one step closer to the terminating condition
    call a "clone" of the recursive module
endif
```

To construct the recursive solution, we need only "plug in" the particulars of our task to this general form. What is our terminating condition? We know that we do not want to move the pointer that points to the head of the list for fear of losing our access to the beginning of the list. Therefore, we need a temporary pointer variable. We'll call it `current_ptr`. Our traversal should terminate when `current_ptr = NIL`, which will indicate that we're at the end of the list. Thus, our terminating condition is

```
(current_ptr = NIL)
```

and we can state our condition for *continuing* the recursion as

```
if NOT (current_ptr = NIL) then
```

or, equivalently,

```
if (current_ptr <> NIL) then
```

Taking one step closer to the terminating condition means "printing and moving the pointer." We can write these steps as

```
print (current_ptr^.data)
current_ptr <- current_ptr^.next
```

The former instruction carries out the required action (printing), while the latter instruction moves us one step closer: It adjusts `current_ptr` to be one position further down the list, perhaps pointing to the next node or perhaps to `NIL`. In either case, with `current_ptr` advanced, we can now call a clone of the recursive module via

```
Traverse_Recurse(current_ptr)
```

That's all there is to it. The following implementation works. However, as we shall soon see, it contains a needless step.

```
procedure Traverse_Recursively (current_ptr isoftype in Ptr
                                    toa List_Node)
// Purpose: traverses a linked list consisting of List_Nodes,
// printing out the value stored in each node in sequence.
```

```
    if (current_ptr <> NIL) then
       print(current_ptr^.data)
       current_ptr <- current_ptr^.next
       Traverse_Recursively(current_ptr)
    endif

endprocedure //Traverse_Recursively
```

There is nothing wrong with this procedure. However, we can streamline its logic. Notice that the second instruction after the `if` updates the procedure's copy of `current_ptr` immediately before passing that new value as a parameter in the next line:

```
current_ptr <- current_ptr^.next
Traverse_Recursively(current_ptr)
```

Example 5.7 shows a cleaner, more streamlined way of accomplishing the same thing.

EXAMPLE 5.7   The task is to traverse the list and print out the values stored in it, which does not involve changing the list in any way. Presumably, when this procedure is called, it is passed the value of `list_head`. Since the task gives us no reason to change the value of `list_head`, we appropriately make `current_ptr` an *input* parameter. What we need is some way to pass the value of `current_ptr^.next` to the next call of the procedure. We can accomplish this directly and simply by replacing the last two instructions of our first attempt with the single instruction

```
Traverse_Recursively(current_ptr^.next)
```

Thus, the procedure is properly written as

```
procedure Traverse_Recursively (current_ptr isoftype inPtr
                                        toa List_Node)
// Purpose: traverses a linked list consisting of List_Nodes,
// printing out the value stored in each node in sequence.

   if (current_ptr <> NIL) then
      print(current_ptr^.data)
      Traverse_Recursively(current_ptr^.next)
   endif

endprocedure //Traverse_Recursively
```

We assume that our algorithm begins at the head of the list. However, this is determined by the calling algorithm. The traversal will begin at whatever location is dictated by the parameter that is initially passed in. Thus, if the calling algorithm sends us a pointer that points to the middle node of the list, we shall traverse only the last half of the list.

When the recursive call is made, `current_ptr^.next` is passed as a parameter. The next clone of the procedure receives `current_ptr^.next` as an in parameter and "knows it" via its parameter identifier `current_ptr`. Thus, when the second call reads the value of `current_ptr`, it is reading the pointer value that was known to the previous call as `current_ptr^.next`.

For each call, if current_ptr is not NIL, we print the data field of the node to which current_ptr points. We then pass current_ptr^.next when we make the recursive call. In effect, what we are doing is calling many clones of the procedure, and each one is passed what is logically a "head" pointer to a smaller list. The reason we call it a "head" pointer is that it does not actually point to the first node of the entire list but rather points to the *first node in the list of nodes that have not yet been visited*. Our algorithm has no way of knowing if anything is to the left of current_ptr. Hence, each clone "thinks" that it is getting a full linked list.

The process is illustrated in Fig. 5.16. In the diagram, we use the thin dotted line to show the source of current_ptr's value (i.e., as the various pointer variables are

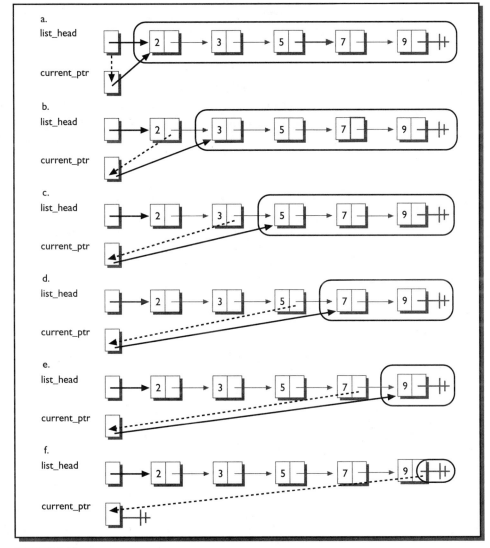

FIGURE 5.16

passed to `current_ptr` as in parameters). This means `current_ptr` obtains its value from those pointer variables that reside in the list nodes, but it cannot modify them.

- The thin arrows show the data passed to `current_ptr` as in parameters.
- Figure 5.16a shows the original list as passed in the first call. The value 2 is printed.
- Figure 5.16b through e shows the list as the traversal progresses: values 3, 5, 7, and 9 are printed.
- At each point in the traversal, `current_ptr` can be thought of as a head pointer to the first node in the list of nodes that have not yet been visited. The bubbles enclose the nodes in `current_ptr`'s list at each recursive call.
- In Fig. 5.16f `current_ptr` is NIL, which means the original list has been exhausted and the terminating condition has been reached.

5.7.8   A Recursive Linked List Search

Searching a linked list to find a particular data value is similar to traversing the list. In fact, we can think of searching a list as traversing a list until either (1) we find what we are looking for, or (2) we exhaust the list without finding it.

We can create a search algorithm by modifying the logic we used in the traversal algorithm in three ways:

- We must add a parameter by which the searching routine receives the *target value* for which it is searching.
- We must change the terminating condition to reflect the two circumstances in which we want the search traversal to halt.
- We must change the actions we take so that the procedure's results indicate whether the search has succeeded or failed.

The following example shows one method for searching a linked list.

EXAMPLE 5.8   Because there *are* actions to take after the terminating condition has been reached, the first of our two formats for recursion is called for:

```
procedure Search_Recurse(current isoftype in Ptr toa
                         List_Node, target isoftype in Num)
// Purpose: searches a list of List_Nodes for the target
// value. Prints out a textual message indicating whether
// the target value is in the list.

   if ((current = NIL) OR (current^.data = target)) then
      if (current^.data = NIL) then
         print ("The value ", target, " is not in the list.")
      else
         print ("The value ", target, " is in the list.")
      endif
   else
```

```
        Search_Recurse(current^.next, target)
    endif

endprocedure //Search_Recurse
```

5.7.9   Short Circuit Evaluation

Notice that in Example 5.8, repetition halts under either of two terminating conditions:

```
(current = NIL) OR (current^.data = target)
```

The particulars of these conditions present a potential difficulty. Observe that if the first conditional expression resolves to TRUE, the second conditional expression is nonsense. That is to say, if current is NIL, current^.data does not exist. If we follow the normal pattern of evaluating complex conditionals, we would first evaluate each of the two individual conditionals and then OR their boolean results as follows:

```
(<boolean value> OR <boolean value>)
```

Given the conditional expressions of our search procedure, if the first condition resolved to TRUE, attempts to evaluate the second condition would cause an error: We would be attempting to obtain the value from a data field that does not exist.
   Different languages handle this in different ways:

- Some languages require the use of different logic in such situations. We'd have to write our logic so that we first test one condition and then test the second condition only if the result of the first condition indicated that we should. For example, here is the logic for a recursive traversal that does not require short-circuit evaluation:

```
if (current = NIL) then
   print ("The value ", target, " is not in the list.")
elseif (current^.data = target) then
   print ("The value ", target, " is in the list.")
else
   Search_Recurse(current^.next, target)
endif
```

- Other languages feature what is called "short-circuit evaluation," which allows us to do what we have done in Example 5.8. Short circuit evaluation recognizes that an OR operator requires that only one of the two conditional expression be TRUE in order for the entire conditional to be TRUE. Therefore, if it saw that (current = NIL) was TRUE, it would know that the entire conditional was TRUE and would stop evaluation without attempting to evaluate the second conditional expression. Because it sometimes eases our job of constructing proper logic, our language allows short-circuit evaluation.

Notice that short-circuit evaluation doesn't change the fact that it is *always* an error to dereference a NIL pointer. Short-circuit evaluation makes our logic easier by preventing the execution of such illegal instructions provided that we construct our conditionals properly.

5.7.10 Building a Linked List

So far, we have seen how to traverse an existing linked list in its entirety and how to search an existing list for a specified value. We have not as yet seen how to construct a linked list. To clearly understand how we go about constructing a list, it is necessary to have the following insights:

- We must consider what attributes we wish that list to have. Do we want to build a list such that each new node is appended to the end of whatever list might already be there? Or do we want to construct a list such that the values stored in the list are in some kind of sorted order (e.g., in ascending order or in descending order)?
- Good abstraction means that we want a single module that will allow us to add a new node to an existing linked list such that it will do its job correctly regardless of how many nodes are already in the list.
- Inserting the first item into an "empty list" is simply a special case of the generic task of adding to a list.
- Inserting an item at the end of a list is another special case of the generic task of adding to a list.
- Inserting an item somewhere in the middle of a list is the general case of adding to a list.

Thus, we require a single module that will deal with each of the aforementioned three cases such that the list is always maintained in whatever order we require. Regardless of the attributes we want the list to have, we must ensure that each of those three cases (at the beginning, somewhere in the middle, and at the end) is successfully handled.

As an example, suppose we are to construct a list that stores a series of numbers in sorted ascending order. Before rushing to code any attempted solution, let's first reason about what we know:

- By adding a node to the list, we will be changing the state of the list; therefore, we know that the module must be a procedure, not a function.
- We also know that we must search the list to locate the appropriate position in the list before we insert the new node into it. Thus, we will start at the beginning of the list and traverse the list until we've found the correct position for insertion. After locating that position, we must insert the new node. Thus, we can tell that we require a recursive procedure of the first of the two forms of recursive modules as follows:

```
if (<terminating condition>) then
    <finish up, i.e., insert the new number>
else
    <take one step closer, i.e., move one step down the list>
endif
```

- To add a new value to the list, the procedure must know what that new value is and therefore requires an in parameter that communicates that new value.
- To add a new value to the list, the procedure must be able to (1) determine if the correct location has been found, and if it has (2) to modify pointers as neces-

sary to connect the new node into the list. Therefore, the procedure requires an in/out parameter that communicates a pointer to the current location.

From this, we know that our first attempt at a solution will look something like this:

```
procedure Insert_In_Ascending_Order (current isoftype in/out Ptr
                        toa List_Node, new_value isoftype in Num)
// Purpose: inserts a node containing new_value into a linked
// list of List_Nodes such that the list is maintained in
// sorted ascending order.

    if (<we're at the correct location in the list>) then
        <insert node containing new_value at current location>
    else
        Insert_In_Ascending_Order(current^.next, new_value)
    endif

endprocedure //Insert_In_Ascending_Order
```

How can we articulate the terminating condition? To answer this, we must enumerate the ways in which we might know that we have arrived at the correct location. To do so, consider each of the three cases we enumerated: first position in the list, last position in the list, and some position in the middle of the list.

1. *General case.* The new node belongs somewhere in the middle of an existing list. In general, we shall traverse down the list from beginning to end until we find that we've detected a location where the value of the *next* node is greater than the new value we wish to add. Observe that we must stop traversing the list when the next node's value is greater than the new value because if we traverse until the current node's value is greater, we've gone too far. We are able to insert a new node *after* the current node, via the next pointer, but we have no way to insert a new node *before* the current node.

   To illustrate this, consider the list shown in Fig. 5.17. It shows that the in/out parameter current has been passed the value of the next field of the third node. Because current is an in/out parameter, it can both obtain and change the value of that next pointer. (We use the thin double-pointed arrow to indicate that current can both read and write to this next pointer.) At the moment current is effectively a pseudonym or alias for that specific pointer: If we retrieve the value of current, we obtain the address of the node that stores 7.

   a. If the new value we wish to add to the list is 6, we are in the correct location, and it's time to insert a new node immediately after our location.

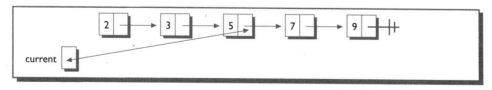

FIGURE 5.17

b. If the new value we wish to insert is 8, we have not yet arrived at the correct location for inserting it. We need to move one more position to the right to arrive at the correct position.

c. If the new value we wish to add is 4, we've gone too far. (While we do have a next pointer, our definition of a List_Node does not include a previous pointer.)

In the general case, then, we know that we've reached a terminating condition if our current parameter has been passed next pointer that points to a node that contains a value greater than the one we wish to add, that is, if (current^.data > new_value).

2. *Special case*. The new node belongs in the first position in the list. There are two circumstances in which our new value belongs in the first position in the list:

a. If there are no nodes in the list (i.e., if it is an empty list). We can detect this situation quite easily: If the original list head pointer passed in by the calling algorithm is NIL, we know that there are no nodes in the list, and therefore the new one *must* be in the first position. Thus, if during the very first call (current = NIL), we have reached a terminating condition.

b. If there are nodes in the list, and if the value of the very first node is greater than the our new value (e.g., if the first node has a value of 2 and our new value is 1), the new value belongs in the first position. Thus, if during the very first call (current^.data > new_value), we have reached a terminating condition.

3. *Special case*. The new node belongs in the last position in the list. Again, there are two circumstances in which the new value belongs last in the list:

a. If there are no nodes in the list (i.e., it is an empty list). In this case, the new node will simultaneously be both the first and the last node in the list. We've already seen how to detect this.

b. If we've exhausted the list without finding any value greater than our new value. In this case, our new value is the largest and thus belongs at the end. We can detect this if, after traversing the list, we reach a state where (current = NIL).

After considering each of our cases, we've encountered only two terminating conditions: (current = NIL) and (current^.data > new_value). Given this, we have what we need to construct our first attempt at a solution:

```
procedure Insert_In_Ascending_Order (current isoftype in/out ptr
                 toa List_Node, new_value isoftype in Num )
// Purpose: inserts a node containing new_value into a linked
// list of List_Nodes such that the list is maintained in
// sorted ascending order.

    if (current = NIL) OR (current^.data > new_value) then
       Insert_New_Value(current, new_value)
    else
       Insert_In_Ascending_Order (current^.next, new_value)
    endif

endprocedure //Insert_In_Order
```

This procedure determines when and where to perform the insertion of the new value into the list, but it defers the specifics of the actual insertion task to another procedure, Insert_New_Value. Let's see what that procedure might look like.

EXAMPLE 5.9 Upon reaching a terminating condition, we call procedure `Insert_New_Value` and pass it both `current` and `new_value`.

```
Insert_New_Value(current isoftype in/out Ptr toa List_Node,
                 new_num isoftype in Num)
// Purpose: inserts new_num into a linked list of List_Nodes
// such that it will be pointed to by current.

    temp isoftype Ptr toa List_Node
    temp <- new(List_Node)
    temp^.data <- new_num
    temp^.next <- current
    current <- temp

endprocedure //Insert_New_Value
```

As with all attempted solutions, it is necessary to trace the execution of our algorithm to ensure that it behaves as intended. Take paper and pencil and create various ascending lists and walk through the execution to verify that (1) it works and (2) you understand what it is doing instruction by instruction.

5.7.11   Deleting Values from a Linked List

In many respects, the process of deleting a specified value from a linked list is similar to the process for inserting a value into a linked list. In particular, we must

- Be mindful of the list's attributes (Is it sorted? If so, in what order?).
- Successfully traverse the list until we are at the correct location to delete the targeted value or have determined that the targeted value is not in the list.
- Be sure that we stop *before* the node containing the targeted value.

While the logic is similar to that used in inserting a new node, there are a few key differences. Again, we must consider both the general case and special cases that can arise at the beginning and end of a list.

- *General case.* The targeted node resides somewhere in the middle of an existing list. In general, we shall traverse down the list from beginning to end until we find that we've detected a terminating condition. What might the terminating conditions be? (1) If `current` points to a node containing the target value, we halt repetition and act to delete that node. (2) If `current` points to a node that stores a value greater than the target, we know that the target is not in the list and we can halt repetition and report failure. (3) If `current` is `NIL`, we know that we've exhausted the list without finding the target value and can halt repetition and report failure. Thus, we have three possible terminating conditions in the general case: (`current = NIL`), (`current^.data > target`), and (`current^.data = target`).
- *Special case.* The target is in the first position in the list. This is easily detected: If, in the original call, the list head pointer that is passed to `current` points to a node containing `target`, our search is done. We need only be sure that we adjust the original list head node to point to the second node in the list or to `NIL`, depending on whether or not the target resides in the list's only node.

- *Special case.* The target is in the last position in the list. This is detected by the same means as in the general case. We need only be sure that, after deleting the final node, the node previous to it has its `next` pointer set to NIL.

Given the above, we can now attempt a solution algorithm for deleting nodes from a sorted linked list.

EXAMPLE 5.10 Let's consider a procedure that will delete nodes from a sorted linked list.

```
procedure Delete_From_Ascending_List (current isoftype in/out
                   Ptr toa List_Node, target isoftype in Num)
// Purpose: determine if the target value is in a list of
// List_Nodes; if so, delete it; if not, print an appropriate
// message indicating failure.

   if (current = NIL) OR (current^.data >= target) then
      if (current = NIL) OR (current^.data > target) then
         print ("Targeted value not found; deletion failed.")
      else
         current <- current^.next  // delete the next node
      endif
   else
      Delete_From_Ascending_List (current^.next, target)
   endif

endprocedure // Delete_From_Ascending_List
```

Again, it is important to trace the execution of the algorithm to ensure that it behaves as advertised. Take paper and pencil and create various ascending lists and walk through the execution to verify that (1) it works and (2) you understand what it is doing, instruction by instruction.

5.7.12 Summary of Linked List Features

Linked lists provide a way to store a *homogeneous* collection of data such that many items of the same type can be associated within the same list structure. Each item in a linked list is a *node*. Each node consists of data and a pointer. The data may be simple (such as a number), or it may be a complex structure (such as a record consisting of numerous data fields). The pointer within each node allows the nodes to be connected to one another into a single list in much the same way that railroad cars are coupled together to constitute a train. Like the cars of a railroad train, nodes may be added, deleted, rearranged, and have their contents changed at will.

The nodes of a linked list are *dynamic variables* that an algorithm may create and deallocate at any time. Thus, a linked list can always be of exactly the right size for any given list of data. Because the dynamic variables that constitute a linked list have no identifiers, they can be accessed only by navigating to them from some *named* pointer variable. At least one named pointer variable must exist and point to the linked list for the list to exist and be accessible. By following a named pointer to the linked list, the nodes of the linked list may be accessed as appropriate to the task at hand.

5.8 The Scope of Linked Data

In Chapter 3, when we gave our rule for the scope of data, we said, "The scope of named data is limited to the module in which it is declared." Notice that we said the "scope of *named* data is limited..." . That is exactly what we meant: Any named variables are limited in scope. Observe, however, that the nodes in a linked list do *not* have names. The named pointer variables (e.g., list_head and current, which are needed to access the nodes) have names, but they are simply pointer variables, not nodes. The nodes themselves have no names. Nodes in a linked structure have the same scope as *types* and *constants*. They are not limited in scope.

5.8.1   Static vs. Dynamic Variables

To understand this, it is helpful to understand something about how and where computers store data. In particular, you should understand the difference between static and dynamic allocations of memory. Earlier, we suggested using a stack to help trace the execution of recursive calls. As each call was made, a frame for that call was pushed on top of the stack, and when each call was completed, its frame was popped off the stack. Actually, this mechanism is more than just a good way to trace execution; it is how most computers operate.

Imagine the computer's memory to be a large rectangular area consisting of many individual cells such that each cell has its own address. As a program begins to execute, a frame is pushed onto the stack. All the *named* variables and constants that are declared within the main algorithm are actually stored within this frame. The more named variables and constants that are declared, the larger this frame will be since it must be sized to accommodate all the named data that have been declared.

The space for the stack uses part of memory. Thus, as more and more memory space is used for the stack, less and less memory is free and available for use.

To understand the difference between static and dynamic variables, let's consider the following example.

EXAMPLE 5.11   Suppose the main algorithm included the declaration of the two variables, list_head and some_num_var. As execution began, memory looked like Fig. 5.18a. If list_head was then initialized to NIL and some_num_var was initialized to 4, memory would look like that shown in Fig. 5.18b.

Now, imagine that within the algorithm is a call to a procedure that inserts a new node into the list. It might look like the one we developed in Example 5.9:

```
procedure Insert_New_Value (current isoftype in/out Ptr toa
                            List_Node, new_num isoftype in num)
// Purpose: inserts new_num into a linked list of List_Nodes
// such that it will be pointed to by current.

    temp isoftype Ptr toa List_Node
    temp <- new(List_Node)
    temp^.data <- new_num
```

```
                    temp^.next <- current
                    current <- temp

               endprocedure //Insert_New_Value
```

For simplicity, let's say that this algorithm has been called directly by the main algorithm via the call shown below:

```
               Insert_New_Value(list_head, some_num_var)
```

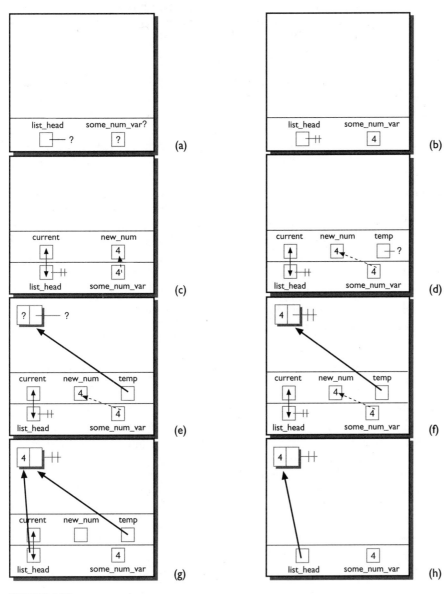

FIGURE 5.18

Thus, it is being called by the main algorithm to insert a value to be pointed to by list_head. We shall now consider exactly what occurs as this call takes place.

As the module is called, its frame is pushed onto the top of the stack, and all its *named* data reside within that frame. Thus, after the call, but before the procedure's code has been executed, the stack would look like Fig. 5.18c.

- We show a thin double-pointed arrow connecting list_head and current to indicate their relationship: current is an in/out parameter and thus may both read and write to the variable passed to it as a parameter, list_head.
- We show a thin dotted arrow connecting some_num_var and new_num to indicate their relationship: new_num is an in parameter and thus receives a copy of the value passed as a parameter from some_num_var, but it may not change the original (i.e., communication is a one-way street with information flowing from some_num_var to new_num but not the other way).

As Insert_New_Value executes, its five instructions cause the following actions to occur:

- The first instruction declares the local pointer variable temp. This instruction declares temp as a local variable; thus temp does not have any initial value passed to it via the parameter. Its value is not defined until an instruction within the procedure assigns a value to it. Thus, we use a question mark to show that its value is undefined, as shown in Fig. 5.18d.
- The second instruction causes the allocation of a new node such that temp points to it, as shown in Fig. 5.18e. Note that, while the new node is allocated, the values of its data and next fields are momentarily undefined.
- The third instruction causes the value stored in some_num_var to be copied into the new node's data field, and the fourth instruction causes the value stored in list_head to be copied into the next field of the new node. This produces the state shown in Fig. 5.18f.
- The fifth instruction causes the value of temp (i.e., the location of the new node) to be written to list_head via the in/out parameter current. The result is shown in Fig. 5.18g.
- Finally, after Insert_New_Value has completed, its frame pops off the stack and all its local variables and parameters vanish. After this happens, memory looks like the drawing of Fig. 5.18h. Although procedure Insert_New_Value has vanished from the stack, observe that it has left behind a different data state than it found: There is now a new node in memory and list_head points to it.

Observe that, because the new node is not a *named* variable (but rather is dynamically allocated and thus is accessible only via following a pointer), it does not reside in a stack frame but rather in the memory space above the stack. This part of memory, the area that is above the stack, is called the *heap*.

All *dynamically allocated variables* do not reside in the stack. Instead, they reside in another area of memory, in the heap.

While real-world computer implementations vary, you may think of the heap as being at the other end of memory from the *stack* (i.e., the stack begins at the bottom and builds upward, while the heap begins at the top of memory and expands downward).

As each procedure or function is called, it gets its own *stack frame,* which is *pushed* onto the stack and thus expands the stack upward. As each subprogram completes, its frame is *popped* off the stack, shrinking the stack and freeing the memory that the stack frame had occupied.

As each piece of dynamic memory is allocated, it partially fills the heap. As each piece of dynamic memory is deallocated, it frees up space in the heap.

If the portion of memory used by the stack and the portion of memory allocated to nodes in the heap grow, in some combination, to the point where the stack and the heap collide with one other, the computer has run out of memory. ▪

This is the kind of thing that really happens, more or less, when a program is run on a real computer. It explains why it is that named variables declared within procedures or functions do not live for the life of the program. They physically exist within the stack frame for the module in which they are declared, and when that module completes and its frame is popped off the stack, the physical locations for the named variables get "blown away." The only reason that the named identifiers declared within the main algorithm "live" throughout execution is because the stack frame for the main algorithm is created when the algorithm starts and does not get popped off the stack until the entire algorithm completes.

As you create algorithms and trace their execution, an awareness of these facts allows you to do just what a computer does: You can follow the creation and deallocation of variables by making sketches of memory, placing named (or static) variables in the appropriate stack frame, placing dynamic variables in the heap, and updating values in the appropriate locations. Such sketches are invaluable tools that help students (and programmers) understand what their algorithms *really* do.

5.8.2 A Loophole in Parameter Protection for Linked Data

Recall that the purpose of parameters is to provide a well-defined interface between the modules of an algorithm. In the header line of a module, the formal parameter list provides a specification of the parameters needed by the module, including a specification of the kind of parameter: in, out, or in/out. Thus, an algorithm that passes one of its variables to a module as an *input* parameter does so with the understanding that it is giving that module a *copy* of its variable's value. The intent is that there is no danger of the module changing the value of the calling algorithm's variable. For a

FIGURE 5.19 The linked list parameter loophole

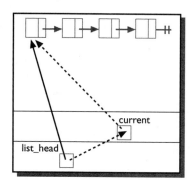

module to change such a variable, it would have to be sent to it as an out or in/out parameter.

When passing a pointer to any linked data structure such as a linked list, there is a loophole in the protection afforded to in parameters: While the module cannot modify the contents of any pointer variable sent to it via an in parameter, the module can modify the data to which that pointer points.

EXAMPLE 5.12 Consider the linked list represented in Fig. 5.19. This shows the state of affairs after the main algorithm has called a module and has passed it list_head as the in parameter current.

Again, we use a thin dotted-line arrow to show the parameter information flow: the data stored in list_head flow to current, but not the other way.

Because list_head was passed as an in parameter, we can indeed rest assured that current cannot modify the contents of the pointer variable list_head. However, this protection applies only to the variable passed as the parameter. Notice that the algorithm did not pass the linked list as a parameter (we have no way to do that). All that was passed was the algorithm's pointer to the linked list. As a result, it is only that pointer that is protected from modification by the module. The module may use current to see where the beginning of the list is and may then modify whatever it finds there. In other words, the instruction

```
current <- current^.next
```

would not change the linked list itself, as it is only modifying the copy of the input parameter. Yet the instructions

```
current^.data <- 0
current^.next <- NIL
```

would indeed modify the linked list itself.

This is a large security loophole since it allows an in parameter to be used to modify or destroy some or all of a linked structure. It arises because the dynamically allocated variables in the heap are beyond the reach of the security protection that is enjoyed by static named variables that appear in the stack. We shall see how to address these and similar problems in Chapter 7. In the meantime, be aware of this pitfall.

Warning: Be very careful to trace algorithm execution when passing and manipulating pointers. Parameter protection is limited to the pointer itself, not to the data items to which it points.

5.9   Binary Trees

In this section we'll discuss a very powerful data abstraction: the binary tree.

Definition: A **tree** is a data structure that is made of nodes and pointers, much like a linked list. The difference between them lies in how they are organized. In a linked list each node is connected to one "successor" node (via a `next` pointer), that is, it is linear. In a tree, the nodes can have *several* `next` pointers and thus are not linear. ■

The top node in the tree is called the root and all other nodes branch off from this one. Every node in a tree can have some number of children. Each child node can, in turn, be the parent node to its children, and so on. Of course, within each node, each of the various pointers requires its own unique field identifier, perhaps `child1`, `child2`, `child3`, and so on. A common example of a tree data structure is the generic family tree used in genealogy; in computers it is the binary tree

 Definition: A **binary tree** is a tree that is limited such that each node has only two such children. ■

To distinguish between the two children of a node, they are referred to as the left and right children. Nodes which have no children (i.e., when both child pointers have been assigned the value NIL, they are called leaves. Thus, we have very sensible nomenclature if we just think of a real-world tree turned upside down: The root is at the top and the leaves are at the bottom.

There are several parallels between binary trees and linked lists:

- The root of a tree is analogous to the head of a list.
- For each node in a binary tree, there can be at most *two* successor nodes, called left and right children; in a linked list, each node can have at most *one* successor, the `next` node.
- In a binary tree, we can follow either of two pointers within a node from the parent to a child; in a linked list, we can follow a single pointer within a node from the predecessor to the successor.

Figure 5.20 shows one example of a binary tree.

EXAMPLE 5.13 The implementation of a binary tree implies declarations similar to those of a linked list. For the example shown in Fig. 5.20, in which each node has only a single numerical data field, the declarations might be:

```
Tree_Node definesa record
    data isoftype Num
    left_child isoftype Ptr toa Tree_Node
    right_child isoftype Ptr toa Tree_Node
endrecord  //Tree_node
```

Figure 5.21 shows the binary tree of Fig. 5.20 in a way that reveals the node structure. ■

In the same way that successful use of a linked list requires that we always keep a named pointer (perhaps called `list_head` or some other descriptive name) pointing to the first node of the list, successful use of trees requires that we always keep a named pointer pointing to the root of the tree. Without such

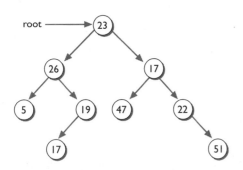

FIGURE 5.20 A Binary Tree

FIGURE 5.21 Implementation Structure of a Binary Tree

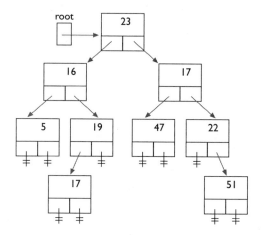

a pointer pointing to the tree, we have no way to access the tree. (Furthermore, if there is no pointer pointing to the root node of a tree, a chain reaction of deallocation would automatically result, just as would happen with a linked list that lost its `list_head` pointer.) Thus, it is imperative that there is always some named pointer (perhaps called `tree_root` or simply `root`) pointing to the root node of the tree. Just as a linked list that has no nodes is still a list (albeit an empty one), so too is a tree with no nodes still a tree: an empty tree, but a tree nonetheless.

For the same reasons that we were careful not to move the `list_head` pointer away from the first node in a linked list, we have the same concern about the `tree_root` pointer of a tree. For tree manipulation purposes, we often use other, temporary pointers so that we do not move the `tree_root` pointer away from the root. Thus, we will often have declarations of named pointer variables such as

```
tree_root isof type Ptr toa Tree_Node
current isoftype Ptr toa Tree_Node
```

To access various locations in a tree, we use pointers just as we did before (i.e., to access the data value stored in the `left_child` of the `root`). We might say,

```
current <- tree_root
current <- current^.left_child
some_num_var <- current^.data
```

The first instruction causes `current` to point to the `root` of the tree. The second instruction causes current to then point to the `left_child` of the `root`. Once it points there, the third instruction copies the value of that node into the variable `some_num_var`.

Trees are invaluable for helping us overcome a universal problem of how to store large amounts of data such that we can combine both:

■ Fast access to any particular piece of data.
■ Flexibility in terms of adding and deleting data from storage.

Without trees, we often have to choose between speed and flexibility. As we shall soon see, with trees we often can have both.

5.9.1   Traversing Binary Trees

Traversing binary trees is a bit more complicated than traversing linked lists because we cannot merely step through a linear sequence. Trees are not linear, and we instead have to navigate through the various branches. For each node in the tree, we must traverse one branch, then return to the root and traverse another branch, and so on, until each branch has been traversed. While trees may have any number of branches, the most widely used tree is the binary tree, and we shall confine ourselves to that topology.

Because of the recursively defined structure of a binary tree, the traversal algorithm is inherently recursive. To see what we mean by a recursively defined structure, think of the three components of a binary tree:

- A root node.
- A left subtree.
- A right subtree.

The left child of the root node is itself the root of the left subtree, and the right child is the root of the right subtree. The same can be said for each and every node in the tree: Each node is the root of the subtree below it. Even the leaves of the tree are roots of their own subtree, albeit trees that contain no further subtrees.

Tree traversal algorithms exploit this fact. We must first traverse one subtree and then return to the root to traverse the other subtree. An ordering of steps that do this can be recursively called each time a new node is visited.

We can break the original tree traversal problem into three smaller parts:

1. Traversal of a single node: the root.
2. Traversal of the left subtree.
3. Traversal of the right subtree.

Traversing a single node is trivial: We simply visit that node and take care of whatever our business might be (processing its value, printing out its value, or whatever). To traverse each of the two subtrees, we simply consider the topmost node of each subtree as the root of that subtree and recursively call the algorithm.

There are three ways to traverse a binary tree, called *inorder, preorder,* and *postorder.* They are remarkably similar to one another, each containing the same three logical steps, listed above. They differ only in the order in which the three steps are carried out.

The ordering of steps is what gives rise to their names. In the preorder traversal, the root node of a tree is the first one visited (hence the prefix "pre"), then the left subtree is traversed, and finally the right subtree. In an inorder traversal, the root node is visited after the left subtree and before the right subtree: It is *in* the middle. In the postorder traversal the root node is visited after both the left and right subtrees have been completely traversed; thus the prefix "post." Because the inorder traversal is used most frequently, we shall concentrate first, starting in Example 5.14, on the algorithm for it.

EXAMPLE 5.14 Given the root of a tree, an inorder traversal traverses the left subtree of the root, visits the root, and then traverses the right subtree. In traversing the left or right subtree, the same rule is applied in a recursive manner. The algorithm is as follows. (Note that the numbers to the left of some lines are not part of the procedure. They are there to facilitate our discussion of the execution of the algorithm.)

```
procedure Inorder (current_ptr isoftype in Ptr toa
                Tree_Node)
// Purpose: performs an inorder traversal on a binary
// tree that stores numbers, printing the data value
// stored in each node}
```

FIGURE 5.22 A Binary Search Tree

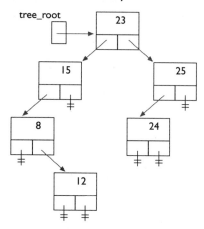

```
1   if (current_ptr <> NIL) then
2       Inorder(current_ptr^.left_child)
3       print (current_ptr^.data)
4       Inorder(current_ptr^.right_child)
5   endif

    endprocedure //Inorder
```

This algorithm looks amazingly simple considering the complicated task it performs: It can traverse any binary tree, regardless of its particular shape, regardless of whether it is symmetrical in shape or lopsided, and regardless of whether it contains one node or billions of nodes. Thus, it provides a good example of the elegant power of recursion.

We shall step through this algorithm, using the binary search tree shown in Fig. 5.22.

5.9.2 Binary Search Trees

Definition: A **binary search tree**, or BST, is a binary tree that has its data values arranged in a particular way: *Each node* in the tree contains a value larger than all the values in its left subtree and smaller than all the values in its right subtree.[2]

This relationship among the values in a BST is important because it allows us to quickly search for a particular value. Beginning at the root, we can exploit the ordering of values to make a series of simple "less than" or "greater than" decisions that guide us to the left or the right at each node as we move from the root towards a leaf in search of a given value. We shall discuss this soon in Section 5.10.5.

5.9.3 Inorder BST Traversal

Recall that an inorder traversal goes about its job according to the following pattern:

- It first visits all the nodes in the left subtree.
- It then visits the root node.
- It then visits all the nodes in the right subtree.

Given the specific pattern in which values are arranged in a BST, an inorder traversal will visit the nodes of a tree such that the values stored in them are encountered in

---

2. The following question naturally arises: Can a binary search tree contain duplicate values? This is a policy question, not an algorithmic question. Sometimes we might wish to allow it, other times not, depending on the nature of the problem. If duplicates are to be allowed in a given instance, one of two simple policies is applied: All duplicates are treated either as greater than or as less than equal values for purposes of inserting them into a tree.

ascending order. When applied to a BST, an inorder traversal achieves a particular pattern:

- It first visits all the nodes that contain values less than the root.
- It then visits the root node itself.
- It then visits all the nodes that contain values greater than the root.

 Because of its recursive nature, an inorder traversal follows this pattern with respect to each and every node in the tree and thus visits all the nodes in the tree in sorted order. ▪

To understand how an inorder traversal of a BST provides a sorted list, consider the tree shown in Fig. 5.22. Given the values stored in this tree, a traversal that outputs the values in sorted ascending order will produce the following output:

```
8, 12, 15, 23, 24, 25
```

To see how an inorder traversal accomplishes this, we shall again use a stack to help us keep track of the recursive execution of the procedure to perform an inorder traversal and print out each node's value, as given in Example 5.14. We know that the tree nodes themselves are stored in the heap, but to save space we will only show the stack. In each stack frame we will keep three pieces of information for each recursive call:

1. The data value stored in the node pointed to by current_ptr.
2. The number of the instruction in which the recursive call was made. Because recursive calls are made only in the lines labeled 2 and 4 (see Example 5.14), each call can only be interrupted by a recursive call in lines 2 or 4.
3. The node to which a pointer was passed in the recursive call; we'll indicate this via the data value stored in that node.

 It might be best to take scrap paper and copy the algorithm from Example 5.14 *and* sketch the tree shown in Fig. 5.22 so you can follow the trace of the recursion without flipping pages back and forth. ▪

The algorithm is initially called via

```
Inorder(tree_root)
```

where tree_root is a Ptr toa Tree_Node that points to the node containing the data value 23. Thus, the algorithm is initially passed a pointer to the node containing 23. Since that node has a left subtree, whose root is the node containing 15, the algorithm is interrupted by a recursive call to traverse that subtree (line 2).

Thus, we put a frame on the stack representing the first call of procedure Inorder (i.e., when current_ptr points to the root node). In this frame, we record information such as the line in which the execution of the algorithm was interrupted by a recursive call and the node to which a pointer was passed to the recursive clone of the algorithm. Thus, with `current_ptr` pointing to the root, and a recursive call occurring in line 2 of the procedure, our stack frame looks like this:

```
current_ptr points to node w/23; Call: line 2; Passes ptr to 15
```

The second clone of the algorithm then begins, with the node containing 15 being *its* root. This node has a left subtree also, so the algorithm is interrupted in line 2. A recursive call is invoked on its left subtree (i.e., the subtree whose root is the node containing 8). Thus we put another frame on the stack:

```
current_ptr points to node w/15; Call: line 2; Passes ptr to 8
current_ptr points to node w/23; Call: line 2; Passes ptr to 15
```

The third clone of the algorithm begins with `current_ptr` pointing to the node containing 8. This clone of the algorithm is interrupted exactly as the previous ones were, and the stack looks like this:

```
current_ptr points to node w/8; Call: line 2; Passes NIL ptr
current_ptr points to node w/15; Call: line 2; Passes ptr to 8
current_ptr points to node w/23; Call: line 2; Passes ptr to 15
```

Next, we find something different. This time, the algorithm is called to act on the tree rooted by a `NIL` pointer. As it begins execution, the stack looks like this:

```
current_ptr is NIL
current_ptr points to node w/8; Call: line 2; Passes NIL ptr
current_ptr points to node w/15; Call: line 2; Passes ptr to 8
current_ptr points to node w/23; Call: line 2; Passes ptr to 15
```

Because `current_ptr` is `NIL`, the condition in line 1 fails. Thus, this clone of the algorithm completes its work without doing anything at all. Its frame (the top one) is popped off the stack.

At this point, we return to the stack and "wake up" the process represented in what is now the topmost frame. This is the clone that has a pointer to the node containing 8 as its root. It was interrupted in line 2. Since that call has now finished, it can proceed to line 3, and its `current^.data`, the number 8, is printed. The algorithm then proceeds to line 4. This causes the algorithm to be interrupted again, this time by a recursive call that passes the current node's `right_child` pointer. Thus, the stack now looks like this:

current_ptr points to node w/8; Call: line 4; Passes ptr to 12
current_ptr points to node w/15; Call: line 2; Passes ptr to 8
current_ptr points to node w/23; Call: line 2; Passes ptr to 15

A new clone of the procedure is pushed onto the stack. Its `current_ptr` points to the node containing the value 12. As it begins execution, it is interrupted in the same way as before, in its line 2, which causes it to make a recursive call passing its `left_child` pointer as a parameter. As this happens, the stack looks like this:

current_ptr points to node w/12; Call: line 2; Passes ptr to NIL
current_ptr points to node w/8; Call: line 4; Passes ptr to 12
current_ptr points to node w/15; Call: line 2; Passes ptr to 8
current_ptr points to node w/23; Call: line 2; Passes ptr to 15

With the call, a new fifth frame is pushed onto the stack:

current_ptr points to NIL
current_ptr points to node w/12; Call: line 2; Passes ptr to NIL
current_ptr points to node w/8; Call: line 4; Passes ptr to 12
current_ptr points to node w/15; Call: line 2; Passes ptr to 8
current_ptr points to node w/23; Call: line 2; Passes ptr to 15

With `current_ptr` having a NIL value, the line 1 test fails, and the fifth frame pops off the stack without doing anything. This wakes up the fourth frame, which had gone to sleep in its line 2. When it wakes up, it proceeds to its line 3 and prints out the value 12. (Thus far, we've printed 8 and then 12).

Execution then proceeds to its line 4, which is a recursive call (passing the `right_child` pointer of the node containing the data value 12). This again puts the fourth frame to sleep and a new frame on the stack:

current_ptr points to NIL
current_ptr points to node w/12; Call: line 4; Passes ptr to NIL
current_ptr points to node w/8; Call: line 4; Passes ptr to 12
current_ptr points to node w/15; Call: line 2; Passes ptr to 8
current_ptr points to node w/23; Call: line 2; Passes ptr to 15

Since a NIL pointer is passed by the fourth frame to the fifth, we once again have a new fifth frame that encounters a failed condition in its line 1 and then pops off the stack without doing any work.

The fourth stack frame reawakens having completed its line 4. It then completes execution and it too pops off the stack. This wakes up the third stack frame, which had most recently gone to sleep via a recursive call in its line 4. When it wakes up again, there is nothing for it do but finish, so it is popped off the stack as well. Thus, in short order, the fifth, fourth, and third stack frames have popped off the stack.

When we return to the second stack frame, we see that it went to sleep in the following state:

```
current_ptr points to node w/15; Call: line 2; Passes ptr to 8
current_ptr points to node w/23; Call: line 2; Passes ptr to 15
```

The recursive call made in its line 2 has completed. Thus, when it wakes up, it proceeds to its line 3, printing out the value 15. (So far, we've printed out the values 8, 12, and 15.) It then proceeds to line 4, which is a recursive call, passing a pointer to the right child of its current_ptr, which is a NIL pointer. This results in a new third frame on the stack:

```
current_ptr NIL
current_ptr points to node w/15; Call: line 4; Passes NIL ptr
current_ptr points to node w/23; Call: line 2; Passes ptr to 15
```

We encounter the same series of behavior we saw before: A recursive call has passed a NIL pointer, causing a new stack frame to be pushed and popped without doing any work. Then, the second stack frame wakes up and, having now completed its line 4, finishes execution, and it too is popped from the stack.

Thus, only the frame for the original call remains on the stack. The traversal of the root's left subtree has now been completed, and all tree values less than the value of the root have been printed. When the remaining frame wakes up, it proceeds to its line 3, printing out the value 23, giving us the values 8, 12, 15, and 23 so far. After printing out its value, it proceeds to the recursive call in line 4, which begins the traversal of its right subtree, and the stack looks like this:

```
current_ptr points to node w/23; Call: line 4; Passes ptr to 25
```

The recursive call gives us a new second frame, which is interrupted in its line 2:

```
current_ptr points to node w/25; Call: line 2; Passes ptr to 24
current_ptr points to node w/23; Call: line 4; Passes ptr to 25
```

This gives us a new third frame:

`current_ptr points to node w/24; Call: line 2; Passes ptr to NIL`
`current_ptr points to node w/25; Call: line 2; Passes ptr to 24`
`current_ptr points to node w/23; Call: line 4; Passes ptr to 25`

We get a quick push and pop of a new fourth frame (which has a `NIL` pointer and thus does no work), followed by the printing of a data value (in this case 24, giving us 8, 12, 15, 23, and 24), followed by another quick push and pop of another fourth frame with a `NIL` pointer. The third frame then finishes and pops off the stack, returning us to the second frame.

The second frame wakes up after having completed its line 2 and proceeds to print out its data value, giving us 8, 12, 15, 23, 24, and 25. It then proceeds to its line 4 recursive call, giving:

`current_ptr points to node w/25; Call: line 4; Passes NIL ptr`
`current_ptr points to node w/23; Call: line 4; Passes ptr to 25`

This leads to another new third frame:

`current_ptr is NIL`
`current_ptr points to node w/25; Call: line 4; Passes NIL ptr`
`current_ptr points to node w/23; Call: line 4; Passes ptr to 25`

The top frame pops off without doing any work, and we return to the stack to find that both processes on the stack "went to sleep" in their fourth line. In turn, they each wake up, complete, and pop off the stack. The traversal is now complete. Observe that it has printed out each value in the tree in ascending order.

Whew! All this from a tree containing only six nodes. Imagine if the tree had a few thousand nodes. And, remember, all this was accomplished by a simple recursive algorithm containing only one `if` statement, two recursive calls, and a `print` instruction.

5.9.4 Preorder and Postorder Traversals

The other two kinds of tree traversal are remarkably similar. The instructions are the same; only the order in which they occur differs. Preorder traversals visit the root, the left subtree, and then the right subtree. The algorithm is almost identical to the inorder case, except the order of the instructions is different. But the change is significant. The output from the example tree of Fig. 5.21 will be 23, 15, 8, 12, 25, 24 for the preorder traversal, as shown in Example 5.15.

EXAMPLE 5.15 The preorder algorithm is as follows:

```
procedure Preorder(current_ptr isoftype in Ptr toa Tree_Node)
    {Purpose: performs a preorder traversal on a binary tree which stores
        numbers, printing the data value stored in each node}

    if (current_ptr <> NIL) then
        print(current_ptr^.data)
        Preorder(current_ptr^.left_child)
        Preorder(current_ptr^.right_child)
        endif

end {Preorder}
```

Postorder traversals visit the left subtree, the right subtree, and then the root. Compare the following algorithm with that of Example 5.15.

EXAMPLE 5.16

```
procedure Postorder(current_ptr isoftype in Ptr toa Tree_Node)
    {Purpose: performs a postorder traversal on a binary tree which stores
        numbers, printing the data value stored in each node}

    if (current_ptr <> NIL) then
        Postorder(current_ptr^.left_child)
        Postorder(current_ptr^.right_child)
        print(current_ptr^.data)
    endif

end {Postorder}
```

This algorithm will print out the values of the tree shown in Fig. 5.21 in the sequence 12, 8, 15, 24, 25, and 23.

5.9.5 Searching a Binary Search Tree

Now that we know how to traverse a binary search tree, let's see how to search for a value in one. The beauty of a binary search tree is that the items in it are arranged in a way that makes searching very fast. Unlike the search of a linked list, the search of a BST does not involve executing a traversal until the value is found. When searching a BST, we can exploit the order in which values are stored in the tree.

For any value in a binary search tree, we know that all the values in its left subtree are smaller than the current value and all values in its right subtree are larger. Therefore, when doing a search, we compare our target to the value in a given node, and if the current node doesn't contain the value for which we're searching, we then move to the node's left or right child depending on the result of the comparison.

In a *balanced* binary search tree this method results in very good search performance.

Definition: A **balanced binary tree** is one that is roughly symmetrical such that there is a difference of at most one level of depth among the various leaves.

In a balanced binary search tree, each such left or right decision eliminates approximately half of the remaining nodes from the search. This process is illustrated in Fig. 5.23 as we search for the value 17.

- We first encounter the root whose value is 23. Since that value is larger than the target, we narrow our search to its left subtree.
- Our second call focuses on the subtree rooted by the node containing 15. Because 15 is smaller than our target, we narrow our search to its right subtree.
- This call discovers that its `current_ptr^.data` matches the target value.

The following example steps through the creation of a recursive algorithm to accomplish this search.

EXAMPLE 5.17 We must first determine which kind of module to use. Because we will be printing messages, we will use a procedure, and since the printing is something we do *after* reaching the terminating condition, we use the first of our two recursive formats:

```
if (terminating condition) then
    do final actions
else
    take a step closer to terminating condition
    call "clone" of module
endif
```

We can now begin to construct the detailed logic of the procedure:

```
if ((value found) or (value not in tree))
then
    print appropriate message
else
    take one step to the right or to the left
    make recursive call
endif
```

Notice that both the `if` and `else` clauses must each deal with two possibilities. The `if` clause must print out one of two messages, as appropriate, and the `else` clause must take one step either to the left or to the right. Thus, both the `if` and `else` clauses imply their own decisions. We might articulate their logic as follows:

```
// the first part: if terminating condition
                satisfied}
    if (at NIL ptr) then
        print "value not in tree" message
    else // at node containing target value
        print "value found in tree" message
    endif
```

FIGURE 5.23

```
   // the second part: taking one step closer
   if (must search left subtree)
      go to the left
   else //must search right subtree
      go to the right
   endif
```

From this logic, we can write the algorithm as follows:

```
procedure BST_Search (current_ptr isoftype in Ptr toa
                Tree_Node, targetisoftype in Num)
// Purpose: search a binary search tree for the given target
// value; print out appropriate message indicating if target
// is in the BST.

   if (current_ptr = NIL) then
      print ("The tree does not contain ", target)
   elseif (current_ptr^.data = Target) then
      print ("The tree contains ", target)
   elseif (current_ptr^.data > target) then
      BST_Search(current_ptr^.left_child, target)
   else //it must be that current_ptr^.data <= Target
      BST_Search(current_ptr^.right_child, target)
   endif

endprocedure //BST_Search
```

5.9.6   Adding Nodes to a BST

As with inserting a value into a linked list, the principle of abstraction means that we want a general algorithm that will correctly insert a new value into a BST under all circumstances. Unlike a linked list, it is not necessary that a BST insertion algorithm traverse the tree. Instead, as in searching a BST, we can exploit the pattern of values in a BST to make the job easier.

In a BST, a new node will *always* be inserted at a NIL pointer. We *never* have to rearrange existing nodes to make room for a new one. For example, given the BST shown in Fig. 5.22,

- The value 16 would be inserted as the left child of the node containing 17.
- The value 21 would be inserted as the right child of the node containing 17.
- The value 26 would be inserted as the left child of the node containing 29 and so on.

In fact, the logic used is very similar to that used in searching a BST. To insert a new value, we search for that value, and upon encountering a NIL pointer, we have located the pointer to which the new node should be attached. The creation of a procedure that implements this logic is left as an exercise.

5.9.7 Deleting Nodes from a BST

Deleting a node from a BST can be a bit tricky. This is because the definition of a BST requires that the proper arrangement of values relative to one another is always maintained. Thus, when deleting a node, we must ensure that the remaining nodes are connected to one another in a way that preserves the proper arrangement of values.

This is easy to do if the node targeted for deletion happens to be a leaf node. We simply change the pointer to it from its parent to NIL. But what if the targeted node has children of its own? We must somehow guarantee that its children are connected to the tree such that the proper arrangement of values is maintained.

To ensure that this is the case, we use the following rule: Any deleted value that has two children must be replaced by an existing value that is one of the following:

- The largest value in the deleted node's left subtree (i.e., the greatest of its smaller descendants).
- The smallest value in the deleted node's right subtree (i.e., the smallest of its larger descendants).

Thus, given the tree of Fig. 5.23, if we were to delete the value in the root node, 23, we would replace that value with either 17 (largest in the left subtree) or 24 (smallest in the right subtree). We would then delete the node that contained the value that we used to replace the deleted value (i.e., the node originally containing 17 or the node originally containing 24). If we use the value 24, its node is a leaf, so no further steps are needed.

If the deleted value is to be replaced by a value that is not in a leaf node, we must be sure to take proper care of that node's "orphaned children." We can be certain that any such node will have at most one non-NIL child pointer. (Why?) We can handle this by connecting the moved value's orphan with its parent. For example, consider the tree of Fig. 5.23:

- Imagine that we are deleting the value 23 from the tree and that we will replace it with the value 17, thus targeting the node that originally held 17 for deletion.
- Observe that the node containing 17 had a left child containing the value 16.
- We copy the value 17 to the root node, thus deleting the value 23 from the tree.
- We then reassign the right child pointer of the node containing 15 to point to the node containing 16.

As a result, no pointer is pointing to the node that originally contained 17, so it is deleted. Its former child (the node containing 16) is now the child of its former parent (the node containing 15), and the structure of the tree is maintained. In effect, we are doing the same thing that a grandparent does when he or she adopts a grandchild who has lost his or her parents.

It is important that you understand deletion at the level of the idea such that you know how to do it with tree drawings. Writing the code to implement this idea is a bit tricky, so we leave it as an advanced, optional exercise.

5.10 Graphs

A graph is a data structure that does not have the restrictions of linked lists and trees.

Definition: **Graphs** are simply sets of nodes connected by pointers. They need not be linear (as do linked lists) nor do they have to have limited parent-child relationships (as do trees).

FIGURE 5.24 A Graph

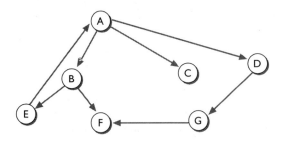

A graph may contain any arrangement of nodes and connecting edges. Therefore, both linked lists and trees are examples of graphs. However, the term is generally used to refer to structures that do not have the restrictions implied by linked lists and trees. Examples of graphs can be found by consulting any road map: The cities are nodes and the highways between them are edges which connect the nodes.

A road map typically represents a nondirected graph, in that most roads are two-way streets. If we imagine a road map on which each road is a one-way street, we have the concept of a directed graph, as shown in Fig. 5.24.

As with other dynamic structures, we implement graphs using records as nodes and pointers as the edges that connect the nodes. Graphs present a new kind of problem, in that we don't know how many pointers each graph node requires. In fact, any given node in a graph may have any number of edges to other nodes, and their number may vary over time. Thus, we require some flexible, dynamic means of representing graphs in terms of data structures. Let's investigate such a means in Example 5.18.

EXAMPLE 5.18 We can have a linked list of *successor* nodes such that a graph node points to the first node in the list of its successors. This can be implemented using two kinds of nodes and two kinds of pointers, as follows:

```
Graph_Node definesa record
    data isoftype Char
    successors isoftype Ptr toa Connector_Node
endrecord //Graph_Node

Connector_Node definesa record
    node_ptr isoftype Ptr toa Graph_Node
    next_node isoftype Ptr toa Connector_Node
endrecord //Connector_Node
```

Because we have no way of knowing how many nodes a given node will point to, we must have a dynamic way to have as many pointers as necessary. Thus, to represent each graph node, we define the record type `Graph_Node` to have a `data` field and a single pointer, which we might call *successors*. If a given `Graph_Node` does not point to any other nodes, then its successors pointer will be `NIL`. If a given node has one or more than one nodes to which it must point, its successors pointer points to a `Connector_Node`.

A `Connector_Node`'s job is to function like the glue that holds the graph together. Each `Connector_Node` contains two different types of pointers: one to point to a `Graph_Node` and the other to point to another `Connector_Node`. By pointing to a single `Connector_Node`, a given `Graph_Node`'s successors pointer is in effect pointing to a linked list of `Connector_Nodes`. Each `Connector_Node` in the list provides access to a successor `Graph_Node` and to the next `Connector_Node` if another is needed.

This dynamic implementation of graphs allows us the flexibility to create graphs of any size or shape. This kind of implementation of the graph represented in Fig. 5.24 is shown in Fig. 5.25.

We shall touch on graphs in later chapters. Do not concern yourself too much with how to create and manipulate them. Instead, be sure that you understand the concept.

5.11   Iterative Control

So far, we have controlled all repetitive actions via *recursion* whereby we achieve repetition by having a subprogram make a call to itself. A second means of controlling repetition is provided by the iteration construct known as a *loop*. To *iterate* means to *repeat*.

Definition: A **loop** construct provides a way to effect iteration without making recursive calls.

Unlike many programming languages that feature a variety of rather odd special-case loop constructs, we use a single, general loop structure. Its form is as follows:

```
<do something>
loop
    <step 1>
    :
    <step n>
    exitif (<conditional expression>)
    <step n+1>
    :
    <step m>
endloop
<do yet another thing>
```

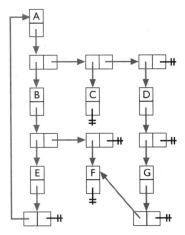

FIGURE 5.25 Implementation
Structure of the Graph

A loop may appear anywhere within a body of instructions. Our loop construct begins with `loop` and ends with `endloop`. All the instructions in between those two are part of the loop body. The execution of instructions proceeds in the normal sequential fashion, from top to bottom. When the algorithm reaches the `endloop` instruction, it *automatically* goes back to the top `loop` instruction and repeats the block of steps all over again. Notice how indentation is used to show which steps are inside the loop.

In most situations, the repetition must not go on forever. It must end when an appropriate data state has been reached. Thus, the loop body includes an `exitif (condition)` instruction, which allows us to break out of the loop when the terminating condition becomes TRUE. The sequence is as follows: Starting at the `loop` instruction, each step is executed in order. When the `exitif (condition)` step is reached, the condition is tested.

■ If it is TRUE, iteration is stopped, and execution resumes at the first step after the `endloop`.

- If the condition is FALSE, the iteration continues in sequence until it reaches the end of the loop, goes back to the top, and repeats the entire process again.

EXAMPLE 5.19 Let's look at an example of a loop, one that might apply to Sisyphus in *Paradise Lost*:

```
1. loop
2.      select a rock
3.      roll the rock uphill
4.      exitif (there are no more rocks at the bottom)
5.      go back downhill
6. endloop
7. celebrate
```

Given the algorithm above, what happens? At step 1 Sisyphus enters the loop. Starting at step 2, he selects a rock, and at step 3, he rolls it up the hill. Then if there are no more rocks to be rolled uphill, the exit condition tested in step 4 is TRUE; if so, he skips the rest of the loop and goes immediately to step 7 to celebrate finishing the job. If there *are* more rocks, however, the exitif condition in step 4 is FALSE, and he must execute step 5 (go to the bottom of the hill). Then, in step 6, he encounters endloop, which signifies that he must return to the top of the loop and perform the loop sequence all over again.

Keep in mind two important facts about the use of the exitif statement:

- Only one exitif statement is allowed per loop.
- The exitif statement can be placed anywhere within the loop body. Where it is placed is determined by the particulars of the repetitive task.

In the example above, we placed the exitif test in the midst of the other loop body statements. Often, such placement is appropriate to the problem at hand. Sometimes, however, it is appropriate to place the exitif at either the very beginning of the loop body or at the very end.

The next three examples illustrate the effect of the different placements of the exitif statement.

EXAMPLE 5.20 Placing the exitif(<condition>) as the first line in the loop body creates what is called a *sentinel loop* because the test is done before any other instructions inside the loop are carried out. In effect, the exitif test serves as a sentinel (or guard) that determines whether or not execution is allowed to enter the loop even one time. Using a structure like this allows the possibility that the loop will be skipped entirely if the condition is TRUE the first time it is tested.

```
loop
    exitif (<conditional expression>)
    <step 1>
    :
    <step n>
endloop
```

For example, our rock-rolling problem should feature a sentinel loop *if* there might be no rocks to begin with.

EXAMPLE 5.21 Placing the exitif(<condition>) as the end of the loop body creates a *test-last loop*, because the condition is tested after all other instructions in the loop are carried out. Using this structure guarantees that all the steps in the loop will be executed at least once before the loop is exited. This form is used when the statements within the loop body *must* be executed in order to obtain the value that is tested in the exitif test.

```
loop
    <step 1>
    :
    <step n>
    exitif (<conditional expression>)
endloop
```

EXAMPLE 5.22 Placing the exitif(<condition>) somewhere in the middle of the loop creates an *n-and-a-half loop*, because the loop body will not all be executed the same number of times. The statements before the exitif will be executed one more time than will the statements after the exitif. While we might not be able to tell ahead of time how many iterations will be performed, we know that if the entire loop is executed *n* times, the statements before the exit if will be executed *n* + 1 times. Thus, we describe the loop as a whole as having been executed *n-and-a-half* times. For example:

```
algorithm Shop_With_$20
// Purpose: Given $20 in cash and a prioritized list of
// items that will cost more than $20 in total, determine
// when no more items may be purchased.

    spent_so_far isoftype Num
    spent_so_far <- 0
    next_item_price isoftype Num
    next_item_price <- 0

    loop
        read(next_item_price)
        exitif ((spent_so_far + next_item_price) >= 20)
        <Place next item in shopping cart>
        spent_so_far <- spent_so_far + next_item_price
    endloop

<Go to cash register to purchase items>

endalgorithm //Shop_With_$20
```

The loop in Example 5.22 illustrates two important ideas:

■ First, notice that certain initialization steps were performed before the loop began (e.g., declaring and initializing the two local variables). Often, some sort of initialization is required prior to the loop so that the loop will begin with appropriate values.

■ Second, observe that each pass through the loop took one step toward the termination condition. Sooner or later, any shopper will have $20 worth of items. Thus, this loop is not an *infinite* loop, which goes on forever.

Warning: When constructing loops, it is imperative that you be careful to ensure that both of the following things are taken care of:

- Appropriate preloop initialization of values.
- Certainty that the terminating condition will be reached.

5.12 Iteration vs. Recursion

In principle, iteration and recursion are equivalent. Anything that can be done with one can be done with the other, as we will illustrate next.

EXAMPLE 5.23 Consider our procedure for traversing a linked list and printing out each value stored in the list. We implemented this in Example 5.7 with recursion as follows:

```
procedure Traverse_Recursively (current_ptr isoftype in Ptr
                                      toa List_Node)
1      if (current_ptr <> NIL) then
2          print(current_ptr^.data)
3          Traverse_Recursively(current_ptr^.next)
4      endif
end {Traverse_Recursively}
```

We can implement the same logic using iteration as follows:

```
procedure Traverse_Iteratively(current_ptr isoftype in Ptr
                                      toa List_Node)
1      loop
2          exitif (current_ptr = NIL)
3          print(current_ptr^.data)
4          current_ptr <- current_ptr^.next
5      endloop
end {Traverse_Iteratively}
```

From the outside, the two procedures in Example 5.23 are indistinguishable (except for their names). Each one is passed some pointer value, and it has the effect of printing out all the values in the list. Thus, from external appearances, there will be no way to tell whether the traversal is implemented iteratively or recursively. In both cases, when it is initially called, a parameter (`current_ptr`) gets passed the value of some pointer to the list, presumably `list_head`. In both cases, it is an `input` parameter, thus ensuring that we do not change the original value of `list_head` (or whatever pointer was passed in).

In the iterative version, the first instruction in the loop is the `exitif` test. Why? Observe that the exit condition would be true at the very beginning if there is nothing in the linked list, that is, if

```
list_head = NIL
```

In both versions, we first check to see if `current_ptr` is NIL. If it is, we must exit immediately: If `current_ptr` is NIL, `current_ptr^.data` and `current_ptr^.next` do not exist. Executing these instructions would be an error. (If we tried to dereference them via a computer program, the program would crash.)

Notice the strong similarity between the logic of the iterative and recursive solutions. For most algorithmic tasks, the recursive and iterative implementations will show strong step-by-step similarities. Given that recursion and iteration are logically equivalent, how do you tell which to use for a given circumstance? Keep the following idea in mind.

Although in principle, iteration and recursion are equivalent, in practice, you can accomplish *some* things a great deal easier with recursion than you can with iteration.

For example, for both linked lists and trees, a search can be readily articulated using either a recursive or iterative approach. The same is true for linked list traversals. However, for tree traversals there is a very real and significant difference. Recall how clear and compact the recursive solution is. The same is not true for an iterative approach. Because a tree traversal "bounces up and down" throughout the tree, its logic is different from the linear paths taken for such searches and for list traversals.

The recursive tree traversal solution *implicitly* exploits the stack to keep track of "where it is" in the traversal process. If you were to write an iterative solution, you would not get this "free benefit" that the combination of recursive calls and the stack provides. (Instead, you would have to code your own stack data structure and the appropriate push and pop routines; you would also have to write code to initialize the stack and to call those push and pop routines at the appropriate places, simply to manage the tree traversal.) We get all this "for free" when we use recursion. Thus, while it certainly is possible to do tree traversals iteratively, nobody seems to want to (except for some students who want to see what an iterative tree traversal might look like). As a practical matter, the tree traversals we've discussed are almost always done recursively simply because it is a lot easier that way.

How do recursive and iterative solutions compare?

- *Recursive solutions often present a clearer, cleaner articulation of the essential logic than do iterative solutions.* Not only is it easier to do tree traversals recursively than iteratively, it is also a great deal easier to see the logic in the recursive approach. This is because the recursive solution is not cluttered up by `loop`, `exitif`, and `endloop` statements; instead, recursive solutions generally present an easily understood `if-then-else` format for expressing the repetitive logic. Thus, for many complex problems, recursion has the advantage of providing easier to understand solutions. Compare the iterative and recursive solutions in Example 5.23 for an example of this.
- *Recursion implies costs in both time and space that iteration does not.* Each time a recursive call is made, a new frame must be pushed onto the stack, and each time a recursive call completes, its frame must be popped off of the stack. Each of these push and pop operations takes some small amount of time. In addition, each stack frame also consumes memory. If the execution of a

recursive routine features enough recursive calls, it is possible that memory will be filled (in which case a stack overflow error will result and the program will crash).

As a result of the time and space costs of recursion, it was not popular when computing resources were rare and expensive. The practical economies of hardware meant that programmers could not afford recursion. However, those economies have changed. The modern affordability of both processors and memory means that time and space costs do not matter nearly as much as they once did. Instead, as algorithm complexity grows, the advantage of cleaner logic gains greater importance, especially at the algorithm design stage.

Often, an algorithm will be developed featuring a recursive approach. If time and space concerns do matter, the algorithm can be translated into an iterative form. Some compilers automatically do this conversion anyway as they translate a program from human understandable source code to machine-understandable object code, in which case there are no extra costs to recursion at all.

It is no accident that we introduced recursion first. Experience has shown us that students who learn recursion first can easily pick up iteration later. Unfortunately, it seems that those who learn iteration first often suffer from a mysterious form of "loop-induced brain damage" that makes it difficult for them to master recursion.

What matters is that you master *both* recursive and iterative approaches so that you can deploy whichever one is best for a given situation. Often, it doesn't matter which one you use. However, when it *does* matter, it should be the problem at hand, and not your personal bias, that determines which approach you use.

As it happens, iteration goes hand in hand with the data structure we introduce next.

5.13 Arrays

Like a linked list, an *array* is a linear structure. That is, it is used to store a *list* of data (i.e., multiple values of one type of data). Unlike a linked list, the capacity of an array is fixed, not dynamic. A given array is declared to have some *fixed number* of identical *cells* placed under one structure.

Thus, while we might think of a linked list as analogous to a railroad train, an array is more similar to an apartment house with a fixed number of apartments, each one having its own apartment number. While we can rearrange the contents of the various apartments, we cannot readily modify the location of apartments relative to one another within the apartment building, nor is it feasible to simply construct or destroy apartments dynamically based on occupancy needs. Arrays have this same limitation.

Because all the data contained in an array are of the same type, an array (like a linked list) is a *homogeneous* data structure. This is a requirement of arrays: Each and every cell in a given array must be of the same data type.

Each *cell* (or *element*) in an array can hold one data item and has its own address, or *index*, within the array. The index of an array cell is the number of its position in the structure. For example, the first cell in the array has an index of 1, the fourth has an index of 4, and so on. This feature gives arrays a benefit that linked structures lack: the capability for *random access* to any item in the list (i.e., we can jump directly to whatever cell index we like).

In this respect, arrays are analogous to CDs, which allow the listener to immediately jump to any musical track, while linked lists are analogous to cassette tapes, which require that you fast forward through songs if you wish to get to a later one.

Let's see how we might define an array data type.

EXAMPLE 5.24   We define an array data type by specifying the identifier for that type and by giving its dimensions and the type of data it can hold. We might define an array to hold a list of five numbers as follows:

```
Five_Num_Array definesa array[1..5] of Num
```

Any variable declared to be of this type will consist of five cells that can hold numbers. For example, we might declare two such array variables as follows:

```
this_array,
that_array isoftype Five_Num_Array
```

To visualize an array, we draw arrays as a group of cells joined together, with the appropriate indices. For example, the structure of variable `this_array` would be

We access the data values stored in an array by referring to the identifier of the array followed by the index of the item we want to access. Thus, to store the list of values 1, 9, 6, 7, and 4 in the array variable `this_array`, we could write

```
this_array[1] <- 1
this_array[2] <- 9
this_array[3] <- 6
this_array[4] <- 7
this_array[5] <- 4
```

which would give the result

Having done this, we might then use the arrays' random access capability to assign certain values from `this_array` to selective elements in `that_array` as follows:

```
that_array[5] <- this_array[3]
that_array[2] <- this_array[1]
```

which would give us

```
               1  2  3  4  5
this_array   | 1 | 9 | 6 | 7 | 4 |

               1  2  3  4  5
this_array   | ? | 1 | ? | ? | 6 |
```

We can assign the entire contents of one array to another array of the same array type. This is something we could not do in a single operation with a linked list (we'd need a procedure to traverse both linked lists, copying values one by one along the way). With arrays, copying can be accomplished by simply referring to the array variables' identifiers *without* reference to individual elements. For example,

```
that_array <- this_array
```

would result in

```
               1  2  3  4  5
this_array   | 1 | 9 | 6 | 7 | 4 |

               1  2  3  4  5
this_array   | 1 | 9 | 6 | 7 | 4 |
```

Arrays are valuable because they allow us to group many instances of the same kind of data together, and they provide rapid random access to each instance.

5.13.1 Arrays vs. Linked Lists

Arrays are *superior* to linked lists in two respects:

- At the level of logic, arrays allow us random access to any cell in the array without having to traverse the structure.
- At the level of implementation in a computer, for a given list of fixed size, arrays require less memory than linked lists since they do not require space for pointers.

Arrays are *inferior* to linked lists in at least two respects:

- They are *static* structures, which means that we must define their size and structure when we declare them. Once an array is declared, we can manipulate the contents of any and all cells in the array, but we cannot change the size or structure of the array. Thus, if we declare an array to store 100 items, and it turns out that we need to store only 2 items, we've wasted space; if we need space for 101, we're out of luck.
- Even if an array has ample space for our needs of the moment, it is sometimes costly to insert new values into an array. Consider an array in which the values are in sorted order. Imagine that we want to insert a new value that belongs at the beginning of the list. In a linked list, we simply create a new node and hook up the pointers in an appropriate fashion. With an array, it is necessary to move

all the values to the right of the insertion point one cell to the right in order to make room for the new node. For large lists of data, this can be very costly.

5.13.2 Traversing Arrays

Traversing an array is typically done with a loop. Here is an example.

EXAMPLE 5.25   We assume the following declarations:

```
MAX_ARRAY_SIZE is <some literal positive num value>
This_Array_Type definesa Array[1..MAX_ARRAY_SIZE] of Num
```

We also assume that the array contains values (i.e., that each of its elements has been initialized to some value). (*Note:* we have insisted on descriptive identifiers for variables. By long standing tradition, it is customary to use the identifier i to name a variable that will represent the current index into an array. Because of this convention, using i for this purpose is indeed descriptive since programmers will know exactly what you mean.)

```
procedure Traverse_Array(trv_array isoftype in This_Array_Type)
// Purpose: traverse array of Num, print out values in the
// order in which they are encountered

    i isoftype Num
    i <- 1
    loop
        print (trv_array[i])
        i <- i + 1
        exitif (i > MAX_ARRAY_SIZE)
    endloop

endprocedure //Traverse_Array
```

5.13.3 Searching Arrays

The simplest search of an array is very similar to a traversal, except that the algorithm compares each data element against the target value and stops when that value is found in the array, as shown below:

```
procedure Search_Array (srch_array isoftype in
          This_Array_Type, target isoftype in Num)
// Purpose: determine if target value is stored in
// srch_array, print out appropriate message}

    i isoftype num
    i <- 1
    loop
        exitif ((i > MAX_ARRAY_SIZE) OR (srch_array[i] = target))
        i <- i + 1
    endloop
    if (i <= MAX_ARRAY_SIZE) then
        print("Found Target")
    else
        print("Did Not Find Target")
    endif

endprocedure //Search_Array
```

This logic is similar to the Example 5.25, except that the loop exit has two conditions: We exit the loop when we've reached the end or found the target.

5.13.4 A More Efficient Array Search

There is a much more efficient way of searching an array *if* the data in the array is sorted. It is called a *binary search*. This method is useful only when array data is sorted. Let's consider an array sorted in ascending order, pictured as follows:

	1	2	3	4	5	6	7	8	9
	2	5	6	11	15	23	25	42	50

The *binary search* exploits the fact that the values are in sorted order.

Because the data in the array are sorted, we can always tell whether the target value is to the right or to the left of the value of any given position. If the target value is larger than the value at a given position, it must be to the right. If so, we can ignore all the values to the left. Conversely, if the target value is less than the value at a given position, it must be to the left and so we ignore all the values to the right.

A binary search implements this logic repeatedly until the search is completed. It begins by examining the value located in the middle of the array. If we get lucky and that middle element contains our target, the search is complete. In the more likely event that we have not found our target, we decide to move right or left depending on whether the target item is greater or less than the value of the element. Thus, approximately half of the array is disqualified.

We then move to the middle of the *remaining* elements and decide again whether to move right or left. With this decision, half of the remaining elements are disqualified. This process is repeated until we either "hit" our target or are left with only one element that is not the target (i.e., the target value is not there to be found).

Before we look at an example, we need to define a convention to use when we have an even number of elements. For a group of n elements, where n is even, the middle element will be defined as the one at the position given by $(n/2)+1$.

EXAMPLE 5.26 Refer to the array we drew above and imagine our target is the number 25, stored in the seventh element. We start looking at the middle element, whose index is 5. Since 15 is less than 25, we must search the right half of the list (i.e., the array from positions 6 through 9). According to our convention, the middle element of the right half is at index 8, so we check there for the target. It is greater than 25, so we must now search the remaining two elements (6 and 7). The middle of these two elements is at index 7. We find our target and stop searching.

This process is represented in the diagrams below. The arrows indicate the element that is currently being compared to the target. The rounded box surrounds the array elements that have not yet been eliminated from the search.

a. At first, the entire array is under consideration.

b. After comparing the target 25 to 15, we know the result must be to the right of index 5. The middle element of that range is 42, so we compare 42 to 25.

c. We eliminated 42 and the element to its right, so there are only two elements left. The middle element is the value 25, which is our target.

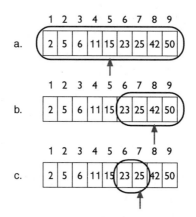

Note the efficiency of this search. With a linear traversal, we would have needed to start at the first element and compare seven elements against the target. With the binary search we need only three comparisons.

Of course, you might well point out that search by traversal would work better if we were looking for the value 5. True enough. Binary search would again require three comparisons, while the search by traversal would require only two comparisons. However, remember that a search algorithm must be *general* (i.e., it cannot make assumptions about which value we might be searching for or about where in the list of values it might be). Thus, we evaluate the efficiency of an algorithm in terms of its *average* or expected performance.

Analysis of efficiency will be covered in more detail in Chapter 9. For now observe that for a sorted array of size n, a successful search by traversal may require from 1 to n searches but will (over many trials for various values) traverse *on average* half the list (i.e., approximately $n/2$ comparisons). This is true regardless of whether the array is sorted or not.

In contrast, a binary search exploits the ordering of a sorted array to require approximately $\log n$ comparisons.[3] For small arrays such as in our example, the difference is trivial. But what would the difference be for an array of 10,000 or of 10,000,000?

You may wonder how we might do a binary search on a linked list. The answer is that we cannot because a binary search requires that we be able to *calculate* the mid-

---

3. When we say $\log n$, we refer to the log in base 2 (i.e., $\log_2 n$). For any n, $\log n$ means the exponent to which 2 must be raised to equal n. For example, $\log n$ equals 3 if n is 8 because 2 raised to the third power equals 8. Similarly, if n is 16, $\log n$ is 4; if n is 32, $\log n$ is 5; if n is 64, $\log n$ is 6; and so on.

dle position of a list of numbers and then jump to it. We can do this with an array since the array indexes give us *random access* capability. But it is impossible in a linked list. We can only move around in a linked list by navigating through it via pointers. Linked structures do not provide any way to achieve random access. However, a binary search tree that is full and balanced can and does offer us the same performance that we obtain from binary search on an array. In fact, it implements the same logic: go to the middle and then throw out half the values with each access.

5.14 The Abstraction Power of Constants

Recall that atomic data structures can be either *variables* (whose value can change) or *constants* (whose value is fixed, such as PI). Constants are useful tools for abstraction much as user-defined data types are. Constants give us ways to easily achieve algorithm modification and readability. Used properly, they allow us to raise the level of abstraction.

5.14.1 Ease of Change

In the example above, we defined the size of our various array data types by using a constant, not a literal value, for the upper size limit, that is, we did something like the following:

```
This_Array_Type definesa array[1..MAX_ARRAY_SIZE] of num
```

instead of

```
This_Array_Type definesa array[1..20] of num
```

To understand why we did this, note that MAX_ARRAY_SIZE was also mentioned in the search and traversal algorithms themselves, as shown below:

```
exitif(i > MAX_ARRAY_SIZE)
```

Thus, had we used a literal value (say, the 5) instead of a named constant, we would have in effect hardwired the size of the array into:

- The array type definition itself.
- The code of *any and all loops* that act upon *any and all variables* that were declared to be of that array type.

Doing things in this manner is an example of a low level of abstraction since the details would not be isolated and hidden but instead scattered about throughout *both* the type definitions *and* numerous decision statements. To achieve a higher level of abstraction, we want to *separate* the details of array size from the particulars of *both* the type definitions *and* the control structures.

By isolating array size in a constant, such as,

```
MAX_ARRAY_SIZE is 5
```

we can write both type definitions and control structures to be *independent of any particular size*. Thus, if we later want to change the array size from 5 to 137, we would need only change the value of one constant, for example,

```
MAX_ARRAY_SIZE is 137
```

This would give us a new algorithm in which *both* the data structure definitions *and* the details of the control structure's decisions would be *automatically updated* to reflect the modified size.

By using constants in this way, we allow for easy algorithm modification. For example, consider my problem with a credit card company: My last name always has the last character missing, perhaps because their character string data type is implemented as an array that is too short to accommodate my entire name (and I'm probably not the only one). If they wanted to correct this problem, they *might* have to search through all their software and change the size of many, many array declarations and control structures. However, if they made proper use of constants and data types, they would only have to change *one* constant declaration.

5.14.2 Readability

The use of constants also improves readability. As we have already seen, the instructions

```
exitif(i > MAX_ARRAY_SIZE)
```

is more natural, and its meaning is more obvious, than is the instruction

```
exitif(i > 137)
```

We can exploit this benefit of constants in many ways as shown in the example below.

EXAMPLE 5.27 Consider an algorithm for tracking how many of a given endangered species exist, state by state. We will need an array of 50 numbers such that each array element stores the size of the surviving population for a given state. We can do this without any constants, but the extensive use of constants can make the entire algorithm more natural and readable.

```
NUM_OF_STATES is 50
ALABAMA is 1
ALASKA is 2
ARKANSAS is 3
...
...
WEST_VIRGINIA is 49
WYOMING is 50

State_Array definesa array [1..NUM_OF_STATES] of Num

endangered_species_populatn isoftype State_Array
```

Given these declarations, we can now write logic in higher-level terms, as follows:

```
endangered_species_populatn(California) <- 734

print("The members of endangered species still alive in ")
print("Alabama number", endangered_species_populatn(Alabama))
```

While this use of constants is motivated by the desire to make the algorithm more comprehendable, it also makes it more adaptable. Imagine that another state is admitted to the union, thus changing the alphabetic position of other states. Had we not used constants for state identifiers and instead had referred to West Virginia as 49 throughout, the entire algorithm would require rewriting. Using constants, we need only revise the constant declarations that assign numbers to state names. All instructions that include the state name constant identifier will not need any modification at all since the change in the number associated with each state name will cascade down from the new constant declarations.

5.15 The Abstraction Power of Creating New Data Types

The ability to create new data types of our own specification is an extremely powerful tool that has relevance beyond just the creation of particular records, arrays, or linked structures.

It is a general principle that we use data types to *raise the level of abstraction of our data structures.* We do so by using data types as building blocks from which we can construct *exactly* what is needed.

We can combine various type definitions, constructing data types from arrays and records in whatever fashion suits us, much like a child builds structures out of blocks. The difference is that the child must make do with whatever blocks come in the box, while we may *define* whatever size, shape, and structure of "building blocks" we want.

5.15.1 Mixing Atomic and Complex Types

The data abstractions needed in an algorithm are determined by the problem at hand. Atomic data types should be used whenever they are sufficient, and complex types should be defined and used as called for by the problem. Let's look at an example in which both atomic and complex data structures are needed.

EXAMPLE 5.28   Consider the details of a Student_Grade_Record data type, below. In it, we combine atomic types (in this case Num) with *user-defined* or *complex* types to create what is wanted:

```
NUM_OF_HOMEWORKS is 14
NUM_OF_QUIZZES is 12
NUM_OF_PROJECTS is 13

Homework_Grades definesa array [1..NUM_OF_HOMEWORKS] of Num
Quiz_Grades definesa array [1..NUM_OF_QUIZZES] of Num
Project_Grades definesa array [1..NUM_OF_PROJECTS] of Num

Student_Grade_Record definesa record
   name isoftype String
   soc_sec_num isoftype Num
```

```
      homework_scores isoftype Homework_Grades
      quiz_scores isoftype Quiz_Grades
      project_scores isoftype Project_Grades
      final_exam_score isoftype Num
      final_grade isoftype Char
   endrecord //Student_Grade_Record
```

Notice that we have a *record* type with seven fields and that three of these fields are *arrays*. Any variable of type `Student_Grade_Record` will have this structure. If we wanted to declare three variables of type `Student_Grade_Record`, we might then declare:

```
   student1,
   student2,
   student3 isoftype Student_Grade_Record
```

This would create three different variables. To access the `soc_security_num` of `student1` we would write

```
   student1.soc_sec_num
```

To access the name of `student3` we would write

```
   student3.name
```

And to access the score earned by the second student on the third quiz, we would write

```
   student2.quiz_scores[3]
```

In this instruction, `student2` is the record, `quiz_scores` is the field within it that consists of an array of Nums, and the 3 specifies the location in that array.

5.15.2   Arrays of Records

In the next three examples, we build on the abstractions of Example 5.28, illustrating how we can use one complex type (a record) as an element of another complex type (an array).

EXAMPLE 5.29   Imagine that we will always have exactly 100 students in a class. We might define a data type for arrays of `Student_Grade_Records` as follows:

```
   CLASS_SIZE is 100
   Class_Grades definesa array[1..CLASS_SIZE] of Student_Grade_Record
```

This declaration creates a data type of an array of 100 elements such that each element in the array is an occurrence of the seven-field record. We could then declare a variable of this type as follows:

```
   this_class isoftype Class_Grades
```

We could then access the social security number of the fourteenth student as follows:

```
   this_class[14].soc_sec_num
```

Here, `this_class[14]` specifies the fourteenth element of the array, the period tells us to look inside that record at that location in the array, and `soc_sec_num` tells us which field inside the record to access. Similarly, to access the score earned by the thirty-seventh student on the fourth homework, we would write

```
this_class[37].homework_scores[4]
```

In this instruction, `this_class[37]` specifies the thirty-seventh element of the array, the period tells us to look inside the record at that location, and `homework_scores` tells us which field inside the record to access. The field `homework_scores` is itself an array of Num, and thus `homework_scores[4]` specifies that we want the fourth such score for the specified student.

If we wanted to print out the project scores earned by the twenty-third student, we might write

```
i isoftype Num
i <- 1
loop
   print (this_class[23].projects[i])
   i <- i + 1
   exitif (i > NUM_OF_PROJECTS)
endloop
```

Of course, this would *not* be a general algorithm for printing project scores. To benefit from procedural abstraction, it would be far better to create the following procedure.

EXAMPLE 5.30

```
procedure Print_Project_Grades (this_student's_projects isoftype
                                    in Project_Grades)
// Purpose: print all project grades for a given student

   i isoftype Num
   i <- 1

   loop
      print (this_student's_projects[i])
      i <- i + 1
      exitif (i > NUM_OF_PROJECTS)
   endloop

endprocedure //Print_Project_Grades
```

This procedure could then be called whenever we wished to print out the project grades for any student. To print out the name of the twenty-third student, we would call it as follows:

```
Print_Project_Grades(this_class[23].project_scores)
```

This passes the appropriate array of project grades to the procedure.

EXAMPLE 5.31   If we wished to print out a list of all the students' names with their project grades, we might create a procedure such as the following:

```
procedure Print_Class_Prj_Grades (grade_book isoftype in
                                    Class_Grades)
// Purpose: traverse grade_book, print each student's name
```

```
// and call Print_Project_Grades to print out the project
// scores for each student.

    i isoftype num
    i <- 1
    loop
       print (grade_book[i].name)
       Print_Project_Grades(grade_book[i].project_scores}
       i < i + 1
       exitif (i > CLASS_SIZE)
    endloop

endprocedure //Print_Class_Project_Grades
```

This combination of records and arrays allows us to take advantage of the power of arrays and loops while dealing with more complicated data structures. Example 5.32 shows the use of such a structure.

EXAMPLE 5.32   We would calculate and print a summary of class performance on the final exam by calling

```
Exam_Score_Summary(this_class)
```

where Exam_Score_Summary is

```
procedure Exam_Score_Summary (class_roll isoftype
                               in Class_Grades)
// Purpose: calculate then print entire summary data re:
// class performance on the final exam, including lowest score,
// highest score, and class average.

    min_score isoftype Num
    min_score <- 100

    max_score isoftype Num
    max_score <- 0

    sum_of_scores isoftype Num
    sum_of_scores <- 0

    i isoftype Num
    i <- 1

    loop
       sum_of_scores <- sum_of_scores + class_roll[i].exam_score

       if (class_roll[i].final_exam_score < min_score) then
          min_score <- class_roll[i]_final_exam_score
       endif

       if (class_roll[i].final_exam_score > max_score) then
          max_score <- class_roll[i].final_exam_score
       endif

       exitif (i = CLASS_SIZE)
       i <- i + 1
    endloop

    average isoftype Num
    average <- sum_of_scores / CLASS_SIZE
```

```
print("The class average on the final exam is ", average)
print("The highest score is ", max_score)
print("The lowest score is ", min_score)

endprocedure //Exam_Score_Summary
```

5.15.3   Records of Records

Not only can we combine records and arrays in any combination, we can also achieve important benefits by creating records of records. In the previous section, we made the unreasonable assumption that classes would always have 100 students enrolled, no more, no less. Because there is no constant number of students for all classes, we would want a dynamic rather than static structure.

EXAMPLE 5.33   We might create the appropriate data structure by incorporating our `Student_Grade_Record` in the definition of the list node itself:

```
Student_Node definesa record
    data isoftype Student_Grade_Record
    next isoftype Ptr toa Student_Node
endrecord //Student_Node
```

This approach gives us a node that consists of a record with two fields, `data` and `next`, just as in our earlier linked list examples. What's different is that `data` is itself no longer a single `data` field but is now a record of `Student_Grade_Record`.

When constructing a data structure with multiple `data` fields, the principle of abstraction implies that it is best to encapsulate all the `data` fields inside a record, such that any pointers related to the data's storage in a data structure are not part of that record.

The reason for this construction is that there is an important, meaningful difference between the `data` fields and the `pointer` fields:

- The `data` fields represent some information about phenomena related to the logical task.
- Any pointers that are required to connect that data to a data structure are implementation details unrelated to the logical task itself.

Thus, the node record has two logical fields: one related to data representation and the other related to how we connect the nodes together. Encapsulating the `data` fields within a record, apart from the pointers, embodies this logical difference between the data itself and the data structure we use to store it.

In addition to supporting logical clarity, this kind of abstraction pays practical benefits. For example, it allows all the `data` fields to be passed between modules via a single record parameter, which is both logically superior and much more convenient than passing each and every `data` field as an individual parameter.

Suppose we are given such a linked list; for the class grades problem of the previous section we might calculate the number of students in the class by modifying our recursive traversal routine.

EXAMPLE 5.34 Because there is some final action to be taken upon reaching the end of the list (returning 0 to complete the final recursive call), we require the first of our two recursive templates:

```
function Enrollment returnsa Num(current_ptr isoftype
                                in Ptr toa Student_Grade_Record)
// Purpose: calculates and reports the number of students
// enrolled in the class

   roll_size isoftype Num
   roll_size <- 0

   if (current_ptr = NIL) then
      Enrollment returns 0
   else
      Enrollment returns (1 + Enrollment(current_ptr^.next))
   endif

endfunction //Enrollment
```

This routine might be initially called as follows:

```
class_size <- Enrollment(this_class)
```

In much the same way, if faced with very large enrollments, we can create the structure for a binary tree of students by changing the definition of our `Student_Node` as shown in the next example.

EXAMPLE 5.35 Instead of using a linear structure to organize student data, let's create a structure to support a binary search tree of students:

```
Student_Node definesa record
   data isoftype Student_Grade_Record
   left_child isoftype Ptr toa Student_Node
   right_child isoftype Ptr toa Student_Node
endrecord //Student_Node
```

By using a tree of such nodes, we might print out the roster of students by making use of a version of a recursive tree traversal:

```
procedure Print_Student_Names(current_ptr isoftype in
                              Ptr toa Student_Node)
// Purpose: perform inorder traversal of tree of student grade
// records to print out each student name

   if (current_ptr <> NIL) then
      Print_Student_Names(current_ptr^.left_child)
      print(current_ptr^.data.name)
```

```
        Print_Student_Names(current_ptr^.right_child)
    endif

endprocedure //Print_Student_Names
```

5.15.4 Arrays of Arrays

The arrays we've seen so far are all one-dimensional arrays. We can also declare and manipulate arrays of more than one dimension. For example, we can create a two-dimensional array (or *table*) by writing the declarations shown below.

Note: Just as it is permissible by convention to use the identifier i for an array index, so too is it convention to use the identifiers i and j for the indices of two-dimensional arrays.

```
DIMENSION_ONE is {some literal positive number}
DIMENSION_TWO is {some literal positive number}

This_Array_Type definesa array[1..DIMENSION_ONE] of num
That_Array_Type definesa array[1..DIMENSION_TWO] of This_Array_Type

two_d_array isoftype That_Array_Type
```

These declarations provide us with an array variable that is a *data table*. It is constructed by declaring an array of arrays. That is to say, each element of an array of type This_Array_Type. Thus, referencing two_d_array[3] accesses the third element of the table, which is itself an array of This_Array_Type. To access the seventh element of this array, we would write:

```
two_d_array[3][7]
```

How might we traverse this array? The next example illustrates a way.

EXAMPLE 5.36 To traverse a multi-dimensional array, we use *nested loops* (i.e., multiple loops nested one inside the other). Thus,

```
procedure Traverse_2D (array_2d isoftype in That_Array_Type)
// Purpose: traverse 2D array of nums, printing out each
// value in turn

    i isoftype Num
    i <- 1

    j isoftype Num
    loop
        j <- 1
        loop
            print(array_2d[i][j])
            j <- j + 1
            exitif (J > DIMENSION_ONE)
        endloop
```

```
        i <- i + 1
        exitif (i > DIMENSION_TWO)
     endloop

   endprocedure  //Traverse_2D
```

This traversal, which prints each array element, starts at element `array_2d[1][1]`, then moves on to `array_2d[1][2]`, and so on. Once j becomes greater than the maximum index of the first array dimension, the inner loop is exited, and the outer loop continues (i.e., i is incremented). Then the outer loop (and hence also the inner loop) is repeated, with j starting over at 1. So, on the second pass through, we traverse `array_2d[2][1]`, then `array_2d[2][2]`, etc. The entire traversal is finished when (i >DIMENSION_TWO) and (j >DIMENSION_ONE).

For higher-dimension arrays we would need more levels of nesting. The rule is that one nested loop is required for each dimension of the array that is to be traversed. For example, if you want to traverse a three-dimensional array, you will need three nested loops.

Dynamic Allocation Is Everywhere

The *dynamic allocation* of memory allows us to write algorithms without deciding in advance how much of our space resources we devote to any data structure. This permits our algorithms to use as much memory as needed at a given moment and then *deallocate* it when it is no longer needed.

As a general principle, dynamic allocation is being used in ways that have nothing to do with computer programming. Modern manufacturing companies no longer want to commit resources in a static way to making a given product. Instead they want flexible manufacturing facilities. For example, automobile manufacturers want to be able to switch their production facilities over to whatever the hottest selling model is. This is far more efficient than the conventional static allocation of production resources. Why have one plant idle just because it makes a slow seller, while another plant is constantly running overtime? The benefits of dynamically allocating production capability are obvious.

We also see the principle of dynamic allocation being applied in the human arena. There is a growing trend toward using temporary employees in jobs that have traditionally been filled by permanent workers for the same reason that we don't want to declare an array of 1000 cells if we might only need to store 40 pieces of data. Companies don't want unskilled workers, but they do want the freedom to bring workers on as they need them and to let them go when they don't. Temporary workers can be hired and fired much more easily and cheaply than can permanent employees and thus offer the same advantages that linked lists offer over arrays.

Before you assume that it's just hard-hearted capitalists who desire dynamic allocation, consider that it's a pervasive theme throughout our society. Until recently, marriages and families were statically allocated. Once a couple was married, they were expected by society to stay that way, and the question of whether or not they were happy together didn't really matter much. Similarly, the normal career path of recent generations was static: Take a job and "gut it out" until retirement. The question of "satisfaction with my job" just didn't come up very often.

All in all, for better or worse, dynamic allocation goes hand in hand with freedom of choice, and both the benefits and costs of that freedom come with the territory. Regardless of the opinion that each of us might hold, it is clear that our society formerly used a static allocation approach (encouraging stability at the cost of personal satisfaction) and that it now supports dynamic allocation (encouraging personal satisfaction at the cost of stability).

This may prove to be one of the more significant evolutionary challenges of modern times because people have never before had to deal very much with choice. This is because there wasn't much of it around. Compared to us, people from previous eras largely had no choice about their jobs, where they lived, or how they lived. The college students of today are the first generation that have spent their *entire lives* inundated with it. "What do I want to do?," "Where do I want to live?," "Do I want to have children or not?" Questions such as these are of the utmost importance to everyone's lives, and surely very few would want to have others imposing answers on us. But these are largely new questions, ones that your grandfathers and grandmothers probably didn't spend much time wrestling with.

This freedom to choose, this freedom to make life choices that are dynamic, not static, is a new phenomenon in human history. And, like most new things, it is evidently both a blessing and a curse because these questions about our own happiness and satisfaction are precisely the things that help contribute to our unhappiness and dissatisfaction. Yet there is no avoiding them. They are part of modern times. How does it feel to be dynamically allocated?

SUMMARY

The goal of *data abstraction* is to allow the logical grouping of related data and to separate the means of naming and using data from the low level details of how that data is organized. Well-designed data structures feature high levels of data abstraction, which is accomplished via extensive use of user-defined data types and constants. Such structures allow significant modifications to an algorithm's data structures via just a few changes to constants and data types. They also pay big dividends in allowing algorithms to be updated easily and cheaply.

Data structures can be designed and created to fit the data requirements of any particular problem. They can take the form of *static* structures (*arrays*) or of *dynamic* structures (i.e., *linked lists, trees,* and *graphs)*.

Linked Lists

Linked lists allow us to collect a list of data that is *dynamic* (i.e., we can change the size of the list at will), and we can rearrange the nodes of the list however we might wish to. Linked lists have the advantage of always being the correct size for the data at hand. The price paid for this is the memory required to store a pointer field for each node in the list. Linked lists also present the disadvantage of requiring traversals to locate data. There is no random access possible with a linked list, and thus we have to examine many items in the list before finding the one we want.

Binary Trees

Binary trees give us all the advantages and many of the disadvantages of linked lists, with two differences:

- They require slightly more space than do linked lists since each node requires space for two pointer fields, not one.
- If they are implemented as a binary search tree, they can be significantly better than linked lists with respect to the time cost of a search: They are not linear in nature and thus far fewer nodes must be examined before we can locate the one for which we are searching. This benefit is obtained only if the binary search tree is full and balanced, or nearly so.

Arrays

Arrays provide a static way to collect lists of data under a single name. We have to declare the size of an array at the very beginning of our algorithm. This means that we have to know in advance how many cells we will need. Sometimes, it is not possible to know this in advance. In such circumstances, arrays are not the best choice. Arrays also require that we plan for *the maximum possible size,* because an array is static (i.e., we cannot change the size of the array as we go along). This can be very wasteful because our array may occasionally be full but often may be nearly empty. This is not a problem on paper, but it used to be a significant problem in computer programming.

The primary advantage of arrays is that they provide a space saving mechanism that supports random access to each element, thus providing easier access than the sequential pointer navigation required by linked structures. Thus, for problems related to fixed-size lists, arrays are often the best structure.

Iteration

Iteration provides an alternative means of repetition to recursion. Logically, they are equivalent, and anything that can be done with one can be done with the other. As a practical matter, iteration is superior to recursion in two respects:

- It is slightly faster since it does not involve recursion's minor time costs of pushing and popping frames off the stack.
- It requires less available memory. Unlike recursion, a loop executes without requiring a stack frame for each recursive call. Should a very large number of repetitions be required, recursion can exhaust the supply of memory, causing failure. Iteration does not present this risk.

Iteration is inferior to recursion in two respects:

- It does not provide the opportunity that recursion provides: With iteration, we cannot automatically exploit the execution stack to temporarily store certain values that can be retrieved later for building partial solutions. Thus, for problems (such as tree traversals) that require that we maintain a series of temporary data or pointer values for future use, iterative solutions can be much more complex.
- Iterative solutions are sometimes "less clean" than are recursive solutions. They require various implementation-related elements such as `loop`, `exitif`, `end-loop`, explicit counter assignments, etc., which can clutter the solution and make it more difficult to quickly understand.

No one data structure is best for all circumstances and thus data structures must be designed to fit the needs of the problem at hand. Often, the best structure is one that is constructed from a combination of complex types. Similarly, neither form of repetition is best, and the preferred one for a given task must be determined based on the problem at hand and the data structure being utilized.

EXERCISES

5.1 Declare a record type called `Class_Grade` that will hold the following information about a students grade in a class:

- Lab average (a number).
- Homework average (a number).
- Quiz average (a number).
- Whether or not current grade is passing (a boolean).

5.2 Create a procedure that will read in (from the user) the information for a record of the type declared in the previous problem and pass that information out of the procedure via a single parameter. For the boolean field in the record, read in a character (Y or N) from the user and then determine whether to assign TRUE or FALSE to the boolean. The procedure should prompt the user as appropriate.

5.3 Create a module that will collect this data for the class as a whole, keeping track of the class average for each of labs, homeworks, and quizzes and maintaining a running total of the number of students who report themselves to be passing or failing. Thus, whenever this module is called, it will accept data for a student and will update the summary data for the class to include the data for the student. Create any additional data structures required.

5.4 Create a recursive module that will accept a pointer to a linked list of numbers and will return the sum of the numeric values in the linked list.

5.5 Create a recursive module that will accept a pointer to a linked list of numbers and will return a count of the numbers that are multiples of 3.

5.6 Create a module that will traverse a linked list of numbers and insert a new node with the value 32 immediately after the first node that holds a value greater than 10. If no such node is found, the module should terminate without doing anything.

5.7 Create a recursive module that will traverse a linked list of numbers and insert a new node with the value 32 immediately after the last node that holds a value greater than 10. If no such node is found, the module should terminate without doing anything.

5.8 Create a recursive module that will accept a pointer to a linked list of numbers and will delete the last node in a nonempty linked list.

5.9 Create a recursive module that will accept a pointer to a linked list of numbers and will delete all odd numbers from that list.

5.10 Create a recursive module that will accept a pointer to a linked list of numbers and will delete all odd numbers from the end of the list (i.e., it will guarantee that, upon completion, the last item in the list is the last even number that was in the original list).

A string is an ordered list of characters. For Exercises 5.11 through 5.15, pretend that our language does not provide the built-in data type String, and therefore you must implement the "string abstraction" yourself.

5.11 Declare the data structure(s) necessary for a linked list implementation of a string.

5.12 Write a recursive module called Read_String that will accept a pointer to a string and will add characters to the end of the string. It will continuously read in new characters and append them to the string. When it encounters a period (.), it will terminate.

5.13 Write a recursive module called Print_String that will take in a pointer to a string and will simply print out the contents of the string.

5.14 Write a recursive module Print_String_Backward that will behave just as the module from the previous problem except that it will print characters in reverse order, from the end of the string to the beginning. Use a recursive module that exploits the stack to do this. Do not build another copy of the string that stores the values in reverse order.

5.15 Do the same task as in Exercise 5.14 but use iteration, not recursion. This time, you may obtain items from one string and build another list that stores them in reverse order. Once this has been accomplished, Print_String from Exercise

5.13 should be able to print the new list, effectively printing the original string in reverse order.

5.16 A palindrome is a word that is spelled the same forward and backward (e.g., dad, mom, sis, madam, toot and kook are palindromes). Use the structures and modules you developed in Exercises 5.11 through 5.15 to create an algorithm that detects if a character string is a palindrome. Do not rewrite the modules that you wrote for those problems, but call them as needed from this algorithm. Your algorithm will:

- Read in a character string (as in Exercise 5.12).
- Traverse the resulting string, reading each character in it, and copying each character into a reversed string (as in Exercise 5.15).
- After creating the two strings, traverse both strings, comparing each character, until it has determined if the original stored is a palindrome.

Exercises 5.17 through 5.20 refer to the binary tree shown in Fig. 5.26.

5.17 Is this tree a binary search tree? Why or why not?

5.18 What is the output of an inorder traversal of the tree?

5.19 What is the output of a preorder traversal of the tree?

5.20 What is the output of a postorder traversal of the tree?

5.21 Draw the binary search tree that would result if we started with an empty tree (root = NIL) and added the following numbers in the order given below:

```
7, 4, 8, 10, 2, 3, 9, 23, 20, 18, 12, 1
```

5.22 Create a module that will determine the largest value in a binary tree of numbers (*not* a binary search tree). Declare any necessary data structures including the binary tree itself. The module will be passed the root of the tree as a parameter and will return the largest value found in the tree. If the tree is empty, return 0 as the maximum value in the tree.

5.23 Create a module that will locate the largest value stored in a binary search tree of numbers.

5.24 Create a module or modules to traverse a binary tree of numbers and compute the average of the values stored in it.

5.25 Create a module or modules to traverse a linked list of numbers and compute the sum of numbers stored in it, using iteration not recursion.

5.26 Create an iterative (i.e., loop controlled) module that will search for a given target value in a BST of numbers.

5.27 Given the following type definition, where MAX is a positive numerical constant that has already been defined,

```
Num_Array_Type definesa array [1..MAX] of Num
```

write a module that will receive, via a parameter, an array called input_array of type Num_Array_Type and, using loops, will return the index of the smallest element in the array.

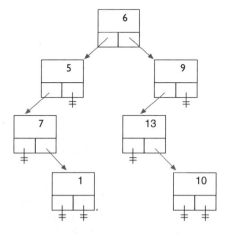

FIGURE 5.26 Tree for problems 5.17 through 5.20

5.28 Use an array to implement a *stack* of numbers. Items may only be pushed and popped to and from the top of the stack. Create modules for Push, Pop, IsFull, and IsEmpty.

5.29 Use an array to implement a *queue* of numbers. The idea of a queue is embodied in any waiting line (e.g., checking out at the grocery store). A queue is a first in, first out list. Items may be added (or *enqueued*) only at the end of the queue and may be processed and removed (or *dequeued*) only from the head of the queue. Since items come and go from the queue, you will be faced with the "wraparound" problem: Instead of relocating any values within the queue, use the MOD operation to handle the wraparound. Create modules for Enqueue, Dequeue, IsFull, and IsEmpty.

5.30 Create a different Enqueue module for your queue (Exercise 5.29) such that it's now a *priority queue*. A priority queue is a first in, first out queue in every respect except one: Items are not always added at the end of the queue. Instead, items are inserted into a priority queue at a position that is based on their priority: The higher their priority, the closer to the front of the line they get.

5.31 Write a procedure that will convert an array of numbers to a linked list of numbers. This procedure should have two parameters: a pointer to the head of the linked list and an array. Use a loop in your answer. Do not use recursion. Assume that the array is already full of numbers—you don't need to read them in. Declare any necessary data types you need to solve this exercise.

5.32 Create a module that will take in an array of numbers and create a BST of the same numbers.

Many of the exercises below build on the answers to others. Be sure to exploit this fact. Reuse your answers to one question if they will help you answer another question. In such cases, do *not* rewrite your code; refer to any previously written module by calling it with appropriate parameters.

5.33 Design a record type Student_Transcript, including fields for

```
Name, Address, Phone, SS#, Major, Class, GPA, and
Academic_Record (a pointer to a linked lists of Terms)
```

5.34 Design a data structure, Academic_Record, for student academic performance data, consisting of a linked list of Terms, with each term having a term_identifier (e.g., fall_95), a term_gpa, and a course_list. The course list should include the courses taken for a given term, including course number, course name, professor, credit hours, and course grade.

5.35 Design a data structure to hold the data for the Student_Body. It should consist of a BST of Student_Transcript with student data organized by student social security number.

5.36 Create a module that will examine the Academic_Record for a given student and determine if that student has ever taken 20 or more credit hours in a single term.

5.37 Create a module that will traverse a Student_Body BST and create a list of social security numbers of all students who have taken 20 or more credit hours in any single term. Students should be inserted into the list in ascending order based on their GPA.

5.38 Create a module to traverse a Student_Body BST and create a list of all Majors together with the effective GPA of each (e.g., total quality points earned by computer science majors divided by total hours taken by computer science majors).

5.39 Create a module to traverse a Student_Body BST and collect data on the grades assigned by a given professor. That is, what is the effective GPA of students in courses taught by that professor?

5.40 Create the necessary data structures and algorithms to create and maintain inventory at a chain of five movie rental stores. Each store will have some number of movie titles. For each title, each store may have zero or more copies. Each copy will always have the status of either rented, in stock, or overdue. Create the data structures and algorithms necessary to support the following transactions:

- At which stores is a copy of a movie in stock?
- How many copies are checked out versus in stock?
- Check out a movie to a customer and update appropriate data.
- Check a movie back in when a customer returns it, updating the appropriate data.
- Print a list of movies that are overdue.

Implement a solution using whatever combination of data structures is best suited for the task. Do not worry about manipulating dates or days. Assume that that is done "by magic." Create a solution that does only what is specified.

CHAPTER 6

Algorithmic Methods

In many ways, algorithms are like buildings: they require plenty of planning in the design process, they are made from fundamental building blocks (instructions and data, decisions, control structures, and abstractions of various kinds instead of bricks, pipes, and wires), and each is designed to fulfill a very specific function. This chapter will deal with the algorithmic methods that are used to fulfill common functional needs.

The choice of the algorithmic method is very important since it influences the efficiency of the algorithm in solving the problem, the amount of computer resources that will be required, and the difficulty of writing the algorithm. In fact, there have been cases where a problem harried scientists for generations until some daring soul tried a different algorithmic method and showed the solution to be practically trivial using that approach.

You will find that writing algorithms is not a cut-and-dried task by any means. It often takes a good measure of creativity and ingenuity, and it appears to be more of an art than a science. In this chapter, we'll explore five particular algorithmic methods that are commonly used for various kinds of problems: *traversing, searching, sorting, divide and conquer,* and *optimization.* Consider them as tools to help in the design of problem-solving processes.

6.1   Traversals

Traversals are ways of accessing data contained in structures such as arrays, linked lists, trees, and graphs. They are among the most widely used algorithmic methods. We saw several examples of them in the previous chapter.

Definition: To **traverse** a data structure means to step through the entire structure in an ordered fashion, displaying or acting upon each data element in turn.

Traversals must be tailored to the data structure that is being examined.

6.1.1   Traversals of Linear Structures

We saw several example of linear traversals in the previous chapter. In the four examples that follow we show traversals of linked lists and arrays via both iteration and recursion.

EXAMPLE 6.1   This procedure is a recursive implementation. A linked list is traversed and the numeric data value of each node is printed in turn.

```
procedure Traverse_List (current isoftype in Ptr toa List_Node)
// Purpose: recursive implementation of a traversal that visits
// each node in a linked list of numeric data values and prints
// out each value in turn.

  if (current <> NIL) then
     print(current^.data)
     Traverse_List(current^.next)
  endif

endprocedure // Traverse_List
```

EXAMPLE 6.2   This procedure is an iterative implementation. A linked list is traversed and the numeric data value of each node is printed in turn.

```
procedure Traverse_List (current isoftype in Ptr toa List_Node)
// Purpose: iterative implementation of a traversal that visits
// each node in a linked list of numeric data values and prints
// out each value in turn.

  loop
     exitif (current = NIL)
     print current^.data
     current <- current^.next
  endloop

endprocedure // Traverse_List
```

EXAMPLE 6.3   The following procedure is a recursive implementation of traversing an array, printing out the numeric data value of each element in turn.

```
procedure Traverse_Array(this_array isoftype in
                Some_Array_Type, i isoftype in Num)
// Purpose: recursive implementation of a traversal that
// visits each element in an array of numeric data values and
// prints out each value in turn. Assumes the first element
// is index 1, the last is index MAX_ARRAY, and initial call
// passes in i of value 1.

   if (i <= MAX_ARRAY) then
      print(this_array[i])
      Traverse_Array(this_array, i+1)
   endif

endprocedure // Traverse_Array
```

EXAMPLE 6.4   The following procedure is an iterative implementation of traversing an array, printing out the numeric data value of each element in turn.

```
procedure Traverse_Array(this_array isoftype in Some_Array_Type)
// Purpose: iterative implementation of a traversal that
// visits each element in an array of numeric data values and
// prints out each value in turn. Assumes the first element
// is index 1, the last is index MAX_ARRAY.

   i isoftype Num
   i <- 1
   loop
       exitif (i > MAX_ARRAY)
       print(this_array[i])
       i <- i + 1
   endloop

endprocedure // Traverse_Array
```

6.1.2   Traversals of Nonlinear Structures

In the previous chapter, we saw three ways to traverse a binary tree: *preorder, inorder,* and *postorder.* Inorder traversal of binary trees was covered in some depth and, in practice, is implemented recursively, as are preorder and postorder traversals.

While preorder, inorder and postorder traversal each visit the nodes of a given in a different order, all three share a trait: they moved through the tree in an up-and-down fashion. They repeatedly follow left child pointers until such time as they reach a NIL pointer "at the bottom" before they consider any of the right children. Thus, the left side of the tree is traversed before the right side.

Definition: Preorder, inorder, and postorder traversals are called **depth-first** traversals because they go "as deep as they can" before they move side to side.

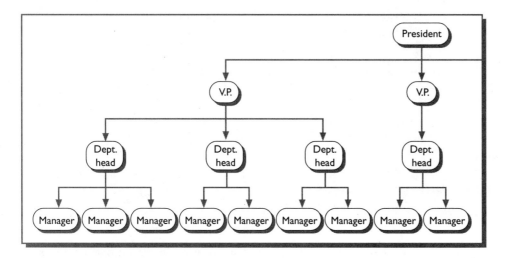

FIGURE 6.1   Graph showing operational management hierarchy

Definition: An alternative means of traversing a tree or graph is via a **breadth-first** traversal. As its name suggests, a breadth-first traversal visits nodes in a side-to-side fashion before it moves up and down in the tree. At each level of depth, it considers each node in left-to-right sequence before considering any of their children.

For example, consider the graph shown in Fig. 6.1. It shows the left portion of the hierarchy chart for the operational management of a company. At the top level is the company president. At the next level are some number of vice presidents. Under each vice president are some number of department heads, under each department head are some number of managers, and under each manager are some number of employees. Because bottom-level employees presumably have no management responsibilities, they are not shown in this graph. In effect, the graph is a tree with each node having an unpredictable number of children.

Assume that we are given this graph and imagine that we want to produce a listing of employees by their rank in the organization. To do this, we would not want to perform a depth-first traversal, as that would cause us to visit various department heads before we visited all the vice presidents, and to visit some managers before we visit all the department heads. Instead, we want to somehow move sideways through the chart, visiting all the nodes at a given level of depth before going down to another level of depth.

To accomplish this requires that we have some means for moving side to side despite the fact that we have no pointers that give us side-to-side linkages. All we have are parent-child links, and we must exploit these to manage a breadth-first traversal.

This circumstance is somewhat analogous to the situation we faced in implementing a depth-first traversal. Then, as now, we had pointers that gave us a means to move downward only. In performing a depth-first traversal, we were able to move both down and up by exploiting a *stack* to keep track not only of where we are but also of to which node we return when it's time to go back to the current node's parent. In depth-first traversals, when we visit a node's child, a frame is pushed onto the stack; when we are finished with a given node, its frame is popped off the stack, and we return to its parent whose stack frame is immediately underneath.

In performing a breadth-first traversal, we require something similar: a data structure that will support our efforts to go side to side instead of up and down.

6.1.3 Stacks and Queues

In the previous chapter, we saw that recursion relies upon, and derives its power from, the stack that is automatically used by a computer as it keeps track of procedure and function calls. This "automatic" stack is known as the *activation stack,* because it comes into play as each module is activated by a call. The idea of a stack is broader than the activation stack, however. In fact, one can create a stack by choosing an appropriate data structure (linked list or array) and writing the modules to perform the relevant push and pop operations. Thus, an algorithm can create and use one or more of its own stacks as appropriate to the problem at hand.

As mentioned in the exercises at the end of the previous chapter, there is another logical data structure that is somewhat similar to a stack; it is called a *queue.*

Definition: A **queue** is a specialized kind of list that features first-in, first-out (FIFO) behavior. Any items removed from a queue ("dequeued") may only be removed from the front. Any items added to a queue ("enqueued") may be added only at the rear.

Queues are ubiquitous in daily life. Examples may be found in check-out lines, waiting lists for tables in a restaurant, or any other "first come, first served" situation. The word itself is used much more frequently in British English than in the American variety. (To buy tickets for a movie, people in America "get in line," whereas people in Great Britain "queue up.")

In our context, a queue is complementary to a stack: A queue is FIFO, and a stack is LIFO (last in, first out). Both a queue and a stack are, first and foremost, ideas, that is, abstractions that we implement via appropriate use of data structures and modules. Unlike the *activation stack,* there is no "automatic queue" available to us, so any queues we use must be explicitly created with data structures and related modules.

At the level of the abstractions:

- *Stacks* have a top and a bottom. *Queues* have a front and a rear.
- For a stack, items are added only at the top via a push operation and are removed only from the top via a pop operation.
- For a queue, items are added only at the rear via an enqueue operation and are removed only from the front via a dequeue operation.

- No other operations that change the state of the abstraction are permitted. The *only* ways to change the data state of a stack are push and pop. The *only* ways to change the state of a queue are enqueue and dequeue.
- Certain information about the data state may be examined without changing the state. This information might be a count of items in the structure, a determination as to whether the structure is empty or full, and the value of the next data item available from the structure (the item at the top of a stack or the front of a queue).

At the level of implementation:

- Both stacks and queues may be implemented in *linked lists* or in *arrays*.
- To satisfy the definitions of stack and queue, the implementation must be constrained. We can do more things to linked lists and arrays than just add and remove data from the appropriate end of the data structure, but to have a stack or a queue we may modify the state of the data structure *only* via the specified operations (push/pop or enqueue/dequeue).
- *To implement a stack in a linked list,* we require only a single pointer, analogous to list_head, to keep track of stack_top. Items are both added to and removed from the top of the stack, so stack_top is the only point of access required.
- *To implement a queue in a linked list,* we benefit from maintaining two pointers, one at the front (analogous to list_head) and another at the rear. While we can get by with only a single front pointer, the fact that we always add to the rear of a queue means that also maintaining a rear pointer (to tell us where to enqueue the next item) saves the work of traversing to the end of the queue each time we do an enqueue operation.
- *To implement a queue or a stack in an array,* we use simple Num variables to do the job that pointers do in the linked implementation; we use them to tell us the indices into the array where the next enqueue and dequeue will occur.
- Using arrays also means that we must deal with *wrap-around*. This is solely an implementation issue that has nothing to do with the ideas of queues or stacks. The nature of this problem and its solution for a queue is discussed in Example 6.5, below. The same issue applies to an array-based stack.

Let's consider a real-life situation as an analogy. When people are in a queue (e.g., waiting in line to buy movie tickets), each time a dequeue occurs (e.g., when somebody purchases a ticket and moves on), the entire queue "moves up." However, suppose we are maintaining a queue in an array. We don't want to move each item in the queue every time a dequeue occurs. If there were 100 items in the queue and one was dequeued, moving the queue itself would require moving each of the remaining 99 data items up one position. For example, the data from index 2 would be copied to index 1, the data from index 3 copied to index 2, and so on, for each and every data item in the queue.

Instead, we can accomplish the same thing while saving a great deal of work by leaving the data items where they are in the array and simply changing the array index that refers to the front of the queue. Thus, for a queue of 100 items with the front of the queue at index 1, a `dequeue` requires only that we change the index value stored in the Num variable `front` from 1 to 2. Thereafter, the `front` of the queue will be at position 2, not position 1. The next `dequeue` will cause the `front` of the queue to become index 3, and so on.

This approach works well and is efficient, but it presents one problem. Over some number of enqueues and dequeues, the queue itself gradually moves to the right in the array data structure. Sooner or later, enqueues will cause the queue to stretch to the right end of the array, where it will "run out of room." At the same time, any dequeues will have created unused locations at the left end of the array. When this happens, we need some way to allow the queue to wrap-around from the right end to the unused spaces at the left of the array, as in Example 6.5.

EXAMPLE 6.5   How does wrap-around work in the case of items in the queue discussed above? (For the sake of brevity, we shall limit our example to a queue of eight items instead.)

After several `enqueues`, the queue will look like

1 2 3 4 5 6 7 8

queue | 15 | 81 | 12 | 78 | 31 | 64 | 28 | | front | 1 | rear | 8 | count | 7 |

Observe that the front index is logically a pointer that tells us where the next dequeued value is to be found. The rear index "points to" the location where the next enqueued item will be stored.

After a `dequeue`, the queue will look like

1 2 3 4 5 6 7 8

queue | 15 | 81 | 12 | 78 | 31 | 64 | 28 | | front | 2 | rear | 8 | count | 6 |

Logically, the `dequeue` removes the value 15 from the queue. However, it is not necessary to explicitly write over it in the array. Simply by changing the value of the `front` index, the value stored in the first array element becomes irrelevant, as the `front` and `rear` indices indicate that the location at index 1 is unused.

After another `dequeue`, the queue will look like

1 2 3 4 5 6 7 8

queue | 15 | 81 | 12 | 78 | 31 | 64 | 28 | | front | 3 | rear | 8 | count | 5 |

Logically, the elements at indices 1 and 2 are free. While they still have old, dequeued values stored in them, the `front` and `rear` indices indicate that the queue occupies locations 3 through 7, leaving elements 8, 1, and 2 free for use.

The next `enqueue` results in wrap-around. If we enqueue the value 34, it will be stored in the next available position, index 8. Because we maintain the rear index to always tell us where the next item will be enqueued, after we add the new value we must update rear, changing its value from index 8 to the index 1, giving us

```
        1  2  3  4  5  6  7  8
queue  15 81 12 78 31 64 28 34   front  3   rear  1   count  6
```

Thus, the queue begins at index 3 and continues to the end of the array at position QUEUE_SIZE (a constant equivalent to MAX_ARRAY). The rear index wraps around to direct the next enqueue operation to index 1.

Another two enqueues, of values 22 and 19, respectively, give us

```
        1  2  3  4  5  6  7  8
queue  22 19 12 78 31 64 28 34   front  3   rear  3   count  8
```

The queue now stretches from the front at index 3, to the end at QUEUE_SIZE, and wraps around to the left of the array, continuing to index 2. At this point in time, the array (and therefore the queue) is full. No more enqueues can occur until one or more dequeues free some space.

Using wrap-around, we save a great deal of work because we need not move all queue items upon each dequeue. However, we need a practical way to handle wrap-around.

1. Each enqueue changes the rear index. Logically, after each insertion it is changed to

   ```
   rear <- rear + 1
   ```

   To handle wrap-around, we update the rear index using the instruction

   ```
   rear <- (rear MOD QUEUE_SIZE) + 1
   ```

   This modification will work for both wrap-around and non–wrap-around circumstances. The same logic is applied to dequeue's modification to the current front index.

2. Unlike a linked implementation, an array implementation is of fixed finite size and thus an array-based queue can become full. A numeric variable, perhaps called count, is used to maintain a count of the number of items in the queue. It allows us to distinguish between full and empty states. The queue is full if (count = QUEUE_SIZE).

   You may question why we need an explicit variable to keep a count of items in the queue. Without wrap-around, we can calculate the count of items in the queue via:

   ```
   count <- rear - front
   ```

If we have wrap-around, however, observe that the situation when

```
(front = rear)
```

is ambiguous. The two indices will be equal in two circumstances: when the queue is full and when it is empty. Thus, we maintain a count to allow us to distinguish between full and empty states.

6.1.4 Breadth-First Traversal

To achieve a breadth-first traversal, we make use of a queue as follows:

- Upon visiting a node in the tree, we `enqueue` pointers to that node's children onto the queue.
- When we finish with a node and must go on to the next one (in breadth-first order), we `dequeue` the next item from the front of the queue.

To illustrate this process, consider Example 6.6, below.

EXAMPLE 6.6   Imagine that you have identified an ancestor who lived a hundred years ago who was an advocate of "higher education for everybody." Because you know that talk is cheap, you're curious about whether this person and his descendants practiced what he preached. In particular, you've decided to investigate the question of who in his family actually went to college in each generation.

This problem naturally calls for a graph data structure, as each generation may have any number of children. For clarity of illustration we'll constrain the problem to a binary tree, simply to avoid the complication of manipulating two kinds of nodes and pointers as might be used to implement graphs. Thus, we'll arbitrarily assume that each person in the family tree can have at most two children.[1] This gives us a family tree that might look like that shown in Fig. 6.2, with the left child being the elder sibling and the right child being the younger. For the sake of brevity, we show only four generations in the diagram, but there might be any number of generations.

A visual inspection of this tree makes clear the systematic process we must engineer. First we consider the top level (`Joseph`), then the second level (`Robert` and `Mary`), then the third level (`Emily`, `Sarah`, `George`, and `Kate`), then the fourth level, and so on. Our traversal ends when we exhaust the tree.

To accomplish this traversal, we follow repetitively use the following logic:

```
if (<we have not examined every node in the tree>) then
    <process the current node as appropriate>
    <enqueue current node's children to the end of the queue>
    <dequeue a new current node from the front of the queue and repeat>
endif
```

---

1. See the description preceding Exercise 6.8 for an alternative data structure for handling an unpredictable number of children.

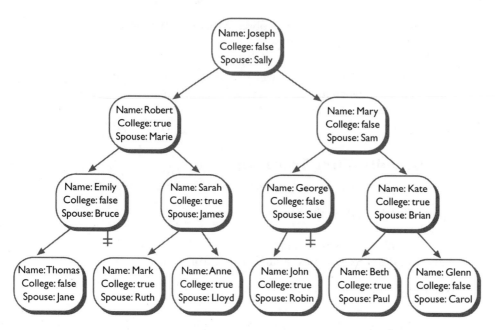

FIGURE 6.2 Breadth-first traversal example

For the problem at hand, the sequence of actions is as follows:

1. We examine the root, determine that `Joseph` did not go to college. Therefore, we do not print his name. We enqueue `Robert` and `Mary`. Thus, the queue contains

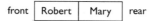

front | Robert | Mary | rear

2. We dequeue `Robert`, determine that he did go to college. We therefore print his name, then enqueue his children, `Emily` and `Sarah`. The queue now looks like

front | Mary | Emily | Sarah | rear

3. We dequeue `Mary`, determine that she did not attend college. We do not print her name. We do enqueue her children, `George` and `Kate`. This gives us the queue

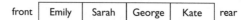

front | Emily | Sarah | George | Kate | rear

4. We dequeue `Emily`, determine that she did not enroll in college, so we don't print her name. We enqueue her child, `Thomas`. The state of the queue is now

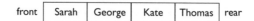

front | Sarah | George | Kate | Thomas | rear

5. We dequeue `Sarah`, determine that she did attend college, so we both print her name and enqueue her children, `Mark` and `Anne`. This gives us the queue

front | George | Kate | Thomas | Mark | Anne | rear

6. We dequeue `George`, determine that he didn't go to college, so we do not print his name. We enqueue his only child, `John`. The queue now looks like

front | Kate | Thomas | Mark | Anne | John | rear

7. We dequeue `Kate`, determine that she did go to college. We print her name and enqueue her children, `Beth` and `Glenn`, giving us the queue

front | George | Kate | Thomas | Mark | Anne | rear

At this point, we have finished traversing the top three levels of the tree in a breadth-first fashion. At this point, too, the queue contains pointers to all individuals of the fourth generation of the family (i.e., the fourth level of the tree).

We continue this process for the remainder of the family tree. The traversal ends as leaf nodes are dequeued from the queue without having enqueued any children on it. When the queue becomes empty, the traversal terminates.

6.1.5 Implementation of Breadth-First Traversal

Given that we can trace the process using pictures, how do we construct the algorithm to implement our logic? First, we assume the existence of modules that implement the enqueue and dequeue operations. Their construction is left as an exercise, based on our previous discussion of their operation. Then, we use those modules in constructing the breadth-first search module as shown in Example 6.7, below.

EXAMPLE 6.7 A breadth-first traversal of the family tree in Fig. 6.2 can be implemented by using a linked list queue implementation.

```
procedure Breadth_First_Traversal (tree_root isoftype in Ptr toa
                                    Family_Tree_Node
// Purpose: performs a breadth-first traversal of a binary tree of
// Family_Tree_Nodes.

    front isoftype Ptr toa Family_Tree_Node
    front <- NIL

    rear isoftype Ptr toa Family_Tree_Node
    rear <- NIL

    Enqueue(tree_root, front, rear)
```

```
          current isoftype Ptr toa Family_Tree_Node
          success isoftype Boolean
   loop
      Dequeue(current, front, rear, success)
      exitif (NOT(success))

      if (current^.data.college) then
         print(current^.data.name)
      endif

      // enqueue ptr to left child if there is one
      if (current^.left_child <> NIL) then
         Enqueue(current^.left_child, front, rear)
      endif

      // enqueue ptr to right child if there is one
      if (current^.right_child <> NIL) then
         Enqueue(current^.right_child, front, rear)
      endif

   endloop

 endprocedure //Breadth_First_Traversal
```

Example 6.7 shows how a complex abstraction (such as breadth-first traversal) can be implemented using simple, everyday ideas (such as a queue). Judging from the actual parameter lists for enqueue and dequeue, what assumptions have we made about the queue's implementation?

6.2 Searches

Definition: To **search** a data structure means to examine it to see if it contains a particular "target" value and, if so, to locate the value within the data structure.

6.2.1 Simple Search via Traversal

The simplest kind of search is merely a traversal in which each data element is compared with a desired "target" value. The traversal abruptly ends when the value is located or when the algorithm determines that the value is not there to be found.

Simple sequential searches of linked lists and arrays can be implemented by extending the traversals shown above. You can add:

- Another parameter by which the target value can be passed in.
- A second terminating condition (e.g., "stop traversal if the target value has been found").
- Appropriate actions based on the result of the transversal.

An appropriate action might be the printing of a message that communicates whether or not the target value was found, or it might be passing an appropriate out parameter that sends a pointer or an array index to the calling algorithm telling it the target value's location, or it might be some other response. What is appropriate is determined by the problem for which searching is required.

6.2.2   Key Fields

Typically, a data structure such as linked list, array, or tree will be used to organize data so that each element in that structure contains multiple data items. For example a list of `employee_records` might be organized so that each item in the list itself contains various data about a given employee. Of these various data fields, one will serve as the *key* field.

Definition: The **key field** provides the value that is used for organizing data records within a larger data structure.

For example, a data structure that stores data about a company's employees might have `employee_records` sorted by social security number, in which case employee `soc_sec_num` would be the key field. Thus, a sequential traversal of a linear structure, or an inorder traversal of a BST, would encounter employees in order by their social security numbers. If employee `name` were the key field, then those traversals would encounter employees in alphabetic order based on their names.

If the search is looking for a value of the key field, then it is generally not necessary to traverse the entire structure to determine if a value is absent. The ordering of values can provide information that allows a failed search to stop sooner. For example, if the last name `Taylor` was encountered while searching for `Smith` in a structure organized by `name`, then we can reason that we have passed the location for `Smith` without finding it. However, if we were searching for `Smith` in a structure that used `soc_sec_num` as the key, then we would have to traverse the entire structure to be sure that `Smith` was not there (the very last social security number might be that of `Smith`).

Thus, simple sequential searches for values of the key field are typically more efficient than are searches for values of nonkey fields to the extent that the search might fail. If the search is guaranteed to succeed (i.e., we know the target is there), we need only find it. Then there is no performance difference between searching for key values and other data via simple sequential searches.

6.2.3   More Efficient Searches

In addition, as we have seen, there are more efficient kinds of searches that do not require a sequential traversal. Such searches exploit the properties of a particular data structure, and how data are arranged within it, to accomplish a search without looking at each and every value in ordered sequence.

The prime examples of complex searches are the *binary searches* that can be performed on either a sorted array or a BST. In the case of a sorted array, binary search is accomplished by exploiting the random access to each element that arrays provide. In the case of a BST, binary search is accomplished by following a linear path from the root towards a leaf, exploiting the BST arrangement of values by making a series of left/right decisions. Binary search of a sorted array is left as an exercise. The following two examples show how searches of a BST are implemented recursively and iteratively.

EXAMPLE 6.8   Here we have a recursive search of a BST returning a pointer to the appropriate node. A `NIL` pointer is returned if the search fails.

```
BST_Search (current isoftype in Ptr toa Tree_Node,
                        target isoftype in Num,
                        location isoftype out Ptr toa Tree_Node)
// Purpose: search a BST for the target value, returns a
// pointer to the node containing that value. If the search
// fails, returns a NIL pointer.

    if ((current = NIL) OR (current^.data = target)) then
        location <- current
    elseif (current^.data > target) then
        BST_Search (current^.left_child, target, location)
    else //current^.data <= target
        BST_Search(current^.right_child, target, location)
    endif

end //BST_Search
```

EXAMPLE 6.9   Here we have an iterative search of a BST returning a pointer to the appropriate node. A `NIL` pointer is returned if the search fails.

```
BST_Search (current isoftype in Ptr toa Tree_Node,
                        target isoftype in Num,
                        location isoftype out Ptr toa Tree_Node)
// Purpose: search a BST for the target value, returns a pointer
// to the node containing that value. If the search fails, returns
// a NIL pointer.

    loop
        exitif ((current = NIL) OR (current^.data = target))
        if (current^.data > target) then
            current <- current^.left_child
        else //current^.data <= target
            current <- current^.right_child
        endif
    endloop

    location <- current

end //BST_Search
```

Observe that "from the outside" an algorithm using these procedures has no way to know whether the search is implemented recursively or iteratively. This is as it should be. Good abstraction means that the idea of a module (e.g., "searching a BST") should be independent of the implementation details (e.g., recursive or iterative solutions) encapsulated within the module.

Because such complex searches exploit the arrangement of values within the larger data structure, they can be performed only on values of the key field. We shall return to the various kinds of searches and traversals in a later chapter to consider their performance characteristics. Complex searches can reduce searching cost by an order of magnitude. If we are assuming a balanced BST or an ordered array, the search need only consider about log$n$ key values in a complex search, as opposed to an average of $n/2$ values for a simple search.

6.3 Sorting

Efficient searches require that the data be arranged in some sorted order. For BSTs, this sorting is performed upon insertion so that the proper relationship of each parent's value to that of its left (less-than parent) and right (greater-than parent) children is maintained. Similarly, linked lists and arrays can be constructed from scratch such that each value is inserted in the proper location, guaranteeing that the values are always in sorted order.

Sometimes a list of data already exists in nonsorted order. In such circumstances, we require some means of transforming an existing unsorted list into a sorted one to allow for efficient searches of that data. There are numerous algorithms for sorting data, some more efficient than others. The most obvious sorts tend to be inefficient, and the efficient ones tend to be more complex and less obvious.

We shall begin by introducing a simple and inefficient sort, Insertion Sort, and will see other varieties later in this chapter and beyond.

EXAMPLE 6.10 Anyone who has played card games has practiced one or more sorting algorithms. The simple process of arranging cards in hand is an example of `Insertion Sort`.

The idea is readily sensible: Pick up the cards, one at a time, and place each card in your hand at the appropriate location relative to any other cards that are already arranged in your hand. If we imagine a card game in which the suits of cards (i.e., spades, hearts, diamonds, clubs) do not matter, then arranging one's hand would be a simple matter of placing each card in the proper location based on the number of the card (with Jacks treated as the value 11, Queens as 12, and Kings as 13. Aces may be either 1 or 14, depending on the rules of the particular card game.).

In algorithmic terms, we can conceive of this situation as calling for a transformation from an unsorted list into a *priority queue* in which cards are placed in the queue at a location determined by their value.

Definition: A **priority queue** is a special kind of queue that features slightly different rules. In a priority queue, an `enqueue` operation does not always add new items to the `rear` of the queue. Instead, it insert each new item into the queue *as determined by its priority.*

An informal example of a priority queue is a school lunch line when the class bully pushes into the front of the line. According to the rules of a standard queue, he should have entered at the end of the line, but he uses intimidation to claim a higher priority and thus inserts himself towards the front.

Another example of a priority queue can be seen when people wait for tables at a crowded restaurant. Those who arrive without reservations go to the end of the queue (i.e., they have a low priority). Those who have made reservations have places closer to the front of the queue as determined by the time of their reservation (i.e., the earlier the reserved time, the higher their priority). Should someone arrive who is a celebrity or a VIP or a friend of the restaurant owner, that person's social status may result in the highest possible priority as they are whisked to the front of the queue for the next available table.

A third example is the mechanism by which jobs are sent to the printer in a college's computing center. Often, a college will rely on one or two printers to handle the bulk of the printing done by students and faculty alike. Since a printer is inherently a sequential device, it can only handle one print job at a time. As more and more students send files to the printer, the files are kept in a queue. This printer queue might be a standard queue or it might be a priority queue. Do you think that the college president's print job will wait in line for all student jobs to finish? Or do you expect that the administration will have a higher priority, allowing their jobs to go to the front of the queue?

In practice, then, the difference between a queue and a priority queue lies in two factors:

1. The recording of a priority for each item to be added to the queue.
2. An enqueue procedure that inserts new items in the queue at a location based on its priority.

The following example shows an implementation of Insertion_Sort that uses the ideas of queue and priority queue.

EXAMPLE 6.10   Suppose we have a card game in which suits do not matter and we wish to arrange the cards. Insertion_Sort can be implemented by repeating a two-step process for each card:

- *Grab a single card* from those dealt to you. You might treat the dealt cards as a stack from which you pop a card (taking the top most card from the stack of face-down dealt cards) or as a queue from which you dequeue a card (taking the cards in the order in which they were dealt).
- *Perform a priority enqueue* to add that card to your hand (placing it in the appropriate location relative to any cards already in your hand).

In this scenario, we ignore the suit of each card and treat the number of each card as the key for sorting.

In card games in which suits do matter, we may wish to arrange cards first by suit, so that all cards of a given suit are clustered together, then by number within each suit. In algorithmic terms, this means we are sorting, by both a *primary key* and a *secondary key*. The primary key would be the suit; upon encountering a card that was, say, a diamond, we would first traverse our hand until we located the first diamond. Once we have located a diamond, we would then insert the card relative to the other diamonds based on the secondary key, the card's number.

Implementations of `Insertion_Sort` may be done utilizing linked lists or arrays or even trees. They may be constructed to work on a single key, or on multiple keys. These implementations are left as exercises.

6.4 Divide and Conquer

Recall that binary search involves exploiting the organization of data to allow us to "throw away" half of the remaining data at each step. Each step reduces the remaining amount of work by approximately half. This idea—repeatedly cutting the problem in half—is used in an algorithmic method known as *divide and conquer*. Unlike binary search, which throws away irrelevant data each time, divide-and-conquer algorithms don't throw anything away. Instead, they repeatedly cut the size of the problem in half and solve for each half. Solving for each half means cutting each half in half again, in a recursive fashion. Eventually, the problem is broken down into small enough chunks that the solution to each chunk is trivial. Once the trivial solutions are found, these various partial results are then combined into the solution to the original problem.

Thus, divide and conquer is a useful strategy when a problem satisfies three criteria:

- The problem can be easily divided into subproblems that are smaller versions of the original, each one solvable by the same algorithm as the original.
- There is a terminating condition at which the subproblems are simple enough to be solved trivially.
- The solutions to the subproblems can be combined to form a solution for the original problem.

A divide-and-conquer algorithm performs the following three tasks:

1. It divides the problem into a number of subproblems that are smaller versions of the original problem. Usually, we divide each problem into two subproblems, each one requiring half the work of the original.
2. It then attacks each subproblem by recursively calling the divide-and-conquer algorithm to divide each subproblem again as in step 1. In other words, each subproblem is broken in two, then each of those subproblems are broken in two, and so on. The recursive calls end when the subproblem cannot be productively broken in two, that is, when each subproblem is small enough to be solved trivially. When each subproblem is small enough to be trivial, a solution to each one is found.
3. Then, the various subproblem solutions are combined into the solution of the original problem.

To illustrate the divide-and-conquer method, we'll describe the workings of the `Mergesort` algorithm. It is used to sort arrays of numbers efficiently. The three stages of `Mergesort` are

1. Divide the unsorted array into two halves. Now we have two subproblems that are one-half the size of the original problem.

2. Conquer the subproblems by calling the `Mergesort` algorithm recursively to divide each half-array into two arrays. This produces four subarrays, each one one-fourth the size of the original array. Recursive calls then divide each of those four arrays, producing eight arrays each of which is approximately one-eighth the size of the original, and so on. The recursive calls stop when each subarray contains only one element each and no more division is possible. The solution here is trivial because a one-element array is, by definition, already sorted.

3. With each one-element array sorted, the subproblem solutions are merged together according to the `Merge` algorithm given below.

Merging means combining two sorted arrays into one larger sorted array. It is very simple. It involves three arrays: the two sorted arrays you wish to merge and a third array into which the resulting larger sorted array is stored. Start at the beginning of each of the two smaller arrays and compare their first elements to each other. Remove the smaller element of the two and place it as the first element into the third array. Next, compare the first two *remaining* elements, remove the smaller one, and place it as the second element in the merged array. Continue the process until all elements have been placed in the merged array. When one of the two smaller arrays runs out of elements, simply place the remaining elements of the other array in their sorted order at the end of the merged array. By the end, the merged array is a sorted list combining all elements from the two smaller arrays. We illustrate the `Merge` algorithm in Example 6.12.

EXAMPLE 6.12   Given the two sorted subarrays shown below, we are to create a merged array by means of the merge algorithm. The first values of each subarray (5 and 3) are compared. The smaller gets copied to the merged array:

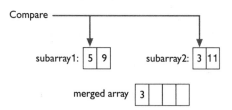

With the 3 copied into the merged array, we compare the smallest *remaining* values from each of the two arrays, 5 and 11. The smaller goes into the merged array:

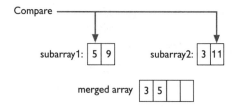

Now the 9 and the 11 are compared and the smaller is copied to the merged array:

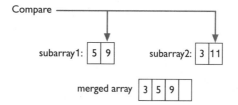

With the left subarray exhausted, the remainder of the right subarray is copied to the merged array, giving

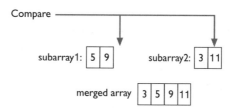

Now let's look at the `Mergesort` algorithm, which uses the `Merge` algorithm. We will need to pass an array into the `Mergesort` procedure. Since we want the array to be changed during the sort, we pass it as an `in/out` parameter. We will pass the entire array during each recursive call, and will also pass array indices that mark the beginning and end of the subarray to be sorted. These can be `in` parameters since we don't have any need to change the original values from which they have come. We can use the following `Mergesort` procedure:

```
procedure Mergesort (sort_array isoftype in/out Array_Type,
                     beginning, ending isoftype in Num)
// Purpose: Sort the array according to the standard
// Mergesort algorithm

   if (beginning < ending) then
      middle isoftype Num
      middle <- (beginning + ending) DIV 2
      Mergesort(sort_array, beginning, middle)
      Mergesort(sort_array, middle + 1, ending)
      Merge(sort_array, beginning, middle, ending)
   endif

endprocedure //Mergesort
```

The array is passed in via the formal parameter `sort_array`. The parameter `beginning` is the first index of the subarray to be sorted, `ending` is the last index of the subarray to be sorted, and `middle` represents the middle index. If `ending` is greater than `beginning`, we have more than one element in the array and should continue the recursive calls. Otherwise, nothing is done and the recursion stops. If continued recursion is called for, the index `middle` is calculated so that we can split the incoming subarray into two pieces. Then we recursively call `Mergesort` for the left and right halves of the array. When these halves have been sorted, we will merge them into a larger sorted array using a call to `Merge`.

FIGURE 6.3 The array is subdivided into its elements.

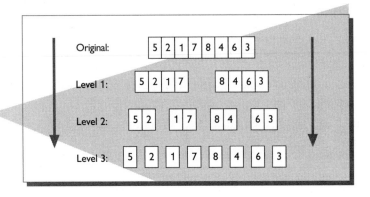

EXAMPLE 6.13 As an example of Mergesort, consider the following unsorted array:

$$sort\_array = \boxed{5\ 2\ 1\ 7\ 8\ 4\ 6\ 3}$$

We first call Mergesort(some_array, 1, MAX_ARRAY). Figure 6.3 shows the array as it is repeatedly divided. The level numbers indicate the level of recursion, and the arrow indicates the level of recursion is getting deeper and deeper.

Notice that each subarray above represents one recursive call. At the first level of recursion, we make two recursive calls—one each for the left and right halves of the initial array—thus creating two arrays of four elements each. At the second level of recursion, we make four recursive calls—one each for the left and right halves of both subarrays in the previous level—resulting in four subarrays of two elements each.

After the subarrays are one element large, we begin to merge them and return back through the recursive path. In Fig. 6.4, the upward arrow indicates that the algorithm is returning through the levels of recursion.

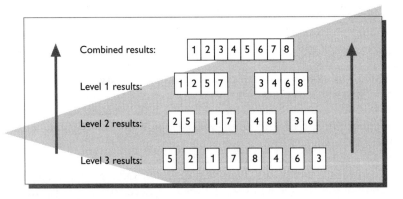

FIGURE 6.4 Sorting is achieved via merging

Given an array of size *n*, observe that at each level of recursion, all *n* items are processed. Thus, for each level of recursion, we do work proportional to *n*. Furthermore, observe that the *number of levels* of recursion is approximately log*n*. Thus, we have log*n* passes over the data with *n* work per pass. Therefore, we say that `Mergesort` requires work proportional to nlogn.

6.5   Optimization

Optimization problems are those in which the aim is to maximize or minimize a given value. Such problems are important to many people, and they arise in various circumstances. Each of the following questions signals an optimization problem.

- How can a delivery service cram the most packages into a truck?
- How can a manufacturing facility that produces several products get the most dollar value out the limited number of production hours?
- How can the phone company route phone calls to get the best use from its limited number of phone lines?
- How can a salesperson visit each of the various cities on a sales route but devote the least amount of travel time?
- How can a university schedule its classes to make the best use of classrooms with a minimum of class conflicts?
- How can a student get the highest grade point average from a specific number of study hours?

Obviously, there are many situations in which people want to optimize a solution. Unfortunately, as we shall see in later chapters, many easily expressed optimization problems have optimal solutions that cannot be computed in a reasonable time. For now, we are concerned with two basic approaches to solving such problems: *approximate solutions* (via "greedy algorithms") and *optimal solutions* (via "dynamic planning").

6.5.1   Greedy Algorithms

Imagine that you are led into a room filled with various piles of coins. Each pile contains coins of equal size but the coins have different values. One pile contains coins worth a dollar, another pile has coins worth a nickel, and so on. Imagine that you are told to fill your pockets with coins of your choice.

You would have no trouble figuring out what you wanted to do: You'd want to fill your pockets with coins of the highest value in order to maximize your gain. If you exhausted that pile, you'd then move to the pile with the next most valuable coins. After grabbing all the coins from that pile, you'd move to the pile of next most valuable coins, and so on, until your pockets were full.

In doing so, you would implicitly be executing a *greedy algorithm*: an algorithm that makes a series of quick "greedy" decisions.

Definition: A **greedy algorithm** attempts to achieve an optimal solution by first deciding how to obtain the greatest immediate gain. When that decision is carried out, it then makes another quick decision to obtain the next greatest gain, and so on. At no time does it evaluate the big picture of the problem it is attacking. Instead, it makes a series of short-sighted decisions.

The greedy method is quite simple and is easy to conceptualize. Hence, the natural instinct is to want to use it for all optimization problems. This is a dangerous instinct, however, because greedy algorithms do not produce optimal solutions for many optimization problems. To demonstrate, let's modify our coin example.

EXAMPLE 6.14   We are to fill our pocket with coins that are, again, of equal size. However, we add some conditions. We specify that only 860 grams of weight can be carried before our pocket breaks, and we specify the weight and value of the various kinds of coins. Here is a list of the coins' properties:

type	value	weight	value/weight
1	$6.00	500g	.0120 dollars/gram
2	$4.00	450g	.0088 dollars/gram
3	$3.00	410g	.0073 dollars/gram
4	$0.50	300g	.0017 dollars/gram

What would happen if we used a greedy algorithm to maximize the amount we carry out of the room?

Well, since we want to get the most value for every gram, we would choose the coin with the highest value/weight ratio on each grab. This means on the first grab we will choose a coin of type 1, worth $6. This uses 500g of our 860g limit, leaving only 360g. Of the remaining choices, the only viable one is to take type 4 coin, worth $0.50, for a total of $6.50. This is our final total, because we cannot pick up any more coins and still stay under the 860 gram limit.

Observe that this outcome is not the optimal solution. An optimal solution would specify that we grab a total of $7, by choosing a coin of type 2 on the first grab and one of type 3 on the second grab.

Warning: A greedy algorithm may or may not produce an optimal solution. A greedy algorithm's solution will be optimal only when we can optimize the final solution by individually optimizing each step without considering the implications upon other steps.

However, a greedy algorithm is often an appropriate solution even when it is not optimal. Why? The reason is that many optimization problems require immense amounts of algorithmic work to obtain an optimal solution. Sometimes the work is so great that it cannot be reasonably accomplished even with the fastest computer. Other times, the work may be "do-able" but simply not worth the trouble. For example, a freight company doesn't want to have to run a complex computer program that requires data about the size, shape, and weight of each and every package each time it packs a truck. In practice, a freight company will have its trucks packed and on the road before such a program could obtain all the required data and produce a result.

In such circumstances, a greedy algorithm can be used to produce an *approximate solution*. In other words, the solution may or may not produce the optimal result, but even if it doesn't, the result may be good enough and will likely be better than if we just used random guesses. We'll discuss these kinds of problems in a later chapter.

FIGURE 6.5 A graph show-
ing distances between cities

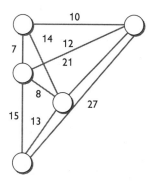

For now, let's look at a common application of the greedy method—its use in solving what is known as a *minimal spanning tree* problem.

EXAMPLE 6.15 Consider the problem of a contractor who needs to construct a telephone network spanning five cities. He is given the distance from every city to each of the other ones, and the only requirements are the following:

- Every city must be able to communicate with every other city.
- The construction must use the least amount of cable possible.

This is an optimization problem in which the amount of cable is minimized. The contractor does not need to connect each city to every other one directly. That would use too much cable and is not a necessary requirement. Instead, he needs to make sure that there is some path from each city to every other one. A given telephone call might not take the shortest conceivable path, but that doesn't matter. All that matters is that the phone company pays for the least amount of cable.

To solve the problem we use a greedy algorithm to decide which cities to connect with cable. We start with a network that contains no connections, choose the shortest available path, and add it to our network. Then on each later step, we choose the next shortest path that has been chosen from all the cities we have reached so far, and we add it—unless it will make a cycle in our network. We do not create cycles because they are inefficient; they add redundant connections between cities that are already linked to the network. Let's walk through an example using the cities and distances given in Fig. 6.5.

Figure 6.5 shows the five cities to be connected by a telephone network. The distances are marked beside each connecting edge. Figure 6.6 shows the steps of finding the network that connects all cities with a minimum investment in cable.

- In step a, we have chosen the shortest path possible (i.e., length 7) and have added it and the cities it connects to our network.
- In step b, we have chosen the next shortest path and added it to the network. Our choices included the paths of length 10 and 14, which emanate from the top city (or "node") in Fig. 6.5, and 12, 8, and 15, which emanate from the bottom node in Fig. 6.5. Of these, path 8 is the smallest, so select it and add the city to which it goes.
- In step c, we have done the same thing. The choices include the same ones as before, less the path of length 8, which has already been added. They also include the paths which emanate from the new node,

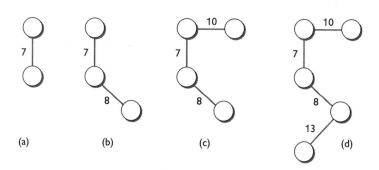

FIGURE 6.6 The steps of finding the optimal network

21, 13, and 14. The last of these was already among our choices (from the top-most node). Of these choices, the smallest path is length 10, so we choose it.

- In step d, we cannot add the shortest path (12) because it would complete a cycle between cities already connected to the network. Instead, we discard that choice and take the next shortest path, whose length is 13.

All cities are connected to the network and there is no need to add any more paths. Thus our solution is complete. Note that a person in any of the five cities can communicate with someone in any other city. Although communication may not be by the most direct route possible, we have used a greedy algorithm to achieve our goal of minimizing the amount of cable needed.

The greedy algorithm we used in Example 6.15 produces an optimal solution for minimal spanning tree problems. Observe that we can view the result as a linked list. A different problem might result in a tree-shaped solution. Also observe that the pertinent information consisted of a listing of the distance of all the possible edges between the nodes. Thus, an algorithmic solution to this problem might construct a linked list or tree and make its decisions based on values (edge distances and the names of the city on each end of each edge) stored in a table.

6.5.2 Dynamic Programming

Dynamic programming is a planning method. Its name has nothing to do with programming in the usual sense of the word. Thus, it may be less confusing if we refer to it as dynamic planning. Regardless of the name, the idea overcomes the weakness of a greedy algorithm approach.

Definition: Dynamic planning laboriously calculates all of the possible solution options, then chooses the best one. Thus, it produces *optimal* solutions, not *approximate* ones.

Fortunately, dynamic planning can be implemented via a recursive approach. Thus, the logic is simple; only the execution is laborious.

EXAMPLE 6.16   Consider the following problem. A traveler is trying to get from point A to point B by the shortest route. He doesn't care how many cities he encounters, only that his distance is minimized. This problem is known as the "weary traveler" problem. We will consider it using the graph of cities shown in Fig. 6.7.

Figure 6.7 shows an *acyclic directed graph*. It is a "directed graph" because each edge has a direction (i.e., is a "one-way street"). It is "acyclic" because, while the edges appear at first to create cycles, the directed nature of them makes it impossible to go around in circles.

Faced with the problem of finding the shortest route from A to B, we know what a greedy algorithm would do. Starting at point A, it would choose the shortest edge (i.e., the path to D). Once at D, it would again choose the shortest path (length of 6) and go to G (total travel so far is 9). Once at G, it would again select the shortest path (6) and go to B, the destination. Thus, a greedy algorithm will plan a route with a total distance of 15.

FIGURE 6.7 Graph showing cities and distances between them

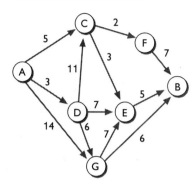

However, upon visual inspection, we can see that this solution is not optimal. A total distance of only 13 can be obtained by taking the route from A to C, then to E and on to B. The greedy algorithm misses this route because the path from A to C is not the shortest path leaving A.

However, a dynamic planning algorithm will discover the optimal path because it does not make any rash decisions. Instead, it considers all the possibilities in a recursive fashion. Given the problem at hand, a dynamic planning algorithm will initially decide only that the best path is the shortest one of its three initial choices: traveling from A to B via points C, D, and G. It knows that one of these routes will be best but doesn't know which one. What it does know is that

```
L(A) = Min((5 + L(C)), (14 + L(G)), (3 + L(D)))
```

where `L(N)` refers to the shortest path from `N` to the destination. As you can see, it makes use of a `Min` function that will reduce to the smallest of the values given.

In order to find the shortest path, it is necessary to know the values for `L(C)`, `L(G)`, and `L(D)`. To find out, the algorithm acts recursively to find the shortest path from each of C, D and G to B. Thus, it must calculate each of:

```
L(C) = Min((2 + L(F), (3 + L(E)))
L(D) = Min((11 + L(C)), (7 + L(E)), (6 + L(G)))
L(G) = Min((7 + L(E)), (6 + L(B)))
```

Once these values are found, they can be substituted in the `L(A)` expression and determine the solution. However, to solve these expressions, it is necessary to know the values of `L(F)`, `L(E)`, and `L(B)`. Thus, we must solve for:

```
L(F) = Min(7 + L(B))
L(E) = Min(5 + L(B))
L(B) = 0
```

Since `L(B)` is quite obviously 0, we can use this knowledge to solve both `L(E)` and `L(F)`:

```
L(F) = 7 via "F to B"
L(E) = 5 via "E to B"
```

We now have enough knowledge to solve `L(G)` and `L(C)`:

```
L(G) = Min((7 + L(E)), (6 + L(B)))
     = Min((7 + 5), (6 + 0))
     = 6 via "G to B
L(C) = Min((2 + L(F), (3 + L(E))) = Min((2 + 7), (3 + 5)
     = 8 via "C to E to B."
```

With `L(C)` and `L(G)` solved, we can now solve for `L(D)`:

```
L(D) = Min((11 + L(C)), (7 + L(E)), (6 + L(G)))
     = Min(((11 + 8), (7 + 5), (6 + 6))
     = 12 via "D to G to B."
```

We have now solved each component of the original expression and can now solve for
`L(A)`:

```
L(A) = Min((5 + L(C)), (14 + L(G)), (3 + L(D)))
     = Min((5 + 8), (14 + 6), (3 + 12)) = Min(13, 20, 15)
     = 13 via "A to C to E to B"
```

Dynamic planning is an example of divide-and-conquer thinking. The routing problem is broken down into each possible route segment. As the distance for each segment is evaluated, its value is stored in an appropriate data structure, then used in calculating the distances for larger route segments, those that pass through one or more points. Eventually, the values for all viable routes are compared, and the optimal one is chosen.

The Limit is Imagination

In 1945, Winston Churchill gave a speech in which he coined the phrase "Iron Curtain" to describe the virtual wall of isolation and control that was being placed by the Soviets around Eastern Europe. It may have been the most powerful *Mechanical Model* metaphor ever spoken. A decade later, U Thant, Secretary General of the United Nations, delivered a speech in which he proclaimed the dawning of a new age, an age which we can see in retrospect as being the Age of the Computational Model.

U Thant announced a watershed change in the very basis of human achievement. He saw that things were becoming fundamentally different in a very particular way. Throughout the entire history of human endeavor, he noted, humankind's accomplishment was limited by available physical resources. The question was always: "Given the material we've got, what can we make out of it?" U Thant announced that that era, an era that dated back to the first human beings, was over.

He was quite clear about the nature of the era that was replacing it. He announced that the essential feature of the New Age is that achievement would be limited primarily by our imagination. In the past people said: "This is what we've got, what can we do with it?" Now humankind would instead ask: "What do we want to create, and how do we invent what's necessary to do it?"

In the decades since U Thant's pronouncement, events have proven him correct. Currently humankind is, through computationally enabled science, going down the road of creation: creating plastic materials that will last for eternity, creating ways to select our own bodily shape and appearance, creating previously unimaginable ways to interact instantaneously with others around the earth, creating new genes to correct genetic flaws and, eventually, perhaps to shape and control the evolution of life itself.

It is difficult to deny the essential point of U Thant's message from 40 years ago: that human accomplishment is no longer governed by the physical properties of available raw materials; that it instead extends outward from our vision, our intention, our ability to conceive of what we want to create. We can make nearly anything we want. So, what do we want to make?

Now, we are engaged in exploring frontiers that are much more daring than putting a man on the moon. It's only a matter of time before the genetic code is mapped and manipulatable. It's only a matter of time before non–fossil-based energy is both safe and available. It's only a matter of time before the biochemical processes that help govern our thoughts and feelings are well understood.

The limit is our ability to get the right conception, to get the right idea, to have the needed insight. Given clarity about what problem we're attacking, we can invent the tools and processes to attack it. So what are the problems we want to attack?

Our own mental clarity is the main limitation of algorithmic power. Once we know what data structure we need to represent some aspect of reality, we can readily create exactly that data structure. Once we know the processing steps by which we wish to manipulate that representation, we can implement exactly those processing steps. Once we know what we're trying to do, we can do exactly what we want.

Algorithmic methods give us the power to manipulate our models, our ideas, our representations however we wish. Computing technologies give us the power to simulate, control, and experiment with whatever conceptions we might have. Within certain limits of complexity, the limitations of algorithms are not in the algorithms. The limitations are instead in our ability to properly envision what we're trying to do. We can implement any logic we want in an algorithm. So what logic do we want to implement? U Thant was right: The limitation of human accomplishment is no longer primarily in our *things,* it's in our *minds.*

SUMMARY

Algorithmic methods provide us with widely applicable solution strategies.

- *Searches* and *traversals* are required with great regularity and, depending on the data structure involved, both iterative and recursive solutions have their place.
- *Sorting* is essential to allow efficient searching of large data structures.
- *Divide-and-conquer strategies* often provide the most efficient and neat solutions to problems that can broken into discrete subproblems. These strategies are often recursive.
- *Greedy algorithms* provide an adequate optimal solution to some optimization problems and a useful "quick and dirty" approximate solution to others.

Depending on the particulars, greedy algorithms can be readily implemented iteratively or recursively.

■ *Dynamic programming* (or *dynamic planning*) provides a means of exhaustively considering all the options and producing the optimal solution to many optimization problems.

Algorithmic methods typically require the appropriate integration of data structures and algorithmic modules to act upon those structures. Thus, the algorithmic method consists of data abstractions that are *combined with* procedural abstractions to affect the data.

In the next chapter, we shall discuss means of encapsulating both data abstractions and relevant procedural abstractions together to create higher-level abstractions.

EXERCISES

6.1 Design and declare the data structures appropriate for storing employee information in a binary search tree. The following data must be stored for each employee: name, gender, social security number, date of hire (including month, date, and year), and salary.

For problems 6.2 through 6.6, create the procedural abstractions to perform the specified task on the binary search tree of employees of problem 6.1.

6.2 Create a module for constructing the tree from scratch. Each time the module is called, it adds an employee such that the tree is always sorted by employee social security number in ascending order.

6.3 Calculate the total payroll for the company.

6.4 Count the number of employees that were born before 1960.

6.5 Print out the employee roster of names and social security numbers such that the list is ordered by *descending* social security number.

6.6 Provide data to permit preliminary evaluation of the question "Is there gender equity in the salaries paid to company employees?" That is, calculate the average salary for male employees and the average salary for female employees. (*Hint:* encapsulate the variables needed to acquire relevant data into a single record that can then be passed as a single parameter.)

6.7 Think critically about the previous question. Does the data called for by problem 6.6 provide adequate information? What information is relevant that is not provided by the data specified in the problem? What relevant information could be readily represented as data in an extended employee record? Is there any relevant information that cannot be easily represented by data?

In Example 6.6, we arbitrarily constrained the family tree so that each parent could have at most two children. We can remove this restriction and still use a binary tree to represent the appropriate relationships among family members. To do so, we use the left child pointer of each node to represent a different kind of information than the right child:

- ■ The left child of a node points to the person's first child.
- ■ The right child of a node points to the person's next-oldest sibling.

Thus, by following left pointers we navigate from one generation to the next in a given subtree, while following the right pointers is equivalent to traversing a linked list of siblings. Stop now and sketch out this idea on paper with boxes and arrows so that you are sure you get the idea.

We refer to this idea in problems 6.8 through 6.12.

6.8 Design and declare the data structure needed to store information about an individual's descendants as described above. Data stored for each individual include name, birthday, gender, hair color, and eye color. Also, each record shall store that same data that are stored for that individual's spouse, if any.

- ■ If you design a "person data" record type properly, you will able to use it in declaring both the variables for each individual and his or her spouse.
- ■ If you designed the date data type you created in problem 6.1 appropriately, you will be able to reuse that type definition in declaring the birthday field.

6.9 Calculate the number of people in the family who have brown eyes.

6.10 Create modules as necessary to find an individual in the family tree, determine his or her eye color, and calculate the number of offspring that have the same eye color as the specified individual.

6.11 Do the same task as in problem 6.10, but this time find out how many children have the same eye color as the specified individual's spouse. (If you used appropriate abstraction in your solution for 6.10, you will be able to reuse one or more of the modules you created for 6.10 without changing them or redeclaring them.)

6.12 Create or reuse modules from previous problems, as necessary, to determine how many of a specified individual's cousins have the same eye color as that individual. *Hint:* You may think of this problem as having the following subproblems:

- ■ For the specified individual, determine his or her eye color and determine to which generation of the family that individual belongs.
- ■ Find the individual of that generation whose node is located at the leftmost position in the tree.
- ■ From that node, traverse that generation to determine how many individuals, other than specified individual and his or her siblings, have that eye color.

For problems 6.13 through 6.16, create algorithms that implement `Insertion_Sort` under the circumstances described in the problem.

6.13 An unsorted list of numbers is provided in a linked list. Traverse the linked list and copy the data value from each item in that list into the appropriate location in an another linked list such that the numbers are stored in ascending order.

6.14 Do the same task as in problem 6.13, but this time insert the values into an array. When you insert a given data value in the array, you will need to move data values already in the array to make room for subsequent elements. You may assume that the array is of sufficient size. You may find it convenient to maintain a counter that keeps track of how many values have been inserted into the array so far.

6.15 Do the same task as in problem 6.13, but this time assume that the original unsorted list is provided in an array. You may reuse portions of previous solutions as appropriate.

6.16 Do the same task as in problem 6.14, but this time assume that the original unsorted list is provided in an array. You may reuse portions of previous solutions as appropriate.

6.17 Solutions to problems 6.13 and 6.15 generate a sorted linked list of numbers. We now wish to print out the numbers in descending order. Create a recursive module that performs this task without requiring the construction of a new list.

6.18 Do the same task as in problem 6.17, but this time use iteration, not recursion. Construct your own stack, and perform pushes and pops as necessary to print out the values in descending order. Use a linked structure for your stack.

6.19 Do the same task as in problem 6.18, but this time use an array to implement your stack. (If you designed your solution to 6.18 with appropriate abstraction, you will be able to create new modules for push, pop, etc., then reuse much of your solution to 6.18 with minimal modification.)

6.20 In Example 6.12, we described the logic of the Merge operation. Construct a module that implements it.

6.21 In Example 6.13, we described the logic of the Mergesort algorithm. In Figs. 6.3 and 6.4, we showed graphic representations of the total work required by Mergesort. However, these figures do not show the sequence in which the various steps occur. Trace the execution of Mergesort on the data from Example 6.13 and make an ordered list of how many times Merge is called. For each call of Merge, specify which values are merged together.

Problems 6.22 and 6.23 each require that you implement a greedy algorithm. Your solution need not provide optimal solutions, but rather appropriate greedy approximate solutions.

6.22 Create a greedy algorithm that solves *bin-packing problems* such as the coins problem of Example 6.14 and other problems like it. Bin-packing problems have the following characteristics:
   a. There is limited capacity (e.g., how much can you carry, fit, spend, use up, or absorb that limits how much you can do). In our coins problem of Example 6.14, the limiting capacity was 860 grams.

b. There are several kinds of items, such that each item has a value (profit), and a cost (how much of the limited capacity is used up by each item of that kind). In our coins example, we had four denominations of coins, each with its own value and weight.

c. The goal is to use the limited capacity in a way that *maximizes profit*.

You may assume an unlimited available supply of each kind of item. Thus, profit is limited only by capacity and the particular way that it is used.

6.23 Create a greedy algorithm that solves the minimal spanning tree problem described in Example 6.15.

Problems 6.24 through 6.27 refer to the dynamic planning approach to optimization. In our discussion of dynamic planning, we described the steps involved but did not present either an explicit algorithm or a data structure.

6.24 How might linked lists be used for keeping track of the various nodes, the available paths to other nodes, and the distance of each path?

6.25 Design a data structure that implements your answer to the previous problem.

6.26 How might a stack be used to help keep track of which points are on the optimal route?

6.27 Implement an algorithm for problem 6.26. You may wish to use a recursive algorithm so that you benefit from the automatic stack management that the activation stack provides to recursive routines.

CHAPTER 7

Tools for Modeling Real-World Objects

Behavioral abstractions are built from both procedural and data abstractions. They provide the basis for *object-oriented programming,* which is the current "state of the art."

The idea of behavioral abstractions is rooted in common sense. Most interesting phenomena in the world can be perceived as combinations of both procedures and as data. Can a baseball shortstop, for example, be perceived as a "set of procedures" or a "set of data"? Quite obviously, a shortstop is a person who embodies both the "procedures" for fielding and hitting and the "data" that convey how good he is at these things. Thus, we can conceive of a given shortstop as *a behavioral entity who manifests data via his procedures.* This is what we mean by a behavioral abstraction: an entity that "has" both data and the procedures and functions that manipulate that data.

In fact, you might think of a behavioral abstraction as a "meta-module," a unit of an algorithm that "has" both procedures and data that are distinct from the rest of the algorithm. They allow us to create abstractions that are superior to what we can create using only procedural and data abstractions. In this chapter, we shall see how to build on what we have learned so far to create behavioral abstractions, and we shall see how they allow us to achieve better encapsulation, greater flexibility, and greater reusability.

253

7.1 The Object-Oriented Paradigm

In our discussion of behavioral abstraction, we will focus on the *object-oriented paradigm* in which instances of behavioral abstractions are known as *objects*. It is the basis of objected-oriented design and programming.

The foundation of the object-oriented approach is human, not technical. It comes from the insight that people manipulate objects quite effectively and naturally, without extensive education or training. As the software industry has watched the complexity of its products grow to the point where they are unmanageable, the need for a better approach has become paramount. What is needed is an approach that supports effective "complexity management" through practical means for delegation of responsibility based on contracts of responsibility. This in turn implies an approach that features a very high degree of abstraction and a naturally human means of both communication and manipulation. The object-oriented (or OO) approach is currently viewed as offering the most promise of satisfying these needs.

At its heart, the object-oriented approach implies the exact opposite of the traditional view of the programmer as a clever, solitary hacker:

- The original motivation for hacking came from a very real need to be clever in order to overcome the limitations of slow processors and tiny amounts of memory. In contrast, the whole point of the OO approach is to exploit the fact that we now have cheap, fast processors and memory that make complex software economically viable and technically manageable. We are willing to sacrifice both memory and cpu cycles in return for effective solutions to both complexity management and software reusability.
- The traditional image of the clever hacker is someone who is more comfortable alone in his room with a computer than he is with people (i.e., he has technical skills but lacks social know-how). In contrast, the entire basis of OO design is social. It is based on communication, delegation, and communication-intensive teamwork among the various members of a society. The "society" isn't composed of people, it's composed of *objects*, that is, behavioral abstractions implemented in software. While undoubtedly OO design is a technical enterprise, its foundation design is social cooperation among objects, and its origin lies in observations of how people effectively cooperate.

As we delve into objects, it is important to distinguish between programming languages that provide object-oriented capabilities and true object-oriented design. In recent years, the phrase "object-oriented" has become a marketing tool for selling software and training. Many things are sold as providing the holy grail of object-oriented features, yet the key to object-oriented design is not in language features or capabilities. The crux of the issue is conceptual—the approach to system design that is taken by the designer and the eyes through which the analyst sees the problem at hand. Facility with programming languages such as C++ has very little to do with effective object-oriented design, just as familiarity with drawing tools does not make one a good artist or architect.

We aim to introduce you to basic concepts and constructs in order to give you an introductory foundation. To the extent that you achieve a foundational understanding, you will be well positioned to build on it, as the demand for OO design continues to grow and extend throughout the software industry and beyond.

7.1.1 The Benefits of the OO Approach

The object-oriented approach to software provides the following three key benefits.

- Superior *encapsulation*. Both a given data structure and the operations that act on that data can be better hidden, better controlled, and more cleanly designed and implemented.
- Superior *reusability* of code. Programmers can readily use libraries of existing code rather than writing everything they need for every program.
- Superior *adaptability* of code. Existing code can be adapted to the job at hand with minimal reengineering.

In later sections of this chapter we will elaborate on each of these benefits.

7.1.2 Required Features

For algorithms to be designed and implemented in the object-oriented paradigm, certain constructs and capabilities are necessary as a starting place. Fortunately, by now you are already familiar with most of them:

- Tools for procedural abstraction, as covered in Chapter 4.
- Tools for data abstraction, as covered in Chapter 5.
- Algorithmic methods, as covered in Chapter 6.

In addition, other capabilities are required. Chief among these are resources that allow intensive communication between an object and the other objects with which it interacts. As we shall see, OO provides a more decentralized model of software behavior. As in other examples of modern decentralized management, higher communication costs are implied. In computing, these higher communication costs are acceptable due to the dramatic improvements that occurred in both price and performance of computing resources. OO would have been quite impossible as a mainstream approach in the early 1980s, as affordable hardware could not have supported the higher memory and intraprogram communication costs implied by effective OO implementations. Thus, not only is OO an idea whose time has come, it also is an idea whose time could not have come any earlier.

7.2 Encapsulation

To understand why we need behavioral abstraction, let's review what we know about procedural and data abstractions to discover where they fall short.

- We use *procedural abstraction* to group together the instructions for a given logical task in order to isolate the details of that task inside a module. This allows us to refer to the task by name, send it appropriate parameters, and receive the benefits of that module's work without being concerned about exactly how it does its work. For example, we've seen both iterative and recursive implementations of the Power function. The two versions go about their business in different ways, but that needn't matter to the algorithm that might use them. All it "knows" is that it called a Power function and received the correct result.

- We use *data abstraction* to isolate the details of a particular data structure. We saw how we could use type definitions and constants to isolate the specification of the size of an array, thus allowing us to easily modify array size without having to make numerous changes to type definitions and module declarations throughout the algorithm.

7.2.1   The Limitations of Procedural and Data Abstractions

For all their benefits, procedural and data abstractions still leave us with things that we cannot hide. For example, the main algorithm shouldn't have to know whether data are stored in an array or a linked structure, yet this is something that cannot easily be hidden. In the case of a linked structure, the main algorithm needs to pass a pointer variable to provide access to the linked list or tree. In the case of an array, the algorithm needs to pass the array by parameter to whatever modules act upon it. Thus, the structure of data is not truly transparent, as various parts of the algorithm get to know more than they should have about the implementation of the data structure.

If an algorithm knows more than it should, it can also *do* more than it should. For example, we know that a queue is a logical data structure that we might implement as an array or as a linked list. We also know that a queue should be operated upon in only certain ways (i.e., enqueue to the rear and dequeue from the front). However, if other parts of an algorithm know what the data implementation is, and know how to get to it, then there is nothing to prevent improper operations from being performed. For example, regardless of how perfectly we implement enqueue and dequeue, there is nothing to prevent another routine from traversing the data structure, sneaking an item into the queue whenever and wherever it pleases and, in doing so, violating the integrity of the queue.

What we want is a means of truly encapsulating both the data and the procedures of logical entities so that their specification *cannot* be violated.

7.2.2   The Encapsulation Concept: Abstract Data Types

When we implement a queue, the queue itself does not really exist in any particular place. The data structure for the queue exists somewhere in memory, but the data structure itself is not "a queue." The data structure used to implement a queue might be a linked list or an array, which are data structures that may be used for any number of purposes. So, while the data structure is most certainly a *component* of the queue, it does not define what we mean by the word "queue."

To understand what a queue is, one must understand a logical idea of a first-in, first-out (FIFO) data structure. This structure implies a set of rules for insertion and deletion, and a means of storing values in the proper order between their insertion and their deletion. Thus, we have some data structure as well as `Enqueue` and `Dequeue` procedures for acting on that data structure. If you look at any one part, you don't see a queue. Only in looking at *all of them together* do you see an implementation of the queue idea.

To refer to all the components—including data and modules—that constitute a given logical data structure, we use the name *abstract data type*.

Definition: An **abstract data type** (or **ADT**) is a logical data structure that implies both data and rules governing how those data are manipulated. Examples of abstract data types include: a *queue,* a *stack,* an *ordered list of numbers,* or *any other abstraction* that is defined in terms of *both the data and the operations* that may be performed on it.

Note that an abstract data type is an idea, a concept, an abstraction. Logically, it enables us to think of a queue as being a thing (a logical entity or essence) despite the fact that it might be implemented in any number of ways (any number of embodiments).

7.2.3 The Encapsulation Constructs: Classes and Objects

To implement abstract data types, we require constructs that support the encapsulation of data abstractions with the procedural abstractions that can act upon those data. In the Object Oriented paradigm, such constructs are known as classes and objects. Each of these terms has a specific meaning:

Definition: A **class** is the construct we use to define an abstract data type. When we create a class, we define both the data and procedural abstractions for a given abstract data type. Thus, a class is similar to a data type, in that it serves as a template.

Definition: An **object** is the construct we use to create an instance of a class. When we declare an object of a given class, we are creating a particular instance that conforms to the template defined by the class. In this way, an object is similar to a variable, in that it is a particular instance of a previously defined template.

Thus, one does not "define an object," nor does one "declare a class." Rather, one "defines a class," so that one may "declare objects of that class," just as one "defines a type," so that one may "declare variable of that type." In both cases, the definition (type or class) provides a template that can then be used to declare entities (variables or objects) that are instances of that template.

A key difference between classes and data types is that, while both include the specification of data abstractions, classes also include the specification of those procedural abstractions that can operate on those data.

In OO terminology, there is a special term for the data and procedural abstractions of a class:

Definition: In OO jargon, we use the word **attributes** to refer to the data structures of a class and the term **methods** to refer to the procedures and functions of a class.

7.2.4   Encapsulation and the Need to Control Visibility

The whole point of encapsulation is to hide the implementation details of an algorithm component. This implies that we can somehow specify which aspects are visible to the user and which are hidden. We need to be able to specify who can see what.

For example, with a queue we want the algorithm that uses the queue to know how to make use of its logical capabilities (e.g., enqueue and dequeue). At the same time, we don't want that algorithm to know the details of how we make those capabilities work (e.g., the data structures used to implement the queue, or the code that implements the enqueue and dequeue methods.).

To accomplish this, we need the capability to specify which parts are hidden and which are not. From this, we have the idea of *public* and *protected* sections.

 Definition: The **public section** contains everything about the class definition that the client algorithm needs to know. This is identical to what the client algorithm is allowed to know. Everything contained in the public section is visible to any algorithm that creates objects of this class.

 Definition: The **protected section** contains everything that is needed to implement the class. The protected section includes the declaration of all the class variables and the implementation details of all the class methods. Everything that is contained in the protected section is hidden from any algorithm that creates objects of the class.

For example, a queue class would consist of both the definition of the data structure used to implement the queue (such as array or linked list) *and* the methods used to implement queue behavior (such as enqueue and dequeue). The data structures and the coded details of the method implementations would be *protected*, as we wish to keep these details hidden. The header lines of the Enqueue and Dequeue methods would be *public*, as these tell others who declare objects of this class how to make use of the queue, which is precisely what we want them to know.

 Any instructions that are not included in the class do not have access to protected data and thus cannot manipulate that data. This allows us to ensure that no part of an algorithm can get to data unless it is supposed to do so.

For example, if a queue class defined Enqueue and Dequeue as the only operations that are permitted on a queue, then it would be pointless to try to violate a queue by writing procedure Sneak_One_In to insert an item to the head of the queue rather than to the tail. Such a method could not access the queue data because it was not defined to be part of the class. By *encapsulating* both data and procedural abstractions together, classes give us the power to control access to data such that only authorized methods are allowed in, as shown in Fig. 7.1.

While the particular example of a queue gives us no good reason to do so, classes also permit us to create methods that are entirely hidden within the class. Such methods would have not only their implementation details but also their header lines protected. They may be called by other methods of the class but cannot be used outside the class because they are only visible from within, as shown in Fig. 7.2.

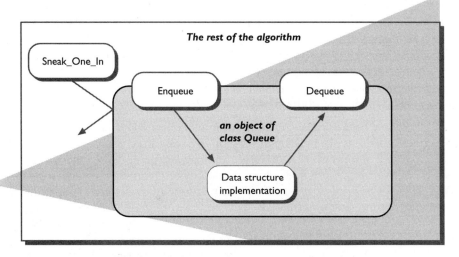

FIGURE 7.1 Encapsulating an ADT

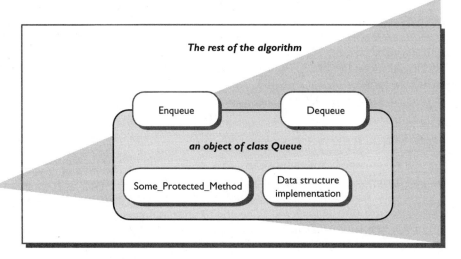

FIGURE 7.2 Public vs. protected methods

7.2.5 The Role of Classes

Classes are more than just data types. They are self-contained implementations of ADTs that can be used by other algorithms. We can implement a logical capability (such as a queue) as a behavioral entity with its data attributes and methods united *within* a single class. The attributes are effectively encapsulated within the class so that no unauthorized code may tamper with the data. The methods that operate on that data are effectively encapsulated so that the rest of the algorithm can use only those methods whose header lines are public.

So far, we have encountered three aspects of classes:

- A class includes both data attributes and the methods by which those attributes can be accessed and manipulated.
- A class limits access to its attributes such that *only the methods defined within the class* can access and manipulate the attributes.
- A class limits access to its methods such that only those that are public can be executed by the rest of the algorithm.

The result is a behavioral abstraction, an implementation of an ADT, which other algorithms may use to achieve the *logical behavior* they want (e.g., managing a queue). Those algorithms that make use of the class (by declaring and manipulating objects of the class) have no idea how that behavior is carried out. The implementation details of both the attributes and the methods are completely hidden from the "client algorithm" that uses the class. The client algorithm is aware of only as much as it needs to know in order to request the services provided by public methods.

 The OO approach allows us to create *client/supplier relationships,* wherein a client algorithm requests service from a supplier, with each party having clearly defined responsibilities and expectations of one another.

In our example, our queue class would be a supplier of services to any client algorithm that needed to declare objects of class queue. As we shall see, the author of the client algorithm would not have to create and manage a queue. Instead, he or she could use an existing queue class to declare queue objects as needed without having to write any of the code for the queue.

We shall see how to define a class soon.

7.2.6   The Role of Objects

Once a class is defined, other algorithms may declare and use objects of that class. For example, with class `Queue` defined, an algorithm may then declare any number of queue objects. An algorithm can declare an object of class `Queue` much like it can declare a variable of type `Num`.

For any algorithm that uses the class, simply declaring objects of the class provides the power of all the behavioral abstraction of that class. A client algorithm may include declarations for any number of objects of the given class, just as it might declare any number of `Num` or `Char` variables.

 Unlike variables, object attributes are protected from direct access and can be manipulated by the client algorithm *only indirectly* via calls to the public methods specified in the class that defines the object.

Thus, if the author of an algorithm declares an object called `this_queue` to be of class `Queue`, that algorithm does not know what data structure is used to implement the queue, nor can it directly access that data structure. All it can do is to ask for public services, such as `Enqueue` and `Dequeue`, to be performed on `this_queue`. The author of the client algorithm does not have to worry about writing or testing or debugging any aspects of the queue. Instead, he gets to reuse code that has already been designed, created, tested, and debugged.

7.3 The Anatomy of a Class

To illustrate what a class is, we will present in Example 7.1 a sample class definition. Then, in the remainder of Section 7.3, we'll walk through this class definition to explain each of its various parts.

EXAMPLE 7.1 Below is a class that defines an implementation of a queue for a given kind of data.. Read through it, noticing its layout and structure.

```
class Queue

public

    procedure Enqueue (new_data isoftype in String)
    // purpose: add new_data to end of FIFO queue
    // preconditions:  the queue object exists and is not full
    // postconditions: new data added to the end of the queue

    procedure Dequeue (served isoftype out String)
    // purpose: remove item from front of FIFO queue
    // preconditions: the queue object exists and is not empty
    // postconditions: data removed from the front of the queue

    function Is_Empty returnsa Boolean
    // purpose: determines if the queue is empty
    // precondition: the queue object exists
    // postcondition: resolves to TRUE if no items are in
    //                the queue, to FALSE otherwise.

    function Is_Full returnsa Boolean
    // purpose: determines if the queue is full
    // precondition: the queue object exists
    // postcondition: resolves to TRUE if the queue is full,
    //                resolves to FALSE otherwise.

    procedure Initialization
    // purpose: initializes object as appropriate
    // precondition: the queue object exists
    // postcondition: the object is properly initialized

protected
    //definition of Queue item node
    Q_Node definesa record
        data isoftype String
        next isoftype Ptr toa Q_Node
    endrecord //Q_Node
    //ptr vars to head and tail of queue
    q_head isoftype Ptr toa Q_Node
    q_tail isoftype Ptr toa Q_Node

    procedure Enqueue (new_data isoftype in String)
        //allocate new node and put new data in it
```

```
         temp isoftype Ptr toa Q_Node
         temp <- new(Q_Node)
         temp^.data <- new_data
         temp^.next <- NIL
         //connect new node to end of the existing queue
         if (Is_Empty) then
            q_head <- temp
            q_tail <- temp
         else
            q_tail^.next <- temp
            q_tail <- temp
         endif
      endprocedure //Enqueue

      procedure Dequeue (served isoftype out String)
         if (Is_Empty) then
            print ("Error: precondition violated;")
             print(" Dequeue from empty queue attempted")
         else
            served <- q_head^.data
            q_head <- q_head^.next
            if (Is_Empty) then
               q_tail <- NIL
            endif
         endif
      endprocedure //Dequeue

      function Is_Empty returnsa Boolean
         if (q_head = NIL) then
            Is_Empty returns TRUE
         else
            Is_Empty returns FALSE
         endif
      endfunction //Is_Empty

      function Is_Full returnsa Boolean
         // dynamic data implementation, so always returns FALSE
         Is_Full returns FALSE
      endfunction // Is_Full

      procedure Initialize
         q_head <- NIL
         q_tail <- NIL
      endprocedure // Initialize
   endclass // Queue
```

7.3.1 The Public Section

In this example, a client algorithm can see the public headers of the methods
Enqueue, Dequeue, Initialize, Is_Empty and Is_Full. That's all. The
procedures Enqueue and Dequeue are public because any client needs to use them
to use of a queue object for its intended purpose. The functions Is_Full and
Is_Empty are public because a client needs to use them to determine if the preconditions for Enqueue and Dequeue are met. Initialize procedures are always public.

Observe that there are no data declarations in the public section. This is no fluke. One of our goals is to encapsulate data such that access to it is controlled. That is, since we do not want the rest of the algorithm to have access to our data, we *prohibit* variable declarations in the public section.

At the same time, note that the header lines for the `Enqueue` and `Dequeue` methods do reveal to the client that objects of this queue class are useful only for data that is of type String. (Later in this chapter, we shall see how to overcome the limitation of having a class handle only a predetermined data type.)

7.3.2   The Protected Section

In the protected section we find the type definitions required to implement the queue. Here, the queue is implemented as a linked list, so type definitions for list nodes and declarations of pointer variables are needed. These are properly *hidden details*. While a client algorithm has a legitimate need to know what kind of data the queue will handle, there is no reason for the client algorithm to know how the queue is implemented. Thus, details of the data structure are hidden in the protected section.

The protected section also includes the full declaration of the methods whose header lines were listed in the public section. Again, while the code is required to implement the queue, there is no reason for a client algorithm to be aware of these details. The client algorithm needs to know *how* it must request service, i.e., it needs to see the public method header lines. Details of their implementation are protected.

Additionally, the protected section could include the declaration of methods whose header lines are *not* found in the public section. This class has no reason to have protected methods, however. If it did, then simply the absence of their header lines from the public section would ensure that no client algorithm could call them. In fact, clients have no way of knowing if such methods even exist. All the clients can do with respect to the queue is make calls to what they see in the public section. It just so happens that, for a queue, all necessary methods are properly public.

7.3.3   Scope of Data Within a Class

Observe that the protected section includes declarations of two global variables (`q_head` and `q_tail`). It is obvious that we need to maintain both head and tail markers for a queue and, indeed, both the `Enqueue` and `Dequeue` procedures contain code that manipulates these variables. It is also obvious that they need to be global, as their values need to live throughout the life of the algorithm. However, observe that these global variables are *not* passed into `Enqueue` and `Dequeue` via parameters. Yet, these procedures manipulate these variables nonetheless.

How can this be? Until now, we have established that *all* data variables that are manipulated by a subprogram *must* be either declared locally within the module or passed to it via parameter. When it comes to defining classes, however, we make a specific modification to the scope rule for variables:

All methods declared in the protected section of a class may directly access any variables that are declared globally in that section without having to receive them via parameter. ▓

We make this exception for a very good reason. Consider what would happen if we did not do so: for each method, all variables needed by that method would have to be included in its parameter list. In the queue example, the public methods Enqueue and Dequeue would have parameter lists that include head and tail pointers to the data structure. Of course, these are precisely the kind of implementation details that we wish to hide. Passing them as parameters would have the bad effect of violating the very encapsulation of implementation details that we want to achieve. To solve the problem of violating encapsulation, we allow global variables declared within the protected section to be directly accessible to the code that is implemented in the protected section *without* requiring them to be passed as parameters. Observe that this does not eliminate scope limits on these variables: Since they are all declared and used within the protected section, their scope and usage are still well controlled.

7.3.4 The Initialize Procedure

At the end of the protected section, there is a `procedure Initialize`. In our example, this code initializes the class variables to appropriate initial values, which is precisely what such a method is for.

It is up to the client algorithm to invoke any Initialize methods. As a general rule, we'd expect such a method to be called exactly once per object, immediately after object creation. Thus, if a client algorithm requires 10 different queues and thus declares 10 objects of class queue, then the client would be expected to invoke the class' `Initialize` method 10 times, once per object. Initialization procedures are optional, based on the needs of the task at hand. If objects of a given class require any initialization steps to be performed when the object is created, then a procedure `Initialize` is a necessary part of the class definition. As with any other method that the client can call, it's header line with formal parameters list should be included in the public section of the class definition.

 In principle, initialization procedures are just like any other procedure. Most classes have attributes that require some initial value, and we can therefore expect most classes to have initialization procedures. For clarity and convenience, we always use the identifier "Initialize" for such procedures.

7.3.5 Contracts

We require that each method include documentation that describes the method's purpose, its preconditions and its postconditions. In OO jargon, we refer to such documentation collectively as being the *contract* for that service.

If the method is public, then the contract must appear in the public section, under the method's header line. This is necessary to allow clients to see what the service the method promises to provide. If the method is protected, then the contract appears there instead.

While documentation is always crucial to effective software maintenance, it is particularly important in the OO world. Since the client algorithm, and perhaps its author, cannot "see" the code of the methods, we must provide the client with a specification of exactly what that client can expect each method to do.

7.3.6 Declaring and Using Objects

Once our `Queue` class is defined, any client algorithm may obtain the benefits of a queue without having to implement one. To make use of the class, the client algorithm need only specify that it is *using* it. By simply including the word "uses," followed by the identifiers of any classes it wishes to use, the client algorithm can make use of whatever code has already been developed. A client may use any number of classes, and a class may itself use another class. Algorithms which are declared to be using a class may then declare objects of that class, much as they might declare variables, as shown in Example 7.2.

EXAMPLE 7.2   Consider the following format for using a class:

```
algorithm Do_Something uses Queue
    temp_data isoftype String
    this_queue isoftype Queue
    that_queue isoftype Queue
    ...
```

With two queue objects declared (`this_queue` and `that_queue`), and with appropriate values stored in record variable `temp_data`, the client might request an enqueue.

```
if NOT(this_queue.Is_Full) then
    this_queue.Enqueue(temp_data)
```

This instruction makes a request to the object `this_queue` to `Enqueue` the current contents of `temp_data`. Since `this_queue` is an object of the class `Queue`, it has the capability to provide that service. Similarly, the instruction

```
if NOT(that_queue.Is_Empty) then
    that_queue.Dequeue(temp_data)
```

would call for service to remove the value at the head of the queue `that_queue` and return it to the client algorithm by storing it in it in the variable `temp_data`. Note that the client algorithm is checking to make sure that object `that_queue` is not empty before it attempts a `Dequeue` and that `this_queue` is not full before it attempts an `Enqueue`. Why does it do this? Because the contracts for the `Enqueue` and `Dequeue` methods in `class Queue` have preconditions: the `Dequeue` method promises to work *provided that the queue is not empty*, and the `Enqueue` method promises to work *provided that the queue is not full*. Thus, the client has to ascertain whether these preconditions are met.

One might reasonably question whether our `Enqueue` method really requires a check to make sure that it is not full. After all, we know that our queue implementation is via a dynamically sized data structure, not a statically sized one. Therefore, isn't it needless to worry about it being full?

To answer this question, recall that the choice of data structure is an implementation issue that is hidden from the client. True, our queue class now features a dynamic data structure. But perhaps tomorrow the decision will be made to change the linked list to an array, in which case the check for Is_Full becomes quite relevant. Since we wish to be able to change implementation details of the class without forcing a rewrite of all client algorithms that may use it, contracts that are independent of implementation decisions are indeed called for.

7.4 Generic Parameters and Reusability

A central benefit of the OO approach is that it allows us to develop and test code separately from the client algorithms, thus supporting the reuse of code among various different clients. Unfortunately, we have yet to overcome an important obstacle that limits reuse. Notice that our class Queue is designed to operate only on data of type String. Thus, class Queue is useful only if we need a queue to store items of type String. If we need a queue to store items that aren't Strings, we're out of luck.

Of course, we might find a way to get around this limitation. For example, if we need to store numbers, perhaps we could "cut and paste" a copy of class Queue, rename the copy class Number_Queue, then do a search-and-replace to change all the references in that class from String to Num. However, it's usually the case in computing that clever attempts to get around something turn out to be messy in the long run. Here, this "clever" process would not only be tedious and error-prone, but also eventually result in the development of countless versions of class Queue. Each of these versions would be identical *except for* the data type (one for String, one for Num, another one for Customer_Rec, one for Employee_Rec, and so on). Then, if we wanted to change how all our various queues are implemented, we'd have to make those changes in each of the many versions. We'd soon have a logistical nightmare built upon a series of minor data type differences, which *have nothing to do* with the behavior we want from a queue!

Fortunately, there is a better way. Our problem is caused by the fact that the class specifies the type of data that the queue stores when, logically, it should be up to the *client* to say what type of data it wants a queue object to manage. This is an example of poor abstraction.

 To properly encapsulate things, it is not enough to prevent the client from concerning itself with details that properly "belong" to the supplier. We must also prevent the supplier from concerning itself with details that properly "belong" to the client.

Good abstraction would mean that the queue would be able to manage whatever data the client is using the queue to store. Logically, class Queue has no business caring what data are stored. It should only need to know *what to do* with the data and be able to make sure that the data are of the type specified.

To achieve a higher level of abstraction, we make use of a new construct, the *generic parameter*. This construct allows the client algorithm to define the type of data that a particular object of a class will store. When the client declares an object of a certain class, it uses the generic parameter to pass a type definition specifying the kind of data that is to be managed by the particular object of that class. Each object provides a template, which manages data of the type specified at the time of its creation. In Example 7.3 we illustrate how a client might use generic parameters to specify what type of data various queues will store.

EXAMPLE 7.3 Within a client algorithm, we might find:

```
Student_Rec_Type definesa record
    student_name isoftype String
    student_num isoftype Num
    student_major isoftype String
    student_gpa isoftype Num
endrecord //Student_Rec_Type

name_queue isoftype Queue(String)
student_queue isoftype Queue(Student_Rec_Type)
number_queue isoftype Queue(Num)
```

Above, we first created the definition of `Student_Rec_Type`. Then, we've declared three objects. Notice the type of each object. Each of the three `Queue` objects is declared such that its class (`Queue`) includes a parameter specifying the kind of data which *that particular queue object* will store. All three objects are of type `Queue`. But each is different from the others in terms of *what type of data* it will store, as specified by the generic parameter:

- Object `name_queue` is declared to be a queue that will manage data of type `String`.
- Object `student_queue` will manage data of type `Student_Rec_Type`.
- Object `number_queue` will be a `queue` of numbers.

Each object has been declared to expect a given type of data. The object need not be concerned with what the data type represents, only that it will receive data of a given type. Once declared, each of the three queue objects will operate independently of one another (just as three ordinary `Num` variables have no bearing on one another).

The client algorithm may then include executable instructions such as

```
if NOT(name_queue.Is_Full) then name_queue.Enqueue(this_name)
if NOT(student_queue.Is_Empty) then student_queue.Dequeue(that_student)
if NOT(number_queue.Is_Full) then number_queue.Enqueue(some_num)
```

Each of these instructions is a request to the specified object to provide a service. For these three instructions to be correct, the actual parameter variables must be of the appropriate type: the variable `this_name` must be of type `String`, `that_Student` variable must be of type `Student_Rec_Type`, and `some_num` must be of type `Num`.

To make use of the generic parameter shown in Example 7.3, we rewrite the `Queue` class as shown in the next example.

EXAMPLE 7.4 Below, we create a class definition in which all references to the type of data stored on the queue are type `Q_Type`. What is `Q_Type`? `Q_Type` is the *formal generic parameter* as specified in the header line of the `class`. Anytime a client algorithm declares an object of class `Queue`, that declaration must pass an *actual generic parameter*. This parameter specifies the type of data that the particular `Queue` object will then treat as `Q_Type`. Note that `Q_Type` is just an identifier. We could use any identifier for this purpose: it's just a placeholder that allows clients to specify what type or class they wish an object of the class to manage.

```
class Queue(Q_Type)

public
    procedure Enqueue (new_data isoftype in Q_Type)
    // contract documentation as before
    procedure Dequeue (served isoftype out Q_Type)
    // contract documentation as before

    function Is_Empty returnsa Boolean
    // contract documentation as before

    function Is_Full returnsa Boolean
    // contract documentation as before

    procedure Initialize
    // contract documentation as before
protected
Q_Node definesa record
    data isoftype Q_Type
    next isoftype Ptr toa Q_Node
endrecord

q_head isoftype Ptr toa Q_Node
q_tail isoftype Ptr toa Q_Node
procedure Enqueue (new_data isoftype in Q_Type)
    <procedure body as before>
procedure Dequeue (served isoftype out Q_Type)
    <procedure body as before>

function Is_Empty returnsa Boolean
    <function body as before>

function Is_Full returnsa Boolean
    <function body as before>

procedure Initialize
    <procedure body as before>

endclass //Queue
```

Generic parameters allow us to transfer responsibility for specifying the kind of data to be managed from the class to the client algorithm. This dramatically improves reusability. A class can be a generic data-handling template that allows clients to declare objects that manage whatever kind of data they wish.

7.5 Tracing the Execution of Object Behaviors

In earlier chapters, we advised you to trace the execution of your algorithms by drawing pictures of their data states. This process allows you to see where variables are ("on the stack" or "in the heap"), to create them as the algorithm allocates space for them, to erase them when they "die," to modify the values stored in them as appropriate, etc. Such drawings are crucial, as they allow you to *see* the logical effects of what would happen in a computer as your algorithm executes.

Objects present nothing really new in this regard, just a new twist. Keep in mind that an instance of all the variables declared in a class exists *for each object* that has been created. For example, in our `Queue` class we see that pointer variables `q_head` and `q_tail` are declared in the protected section. Instances of these two variables are created *for each instance* of the class `Queue`. If the client algorithm creates two objects via

```
one_queue isoftype Queue(Num)
another_queue isoftype Queue(Char)
```

then both `one_queue` and `another_queue` will each have their own head and tail pointers. In other words, *each of these two objects contains its own internal variables.* You may think of their head pointers as having the identifiers `one_queue.q_head` and `another_queue.q_head`, respectively, and you might use these names as you keep track of their values as you trace your algorithms' execution. Just remember that you cannot actually access the head and tail pointers that way. Only those methods defined in the class (such as `one_queue.Enqueue`, `another_queue.Dequeue`, or `one_queue.Is_Empty`) may do so. In fact, the name `one_queue.q_head` will never appear in any part of the algorithm. The object identifier specified in the call determines the head pointer that will be accessed. To apply the `Enqueue` method to `one_queue`'s internal variables, call `one_queue.Enqueue`.

Otherwise, everything else can be drawn just as before. All statically allocated (named) variables exist on the *activation stack* within the *frame* in which they were declared. Whenever that frame is popped off the stack, the named variables "die." All dynamically allocated (i.e., unnamed) variables exist in the heap. For example, if `one_queue` and `another_queue` are declared within the client's main algorithm, then their named head and tail pointers will survive throughout the entire execution of the client algorithm. On the other hand, if they are declared within one of the client algorithm's procedures, then they will "die" as soon as that procedure completes and has its frame popped off the activation stack. In either case, the dynamically allocated nodes that constitute the actual queue itself will live in the heap until such time that no pointer points to them, at which time they are automatically deallocated.

EXAMPLE 7.5   Given the algorithm below, how might we draw its state as it nears completion (after the last instruction has completed but just before the algorithm ends and all stack frames "die")?

```
algorithm Sample_Queue_Client uses Queue
// purpose: nonsense algorithm to illustrate
// drawing trace of object state
    fred isoftype Num
    fred <- 7

    this_queue isoftype Queue(Num)

    if NOT(this_queue.Is_Full) then
     this_queue.Enqueue(fred+2))
    if NOT(this_queue.Is_Full) then
       this_queue.Enqueue(fred+1)
```

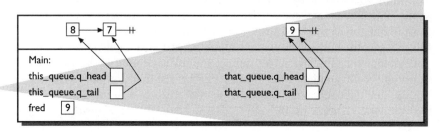

FIGURE 7.3 The permanence of object variables

```
if NOT(this_queue.Is_Full) then
    this_queue.Enqueue(fred)
if NOT(this_queue.Is_Empty) then
    this_queue.Dequeue(fred)

that_queue isoftype Queue(Num)
if NOT(that_queue.Is_Full) then
    that_queue.Enqueue(fred)
endalgorithm //Sample_Queue_Client
```

We might draw the final data state as shown in Fig. 7.3.

7.6 Copy and Clone Operations

There is frequently a need to assign the value of one variable to another. With objects, we do this via *copy* and *clone* operations. To see why we need two operations, consider that a client algorithm uses our Queue class, declares two objects of that class, and manipulates them as shown below:

```
Some_Client_Algorithm uses Queue
    this isoftype Queue(Num)
    if NOT(this.Is_Full) then
    this.Enqueue(7)
    if NOT(this.Is_Full) then
    this.Enqueue(9)
    if NOT(this.Is_Full) then
    this.Enqueue(11)
                              . . .
endalgorithm // Some_Client_Algorithm
```

So far, the queue object this has the values 7, 9, and 11 stored in it (head to tail). The data state of this object might be drawn as shown in Fig. 7.4. Now, consider that the client's next instructions are:

```
that isoftype Queue(Num)
that <- copy(this)
```

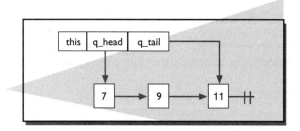

FIGURE 7.4 Each queue object has its own *head* and *tail*.

Definition: The **copy** operation copies the values of the *internal* variables of one object to another. In the case of pointers, it provides a copy of the pointers themselves. It does *not* provides a copy of the data to which those pointers refer. Thus, subsequent operations of one object can affect the other object's data.

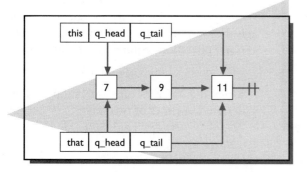

FIGURE 7.5 Two objects share data after a *copy* generation.

The result of the `copy` operation is that internal variables of each object now store the same value, as shown in Fig. 7.5. Now, consider the effect if the client algorithm now executed:

```
if NOT(that.Is_Full) then that.Enqueue(2)
```

It would attach a new node containing the value 2 to the end of the linked list, as shown in Fig. 7.6. We now have two different objects, ones that are supposed to feature well-encapsulated data, sharing data! While this may be useful for certain tasks, it is also quite dangerous. Can you see why? What would be effect of `this.Enqueue(1)`?

If we want a copy of the dynamic data itself, then we use another operation created for that purpose: the `clone` operation.

Definition: The **clone** operation copies the internal variables declared within the object itself; it also follows any pointers and completely replicates any data to which those pointers refer.

FIGURE 7.6 Shared data can cause data integrity problems.

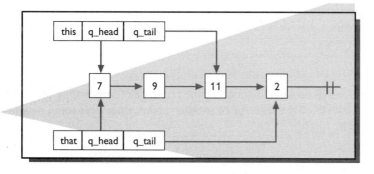

Thus, given our original 7-9-11 list, the operation

```
That <- clone(This)
```

gives the state shown in Fig. 7.7. The `clone` follows the internal pointer variables of `this` and ensures that the internal pointer variables of `that` point to their own copy of whatever `this`' pointers referenced. Now, the two objects *each have their own queue* and changes to one will not affect the state of the other. To prevent cloning from having unintended side effects, we specify that the `clone` operation never overwrites anything and instead makes fresh copies of what it finds.

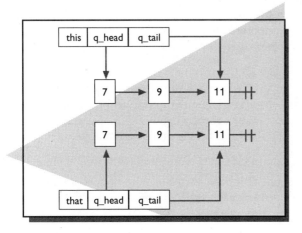

FIGURE 7.7 The *clone* operation gives each object its own data.

The `copy` operation can be considered to be *shallow* (copying only the object's internal variables), while `clone` can be considered to be *deep* (following pointers and literally cloning, not copying, whatever it finds). Obviously, `clone` is the safer of the two operations. Copy is useful only when engaged in advanced data modeling, which is beyond the scope of this course. The `copy` operation requires explicit notation,

```
this_guy <- copy(that_guy)
```

while the safer `clone` operation can be denoted in either of two ways:

```
this_guy <- clone(that_guy)
```

or

```
this_guy <- that_guy
```

<h2>7.7   Inheritance</h2>

So far, we have seen one kind of relationship that may exist between objects: the client/supplier relationship. A client algorithm requests service, which a supplier object makes available. Rather than directly manipulating the implementation of a data structure, the client asks the supplier object to perform a logical operation on it. The supplier then takes care of all the implementation-related particulars. The client/supplier kind of relationship is quite natural to people, and many instances of it can be found throughout everyday life. Objects often feature this same kind of relationship among themselves. If you grasp the concept and purpose of objects' client/supplier capabilities, you're ready to learn more. If not, it's best to review now before proceeding further.

A second kind of relationship between objects is, in principle, quite simple: One object can be declared so that it *inherits* all the features of another object, then adds some new features or capabilities to it.

This has the benefit of saving a great deal of coding. Not only can you easily customize existing code, but this paradigm encourages the development of libraries of code. Frequently, programmers discover that the capabilities they want have already been written and tested, and may be easily modified to suit special needs.

7.7.1 Inheriting and Extending Behaviors

Suppose that we have implemented our `queue` class and we now want to know how many items are currently stored in the queue. One way to do this would be to have the client algorithm maintain a count, but that would be an example of poor abstraction. The number of items in the queue is properly a property of the queue and thus the queue abstraction should be responsible for keeping track of it. Thus, we now want a kind of queue that will keep a count of the number of items currently in it.

Without inheritance, either we'd have to revise our original queue abstraction, `class Queue` (which we might not want to do; perhaps we want clients to be able to declare some queue objects that don't keep count) or we'd have to create a whole new abstraction with similar-but-different code (This would result in the same kind of problem that lead us to generic parameters: many similar-but-different classes, such that any improvements to their common components would have to be made to each of the many different classes.).

By using inheritance, we have neither problem. Instead, we take an existing queue class (the *superclass*) and use it as a basis for defining a more specialized class (the *subclass*). An example is shown below.

EXAMPLE 7.6 Consider the definition of `class Counting_Queue` as a subclass that inherits from `class Queue`:

```
class Counting_Queue (Q_Type) inherits Queue

public
   function Count returnsa Num
   // purpose: returns the number of items currently stored
   //          in a FIFO queue object
   // precondition: object has been initialized
   // postcondition: function Count will resolve to the
   //                correct Num value
protected
   function Count returnsa Num
      temp_count isoftype Num
      current isoftype Ptr toa Q_Node
      temp_count <- 0
      current <- q_head
      loop
         exitif (current = NIL)
         temp_count <- temp_count + 1
         current <- current^.next
      endloop
      Count returns temp_count

   endfunction //Count

endclass //Counting_Queue
```

We've created another specialized version of a queue with minimal effort or code. All we did was:

■ Specify that this new subclass shall inherit from `class Queue`.

- Provide the header line and contract for the new capability in the public section. (We did this because we want client algorithms to be able to use it.)
- Provide the implementation of the method in the protected section.

Notice what we *didn't* do. We said nothing about data types or Enqueue or Dequeue operations or anything else that a queue requires because inheritance made it unnecessary. Since this class inherits from the Queue class, *it gets all of the* Queue *data and methods for free*. Our Counting_Queue class now includes *all* the features of its ancestor class, including anything and everything that was in its public and protected sections. In addition, its repertoire of behavior has been expanded beyond that of its ancestor class by the new capability we added. We've managed to build on previous work to easily create an enhanced class through inheritance.

We call the resulting class a *subclass* of its ancestor because it has inherited features from it, much as we consider dog to be a species and then consider Golden Retriever to be a subspecies of dog.

Definition: A **subclass** is a class that inherits from another class. It has all the attributes of its ancestor and, in addition, has whatever new features are provided in its definition.

7.7.2 Redefining Inherited Capabilities

We've seen how to extend the capabilities of a class (Queue) by defining a new subclass (Counting_Queue) that inherits from the original. Of course, someone might disagree with us about how we've implemented our new subclass. For example, you might reasonably say that, for some given problem, Count will be called much more often than will Enqueue and Dequeue and, thus, it makes more sense to always maintain a count rather than traverse the queue and recompute the count each and every time a count is needed. Such an approach would require that we modify the Enqueue and Dequeue services such that they update a counter variable.

In Example 7.7 (below), as in Example 7.6, we provide a function that returns the number of items in the queue. However, in Example 7.7, we have redefined the particular implementations of Enqueue and Dequeue so that they maintain the correct value in the hidden variable counter_var. We also redefine the Initialize method to provide an initial value for that variable. With these things done, we can define the Count method to simply return the value of that attribute.

Be sure to notice the methods we have redefined. In each case, we've wanted to make use of the code from the superclass' methods and add other instructions to it. Obviously, we don't want to copy the instructions from the parent method (as that would create redundant code). Instead, we invoke the parent method from the redefined method, i.e., we first call the original method from the superclass (via the keyword "super") and then specify the additional instructions needed. Consult the protected sections of Enqueue, Dequeue, and Initialize for examples.

EXAMPLE 7.7 Suppose we decide to change our implementation of Counting_Queue so that Enqueue and Dequeue update a counter variable. We still need `Enqueue` and `Dequeue` services, but we need to *redefine* the particulars of what they do. In the OO paradigm, we can do this as follows:

```
class Counting_Queue(Q_Type) inherits Queue

public
    function Count returnsa Num
    //insert contract from previous example

protected

    counter_var isoftype Num
    procedure Enqueue (new_data isoftype in Q_Type)
        //modified to increment counter_var upon each Enqueue
        super.Enqueue(new_data)
        counter_var <- counter_var + 1
        endprocedure // Enqueue

    procedure Dequeue (served isoftype out Q_Type)
        // modified to decrement counter_var upon each Dequeue
        super.Dequeue(served)
        counter_var <- counter_var - 1
        endprocedure // Dequeue

    function Count returnsa Num
        Count returns counter_var
    endfunction //Count

    procedure Initialize
        super.Initialize
        counter_var <- 0
    endprocedure // Initialize

endclass //Counting_Queue
```

This is an example of another object capability that we can state as a general idea:

We can not only take what we want from ancestor classes and add whatever new data or services we need, but we can also *redefine* existing attributes and/or methods.

This capability gives us a great deal of power, which must be used wisely and with care. Keep in mind that we cannot violate any contracts that we make with clients. Services such as `Enqueue`, `Dequeue`, and `Count` must deliver what is promised.

Redefinition of services is acceptable as long as the new definitions still do what they are supposed to do from the client's perspective. However, should a redefinition change the service that is provided to client algorithms, then a serious breach of contract may occur.

Whenever you create a subclass that redefines an inherited identifier, it is appropriate to "be paranoid" about changing the functionality provided to the client. The new subclass must honor the contract which its ancestor class has made. If it does not, it must provide clients with a new contract, specified in the subclass' public section for the redefined service.

7.7.3 Summary of the Kinds of Inheritance

We've seen two kinds of inheritance relationship among classes.

- *Extension:* The subclass inherits all traits supplied by its ancestor, then extends or expands the repertoire of behavior by adding one or more new services.
- *Redefinition:* The subclass inherits all traits supplied by its ancestor, then changes what one or more of them mean, in terms of either implementation or functionality, or both.

    Any combination of these kinds of inheritance may occur in a single subclass.

7.7.4 OO Modeling of Real World Attributes

So far, we've used classes to model only *collections* of data, e.g. queues. The data themselves, those things that we stored in the queue, were conventional data structures. Classes, and the inheritance relationships they allow, are also useful for modeling the data aspects of real world objects. Of course, when modeling such data, we want to take care to do so in the OO paradigm, which means that we shall design our classes so that the attributes we're modeling are well encapsulated: hidden from outside access and available only through prescribed methods.

It is now generally accepted that it's good to protect class attributes from direct access. This is best accomplished by defining **accessor** ("Get") and **modifier** ("Set") methods through which all access occurs. This practice eases program debugging and maintenance by ensuring that there is exactly one way to access, and one way to modify, each attribute. Furthermore, since all access is through these methods, one can design these methods to help protect the integrity of the data.

In the OO world, this practice has become standard to the point that contract documentation is typically not required for simple accessor and modifier methods. This is because everyone knows to expect such methods and understands the purpose they serve.

In Example 7.8, below, we show the use of such methods in solving a simple data-modeling problem. Suppose we must manage certain data about vehicles: vehicle ID number, manufacturer, year, and model. We provide an OO implementation below, utilizing accessors and modifiers to limit access.

EXAMPLE 7.8 This class provides methods for obtaining, storing, and displaying four pieces of information for any vehicle.

```
//-----------------------------------

class Vehicle

public

    procedure Initialize
        // purpose: interactively obtains information on the vehicle
        // preconditions: the object exists
        // postconditions: Vehicle contains valid data

    procedure Display
        // purpose: display information on the vehicle
```

```
              // preconditions: vehicle has valid data
              // postconditions: information displayed on screen

      protected

          vin isoftype Num
          make isoftype String
          model isoftype String
          year isoftype Num

          procedure Set_VIN(new_vin isoftype in Num)
              vin <- new_vin
          endprocedure // Set_VIN

          function Get_VIN returnsa Num
              Get_VIN returns vin
          endfunction // Get_VIN

          // Add similar Get and Set methods for Make, Model, and Year

          procedure Initialize
              new_vin isoftype Num
              new_make isoftype String
              new_model isoftype String
              new_year isoftype Num

              print("What is the Vehicle Identification Number?")
              read(new_vin)
              Set_vin(new_vin)

              print("What make is this vehicle?")
              read(new_make)
              Set_make(new_make)

              print("What is the model type of this vehicle?")
              read(new_model)
              Set_model(new_model)

              print("What year is this vehicle?")
              read(new_year)
              Set_Year(new_year)
          endprocedure // Initialize

          procedure Display
              print("VIN: ", Get_VIN, "Year: ", Get_Year)
              print("Make: ", Get_Make, "Model: ", Get_Model)
          endprocedure // Display

      endclass //Vehicle

      //-----------------------------------
```

What we are representing here is a set of facts about vehicles. Notice that the attributes are protected from (and invisible to) any client algorithm that may use this class. Clients are permitted to initialize vehicles (which triggers a process that gathers all the needed data) and to display the data so gathered. In this implementation, clients are not allowed to otherwise access or modify the vehicle attributes.

Of course, one might argue that, depending on the application at hand, it might be quite sensible to allow client algorithms to access and perhaps modify each vehicle attribute independent of the others. If such were the case, the only modification needed would be to include the header lines for the *accessor* (i.e., "Get") and *modifier* (i.e., "Set") methods in the public section. This would still prevent the client from interacting directly with the attributes, but would allow them to call those accessor and modifier methods, which do. If we wished to provide clients with this ability, we could do so by modifying this class or by defining a new subclass, which includes those things in its public section.

Imagine that we have now been given the job of creating two subclasses of vehicle: Car and Truck, each with their own special data needs.

EXAMPLE 7.9 Our job is to extend the Vehicle class into a subclass for Cars that will store standard vehicle information, plus information about body style (e.g., sedan, coupe, convertible, etc.) and the number of doors. We can do this via the subclass, below:

```
//------------------------------------

class Car inherits Vehicle

public

protected

   body_type isoftype String
   num_doors isoftype Num

   procedure Set_Body_Type(new_body_type isoftype in String)
      body_type <- new_body_type
   endprocedure // Set_Body_Type

   function Get_Body returnsa String
      Get_Body returns body_type
   endfunction // Get_Body

   procedure Set_Num_Doors(new_num_doors isoftype Num)
      num_doors <- new_num_doors
   endprocedure // Set_Num_Doors

   function Get_Num_Doors returnsa Num
      Get_Num_Doors returns num_doors
   endfunction // Get_Num_Doors

   procedure Initialize

      new_body_type isoftype String
      new_num_doors isoftype Num

      // First obtain the general vehicle info
      super.Initialize

      // Then get the additional data specific to cars
      print("Enter body style: ")
      read(new_body_type)
      Set_Body_Type(new_body_type)
```

```
            print("Enter number of doors: ")
            read(new_num_doors)
            Set_Num_Doors(new_num_doors)

        endprocedure // Initialize

        procedure Display

            // First display data common to all vehicles
            super.Display

            // Then print car-specific info
            print("This car is a ", Get_Num_Doors,"-door", Get_Body_Type)

        endprocedure // Display

    endclass // Car

    //------------------------------------
```

Notice that we do not have anything in the public section of class Car. We inherit the public section from class Vehicle and our extensions to that class do not create any new public methods, nor are we making any changes that violate the original contracts. All we are doing is adding to the list of information that an object of class Car will manage. With the old headers and contract still good, there is no need for new ones.

Now, imagine that we are given the job of creating a class for Truck objects such that each such object will obtain, store, and display both standard Vehicle data plus gross_weight. We might do this as shown in Example 7.10.

EXAMPLE 7.10   An implementation of a Truck subclass extending Vehicle as described above.

```
    //------------------------------------

    class Truck inherits Vehicle

    public

    protected

        gross_weight isoftype Num // weight in tons

        procedure Set_Weight(new_weight isoftype Num)
            gross_weight <- new_weight
        endprocedure // Set_Weight

        function Get_Weight returnsa Num
            Get_Weight returns gross_weight
        endfunction // Get_Weight

        procedure Initialize

            new_weight isoftype Num

            // First get the normal vehicle info
            super.Initialize

            // Then get the additional info specific to trucks
            print("What is the truck's gross weight in tons?" )
```

```
        read(new_weight)
        Set_Weight(new_weight)

    endprocedure //Initialize

    procedure Display
        // First display info common to all vehicles
        super.Display

        // Then print truck-specific info
        print( "This truck has a gross weight of")
        print( Get_Weight, ' tons.")
    endprocedure //Display

endclass // Truck

//------------------------------------
```

Both the Car and Truck subclasses make use of inheritance from their parent, the superclass Vehicle. As a result, we had to do only as much coding as needed to specify the differences between them.

This approach of "programming only the differences" is one common characteristic, and main benefit, of the object-oriented programming paradigm. ▪

We could exploit this to rapidly create what we might call a "vehicle tree," a network of automotive data, in which the various properties and attributes of various families of cars, racing cars, light trucks, commercial trucks, busses, motorcycles, bicycles, etc. might be specified in relation to one another. If we were to do this, the big design challenge would be to first do the proper abstractions ourselves, on paper.

The class abstractions are only as good as the designers' thoroughness at abstracting the points of commonality and difference among items. With poor designs, you'll likely be programming a great deal more than "just the differences" if common components were not identified, abstracted and assigned to the correct place in the class hierarchy. ▪

7.7.5   Class Hierarchies

Inheritance allows us to share code, to build on previous work, and to create libraries of code that we can then modify to particular needs. We can obtain these benefits because inheritance allows us to establish and exploit relationships among various behavioral abstractions. The relationships between classes can become complicated. It is necessary for the algorithm designer to be clear about what relationships exist and what the ramifications of them are. It is very important that components common to various subclasses be abstracted out and placed as high in the hierarchy as possible. If this is not done, then all the problems of redundant code will sneak in, as

FIGURE 7.8 A simple inheritance hierarcy.

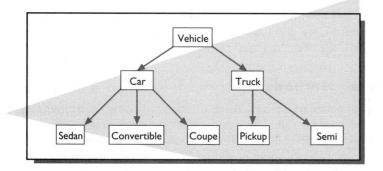

tasks are coded again and again in different subclasses. If the proper abstractions were first done, then these tasks could have been coded once in the appropriate parent class, with all subclasses sharing that single original.

Fortunately, there is a natural way of representing these relationships among classes. It is one of our more basic data structures and also happens to be the very representation that people have used for hundreds of years to keep track of their ancestry: a family tree. We see such a diagram in Fig. 7.8. It shows the relationships among the three classes defined in Examples 7.8, 7.9, and 7.10, as well as among some other possible subclasses that we have not yet defined.

7.7.6   OO Modeling of Real World Behaviors

In our example concerning Vehicles, we modeled only data attributes of Vehicles, Cars and Trucks. While those classes evidenced some behavior (i.e., the classes provided `Initialize` and `Display` methods), the real world objects we modeled didn't, e.g., we didn't drive a car or haul things in a truck. We modeled simple facts, not actions. Let us now consider the challenge of modeling behaviors.

First, we must come to terms with the limits of this medium. Behaviors are active, while books are static. Thus, we will not be able to see actions occur and will instead have to settle for textual reports of actions. You cannot see me type these words or see the mess on my desk as I do it, but you can read a message from me saying, "I am now typing away lickety-split." We'll have to settle for those kind of actions here.

Second, we must realize that the chief challenge we face is to establish the proper hierarchy for behavior. Any method that occurs at it's maximum height in the class hierarchy will have to be designed, coded and tested only once. Any method that is lower in the hierarchy than it can be will have to be designed, coded, and tested multiple times. Maintenance on the former will be cheap; maintenance on the latter will be expensive (and annoying). There is no doubt on this point: we want to locate behaviors as high as possible in the class hierarchy as we *reasonably* can.

As an example, let's consider that problem of creating a class hierarchy for animals, perhaps for a veterinarian's office. For simplicity's sake, let's limit ourselves to only three kinds of pets: dogs, cats and birds. All three have behaviors that are typical of their species: dogs bark and birds chirp, cats slink around and birds fly, and so on. So, how do we represent these behaviors in our hierarchy?

If we limit ourselves to the two kinds of behavior we've just mentioned, we can identify their appropriate categories, say, "moving" and "speaking." Thus, we want our `Animal` class to specify at least these methods for `Move` and `Speak`. Yet, at the abstract level of "Animal", we don't know how to specify what those behaviors will actually be. This is why we need "deferred methods."

7.7.7 Deferred Methods

Deferred methods are necessary because there are many situations where we can see what categories of behavior are called for but we don't yet know how to specify those behaviors. Suppose we were describing pets. In this case, there is no good way of saying how a generic Animal should speak or move. Yet, we know quite well that these are appropriate categories of behavior for our subclasses of dogs, cats, and birds. Thus, we refer to these as deferred methods.

 Definition: A **deferred method** is a method which is incompletely specified because needed details are not known or not knowable, and therefore the class containing them cannot be fully implemented. However, it can serve as a category header in a class which is the parent for various subclasses.

Different languages deal with deferred methods in different ways. At the moment, for simplicity, we will assert that the body of a deferred method in the parent class must do something "safe" to cover the case where a subclass fails to implement a deferred method, and executes that method on the parent. For example, an animal asked to move or speak might just do nothing.

EXAMPLE 7.11 We will model simple behaviors for household pets. Each species has it's own way of moving through the world, and each makes it's own characteristic sounds. Each pet also has its own name. We use both inheritance and deferred methods to model these creatures, below:

```
//-----------------------------------------------

class Animal is deferred

public section

   procedure Speak
      purpose: elicits a sound from the animal
      preconditions: the animal exists
      postconditions: the animal makes an appropriate sound

   procedure Move
      purpose: elicits a description of movement appropriate to the animal
      precondition: the animal exists
      postcondition: the animal's species and its movement are reported

   procedure Get_Name
      purpose: reports the name of the animal
      precondition: the animal has been initialized
```

```
        postcondition: the animal's name is printed
     procedure Initialize
        purpose: obtain and store the pet's name
        precondition: the animal exists
        postcondition: the pet's name is recorded

  protected section

     name isoftype String

     procedure Set_Name(new_name isoftype in String)
         name <- new_name
     endprocedure // Set_Name

     function Get_Name returnsa String
        Get_Name returns name
     endfunction // Get_Name

     procedure Move
         // do nothing
     endprocedure // Move

     procedure Speak
        // print("I cannot speak until you tell me what kind of animal I
               am!")
     endprocedure // Speak

     procedure Initialize
        new_name isoftype String
        print("What is the pet's name?")
        read(new_name)
        Set_Name(new_name)
     endprocedure // Initialize

  endclass // Animal

  //----------------------------------------------
```

In class `Animal`, much was specified: the contracts for speaking, moving, name
reporting, and initialization were provided. In addition, all data and methods for
dealing with the pet's name were completely implemented. The particulars of what it
means to speak and move were deferred.

Subclasses of `Animals` would fill in precisely these methods. They would inherit
from `Animals` and, thus, not have to do anything about those parts of `Animals` that
were not deferred. Completing the deferred methods is all that any subclasses must
do. We show a single example, below.

```
  //----------------------------------------------

  class Dog inherits Animal

  public

  protected

     procedure Move
        print("I am a dog sniffing around")
     endprocedure // Move
```

```
        procedure Speak
            print("Arf")
        endprocedure // Speak

    endclass // Dog

    //-----------------------------------------------
```

We now have an implementation of two simple classes, one each for the superclass `Animal` and its subclass `Dog`. Each attribute and method was located as high as possible in the class tree.

7.7.8   Standard Interfaces for Differing Behaviors:

Some might reasonably question whether it was worth it to establish the categories of behavior in the `Animal` class, where they couldn't be completed. Why bother with the deferred methods? Why not just allow each subclass to handle its means of speaking and moving on it's own? Good questions, all.

By using deferred methods, we have established categories of behavior to which each subclass must conform. The author of the `Dog` class cannot finish his work unless he completes the job of telling us how a dog speaks. Someone defining subclass `Cat` can't finish until she tells us how a cat moves. In effect, we've used deferred methods to establish a standard interface for getting animals to speak or move. We can elicit different behaviors from the same method call because these calls were published in the public section of the shared ancestor of the fully implemented classes. As a result, we know that we need only invoke the single identifier `Speak` in order to hear "Arf," "Chirp," or "Meow." Without the class hierarchy, we'd likely see an evolution of numerous method names that do the same things but with greater confusion, e.g., "Bark" for Dogs, "Tweet" for Birds, "Oink" for Pigs, and so on. By moving the method definition high enough in the hierarchy, we were able to bypass all the species-specific differences and instead build a basis for standard client interfaces.

7.7.9   Resolving Ambiguity

Inheritance allows for great flexibility. It also requires that we know how to resolve any ambiguities that might arise. For example, consider that a parent class (`Vehicle`) and a subclass (`Car`) each have their own definition of what it means to provide the service `Display`. For objects that are of class `Vehicle`, `Display` will print only those attributes of which it has knowledge (e.g., the attributes defined in class `Vehicle`), while the subclass extends `Display` to output all related information, including both the data defined in the ancestor class *and* the data extensions defined within the subclass (e.g., the attributes defined in `Vehicle` and those defined in `Car`).

 When a method is defined in both a subclass and its ancestor, how do we know which version is used? To resolve any possible ambiguities, we always follow a simple rule: Each service request is satisfied according to the definition found at the lowest, most specific level beginning with the class of the object on which the method is invoked.

This means that, whenever a service is requested from any instance of a subclass, we first see whether that service is explicitly defined or redefined for that subclass. If it is, we use that definition. If it is not, we then look to the parent of that subclass and use whatever definition is provided there. If the parent of that subclass doesn't explicitly define the service, then we look to the "grandparent" and so on, in a bottom-up fashion. Sooner or later, we will either (a) encounter a definition for that service (in which case we stop looking and use it) or (b) exhaust the "family tree" of the class without finding a definition (in which case an error has occurred).

7.8 Polymorphism

In addition to *Encapsulation* and *Inheritance*, the OO paradigm provides a third powerful capability: *Polymorphism*.

Definition: **Polymorphism** is the ability to take different forms. In the object-oriented context, it refers to the ability of an object to represent not only an instance of its own class, but also an instance of any of its subclasses.

Polymorphism allows us to maintain the benefits of strong typing while simultaneously allowing us some limited degree of type flexibility provided that we are dealing with objects from the same class lineage. With it, an object can handle not only a representation that conforms to its own class definition but also one that conforms to the definition of any of its descendent subclasses. Polymorphism is limited, as it only applies to those classes that share ancestry. Thus, it is a freedom that is essentially kept "within the family" of a given class hierarchy.

7.8.1 Polymorphism Among Simple Objects

To see what polymorphism is, and how it works, consider the following problem: Imagine that I have found it necessary to pawn my car title to raise money. You, being my best friend, hear of my plight, know how much I love my car, and offer to liberate my car's title by pawning the title to your old truck (to which you are not emotionally attached). We shall represent this series of events in the client algorithm, shown in Example 7.12. The client algorithm makes use of our `Vehicle` class and its `Car` and `Truck` subclasses (from Examples 7.8, 7.9, and 7.10).

> **EXAMPLE 7.12** The situation described above might be represented by the following sequential algorithm:

```
algorithm Title_Loans uses Vehicle, Car, Truck

    // Purpose: demonstrate simple polymorphism
    // via an example of pawning car titles.

    //declare a Vehicle object, used for
    //record keeping by the pawn broker
    pawned_vehicle isoftype Vehicle
```

```
//declare and initialize a Car object
//used to represent my car
my_car isoftype Car
my_car.Initialize

// represent the amount of loan
loan_amount is 1000

// represent the transaction between pawnbroker
// and me: I get $1000, he holds title to my car
brokers_wallet <- broker's_wallet - loan_amount
pawned_vehicle <- my_car
my_wallet <- my_wallet + loan_amount

// at this moment, the Vehicle object
// pawned_vehicle is storing my_car's data

// declare and initialize a Truck object
// to represent your truck
your_truck isoftype Truck
your_truck.Initialize

// represent your heroic deed, whereby you liberate
// my car's title by putting your own truck in hock
pawned_vehicle <- your_truck

// pawned_vehicle no longer represents my_car;
// pawned_vehicle now represents your_truck instead.
// at different moments the Vehicle object, pawned_vehicle,
// has taken the form of a Car and a Truck.

endalgorithm  // Title_Loans
```

In this example, the Vehicle object, pawned_vehicle, has had a Car object and a Truck object assigned to it at various moments. It has literally taken on different forms: it assumed the form of a Car, then the form of a Truck. Note that any given class has this polymorphic ability only with respect to its subclasses. A Car object could not polymorphically take the form of a Vehicle, nor the form of a Truck, because neither Vehicles nor Trucks are subclasses of Car.

7.8.2 Polymorphism and Collections

One place where polymorphism provides meaningful benefits is when we need to manage collections of a objects from within the same class family. Consider, for example, the problem of running a service department in a dealership that sells and services both cars and trucks. Such a business is likely to have some sort of queue of vehicles waiting for service, but how to manage them?

Without polymorphism, we might declare a Queue object to manage information about Car objects (e.g., car_queue isoftype Queue(Car)) and another queue object to manage Truck objects (e.g., truck_queue isoftype Queue(Truck)). If we did this, the car_queue would not be able to manage

Truck objects, and `truck_queue` wouldn't be able to manage `Car` objects. Each of the two `Queue` objects would be able to store information about only the subclass that it was declared to manage as specified via the generic parameter.

However, it could be more useful for the dealership's service department to have a single queue, thus insuring that customers were always treated on a first in, first out (FIFO) basis.

EXAMPLE 7.13 We exploit polymorphism to manage objects of class `Car` and objects of class `Truck` in the same structure. How? By declaring a `Queue` object to manage data of class `Vehicle`:

```
vehicle_queue isoftype Queue(Vehicle)
```

A `Queue` object declared in this way can, quite obviously, manage data about objects of class `Vehicle`. In addition, it can manage information about any subclass of `Vehicle`, that is, `Car` and `Truck` objects. Thus, at any particular moment, vehicle_queue can store a FIFO list containing any combination of `Car` and `Truck` objects.

As we have seen, any object of class `Vehicle` can be used to store and retrieve information about any `Vehicle` or of any subclass of `Vehicle`. Thus, the object declared as

```
next_in_line isoftype Vehicle
```

might be used to store data about whatever vehicle is to be serviced next, regardless of whether it is an object of class `Vehicle`, `Car` or `Truck`. Then, when we have some number of objects stored in vehicle_queue, the instruction:

```
vehicle_queue.Dequeue(next_in_line)
```

will remove *whatever class* of `Vehicle` was at the front of vehicle_queue and associate it with object next_in_line.

Once an item (say, a `Car`) is enqueued on the queue of `Vehicles`, then is dequeued into next_in_line "itself an object of class `Vehicle`" exactly what has become of our `Car` object? Is it still a `Car`? Or has it been transformed into the less-specific `Vehicle`. When we ask it to `Display`, will it report the four attributes of a `Vehicle` or the six attributes of a `Car`?

In truth, different programming languages have different conventions about this. For our part, we want to keep it simple: an object knows what it is and knows what it can do. Thus, if you dequeue one of our pets from a veterinarian's waiting list, and if you tell it "Speak," then it will speak according to its nature: a `Dog` will say "Arf" while a `Cat` might say "Meow." Should we have more specialized capabilities, and you ask an object to do something it can't, then it won't, just like a `Dog` won't fly (nor will it report a system error) just because you tell him to fly. Rather, he'll just look at you. That's how we think objects should be.

7.9　Hybrid OO vs. Pure OO

So far, we have seen how objects provide a range of features that support *encapsulation, reusability, adaptability,* and *polymorphism*. What we have only hinted at, however, is the essential transformation that these capabilities imply for design:

Every component of an algorithm becomes an object!

In our examples so far, we have followed the typical chain of progression that a given programmer or software organization will go through. First, we used OO constructs to encapsulate our *collections* of data. In our earlier examples, we developed queue classes that offered us radically improved levels of encapsulation, reusability, and adaptability. Yet these queues were used to manage collections of conventional, unencapsulated data structures.

Following this, our next step was to extend OO attention to those *individual data structures* themselves. At this stage, we created relationships among classes that represented the attributes of different kinds of vehicles and household pets. With both our data and our collection structures adapted to the OO paradigm, what's left?

The main algorithm, that's what. In example 7.14, below, we take this final step and create a class that coordinates the activity of a Dealership program, as customers leave their vehicles for service, then are notified when their vehicles are ready.

EXAMPLE 7.14　We create a system that allows car dealerships to receive customer orders for servicing their cars or trucks, and to find out which of the serviced vehicles have been worked on and are now ready for pick up their owner.

The system itself is quite simple. There are five classes: `Vehicle`, its subclasses `Car` and `Truck`, the `Queue` class, and the `Dealership` class. We have seen implementations for four of these five classes. Thus, we already know that:

- The `Vehicle` class provides the data that are relevant to all vehicles, as well as the services that allow this data to be obtained and printed.
- The subclasses `Car` and `Truck` inherit from class `Vehicle`, then add the additional data items that are specific to the subclass. In addition, they redefine the services for obtaining and printing information as appropriate to their extended data.
- The `Queue` class provides generic queue behavior for whatever data type is specified for a given queue object.

The fifth class is the only one that is new to us: class `Dealership`, provided below. It includes the declaration of two objects of class `Queue` which, via generic parameter, are specified as managing items of class `Vehicle`. Note that `Dealership` does *not* inherit from any of these classes. Rather, it is a *client* of them (i.e., it declares object of these classes and makes use of the services which they provide).

```
//-----------------------------------
class Dealership uses Queue, Vehicle, Car, Truck

    protected
      order_queue isoftype Queue(Vehicle)
```

```
order_queue.Initialize
ready_queue isoftype Queue(Vehicle)
ready_queue.Initialize

procedure Place_Order
// purpose: allows a customer to place his vehicle in line for
//          service.
// preconditions: order_queue exists
// postconditions: information about customer vehicle resides on
//     request resides on the FIFO queue so that his car is next in
//        line for service

choice isoftype Char
print("What type of vehicle do you want to have serviced?")
print("(C)ar or (T)ruck: ")
read(choice)

if(Choice = 'C' or 'c') then
    // They want enqueue a car
    new_car isoftype Car
    new_car.Initialize
    if NOT(order_queue.Is_Full) then order_queue.Enqueue(new_car)
else
    // They've got a truck that needs service
    new_truck isoftype Truck
    new_truck.Initialize
    if NOT(order_queue.Is_Full) then order_queue.Enqueue(new_truck)
endif

print("Your order has been successfully processed.")

endprocedure // Place_Order

procedure Ready_Vehicle
// purpose: inform the customer when vehicle is ready
// preconditions: ready_queue exists
// postconditions: a Vehicle is dequeued from the
//     ready queue, its info is displayed

    serviced_vehicle isoftype Vehicle

    ready_queue.Dequeue(serviced_vehicle)
    print("A vehicle of the following description")
    new_vehicle.Display()
    print("has had its service tasks completed.")
    print("Please notify the customer that his order")
    print(" is ready.")

endprocedure //Ready_Vehicle

procedure Menu

    loop
        choice isoftype Char
        print("Welcome to the dealership.")
        print("Choose an option:" )
        print("(P)lace an order")
        print("(G)et the next vehicle that's ready to go")
        print("(Q)uit")
        read(choice)
        exitif(choice = 'Q')
```

```
            if ((choice = 'P') OR (choice = 'p')) then
                Place_Order
            else if ((Choice = 'G') OR (choice = 'g')) then
                Ready_Vehicle
            else //have selected invalid option
                    print ('Please try again!')
            endif
        endloop
        print( 'The dealership has closed. Goodbye!' )

    endprocedure //Menu

    procedure Initialize
        Menu
    endprocedure // Initialize

endclass //Dealership

//-----------------------------------
```

From this example we can see how activity flows through an OO implementation. The `Dealership` class merely needs a rudimentary main algorithm which declares and then initializes an object of type `Dealership`. Its `Initialize` method then retains control of the operation until the whole algorithm is completed.[1]

- First, the objects declared by dealership are *instantiated*. There are two such objects: `order_queue` and `ready_queue`. Each of these objects is created. Where? They are created in the data space in the stack frame belonging to `Dealership` (i.e., at the bottom of the activation stack).

- Following the instantiation of those two objects, we find the definitions of three protected methods within `class Dealership`: `Place_Order`, `Ready_Vehicle`, and `Menu`. (All three are protected and thus cannot be seen by anyone outside of `class Dealership`.)

- Finally, the initialization portion of `class Dealership` does only a single thing: It calls the method `Menu`. This method takes effect in the usual way: It gets its own frame on the activation stack, and its local variables are allocated within that frame. (In the case of `Menu`, we can see that it requires only a single `Char` variable named `choice`.) It then begins to execute. Examination of `procedure Menu` shows that it will continuously prompt the user for a choice ("placing an order" or "retrieving data on a ready vehicle" or "quitting"). The choice `quit` is the only one that terminates the execution of the algorithm. In other words, `Menu` continues to operate forever unless someone selects the `quit` option. When either of the other two options is selected, either the

---

1. Some languages go further and allow for automatic initialization of objects, thereby eliminating the main algorithm altogether.

`Place_Order` or `Ready_Vehicle` methods of `Dealership` are invoked. In the case of the former, a vehicle is `Enqueued` on the `order_queue`, while the latter causes a vehicle to be `Dequeued` from the `ready_queue`. And so on.

When invoked, `Dealership`'s method `Ready_Vehicle` will ask the `Vehicle` object that is ready to `Display`. Because any particular `Vehicle` may be a `Car` or a `Truck` object, and since both `Car` and `Truck` classes have redefined `Display` services, the complete data for each car or truck will be printed without the `Dealership` having any explicit knowledge of whether it is a `Car` or `Truck` object that is responding to the `Display` request.

In summary, we have used a total of five classes: a `Dealership` class, a `Vehicle` class and its two subclasses `Car` and `Truck`, and the `Queue` class. Given the existence of the other classes, the functionality of `Dealership` required minimal coding. All that was needed was a method for placing orders, a method for receiving news that vehicle is ready, and a menu to control the user interface.

This simplistic example gives just a hint of how powerful processing tools can be built upon other coded abstractions *without knowing about their implementation details*. This mode of programming is the current state of the art, supporting excellent software engineering practices, especially the extensive reuse of existing code.

As OO spreads throughout the software community, you can expect programmers to follow the same progression we have followed here. Initially, those who jump into OO often don't realize all the ramifications. They begin by doing what is known as "Hybrid OO," wherein they use OO constructs to encapsulate their data collections, and perhaps their underlying data elements as well. Yet they continue to think in terms of the "normal" structured paradigm, as evidenced by the presence of traditional "main" algorithms which exercises centralized control over the program. It is generally only after some considerable experience with the Hybrid OO approach that experienced programmers reach the "aha" experience and begin to write Pure OO.

Definition: **Hybrid OO** refers to the use of OO constructs to encapsulate data collections, and perhaps the underlying data elements, while maintaining the traditional design approach of having a main algorithm that exerts centralized control.

Definition: **Pure OO** refers to the use of OO constructs to effect a complete transformation to the OO paradigm. Pure OO programs feature a main algorithm (or "root class") which exists only for the purpose of starting up what is otherwise a system of distributed control and coordination mechanisms.

Interactive programs (including those on the internet), graphical-interface operating systems (such as the Windows and Mac operating systems), and complex database applications are the applications that most call for a Pure OO approach. Traditional data processing applications can do quite fine with Hybrid OO, provided that they stay within the paradigm of single, monolithic control as opposed to distributed resources and control. Increasingly however, the world is making this harder to do.

FOOD FOR THOUGHT

What Science Can't Do (Yet)

In creating behavioral abstractions, we combine a specification of *what an entity is* (its data and structure) with *how it behaves* (its actions). In doing so, we create an algorithmic paradigm that is inherently social in nature. Objects interact according to how they are defined.

We have now come to a point that touches on many, if not most, of the challenges faced by both science and society. In the realm of social phenomena, society turns to science for answers and finds little of substance. To date, science has been most successful in helping us understand the material world. It has been significantly less useful for understanding human phenomena. Sociology, psychology, anthropology, management, economics: these are the new sciences that emerged about the time of electronic media. They are *human sciences* and their success has been limited by the complexity of human phenomena.

As our algorithmic paradigm becomes more and more focused on behavioral abstractions, we find ourselves at an important threshold. Such a paradigm means that our algorithms are based on *social contracts among behavioral entities*. As we learn more and more about how to abstract, design, and implement such contracts successfully, we may well get better at being able to abstract and articulate the social contracts that are implicitly at work throughout our human world.

We hope this is so, because it is in precisely this arena that society faces its pressing dilemmas:

- We seek to understand the workings of our immune systems and our internal "genetic programs." Recent research has discovered that these systems involve a great deal of complex interaction among their constituent parts. What are the *implicit contracts* that govern our genetic processes, our biological clocks, our aging mechanisms, and so on?
- We seek a humane society such that fellow citizens do not go without food and shelter. Yet our efforts at social welfare have resulted in unintended consequences that subvert our humane goals. What are the *implicit contracts* that govern human responses to societal systems? How can we support the needy without creating ghettos of dependence that are lacking in hope?
- We seek to educate our populace such that everyone has the basis for a full and productive life. Yet our schools are increasingly unsuccessful at fulfilling their function. What are the *implicit contracts* that determine a student's learning experience? In a world where many students focus on career preparation, how can we support both their needs and the needs for broad knowledge acquisition and critical thinking?

If we enumerate the challenges that society faces, many of them involve crucial elements of *implicit contracts of interaction* among many entities in a complex system. To date, the human sciences have not achieved enough rigor to produce much useful information about this kind of phenomena. As we gain more and more experience with explicit social contracts as the very basis that underlies our algorithmic models, we may be able to better abstract and effectively simulate those implicit contracts that are at work in shaping daily human experience. Developing these abilities seems essential if the human sciences are to reach maturity.

Indeed, this is why affordable computing has brought with it a great increase in research being done with computer simulations in all the human sciences. Researchers are hoping to develop algorithmic models that adequately describe the behavior and experience of human beings and their communities and institutions. In the absence of such models and simulations, our understanding of human phenomena will remain limited by complexity. Computing may help us gain breakthrough insights into human phenomena, or we may discover that much human phenomena prove too complex for even algorithmic models to handle. It is still too soon to tell.

Imagine yourself to be a researcher in one of the human sciences. What about the human condition would you want to investigate? Whatever it is, how might you model the relevant human states as data? How might you specify the algorithm for transformations from one state to another? What are the necessary and sufficient conditions for such state changes? How would you go about seeing if your model of human phenomena was useful?

SUMMARY

The import idea of behavioral abstraction is the encapsulation of data with methods. By encapsulating both within a behavioral abstraction, we improve our ability to hide the details and to allow algorithms to be expressed at a higher level of abstraction.

We achieve behavioral abstraction by using two new constructs: *classes* and *objects*. We define behavioral abstractions by creating classes. A class may include the definition of data types but is more than a data type. A class also includes a specification of all the actions that may be performed on its data. Data defined within a class may be accessed only by those procedural abstractions (or "methods") that are created as part of the class.

Once we have defined a class, client algorithms may declare objects of that class. An object is somewhat similar to a variable, in that it stores some state of data. However, unlike a variable, an object's data cannot be directly accessed. Instead, it may be accessed only by invoking a method that is defined as part of the object's class. Since a client algorithm may only manipulate an object's data by calling predefined methods, the client must know what those methods are, what they do, and how to call them. This information is provided in the *public section* of a class. The public section includes all the information a client needs to know about using objects of the class. It includes each method's contract, which specifies the purpose, the preconditions, and the postconditions for that method. Given this information, the client algorithm knows what it can do with an object of that class and how to do it. All other information about a class is hidden in the class' *protected section*. It includes all data declarations and the body of all procedures and functions.

Thus, clients may see those aspects of a class that it needs to know but may not see the implementation details. This supports a higher level of abstraction in the client algorithm. The client need not (and cannot) be concerned with low-level implementation details. Instead, it can request that higher-level logical operations be performed.

Utilization of these capabilities permits object-oriented design, in which all abstractions are raised to the level of behavioral abstractions such that an algorithm is a specification of various objects and of how they interact with one another. Inheritance allows these higher abstractions to be more easily constructed from one another, supporting easier reuse. There are two kinds of inheritance:

- Extension, in which a new subclass inherits all the capabilities of its parent class and then adds new capabilities to those it inherited;
- Redefinition, in which a new subclass inherits all the capabilities of its parent class and then redefines how one or more of them are implemented.

Inheritance allows us to minimize coding. Instead of having to code each new capability from scratch, inheritance allows us to reuse existing code such that we need only write code for the differences between the existing code and the new or different capabilities we want to implement.

EXERCISES

7.1 Create a class for a simple counter. A counter may be incremented by 1, decremented by 1, and initialized or reset to 0. In addition, the value of a counter may be returned at any time. No other operations are permitted on an object of class counter.

7.2 Pretend that we do not have the built-in type String available to us. Create a class for Strings that manipulates characters. Objects of class String should be read via method Read_String() and printed via methods Print_String(). To read, you may prompt the user to enter text and signify the end by hitting the Enter key. Blank spaces may be legitimate elements of a String. Blank spaces are not delimiters that separate one String from another; the Enter key serves that role. You may assume that a press of the Enter key can be detected by an algorithm via the built-in constant EOL (for end-of-line), for example, "if (this_char = EOL)..."

7.3 Create an class for an ordered (in ascending order) list of numbers by declaring an appropriate class. Objects of this class should be accessible to clients only via these logical operations:

Add_To_List	Inserts a new item in the appropriate order.
Delete_From_List	Removes the indicated item from the list.
List_Size	Returns a number indicating the number of items currently in the list.
Current_Data	Returns the data stored in the current list item.
Is_In_List	Determines if a given value is in the list.
Find_Item	Makes the list item storing the value passed in by parameter the "current" item; does not do anything else.
Smallest_Item	Makes the smallest item in the list the "current" item; does not do anything else.
Largest_Item	Makes the largest item in the list the "current" item; does not do anything else.
Next_Item	Makes the successor to the current item the new current item; does not do anything else.
Previous_Item	Makes the predecessor of the current item the new current item; does not do anything else.

7.4 Take your solution for problem 7.3 and modify it to be more generic. Rather than managing an ordered list of numbers, your class should manage an ordered list of any kind of data item. To do so, it will require two generic parameters: one specifying the kind of data item to be stored, another specifying which field of that data item shall serve as the key.

7.5 Create a class for keeping track of the student body of a given college or university, ordered by grade point average (GPA). Include student name, ID number, major, number of credit hours completed to date, and GPA. You may solve this problem using your answers to previous problems.

7.6 Create a stack class in its entirety that includes public methods for push, pop, and retrieve top (without removing it). It may include additional protected methods as appropriate.

7.7 Using an object of your stack class from problem 7.6, write an iterative version of the depth-first traversal In_Order for a binary tree.

7.8 From Chapter 5, we know that arrays and linked lists each have advantages and disadvantages relative to each other. For many problems, it would be convenient to have the random access capability of arrays coupled with the dynamic sizing that linked lists offer. Create a class called Vector that implements this idea and includes the following methods. Your solution should reflect your judgment as whether each method should be public or protected.

7.9 As we have discussed, a priority queue is a queue with a somewhat different Enqueue operation. Create a class for a priority queue, assuming that each enqueued item has some data field containing a numerical priority associated with it (perhaps in a field named "Priority") such that the smaller the priority rating, the higher the priority. You may use your answers to any previous questions as appropriate to lessen how much code you write here.

7.10 Create an OO representation of a movie theatre. Model the behavior of customers, the ticket seller, and the concession-booth worker. You may assume that the theatre has only a single screen, one ticket seller, and one concession-booth worker.

7.11 Use your work from problem 7.10 to model a multi-screen theatre with several concession-booth workers. *Note:* If your work for problem 7.9 features good abstraction, this should be trivial.

7.12 Create an OO representation of a fast food restaurant "drive-thru" window. Do not consider customers who go inside the restaurant; consider only the drive-thru part of the business. You may limit the size of the menu to a few items of each category: sandwiches, fries, drinks, desserts. Be sure to model the two interactions that typically occur: first, an interaction whereby the order is placed, then a second interaction involving payment and delivery of the ordered items. Be sure to model the waiting list in between those interactions.

7.13 Create a class that models the operations of a bank account, including deposits, withdrawals, interest accumulation, overdraft protection (with penalty fees), and service charges.

7.14 Design and implement an OO representation of a drive-thru-only bank. Model the behavior of customers and tellers. Be sure to allow for a line of waiting cars.

7.15 Design and implement an OO representation of a card game of Solitaire. There are many such games; you may implement your choice. You may assume the existence of a "random-card dealer" that will support random dealing of cards and that will ensure that each card is dealt only once. For example, you may call Next_Card, which will return a record with fields for suit and denomination; if the deck is exhausted, it will return the String constant EOD (for "end of deck") as the suit and the number 0 as the denomination.

7.16 Design and implement an OO representation of the board game Monopoly. You may assume the existence of a random number generator that will serve as dice. For example, you may call the method Roll_Dice, which returns a single record containing two numbers, each between 1 and 6, inclusive. You may also restrict the number of properties as you see fit.

7.17 Design and implement an OO representation of a small airport that serves only private pilots (i.e., there are no paying passengers, security checks, etc.). Think carefully about this problem before requesting further specification.

7.18 Design and implement an OO representation of an airport that features commercial flights (i.e., paying customers must be boarded, their bags checked, etc.). Your solution should extend your answer to the previous problem. Think carefully about this problem before requesting further specification.

CHAPTER 8

Tools for Verifying Correctness

Computers have one particular attribute that is both a blessing and a curse: They do *exactly* what we tell them to do. Ordinarily, you might think this is a good thing, and in many ways it is. It is unfortunate only when what we tell them to do is wrong.

Because we are people, it often happens that we accidentally tell computers to do the wrong thing. And, because computers are so literal and stupid, they have no talent whatsoever for figuring out what we meant to tell them. As a result, computers can be counted upon to reliably repeat each and every mistake, again and again, exactly as we (erroneously) have told them to do!

Obviously, algorithmic errors must be located and corrected. However, as computing is used to attack problems that are more and more complex, it naturally happens that our algorithms themselves become more and more complex. The great complexity of modern algorithms makes it difficult to know when all the errors in an algorithm have been detected and repaired. Diagnosing and locating the errors that we accidentally build into our algorithms, or (better yet) preventing and avoiding those errors to begin with, is the single most difficult challange that faces the software industry today, with associated costs running into many billions of dollars per year.

In this chapter, we define and describe the four basic kinds of algorithmic errors that can and do occur. We discuss which kinds of error can be located by automated means versus those that require human judgment to be detected. We also describe the two main approaches for showing that an algorithm is correct: proving the correctness of an algorithm logically, and verifying the correctness of an algorithm by rigorous testing.

8.1   Bugs and Debugging

During World War II, U.S. Navy officer Grace Hopper and her colleagues were calculating trajectories using one of the first computers ever built. At some point, the vacuum-tube behemoth stopped working and the scientists began an exhaustive search for the source of the problem. After much work, they finally discovered that an insect was stuck in the circuitry of the computer. Ever since then, hard-to-find sources of error in computer programs have been called "bugs."

"Debugging," then, means finding all errors in a program and correcting them. In this chapter we shall focus on some techniques for debugging. These techniques are invaluable to any computer programmer because it has been estimated that over 70 percent of a programmer's time is spent dealing with errors. In fact, it is almost unheard of to write a program of any size that is completely correct in the first draft. No programmer is expected to write a bug-free first draft, but he or she is expected to do enough testing so that all of the errors are detected and corrected.

Occasionally, a major error escapes detection, often with terrible results. We rely on computers to carry out all sorts of critical tasks, and if a computer is programmed incorrectly there can be dire consequences. For example, consider the Hubble Space Telescope project. After the telescope had been launched by NASA, it became evident that there was a problem in the optics. Upon examination, an error was discovered in the computer program that monitored the lens grinding. It was a very small error, and would have been simple to correct—had someone found it in time! This expensive incident illustrates how important it is for programmers to carefully check their work.

Definition: An **algorithmic error** is any error in an algorithm that causes the algorithm to fail to fulfill its intended purpose. There are four basic types of algorithmic errors: *ambiguity, syntactic errors* and *semantic errors* (which are different aspects of *language errors*), and *logic errors*.

8.1.1   Ambiguity

Ambiguity is the easiest type of error to eliminate from an algorithm.

Definition: **Ambiguity** means imprecise or unclear instructions. Such instructions yield many interpretations and will lead to an unpredictable final outcome of the algorithm.

Human beings are quite good at making educated guesses to overcome ambiguity, but computers are notoriously incapable of doing so. A computer would not be able to execute an ambiguous algorithm. To guarantee that an algorithm written for a computer is sufficiently clear and precise, we translate it from natural language (such as English) to a special language called a programming language.

Programming languages, including BASIC, Pascal, Fortran, and C, have a very limited vocabulary of words and symbols (other than identifiers) that a computer can recognize. This means that there are fewer ideas that can be expressed in such languages than in English. Programming languages have one great advantage, however; it is much easier for a computer to understand a limited language than a rich one such as English.

EXAMPLE 8.1 Consider a simple instruction that adds two numbers and places the result in a variable called x. In English, there are a plethora of ways to express this operation:

- x equals the sum of 2 and 2
- x equals the addition of 2 and 2
- add 2 plus 2 and place the result in variable x
- take 2, add 2 to it, then write the answer in x

and so on.

In the Pascal programming language, however, there is exactly one correct way to express the operation:

```
x := 2 + 2;
```

It is obvious that it is easier to create a computer program capable of understanding this one form of addition instruction rather than the various forms expressible in English. The Pascal instruction is not ambiguous because only one meaning is associated with it.

8.1.2 Syntax Errors

Once we have translated an algorithm into a programming language, another category presents itself: language errors. There are two types of language errors: *syntax* errors and *semantic* errors.

Definition: A **syntax error** can be thought of as a "typo" or a similar kind of mistake, such as a misspelling, a use of words that are not part of the language, or a use of words in a pattern that violates the grammar of the language.

For instance, if the language we are using is Pascal, a semicolon is required at the end of most instructions. Leaving the semicolon off constitutes a syntax error. Other examples include using '×' to indicate multiplication rather than the asterisk '*', and typing a capital letter ('O') where a zero ('0') is called for. Such errors are done primarily by novices. Once a person is familiar with the programming language and the symbols on the keyboard, he/she can avoid most syntax errors if careful.

8.1.3   Semantic Errors

The other kind of language error is not related to grammar of the language but rather with the meaning expressed in it.

Definition: A **semantic error** is an error in the meaning of an instruction. An instruction may be precise and have no typos, and yet may not make sense, or may be illegal in the context in which it appears.

EXAMPLE 8.2   Consider the following code in which there are two attempts to make improper assignments.

```
MAX_ARRAY_SIZE is 100
Number_Array definesa array[1..MAX_ARRAY_SIZE] of Num
this_array isoftype Number_Array

y isoftype Char
read(y)

x isoftype Num
x <- y
this_array[150] <- x
```

According to the syntax of our pseudocode, there are no syntax errors. Each individual symbol is valid, but they are arranged such that their meaning is improper, that is, after a Char value is read into variable y, the next statement attempts to assign that character value to x, which is a Num variable. Then, an attempt is made to assign a value to cell 150 of the array variable this_array. We know from the declarations that the type of this array has locations 1 through 100; position 150 does not exist. In both of these cases, syntactically correct symbols are used in an improper manner with regard to the meaning they have. These are semantic errors: errors with respect to the meaning of syntactically correct instructions.

Both syntactic and semantic errors are fairly easy to deal with, because the computer itself can detect them. This detection is accomplished by software that translates algorithms from their human-readable form (written in a programming language and know as "source code") into a binary machine-readable form (appropriate to the computer and known as "object code").

There are two kinds of such special-purpose translation software: compilers and interpreters. For most programming languages, translation is performed by a *compiler*, which scans the entirety of the source code and produces either a listing of errors (if there are any) or executable binary code (if there are no errors). In the presence of any errors that are detected by the compiler, the program being compiled cannot be run until all the "compile-time" errors are corrected and the source code is successfully recompiled. Often, it takes multiple "compile-repair-recompile" cycles before a programmer can actually run the program for the first time.

The other kind of translation software is called an *interpreter*. Unlike a compiler, an interpreter does not try to translate the entire program and make a list of all the errors in one step. Instead, an interpreter begins to translate-and-run the program one step at a time. Thus, the first instruction is examined and, if correct, it is executed; then the second instruction, and so on. Thus, using an interpreter, if a program is correct except for a single error near the end, the program will appear to run, then abruptly stop near the end and give the programmer an error message.

Regardless of whether translation is accomplished by a compiler or an interpreter, if a statement contains either a syntactic or semantic error that the translation software can recognize, the computer will halt processing and print an error message to the programmer stating the location at which the offending element resides. The programmer then checks that part of the program for errors and corrects the indicated error or errors. At worst, the programmer may need to consult a language reference manual and/or play detective to compensate for the imperfect ability of translation software to correctly identify the cause of each error it finds.

These kinds of errors are *not* the difficult kind. Yet, for novices, they prove to be a big distraction. When novices are introduced to programming, it is usually the case that they spend countless hours "wrestling" with the compiler, writing a poor program, then relying on the compiler to find their errors. Unfortunately, what usually happens is that the repair of some errors makes the program only slightly better and allows the compiler to then find more errors that had been effectively masked by earlier errors. The net result is that novices can spend two hours writing a program but 15 hours debugging it. In our experience, it is far better to make sure that novices know how to write decent programs *before* they try to compile them and run them. Then, instead of spending two hours writing and 15 hours debugging, a novice might spend four hours writing and two hours debugging.

8.1.4 Logic Errors

The fourth type of error, an error in logic, is often much trickier to find than other types of errors, and plagues veterans as well as novices.

 Definition: A **logic error** is a flaw that causes the algorithm to do something other than what it is supposed to do. The error might be located in a single instruction, or it might be found in the interaction between two or more instructions. An algorithm may have logical errors even when it is syntactically and semantically correct.

EXAMPLE 8.3 Consider the following algorithm intended to sum the numbers from 1 to 10:

```
algorithm Add_One_To_Ten

    total isoftype Num
    total <- 0

    i isoftype Num
    i <- 1

    loop
       i <- i + 1
       total <- total + i
       exitif ( i >= 10 )
```

```
        endloop

   endalgorithm // Add_One_To_Ten
```

The way that the algorithm is written, it will be understood by a computer and will execute. However, it has a logical error and will therefore give an incorrect result. To see why, trace through the loop by hand, using paper and pencil. Notice that the loop begins when i equals 1 and ends when i equals 10. Also notice that it terminates when the value of i reaches 10. Thus, it might appear to work correctly. Unfortunately, we have incremented i inside the loop *prior to* its addition to the total. Hence, our algorithm produces the following result:

```
   Total <- 2 + 3 + 4 + 5 + 6 + 7 + 8 + 9 + 10 = 54
```

This is obviously an incorrect answer to the task the algorithm was designed to perform: it fails to add the value 1 to total. The loop contains a logical error.

Observe that there is no single cause of the error in Example 8.3. Rather there are two different possible causes and thus there are two ways that we can correct the logical error: We can leave the loop as is and initialize variable i to 0, not 1; or we can leave the initialization of i alone and move the first in-loop step (which increments the value of i) to the last in-loop position. Many logical errors are like this; it is not one thing that causes them, but rather an error-producing combination of two or more statements.

Notice that, without any changes, the algorithm of Example 8.3 provides a perfectly valid answer to a different question—namely, "What is the sum of the numbers from 2 to 10?" Many logic errors can be looked at in this manner. They result in an algorithm that answers a different question than the intended one. For this reason, such errors are often hard to recognize because the program appears to work correctly.

 Warning: Check all algorithms carefully "by hand and mind" before accepting them as correct. Do not merely write an algorithm and assume it is correct just because it will get through the compiler, execute, and return a result!

Programmers have a phrase that accurately describes the effect of logic errors: "garbage in, garbage out." This states the truth that a computer is only as correct as the program it is running. If you write your algorithm carelessly and it contains logical errors, the computer will nonetheless do exactly what you tell it to do.

To avoid logic errors, it is necessary to do four things:

1. Understand the problem.
2. Use abstraction to break down the problem into manageable subproblems so that the solution will be modular.
3. Anticipate all possible input data.
4. Trace your code.

Here's why each of the four is important.

1. *Understand the problem.*

Often, when an algorithmic task is assigned, the people who are to write the algorithm are left wondering about *exactly* what is being asked of them. *This is no accident.* It is normal for a person who assigns an algorithm-writing task (perhaps a software product manager, or a software consultant's client, or a faculty member) to have a general idea about what they want the algorithm to do without having considered all the details. The general idea may well be clear, but it often happens that in the course of solving the general problem many smaller issues pop up.

When issues and questions do pop up, the algorithm writer can make assumptions about how such issues should be resolved, but doing so is risky and error-prone. Often, the result is an algorithm that does not perform to specification because an adequate specification was never formulated. Rather than make assumptions, it is imperative that you ask as many questions as necessary to achieve clarity.

This is a primary skill for writing algorithms: finding out *exactly* what is being asked of the algorithm. You must get accustomed to asking questions about particular requirements, as it will be impossible to create successful algorithms without doing so. If you do not have an adequate specification, it is unlikely that you will satisfy it!

2. *Use abstraction to break down the problem into manageable subproblems so that the solution will be modular.*

Not only is it imperative that you understand what the algorithm must accomplish as a whole, it is equally necessary that you have clarity about what is involved in each part of the solution. This is another reason why modularity, by way of good procedural abstraction, is so important in programming. Earlier, we saw that abstraction and modularity are important in helping us solve complex problems by breaking them into simpler ones. The need for correctness provides another reason: Abstraction enables modularity, and modularity localizes the effect of instructions. Localizing the effects of instructions aids programmers in tracking down hard-to-find logical errors. So, by using abstraction well, we make it easier to ensure that our algorithms are correct.

For example, recall that the error in Example 8.3 (our Add_One_To_Ten algorithm). It was caused by an interaction of two parts of the algorithms: the initialization of i and the incrementing of i. Neither of these two parts was wrong in and of itself; the error was caused by the fact that these two parts did not coordinate things properly. Now, imagine that these two lines were not so close together. Imagine that they were spread apart by several pages of other instructions. How long do you think a novice might spend before he found the problem? Good procedural abstraction forces us to put things together in small logical chunks to make each chunk and the whole algorithm far easier to diagnose and repair.

3. *Anticipate all possible input data.*

One must also examine the kinds of input data that the algorithm will need to handle. An algorithm that works for most input values but fails for one value is like a time bomb waiting to explode. For example, a program that takes the logarithm of an input value n will fail when n is 0... *if* the programmer forgot to check if $(N = 0)$ and deal with it. Imagine the chaos if this system was being used by a national bank when someone input a value of zero and caused the program to crash.

This is not just a hypothetical concern. There have been numerous occasions of this kind of error having disastrous consequences. For example, a few years ago, the entire AT&T long distance telephone network crashed (see "The Day the Earth Stood Still" in Food for Thought at the end of this chapter), crippling communications throughout the entire North American continent and costing literally billions of dollars. The cause was a piece of software whose author assumed that his code would always be sent correct values as parameters. For years, that code worked just fine. Then, one day, a value was passed by parameter that shouldn't have been, and the whole North American telephone system crashed.

At first, you might think that the problem lies with the source of the "bad value." However, it is virtually impossible to guarantee that a program will never encounter a bad value. What *is* possible is algorithmic means to stop such errors from having bad consequences. In fact, standard programming practice calls for very simple and easy ways of handling such things, for example, by having a simple "guard statement" in the program that says, in effect, "If a bad value comes in, print the appropriate error message; else process the good values."

To make sure that bad data don't cause computer systems to fail, programmers create *exception handlers* in their programs and create a series of test runs using many different input values. If an input is valid, the program should produce a correct result. If the input is invalid, the program should detect it and handle it in a "graceful" manner and not crash. In a subsequent programming course, you should learn methods and techniques for creating appropriate exception handlers. In this course, make sure you are clear about whether or not your algorithmic solutions may assume good data or whether you are expected to write them so that they can handle bad data as well.

4. *Trace your code, then test it.*

Unlike language errors, logical errors can not be detected by a computer. The computer sees only the algorithm, not the original problem. Hence, it cannot detect that the algorithm is unsuitable for solving the problem at hand. It is left to the programmer to demonstrate the correctness of the algorithm.

Both experience and research has shown that the single most important thing an algorithm author can do to find and remove logical errors is to systematically trace the code of the algorithm. Tracing is performed "by hand and mind" as the author creates a set of input values and executes the algorithm as if he or she were the computer. Even senior software engineers who have decades of experience routinely catch their own errors this way.

Testing refers to the idea of running a computer program with specially designed sets of test input data. The idea is that the programmer carefully chooses the kinds of data values (both good and bad) that will be most likely to expose flaws in the program, then inputs those values to see how the program handles them. Such testing can be done most comprehensively in an automated fashion. In a later programming course, you should learn how to construct appropriate sets of test data. With pseudocode, you can do a reasonably thorough job by being thoughtful in choosing the values you use for tracing.

8.2   Proving Correctness

Obviously, we want to be able to know that our algorithms are logically correct. But how can we truly know that they are? If we want to be sure, we require some means of proving that they are. One such approach comes from logicians and is based on the fact that an algorithmic problem can be divided into two parts:

1. The specification of legal input data.
2. The relationship between the inputs and the desired outputs.

For example, the input might be an integer between 1 and 100, and the desired relationship between input and output might specify: "The output is the cube of the input value." For an algorithm to be correct, we would expect that the second criterion must be met when input satisfying the first criterion is entered.

There are two classes of correctness of algorithms: total and partial.

- *Total correctness* implies that, for all valid input values, an algorithm will reach a stopping point, and when it halts, it will have obtained a correct result (one that satisfies the second criterion).
- *Partial correctness* means that an algorithm will not always halt for legal input values, but when it does, it will have obtained a correct result. Hence, it will not always return a result, but if it does, then we know the result is correct.

Under what condition will an algorithm be partially correct? Well, if for some input values the algorithm enters an infinite loop, it will not halt. For other values, the algorithm does not loop endlessly and instead produces a correct result.

Our method for proving correctness of an algorithm has two stages:

- Stage 1: We prove partial correctness with the use of *invariants*. An invariant is a statement attached to a given instruction in the algorithm that makes an assertion about the state of the calculation at that point.
- Stage 2: We then prove total correctness using *convergence*. Convergence is a way of proving that the algorithm will always terminate, given valid data.

EXAMPLE 8.4   To illustrate the two stages of proving correctness, let's look at an example. Consider a nonrecursive algorithm for calculating exponents. We will limit the valid input data to be any number for the base, and a positive integer for the exponent. Instead of presenting the algorithm in text, we shall use its flowchart diagram in Fig. 8.1.

In the flowchart, the starting and stopping states are indicated by ovals, decision points are indicated by diamonds, and other executable statements are shown as rectangles. The arrows indicate the ordering of steps.

We have attached assertions at certain key checkpoints where we are sure that the data match certain criteria. These assertions are shown as rounded, shaded boxes. You

FIGURE 8.1 An algorithm with assertions

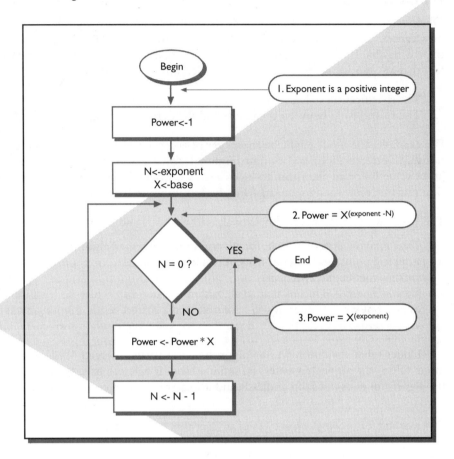

can probably convince yourself that these assertions are true for the first iteration, but we need to prove that the instructions between checkpoints do not invalidate the assertions at any time. Hence, we show how we can start at each assertion and, traversing the algorithm, arrive at the next assertion. Notice that from assertion 1 we can only reach assertion 2, from 2 we can reach 2 or 3, and from 3 we can not reach any other assertions. The proof is shown below.

In Stage 1 we must prove partial correctness with the use of invariants.

1 -> 2: After carrying out the instructions between assertion 1 and assertion 2, we know that $Power = 1$, $X = base$, and $N = exponent$. Hence, it is true that $Power = X^{(exponent - N)} = X^0 = 1$.

2 -> 3: If $N = 0$, and $Power = X^{(exponent - N)}$, then $Power = X^{(exponent)}$

2 -> 2: If `Power` = `X(exponent- N)` and if we carry out the instructions `Power = Power*X` and `N = N-1` between successive encounters of assertion 2, then

$$\text{Power}' = X * \text{Power} = X * (X^{(\text{exponent} - N)})$$
$$= (X^{(\text{exponent} - (N - 1))})$$
$$= (X^{(\text{exponent} - N')})$$

Here, `Power'` and `N'` are introduced to show that the values of those two variables have been updated since the last pass through the loop. This proof has shown that the relationship between `N`, `X`, and `Power` is always maintained.

Now we have made our assertions and proven that they do not change as the algorithm progresses in time. Hence, we call them invariants. Our algorithm is now proven to meet the requirements for partial success.

In Stage 2 of the proof we must prove total correctness using convergence. We must show that the algorithm is totally correct by proving that it terminates for all legal input values. The only way it could avoid terminating is by iterating through the loop infinitely many times. Hence, checkpoint 2 would be traversed infinitely many times. To show that infinite traversing is impossible, we must demonstrate that there is some variable that converges towards a value that will allow us to exercise the exit condition and drop out of the loop. In the algorithm above, the variable is `N`, and we must show that it converges to zero. Indeed, this is the case. Each time we pass through the loop, `N` is decremented. It gets smaller and smaller, until it reaches zero and the loop terminates. Hence, our algorithm is proven to be totally correct.

Notice that if we had allowed inputs such as negative exponents, our algorithm would only be partially correct because it would not terminate for such values; `N` might start out less than zero, and each time it was decremented it would diverge away from zero, becoming increasingly negative.

8.3 Verification

A simpler alternative to the rigorous approach above is an "as you go" verification method.

When performing an "as you go" verification, one verifies that each part of an algorithm is correct as soon as it is designed. After all modules of the algorithm have been verified this way, one must check that the interfaces between modules (the parameters) are not flawed.

For this type of verification, good modularity is essential because it allows each module to be analyzed separately from the others; the algorithm is not treated as a single huge monolith of complex code.

This is why we emphasize both aspects of verification:

- The construction of narrowly focused, task-specific modules.
- Precisely defined interfaces between modules, with all data passed by explicitly defined parameters.

Such designs allow you the chance to create complex algorithms that are correct, maintainable, and extendible. Without these techniques, you have little chance of doing so.

8.4 The Most Important Thing You Can Do

For many years, efforts have been made to improve the extent to which software can diagnose software. Researchers developed better and better compilers such that the compiler provides stronger and stronger help to the programmer in locating algorithmic errors. Progress in this regard has been significant, and today many very inexpensive programming languages come with an excellent *environment*. The word "environment" here refers to the various online features that are provided to the programmer to locate errors and trace execution.

In a related trend, programmers have been able to rely increasingly on software tools to help locate and repair errors. This second trend is quite understandable; after all, if we can implement algorithms to help us find errors in algorithms, why not use them? Indeed, such software tools can make programming much more convenient than it once was.

However, modern research is showing that programmers have moved indiscriminantly in this direction. That is to say, while there are certain benefits that software tools can and do provide, there are also activities that are best done by people, not machines. In particular, we are now discovering that it is far less efficient to use software tools to find most errors than it is for a human being to find them by tracing the code that he or she has created. A programmer who does not thoroughly trace the written code and instead uses a compiler to find errors will spend *more* time than does the programmer who invest some up-front time in design and tracing *before* attempting to compile a program.

It is largely for this reason that we opt to use pseudocode. We do not want you to be distracted by a compiler until *after* you have become practiced at both writing and tracing algorithms.

In subsequent programming courses, much more emphasis will be placed on the use of invariants and other techniques to prevent and avoid errors, and on specific strategies for effective debugging. For now, however, the single most important thing you can do is to become practiced and accomplished at tracing your algorithms. More than any other single factor, effective tracing before compilation, coupled with proper design, significantly reduces the time it takes to achieve an error-free algorithm. If you learn any one thing about correctness, learn to trace your algorithms, and get in the habit of always doing it *before* using a machine for diagnostic help.

FOOD FOR THOUGHT

The Day the Earth Stood Still

In 1951, the landmark movie (and now a cult film), "The Day the Earth Stood Still" was released. In the film, a pleasant young man from Outer Space arrives on Earth (with his robot) to give earthlings a strong message. He uses his alien powers to interrupt all electrically powered activity, bringing earthly activity to a standstill. This gets him the attention he needs to deliver his message: Spacelings had been observing Earth for some time, and were quite prepared to let us do all manner of stupid things to one another, but the advent of our nuclear capability meant that we now had the power to cause damage beyond Earth, so it was time for us to grow up ... or else! Of course, while most earthlings agreed with this message, there were a few nasty earthlings in power who didn't appreciate this sort of alien meddling, and so the plot thickened ("*Klaatu berada nikto*").

In 1989, North America experienced its own version of a day when things stood still. It was the day the phone system crashed, bringing business in North America to a halt, causing all manner of uproar, and resulting in several billion dollars of lost revenue. American business was not amused.

Witnesses at the AT&T Long Lines control center reported an amazing sight. The large electronic map of North America (much like a war room you'd see in a movie) showed the state of telephone traffic in the various sectors around the continent. First, one sector went dark. Seconds later, another sector blacked out. Within minutes, the entire continent went blank, as sector after sector "went down" in a chain reaction. The entire North American long-distance network had crashed.

The first job was to get it "rebooted." As it turned out, nobody was quite sure how to do this. Why? It seems that the network had never actually been started up before. The complex computer-controlled network had *evolved* into being over a period of years, as human-controlled functions were gradually shifted to computer. Thus, there had never been an occasion when the system officially started, which means that since it had never before been "off," no one knew exactly how to turn it on!

AT&T engineers soon figured out how to restart the system (which is why you can call home today), and their attention shifted to figuring out exactly what had happened. As mentioned earlier, they found a "bug of omission": the software had failed to anticipate a particular "bad data" state and, though it took years for that data state to occur, when it finally did occur, it brought the international communications backbone crashing down.

This monumental communications catastrophe was caused by an extremely trivial error. A module within their network control program had the job of making decisions about "what to do next" based on the value it received by parameter. The code was written so that it anticipated all the possible values that were *supposed* to be passed to the module. As long as the incoming parameter value was anticipated by the module everything worked properly. However, as soon as an unanticipated value arrived, the program simply stopped altogether.

This factual story exemplifies one of the chief problems facing us today. We are enmeshed in many complex interdependent systems, each with innumerable details, and the consequences of all the details are impossible to anticipate. This problem shows itself in a couple different ways that each have implications for the future.

First, the story demonstrates the necessity of being extremely thorough in creating effective exception handling. It's not all that hard to create correct algorithms to do whatever we intend them to do *if only we could count on everything going right*. We cannot. As the saying goes, anything that can go wrong will go wrong. Thus, in addition to the algorithmic necessity to articulate the intended recipe of behavior, we must also articulate the behavior of the algorithm for all unintended states that might possibly occur. This is a major challenge and demands a measure of thoroughness that no mainstream human activity has ever before demanded. In effect, we must be better at "expecting the unexpected" than we ever have been before. In practice, this means that a great deal of our software methodologies are focused not on achieving what we want, but instead on *avoiding unintended consequences* that we don't want.

Second, the story brings into focus the difficulty of making sure our decisions are correct when there are so many of them to make. Had the AT&T system had only a small number of decision points, chances are excellent that they all would have been appropriately protected. The fact that this one wasn't is primarily due to the fact that it was *one among so many*.

This same problem shows up in people's lives in ways that have nothing to do with software systems. We live in a time when people have an immense number of choices to make, choices about things both important and trivial, that people have never had before. Should you buy this brand of toothpaste or that one? Should you work on your relationship with this person, or end it and pursue a relationship with that person? Is it worth it to repair the old car one more time, or should you get a newer car? And on and on and on. In modern times, the decisions never stop. Choices to be made everywhere, so many of them, all the time.

Some suspect that this is one the reasons that people feel so hectic and pressured. At my drive-through bank out in the country, an elderly woman teller I know spoke to me about how pressed she feels. "I grew up over there, back before we had plumbing or electricity. Every day, I'd have to walk from here to that blue house to get water from the well. But we were done by dark and would sit around and pass the time together. Nowadays, I only work here 'til noon, then I go on home. But by the time I'm done most nights, *it's after midnight! And I don't know why!*"

And neither does anybody else. This woman used to wash laundry by hand and cook over a wood-fueled stove. Even though these activities were harder and took more time, she had time and energy. And now she doesn't. She wasn't harried, or pressured, or tense. And now she is. Perhaps it's because we spend so much of our lives having to make so many choices and then trying to make the *correct decision for each of them*. Perhaps we don't spend as much physical energy, but we're spending a great deal of psychic energy just trying to make all those "right" decisions.

The story here is a human story. It is not a science fiction story about aliens from outer space, nor a computer network story about the phone system crashing. In human terms, we can't anticipate all the possible consequences, nor can we always be sure which decisions are the right ones. Perhaps the best we can do is to:

- Realize that we're constantly innundated with many choices.
- Distinguish between the ones are worth worrying about and ones that aren't.
- Make sure that we carve out some time for ourselves during which we are free from having to make any decisions at all.

For some people, this last item means meditation. For others, it means swimming or running. For others it means a weekend per month with literally nothing to do. For others, the demands of job and family mean that they haven't found any way to escape the constant psychic pressure of modern times. What is your algorithm for dealing with stress? How well does it work? What are the bugs in it? Are there unintended consequences? How might you get the bugs out? Do you know someone whose algorithm is better than yours? How is it better?

SUMMARY

The cost of algorithmic errors is enormous. By far the greatest portion of programmer time is devoted to finding and correcting them. Due to this immense cost, increasing effort is devoted to preventing them.

There are four kinds of algorithmic errors:

- *Ambiguity:* the meaning of a statement is unclear or subject to interpretation.
- *Syntactic errors:* the grammar of a statement is illegal in the language.
- *Semantic errors:* the statement is legal syntactically but its meaning is incorrect.
- *Logic errors:* the meaning of one or more statements is clear, and the statements are legal, both syntactically and semantically, but their effect is not correct.

Programming languages, by their nature, preclude ambiguity errors. Syntactic errors and most semantic errors can be detected by software translation tools. Logical errors are the most difficult to prevent and to locate, especially in large complex systems, and are the main source of the huge cost of algorithmic errors.

One approach to the prevention of errors is that of *proving correctness*. The goal of this approach is to prove that an algorithm is logically correct with respect to its task. This proof is done by rigorously articulating the relationship between legal input to an algorithm and the resulting output, and by establishing invariants at various key parts of the algorithm. An *invariant* is an assertion about what is necessarily true about the state of computation at that given point in the algorithm. With appropriate invariants established, it is then necessary to logically demonstrate that (a) the algorithmic steps between invariants do not violate the invariants, and (b) the algorithm will terminate for all legal input. This approach is extremely costly and time intensive.

Another approach is as-you-go *verification*. This approach relies on effective modularity and the requirement that each module be individually and extensively tested to make sure that it performs its designated task. With each module verified, it is then necessary to test and verify that the interfaces between the modules are correct and effective at coordinating their joint effort to accomplish the algorithmic task.

Such formal approaches become increasingly important as we implement algorithms in software. However, at the level of basic skill, the single most important and effective means of achieving correctness is to become well practiced and disciplined about tracing code "by hand and mind."

EXERCISES

Each problem from 8.1 through 8.6 has an intended purpose and the corresponding pseudocode solution. It is your task to do the following:

1. Identify all the errors in the given solution. There may be zero, one, or more.
2. For each error, identify what kind of error it is from the list of errors, below, and provide a brief explanation of the error. Your explanation must concisely describe why/when the error might occur, including all error-producing circumstances not ruled out by the question itself.
3. Make corrections to the pseudocode solution to fix the error. These corrections should affect only one or two lines of code per error. After you have made the necessary corrections, the solution should work perfectly for the problem given. Do *not* completely rewrite the solution algorithm.

Note that a single error in the algorithm may be an example of more than one error type. Give *all* error types that might apply to each error.

(Documentation has been intentionally omitted from the problem code, and thus documentation omissions do not qualify as errors in these problems.)

Kinds of errors:

- a. Incorrect initialization
- b. Missing initialization
- c. Using an undeclared variable
- d. Accessing an array incorrectly
- e. Using/calling a function incorrectly
- f. Mismatching types (Assigning one type of variable to another type of variable)
- g. Dereferencing (e.g., trying to follow) a nil or undefined pointer
- h. Inappropriate kind of parameter (in, out, in/out)
- i. Inappropriate kind of module (procedure vs. function)
- j. Failing to increment loop control variable (e.g., Index or Current)
- k. Logical error (Algorithm does the "wrong thing" correctly)
- l. Error not listed above. Specify the nature of the error.
- m. No error

For each error that you find, write the line number in which the error occurs in, the letter corresponding to the type of error, and your correction. Use the following type declaration for all the problems (there are no errors in this section):

```
MAX is 10

Array_Type definesa array [1..MAX] of Num

List_Node definesa record
   data isoftype Char
   next isoftype Ptr toa List_Node
endrecord // List_Node
```

8.1. Intended purpose: Counts the number of nodes in a linked list.

```
1: function Count_Nodes returnsa Char (list_head isoftype
                          in Ptr toa List_Node)
2:    if (list_head = NIL) then
3:       Count_Nodes returns 1
4:    else
5:       Count_Nodes(list_head^.next) + 1
6:    endif
7: endfunction //Count_Nodes
```

8.2. Intended purpose: Return the minimum value found in an array of numbers.

```
1: function Find_Min returnsa Num (the_array isoftype
                       in Array_Type)
2:    the_min isoftype Num
3:    the_min <- The_Array[1]
4:    index <- 0
5:    loop
6:       exitif ((index + 1) > MAX)
7:       if (The_Array[index] < The_Array[index + 1]) then
8:          the_min <- The_Array[index]
9:       endif
10:       index <- index + 1
11:    endloop
12:    Find_Min returns the_min
13: endfunction //Find_Min
```

8.3. Intended purpose: Create a linked list of 20 nodes all having their data field initialized to the letter M.

```
1: procedure Create_List (list_head isoftype in/out
                        Ptr toa List_Node)
2:    current isoftype Ptr toa List_Node
3:    counter isoftype Num
4:    counter <- 1
5:    current <- list_head
6:    list_head <- new(List_Node)
7:    list_head^.data <- 'M'
8:    list_head^.next <- NIL
9:    loop
10:       counter <- counter + 1
11:       current^.next <- new(List_Node)
```

```
12:          current <- current^.next
13:          current^.data <- 'M'
14:          current^.next <- NIL
15:          exitif (counter > 20)
16:      endloop
17: endprocedure //Create_List
```

8.4. Intended purpose: Count the number of A's in a linked list and return that number.

```
1: procedure Count_As (list_head isoftype in Ptr toa
                        List_Node,the_number isoftype out Num)
3:      count isoftype Num
5:      count <- 0
6:      loop
7:          exitif (list_head^.next = NIL)
8:          if (list_head^.data = 'A') then
9:              count <- count + 1
10:         endif
11:     endloop
12:     the_number <- count
13: endprocedure //Count_As
```

8.5. Intended purpose: Create a new node and add it to the end of a linked list. Initialize the newly created node's data field to store the letter C. If the linked list is empty, then have list_head point to the new node.

```
1: procedure Add_End (list_head isoftype in Ptr
                       toa List_Node)
2:      temp_node isoftype Ptr toa List_Node
3:      if (list_head = NIL) then
4:          temp_node^.data <- 'C'
5:          temp_node^.next <- NIL
6:          list_head <- temp_node
7:      endif
8:      if (list_head <> NIL) then
9:          Add_End (list_head^.next)
10:     endif
11: endprocedure //Add_End
```

8.6. Intended purpose: Sum the values in an array of numbers and return that sum.

```
1: function Sum returnsa Num (the_array isoftype in
                              Array_Type)
2:      temp_sum isoftype Num
3:      index isoftype Num
4:      index <- 1
5:      loop
6:          exitif (index > MAX)
7:          temp_sum <- temp_sum + the_array
8:          index <- index + 1
9:      endloop
10: endfunction //Sum
```

8.7. Take one "normal" (for you) day, and carry a piece of paper or a small tape recorder with you. Record each time you are faced with a choice (or contemplate one, even if you don't make a decision about it). Record all choice points, no matter how trivial each might be. Do this from the time you wake until the time you go to bed for a single day.

a. How many choices confronted you?
b. How many of them were trivial "no brainers"?
c. How many of the trivial no brainers were truly automatic decisions. How many actually required a little thought or reflection. Give examples of each kind.
d. How many choices presented themselves that were not resolvable, that is, concerned things that bother you in an ongoing way, about which you haven't yet made a clear decision? What were they about? Work? Personal relationships? Your appearance? What?
e. How many choices did you make without caring whether they were the "right" decisions or not?
f. How many choices caused you to really worry about making the "right" decision?

8.8. With respect to whatever you consider to be the important decisions in your life, how many of your decisions do you consider to have been the "right" decision? How many have been the "wrong" decision? In each case, what aspect of your life were they about? For the "wrong" decisions, what were the "bugs" in your decision algorithm? Were they "syntactic" (i.e., were they about the patterns of life)? Were they "semantic" (i.e., were your errors based on a misunderstanding of the meaning of things)? Were they ambiguity errors? Logical errors?

8.9 Looking back on your life decisions, how has your life experience helped you "debug" your decision algorithms? In what ways?

CHAPTER 9

Tools for Estimating Cost and Complexity

Algorithms are our creations. The current revolution in science and human understanding is, in large part, due to our ability to do more than create algorithms: computer technology allows us to implement these creations (in computer programs) and execute them (by "running" such programs). In short, we not only create algorithms, we can also observe how they perform.

Despite the abstract nature of algorithms, we want to understand their *performance properties*. Just as automotive engineers need to know about the performance of cars, we require knowledge of performance-related attributes if we are to engineer desirable algorithms. Many of the performance attributes of automobiles (miles per gallon, maximum speed, etc.) are readily understood by nontechnical people. In a similar way, we can understand the performance of algorithms without having a great deal of technical knowledge.

To understand the application of computing to the problems of modern times, and to understand what computing can and cannot reasonably do, it is necessary to have a basic foundation in important principles and rules of thumb, just as an educated car-buyer will know what is meant by "miles per gallon" and will have a general idea about realistic versus ridiculous expectations of performance and fuel economy.

In this chapter, we introduce you to the key measures of algorithmic performance and to the general categories of performance that are considered reasonable. To continue our automotive analogy one step further, we would not expect someone who isn't an engineer to be able predict whether a car gets 27 mpg versus 32 mpg, but we would expect everyone to know the difference in both practical value and "reasonableness" between 25 mpg and 250 mpg. We want to provide you with a similar degree of basic knowledge about algorithmic performance.

9.1 Measures of Performance

We are interested primarily in only two aspects of an algorithm's performance: "How fast will it go?" and "What resources does it consume?". Unlike cars, where motion is produced and fuel is consumed, the key algorithmic measures are *time* and *space*. An algorithm or program uses time (cpu cycles) in some proportion to how much work it performs, and it uses space (memory) in some proportion to how much data it manipulates.

Note that the *speed* of a cpu cycle is dependent on the computer, but the *number of cycles required* to process a given amount of data is largely a property of the algorithm (and the program in which it is expressed).

We characterize the performance attributes of algorithms as an empirical issue of time (or work, that is, number of cycles irrespective of their speed) and space.

EXAMPLE 9.1   For a rudimentary analysis of time and space costs, let's consider an algorithm that makes use of the if-then-else construct: an algorithm for a simple calculator. It is specified as having the following behavior:

a. It performs the four basic arithmetic operations on two numerical operands.
b. It prompts the user to input three pieces of data: operand_1, operand_2, and operator, respectively.
c. It produces the output, The answer is [answer].
d. For simplicity, we specify that it need not cope with the divide-by-zero error.

One such algorithm is provided in Fig. 9.1. It is correct for the specified problem. Assuming that the input values conform to what is expected, it will behave as required by the specification. But how do we evaluate its performance? At the most obvious level, we need to ascertain how much memory it requires for its data (space) and how many instructions must be carried out (work).

In this example, the space required is no mystery. We have declared four simple variables and their space is all the data space required. But what about time? Observe that the algorithm contains a sequence of four if statements. Each if statement requires the test of a condition. If the condition is TRUE, then one arithmetic operation and one assignment operation will be performed. Finally, one print operation is performed.

Notice that all four if statements are evaluated, no matter which operator has been input. When the indicated operation is addition, the first if statement is

```
algorithm Calculator
// Purpose: performs four basic calculator functions, but does
// not handle divide-by-zero error

   // read in the 2 operands and the operator
   operand_1 isoftype Num
   print("Enter the first operand:  ")
   read(operand_1)

   operand_2 isoftype Num
   print("Enter the second operand:  ")
   read(operand_2)

   operator isoftype Char
   print("Enter the operator:  ")
   read (operator)

   //perform the indicated calculation
   answer isoftype Num
   if (operator = '+') then
      answer <- operand_1 + operand_2
   endif

   if (operator = '-') then
      answer <-operand_1 - operand_2
   endif

   if (operator = '*') then
      answer <- operand_1 * operand_2
   endif

   if (operator = '/') then
      answer <- operand_1 / operand_2
   endif

   // generate the output
   print ('The answer is', answer, '.')


endalgorithm // Calculator
```

FIGURE 9.1   A simple calculator algorithm, version 1

executed. Then, even though the tests for the remaining three operations are unnecessary, the program tests for them nonetheless.

Without measuring performance in any way, we can intuitively see that we can improve the efficiency of the program by nesting the `if` statements.

EXAMPLE 9.2 We have rewritten the algorithm (see Fig. 9.2) to take advantage of nesting. By nesting the `if` statements one inside the other we have made the number of tests that will be performed dependent upon the input data.

```
algorithm Calculator
// Purpose: performs four basic calculator functions, but does
// not handle divide-by-zero error

   // read in the 2 operands and the operator
   operand_1 isoftype Num,
   print('Enter the first operand:  ')
   read(operand_1)

   operand_2 isoftype Num,
   print('Enter the second operand:  ')
   read(operand_2)

   operator isoftype char
   print('Enter the operator:  ')
   read(operator)

   // perform the indicated calculation
   answer isoftype Num
   if (operator = '+') then
      answer <- operand_1 + operand_2
   elseif (operator = '−') then
      answer <- operand_1 − operand_2
   elseif (operator = '*') then
      answer <- operand_1 * operand_2
   elseif (operator = '/')
      answer <- operand_1 / operand_2
   endif

   // generate the output
   print('The answer is', answer, '.')


end [end of algorithm Calculator]
```

FIGURE 9.2   A simple calculator, version 2

- In the case of an addition operation, the first `if` statement is evaluated, the boolean expression (`operator = '+'`) evaluates to `TRUE`, and the addition operation is performed. The remaining tests, nested inside the `else` clause are bypassed. Thus, when input calls for addition, our new version of the program performs only one test, not four.
- In the case of subtraction, two tests are executed. The first `if` statement is evaluated, the boolean expression (`operator = '+'`) evaluates to `FALSE`, and the `elseif` clause is executed. Within the `elseif` clause, the boolean expression (`operator = '-'`) evaluates to `TRUE`, and the subtraction operation is performed. The remaining tests, those for multiplication and division, are bypassed.
- By the same logic, multiplication requires that three of the four tests are performed.
- In the case of division, all four tests are executed.

Thus, where our earlier versions of the program guaranteed that four tests would be performed each time, our new version makes the exact number of tests unpredictable. The unpredictability of the amount of work required that we have observed in our `Calculator` algorithm is quite normal.

It is a general principle that we cannot predict the path of execution through a given algorithm. This is a consequence of the fact that flow of control can be altered, based on the decisions made by the algorithm as determined by the value of tested variables. Because an algorithm's path of execution is not predictable, and because different paths may involve different amounts of work, it follows that we cannot predict exactly how much work a given algorithm will do.

9.2 Measures of Work

The fact that the work done by an algorithm is unpredictable does not mean that we shy away from trying to measure it. On the contrary, evaluating and comparing the work required by various algorithms is a very important component of software engineering. In fact, it is only by such measures that we can identify which of various possible algorithms for a given task is preferable.

In general, there are three different metrics by which we evaluate algorithms:

1. *Best case:* If we consider only the number of tests performed, the best case for our improved `Calculator` algorithm is one test. It occurs when an addition operation is called for.
2. *Worst case:* Considering only the number of tests performed, the worse case for our improved `Calculator` algorithm is four tests. It occurs when a division operator is called for.

3. *Average case:* This refers to the amount of work required "on the average." We assume some suitably large number of trials with various input, and we determine the mean. In the absence of knowledge about the specifics of the data to be input, we might assume that input is random.

9.3 Analysis of Work Done

Let us now evaluate the work done by our simple `Calculator` algorithm.

EXAMPLE 9.3 We will consider the operations visible to us at the level of a high-level language and won't worry about any underlying machine-level detail (i.e., we are concerned here with an algorithm and not a program). We also will ignore the `reads` and `prints`, as they involve dealing with the "outside world" and, for now, we don't know what work might be involved them.

Each conditional statement includes a test that determines if a given condition is `TRUE` or `FALSE`. Each such test involves two steps.

- First, the condition (a boolean expression, e.g., `operator = '*'`), is evaluated. This evaluation is itself an operation. It always resolves to a boolean value (`TRUE` or `FALSE`), and the boolean result effectively replaces the tested condition as the test is performed.
- Secondly, after the boolean expression has resolved to a boolean value, this value is examined to see whether the `if` or the `else` clause is to be executed. This examination of the boolean result (to determine which path execution will follow) is a second operation.

Thus, each `if-then-else` statement requires two logical operations to determine the flow of control: one operation to resolve the boolean expression to either `TRUE` or `FALSE`, and a second operation to examine this boolean result and select the execution path based upon it.

Apart from the various `if-then-else` statements, our code also includes statements that evaluate arithmetic expressions and assigns the result to the appropriate variable (e.g., `answer <- operand_1 + operand_2`). These also involve two steps:

- First, the arithmetic expression to the right of the assignment operator is evaluated. It resolves to a value, as determined by the specifics of the operands and operator. The evaluation of our simple single-operator arithmetic expressions requires one operation. (More complex arithmetic expressions would require more operations.)
- Then, after the operation is performed (reducing the expression to a value), the result is then assigned to the variable to the left of the assignment operator. This assignment is a second operation.

Thus, each of the assignment statements in our program involves two logical operations: the evaluation of the simple arithmetic expression, and the assignment of the result to the specified variable.

Given this, what can we conclude about the work involved in our algorithm? We know that only one arithmetic operation will be performed each time the program is run. We also know that doing the arithmetic operation will require two logical operations (one to resolve the value, the other to assign it). Thus, we know that two operations will be performed for any legal input.

We also know that some number of condition tests will be performed, and that each such test also requires two operations (one to resolve the boolean expression to a boolean value, the other to test the resulting boolean value).

Before nesting our `if` statements, the algorithm involved four condition tests each time, resulting in eight operations. In addition, the calculation itself involved two operations, for a total of 10 operations. The same number of steps were involved, regardless of the input data. Thus, best case, worst case, and average case all required 10 operations.

After nesting our `if` statements, the worst case is unchanged. In the worst case, we still have to perform all four tests and one calculation, for a total of 10 operations. However, the best case is reduced dramatically. In the best case, we will perform only one test and one calculation, for a total of four operations. Nesting also improves the average work considerably. If we assume random input, we can expect a random distribution of cases requiring one, two, three, or four tests each. This translates to an average of 2.5 tests [i.e., $(1+2+3+4)/4$] and one calculation, all at two operations apiece, for an average work of seven operations.

Thus, while the worst case is unchanged, nesting has reduced the best case work by 60 percent and the average case work by 30 percent. As you can see, these are considerable improvements. They may or may not be significant, however, as determined by other factors, which we will consider later.

As a practical matter, we are usually concerned with average or "expected" work and the worst case more so than the best case. In other words, we rarely worry about things "going right." Furthermore, in most circumstances, we do not attempt to count operations as precisely as we have here. You shall soon see why.

For now, make sure that (a) you understand what we mean by these terms and (b) you can compare the work required by two algorithmic versions of the simple calculator as we have done here.

9.4 Actual vs. Random Input

In many circumstances, the assumption of random distribution of input values is a faulty one, and we must be alert to any properties of the data or of the operational situation that will impact what constitutes an average case.

EXAMPLE 9.4 Let's consider why a calculator component of a cash register system will not have a random distribution of arithmetic operators. Rather, when we shop at the grocery store, addition operators predominate. Multiplication occurs only with respect to buying multiples of an item and when computing sales tax. Subtraction occurs only if we hand the clerk coupons, or if an item has been entered erroneously and must be "backed out." Division rarely occurs at all. In such circumstances, the best and worst cases are unaffected, but we need to consider the average case with more care.

In the case of a cash register program, when determining the order in which we want the operators to appear in our code, we clearly would want addition (the most frequent) to appear first and division (the least frequent) to appear last. We might, however, be unsure as to whether multiplication or subtraction should appear second. In fact, we would need some knowledge about which occurs more frequently in the real world.

In either case, the preponderance of addition operations would suggest that the average work in this situation would migrate somewhat towards 4 from the mean of 7 suggested by the assumption of random data.

This kind of phenomena is not limited to the grocery store. In fact, it occurs quite frequently in many things related to "real life" computing problems. Thus, you should be very thoughtful before assuming that a truly random distribution of any phenomenon will occur.

9.5   Increasing the Complexity

The revised `Calculator` algorithm of Fig. 9.2 features unpredictable performance even though we know that input will consist of a certain number of items (two operands and one operator). For most useful algorithms, things are not quite so easy.

Consider, for example, the task of searching a list to see if it contains a particular value. Obviously, we wouldn't want to write special algorithms for a list of 8 items, a list of 213 items, and a list of 1,316,203 items. A useful search algorithm will be written so that it is general (i.e., it will handle lists of any length). We speak of such algorithms as being designed to search a list of length N, where N is whatever number of items happen to be in any particular list.

Common sense tells us that the amount of work involved will vary based on the size of the list. It will be cheaper to search a list of five items than to search a list of a billion items. In short, common sense tells us that the work we have to do is somehow *proportional* to the length of the list. In this instance, common sense is correct.

In measuring performance, we are generally concerned with how the amount of work varies with the data, for example, the size of the input.

Fortunately, as it turns out, we generally don't need to be concerned with an exact measure but rather an *approximate* measure of the rate at which the work grows. For example, as the size N of a list grows from 5 to 1,000,000,000, we want to know *about how much* the required work will increase. To see why we can settle for an approximate measurement, let's consider an example.

EXAMPLE 9.5   Let's imagine that we have list of numbers of size N and that we must create a search algorithm that will tell us if the value stored in the variable `target_value` is in the list. This is all the algorithm has to do: look in the list of *N* items and decide either "Yes, the target value is there" or "No, the target value is not there." How much work will it take to do this? It depends on two things: *properties of the data* (Is the list sorted or not?) and *properties of the search algorithm.*

As we saw in Chapter 6, to perform a linear search we start at the beginning of the list and work our way towards the end (or vice versa). The search will end when either (a) we find the target value `target_value`, or (b) we reach the end of the list without finding the `target_value`. If we are reading the values in the list from input, the algorithm might look like:

```
// search the list
loop
   read(current_value)
   exitif ((current_value = target_value) OR (no more new data
           to be read))
endloop

// determine if we've found the target
if (current_value = target_value) then
   print ("the target value is there")
else
   print ("the target value is not there")
endif
```

We know that the `if-then-else` will be executed in any case. Thus, the work of the latter part of the algorithm does not vary with *N*. The only thing that varies with *N* is the amount of work we can expect the loop to do.

- Regardless of *N*, the best case performance is 1. This will occur only when we get lucky and the target value happens to be the first item in the list.
- The worst case will be *N* passes through the loop. This will occur only when either the target value is not in the list or it is in last position in the list.
- The average case is impossible to determine unless we know the probability of the target value being in the list. If we assume that it will always be in the list (i.e., we only have to verify that it's there), and if we assume that its position in the list is randomly distributed, then the average case will require approximate *N/2* passes through the loop.

Thus, we can say that:

Best case: One pass through loop

Worst case: *N* passes through the loop

Average case (if the target value is present): *N/2* passes through the loop

Observe that we've ignored the work of the `if-then-else` statement. Why? Because it is constant regardless of *N*. It has no effect on the rate at which the work grows with *N*. Thus, we throw it out of our estimate. Similarly, the fact that we're estimating means that we can also throw out *any other* constant or literal factors (we'll see why soon), for example, the "2" in "*N/2*." Thus, we say that for linear search, best case is 1, while both worst case and average cases grow in proportion to N. In our estimation jargon, we denote this by saying:

- *Best case* is "Order 1," which is written $O(1)$.
- *Worst case* is "Order N," which is written $O(N)$.
- *Average case* is also "Order N".

As mentioned earlier, we generally don't care about the best case, so we refer to linear search as being an "Order N" algorithm. This simply means that the amount of work done by such an algorithm grows at a rate that is more or less proportional to N.

Can we do better? Perhaps, depending on what assumptions we make.

EXAMPLE 9.6 Imagine that the numbers stored are the social security numbers of students, and that we have them stored in a huge array so that each number is its own index into the array. For example, if your social security number is 123-45-6787, then it would be stored at location 123456787 of the array. This scheme would require an array of one billion elements. To find whether a student is in the class, we need only execute the following:

```
if (array[target_value] = target_value) then
    print ("yes, the target value is there")
else
    print ("no, the target value is not there")
endif
```

With this scheme, the work doesn't vary with N (the number of students) at all. We have random access to each number and, regardless of the size of the list, we can do our job with only a single `if-then-else` statement. Thus, we would say that best case, worse case, and expected case are all $O(1)$.

In our Big Oh notation, constant costs are *hidden*. Thus, $O(1)$ does *not* mean that only one operation is required. $O(1)$ means that work will be at most $1 *$ (the constant costs hidden by our Big Oh notation). Remember: With Big Oh, we're concerned with the *rate* of growth. $O(1)$ is our way of saying that the work is constant (i.e., it does not change at all as N grows).

In Example 9.6, the problem with our random access solution that utilizes a huge array is its extreme waste. If we have a class of only 25 students, we still require an array large enough to hold the range of possible social security numbers. This means we require a billion cells but use only 25 of them to store data; 999,999,975 of the cells are wasted. We are only using 1/40,000,000 of the space resource our array is occupying—obviously, an absurd situation. However, it does give us an example of *ideal performance* with respect to work. We'd like to get closer to $O(1)$ than to $O(N)$ performance, especially when dealing with big lists, but without ridiculous space demands.

We can do better than $O(N)$ if we assume that the list is sorted and stored in an array of size N. We have already seen the algorithm in Chapter 6—binary search. Recall what the binary search algorithm does: It repeatedly jumps to the middle of the remaining list and makes a comparison with the value stored there. It either finds the target value or determines which half of the list can be ignored. As with the others, best case is $O(1)$; it might get lucky and find the target value on the first try. But what about worst case and expected case?

EXAMPLE 9.7 Suppose we have a sorted list of 16 numbers stored in an appropriately sized array, and we will assume that we do *not* get lucky and encounter the target value any sooner than worst case.

With its first comparison, the algorithm can dismiss half of the numbers, leaving about eight. On the second comparison it can eliminate half of those, leaving about four. On the third comparison, it can eliminate approximately half of the remaining four, leaving two. On the fourth comparison, it can eliminate half of the remaining two, leaving one. Either the target value will be in that one remaining cell or not. Thus, it takes four comparisons to do the work for a list of size 16.

Observe that $\log_2$ of 16 is 4. (For the mathematically challenged, all we're saying is that 16 is obtained by raising 2 to the fourth power.) Similarly, if the list contained more than 16 elements, but no more than 32 elements, binary search would require about five comparisons (i.e., $\log_2$ of 32). (We always assume base 2, but it really doesn't matter which base number system we use. They differ in a constant way and we throw away all the constants). We call algorithms that perform in this way "Order $\log N$" algorithms, which is written as $O(\log_2 N)$, or henceforth, $O(\log N)$.

We observe that binary search (or any algorithm that repeatedly cuts its remaining work in half) involves work that grows at a rate proportional to the log of N, not N. How much better are $O(\log N)$ algorithms than $O(N)$ algorithms? As Table 9.1 shows, for small numbers the difference doesn't amount to much, but as N grows the difference becomes dramatic.

Table 9.1 should give you a strong hint as to why we're willing to simplify our estimates by throwing out the constant factors. *Who cares* what they are? Their effect is minor compared to the way in which growth is proportional to N.

The following example illustrates why constant costs can be discounted when considering the growth rate of an algorithm's work.

EXAMPLE 9.8 Imagine that two algorithms do the same task—the first requires 325 instructions for each pass, while the second requires only a single instruction for each pass. However, the first algorithm is $O(\log N)$, while the second is $O(N)$. For an N of one billion, the seemingly "expensive" first algorithm would require 325 instructions for each of 30 passes, or 9,750 total instructions, while the seemingly "cheap" second algorithm would require a single instruction for each of one billion passes. Final score: 9,750 vs. 1 billion!

In short, for purposes of estimation, we assume that the constant costs don't amount to much in the big picture. Thus, we throw them away in the interest of giving ourselves a "quick and dirty" estimation tool.

TABLE 9.1 $O(1)$ vs. $O(\log N)$ vs. $O(N)$ performance

N of no more than:	O(1)	O(logN)	O(N)
16	1	4	16
64	1	6	64
256	1	8	256
1,024 (1K)	1	10	1,024
16,384 (16K)	1	14	16,384
131,072 (128K)	1	17	131,072
262,144 (256K)	1	18	262,144
524,288 (512K)	1	17	524,288
1,048,576 ($1K^2$=1M)	1	20	1,028,576
1,073,741,824 ($1K^3$=1G)	1	30	1,073,741,824

Of course, we can contrive a situation where this assumption would be wrong. For example, if the constant costs were one billion, then our estimate would be hiding a considerable cost component! Such an algorithm that offered $O(\log N)$ performance would be far worse than many $O(N)$ algorithms until N grew to be huge. (How huge?) However, in most cases, our assumption is useful. But, be sure to remember that it is an assumption, one that must be questioned from one circumstance to the next.

Remember the following important distinction between measuring and estimating performance.

- When we *measure* performance, we care about the actual time and space resources used by an algorithm.
- When we *estimate* or characterize performance, all we care about is the *growth rate* of an algorithm's work. We do this by tossing out the constants and paying attention only to the dominant factor (e.g., the way in which growth is proportional to N).

9.6 Performance and Data Structures

We have seen that we can find big performance gains in searching by deploying a $O(\log N)$ algorithm rather than an $O(N)$ algorithm. However, our examples of good performance assumed that we had the data sorted and stored in an appropriately sized array. How can we make assumptions like that? In truth, we cannot. We can only say that *if* the data is sorted and *if* the data is in an appropriate data structure, then we can get $O(\log N)$ performance; otherwise we may have to settle for $O(N)$ performance.

Many times, the data will be sorted anyway due to some other part of the algorithm. Long before the advent of computers, good common sense practices for organizing things dictated that lists of names be kept organized in alphabetical order, numerical identifiers (such as invoices or inventory numbers) be kept in ascending order, and so on. Thus, many times data will be sorted already. If so, then we will exploit that fact. If the data are not sorted, then we have to compare the cost of sorting the data and then applying an $O(\log N)$ search versus the cost of applying an $O(N)$ search to unsorted data. We'll get to the costs of sorting soon.

With respect to data structures, we want an algorithm that is general (i.e., will work for whatever size N happens to be). However, we consider arrays to be static. In other words, we cannot make them be general; instead, we have to specify the size of the array in advance. In a given particular situation, this might be done via a constant that determines array size. For example, we might have

```
MAX_ARRAY_SIZE is 30
This_Array_Type definesa array[1..MAX_ARRAY_SIZE] of Num
```

In such a situation, we can use `MAX_ARRAY_SIZE` in place of N in our searching algorithm. Or, we might use some variable to keep us informed of how much of the array is being used. Perhaps `MAX_ARRAY_SIZE` is 10,000, yet our algorithm might keep track of how many values have been read in to it and thus "know" that only the first 125 elements are occupied. In this case, we could use that variable in place of N.

However, there is often no getting around the fact that arrays are static and thus cannot support a general "who knows what N is?" algorithm. An array needs to know the maximum possible N ahead of time, and often N is not predictable. This is where a binary search tree (BST) can be very valuable. A binary search tree allows $O(\log N)$ search performance if certain conditions are met.

For any binary search tree that is approximately full and balanced (i.e., symmetrical and fully populated) the height of the tree is approximately $O(\log N)$. If a BST is full and balanced, $O(\log N)$ search performance can be obtained. But if a BST is not full and balanced, a far different result can occur, as shown in Example 9.9.

EXAMPLE 9.9   Consider a full and balanced tree with seven nodes. It will have three levels of depth: the root, the root's children, and the root's grandchildren. A search to locate a particular value will have to do at most three comparisons (the root, the appropriate child of the root, and the appropriate grandchild of the root). And, of course, 3 is $\log N$ of 8 (i.e., of $N + 1$). Thus, a binary search tree *can* give us $\log(N + 1)$ search performance, which is $O(\log N)$, without any advance knowledge of N.

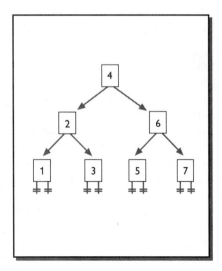

FIGURE 9.3 A full and balanced BST

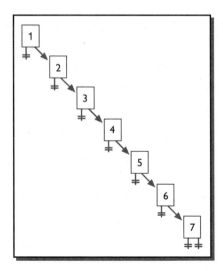

FIGURE 9.4 BST can deteriorate to a linked list

The obstacle to achieving this is that a BST may or may not be full and balanced. Observe that we can take the integer values 1 through 7 and build a variety of BSTs. The exact shape of the tree is dependent on the order in which those values arise. For example, if the values arrive in the order 4, 2, 6, 1, 3, 5, 7, then the result is a BST that's perfectly full and balanced as shown in Fig. 9.3. However, if those values arrive in sorted order, then the tree becomes lopsided and linear, like a linked list that's turned on its side, as shown in Fig. 9.4.

Thus, to be sure that a BST will provide optimal performance, we require some algorithm that will guarantee that the tree is full and balanced. Such an algorithm will manipulate the shape of the tree as necessary upon the insertion or deletion of nodes. There are a few such algorithms, and each of them has their own costs (i.e., we cannot achieve guaranteed balancing for free). We will not concern ourselves with the particulars of such algorithms. However, be sure that you understand what BSTs can do for us *and* that you understand the requirements that must be met for a BST to deliver optimal $O(\log N)$ performance.

A FORTUNATE FACT

For *large data sets of randomly arranged data* (unsorted and not ordered in any way), we need not be too concerned about deploying algorithms to keep the tree balanced. Random data will usually result in a tree that is close to being full and balanced. It will rarely be perfectly full and balanced and, on rare occasion, it may result in a skewed tree, but most of the time random data will produce a nearly optimal BST. Thus, for truly random data sets, the easiest course of action turns out to be close to the best!

9.7 Increasing the Complexity Some More

So far, we've seen the powerful performance gains that can be achieved via an algorithm that is "better than obvious." In other words, we've improved from the "common sense" linear search, which is $O(N)$, to the more efficient binary search, which gives $O(\log N)$. Given the speed of computers, this is the difference between search performance that's very good and performance that's excellent.

Unfortunately, the choices are not always so pleasant. For example, let's consider the task of sorting a list of numbers. You probably have software applications that are already programmed to perform sorting for you. Why, then, do we insist that you look at the logic of sorting algorithms? We choose sorting examples because sorting is a straightforward problem that can be solved with a variety of different approaches. Thus, sorting gives us a chance to compare the performance that different approaches offer.

Let us assume that we have a list of eight unsorted numbers stored in an array, as shown in Fig. 9.5a. How might we sort them? In Example 9.10 we'll show how one

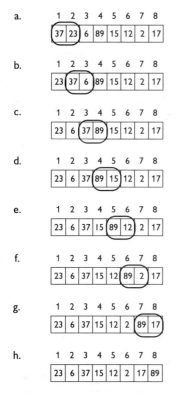

FIGURE 9.5 One pass of `Bubblesort`

sorting algorithm works. Then in Examples 9.11 and 9.12 we'll further analyze that algorithm.

EXAMPLE 9.10   Let us consider a fairly simple or "naive" sorting algorithm, Bubblesort. Bubblesort works in a simple fashion, as shown in Fig. 9.5 and as described below.

- The algorithm begins at the leftmost position and compares the contents of that cell (in this case, 37) with the contents of the cell one position to the right (in this case, 23). If those two values are in proper sorted order relative to each other, the algorithm leaves them alone; if not, it swaps them. In our example, the values are not in the correct order, so they are swapped, giving the array as shown in Fig. 9.5b.
- The algorithm then moves one position to the right and repeats the same process (i.e., comparing the values in the second and third cells). In our example, it finds that the 37 and the 6 are not in the proper order, so it swaps them, producing the state of the array as shown in Fig. 9.5c.
- It then moves one position to the right and repeats the process. In our example, this means that it compares the 37 and the 89, finds that they are in the correct order, and thus leaves them alone (Fig. 9.5d).
- Then, moving to the right again, it compares the 89 and 15; because they are not in the right position, it swaps them, giving the array as shown in Fig. 9.5e.

This process is repeated until, for an array of N items, it compares the values stored at positions $N - 1$ and N, swapping them if necessary (Fig. 9.5f, g). In our example, the final result of this repetitive process would be the array as shown in Fig. 9.5h.

The next example shows what happens in a single pass of `Bubblesort`.

EXAMPLE 9.11   We might express the logic for a single pass through the array as shown below:

```
last_compare_at isoftype Num
last_compare_at <- n - 1

index isoftype Num
index <- 1

loop
    exitif (index > last_compare_at)
    if (s_array[index] > s_array[index+1]) then
        Swap(s_array[index], s_array[index+1])
    endif
    index <- index + 1
endloop
```

Each time through the loop, the variable `index` is incremented, thus shifting the algorithm's attention one location to the right. By the time the algorithm stops, it will have performed $N - 1$ comparisons and somewhere between 0 and $N - 1$ swaps (depending on the particular values in the list). It will also have guaranteed that the highest value in the list is in the rightmost position.

Notice that our single pass through the array has not sorted the entire list. It has only found the proper sorted position for the largest value in the list (i.e., in the rightmost element). But we don't know about any of the other list values or positions.

To sort the remainder of the list, the Bubblesort algorithm then takes the partially-sorted list (with the largest value now in the rightmost position) and begins all over again. It goes back to the first position, compares the first and second values, swaps them if necessary, then compares the second and third values, and so on. In short, it makes a second pass through the list, comparing and swapping, just as before. The only difference between this second pass and the first pass is that the algorithm can stop one position sooner. Because it has already moved the largest value all the way to the right, there is no point in comparing the values at position $N - 1$ and N. Instead, the second pass can end after the comparison (and, if necessary, swap) of values in the $N - 2$ and $N - 1$ positions. After the second pass ends, we know that the two largest values are in their appropriate positions at the end of the list.

After the second pass, Bubblesort starts over again and makes a third pass. By now, the two rightmost positions already hold the appropriate values, so the third pass aims to move the third-largest value into position. It can end after it deals with the values in $N - 3$ and $N - 2$ positions. And so on. Thus, we can see that Bubblesort will make $N - 1$ passes through the data. We can also see that each pass will require one fewer comparison than the pass before it (i.e., the first pass will make $N - 1$ comparisons, the second pass will make $N - 2$ comparisons, and the last pass will make only a single comparison. We might express the entire Bubblesort algorithm as shown in Example 9.12.

EXAMPLE 9.12 The following algorithm features nested loops.

```
procedure Bubble_Sort (n isoftype in Num,
                       s_array isoftype in/out Array_Type)

    remaining_passes isoftype Num
    remaining_passes <- N - 1
    loop
       exitif (remaining_passes = 0)
       index isoftype Num
       index <- 1
       loop
          exitif (index > remaining_passes)
          if (s_array[index] > s_array[index+1]) then
             Swap(s_array[index], s_array[index+1])
          endif
          index <- index + 1
       endloop //inner loop
       remaining_passes <- remaining_passes - 1
    endloop // outer loop

endprocedure // Bubblesort
```

Notice that each of the nested loops has its own job: The inner loop governs each pass through the data, while the outer loop governs how many such passes are made.

In Example 9.12 we have changed the terminating condition of the inner loop. In Example 9.11, the terminating condition was (index > last_compare_at) where `last_compare_at` had been assigned the value of N-1. In Example 9.12, the terminating condition is (`index > remaining_passes`). This was done so that each "inner loop" pass through the data will stop one step sooner than the pass before. We initialize `remaining_passes` to N-1, then decrement it after each pass.

Warning: If algorithms are new to you, make sure that you take scrap paper, draw an array of unsorted numbers, and trace the execution of this algorithm on that array. It is imperative that you be able to trace the execution of algorithms, understand their operation, and be able to reproduce their results as you trace them. If you cannot do this, then you will be unable to make sure that the algorithms you create work as intended. If you find that you are unable to trace the execution of the algorithm, make sure that you get help *promptly* from a classmate, from a TA, or from the instructor.

9.8 Estimating Bubblesort's Complexity

What can we say about the performance of the `Bubblesort` algorithm? It is "Order what?" To estimate the amount of work an algorithm implies or its complexity, examine the algorithm for repetitive structures (i.e., loops or recursive calls that are influenced, directly or indirectly, by N). In the case of `Bubblesort`, we find such two repetitive structures: the loops that are nested one inside the other. Let's consider each in turn.

The inner loop controls each pass through the list of numbers. Each pass involves some number of comparisons and, if necessary, some number of swaps. Each comparison will have some cost, as will each swap. However, in estimating complexity we are not concerned with these details. We are only concerned with how the work *grows in relation to N*. Thus, we are content to consider the number of comparisons without worrying about their exact cost or about how many of them result in swaps.

How many comparisons will the inner loop do? Well, it varies. On the first pass, it does $N - 1$ comparisons to move the largest value to the rightmost position, on the second pass it does $N - 2$ comparisons to move the second-largest value to the next-to-rightmost position, on the third pass it does $N - 3$ comparisons, and on the last pass it does $N - (N - 1)$ or one comparison. This is an average of $N/2$ comparisons. Because we are estimating, we can throw away numeric factors and say that each pass is $O(N)$.

We now have an estimate of "work per pass." But how many passes will there be? This number is controlled by the outer loop. According to the algorithm as given, there will be exactly $N - 1$ passes. (Can you see why?) We again toss out any specific numeric values and thus say that there will be $O(N)$ passes through the list.

So far, then, we see that each loop involves $O(N)$ work. But what does this say about the algorithm? To answer this, we must notice the relationship between the two loops. In this case, they are nested (i.e., each of the $O(N)$ passes through the outer loop causes the inner loop to do its $O(N)$ work). We have $O(N)$ "inner loop work" that is performed $O(N)$ "outer loop times," which is $O(N)*O(N)$ or $O(N^2)$. Thus, we say that `Bubblesort` is an "Order N-squared" algorithm.

Observe that we arrived at an estimate of $O(N^2)$ complexity because the two $O(N)$ loops were nested one inside the other. The estimate would be very different if they were not nested but instead followed one after the other, as shown in Example 9.13 below.

EXAMPLE 9.13   An example of an algorithm with sequential loops follows.

```
this isoftype Num
this <- 1

loop
   exitif (this = n)
   Do_Some_Thing
   this <- this + 1
endloop

that isoftype Num
that <- 1

loop
   exitif (that = n)
   Do_Some_Thing_Else
   that <- that + 1
endloop
```

In this case, we have an algorithm that features a *sequence* of loops each of which is $O(N)$. Since they are not nested, neither influences the amount of work done by the other. Thus, we have $N + N$ work, or $2N$ work. Of course, the constant factor 2 has no place in our estimates, and so we would say that the estimate or our algorithm is simply $O(N)$.

The implications of $O(N^2)$ algorithms can be seen in Table 9.2. Again, for small numbers, the differences between $O(\log N)$, $O(N)$, and $O(N^2)$ algorithms don't matter much. However, imagine that you have to process 16,000 numbers (as is a common task concerning the records of many universities or corporations):

- An $O(\log N)$ or "sublinear" solution would require only about 14 times whatever the constant costs might be.
- An $O(N)$ or "linear" algorithm would require about 16,000 times constant costs.
- An $O(N^2)$ or "quadratic" algorithm would require about 268 million times the constant costs.

Now, consider a company that must process data regarding more than 100,000 stockholders:

- A sublinear algorithm implies about 17 times constant costs.
- A linear algorithm implies about 100,000 times constant costs.
- A quadratic algorithm requires more than 17 billion times the constant costs.

We trust that you are beginning to see why we care about estimates of algorithmic complexity!

Of course, you might think, "Well, ok, let's just go to work and devise sublinear algorithms to solve all our problems." We'd like to do that but, unfortunately, we

TABLE 9.2 $O(\log N)$ vs. $O(N)$ vs. $O(N^2)$ performance

N of no more than:	O(logN)	O(N)	O(N²)
16	4	16	256
64	6	64	4K
256	8	256	64K
1,024 (1K)	10	1K	1M
16,384 (16K)	14	16K	268,435,456 (256M)
131,072 (128K)	17	128K	17,179,869,184 (16G)
262,144 (256K)	18	256K	6.8719E+10
524,288 (512K)	17	512K	2.7488E+11
1,048,576 (1M)	20	1M	1.0995E+12
1,073,741,824 (1G)	30	1G	1.1529E+18

cannot. Nor can we devise linear algorithms for all our problems. In fact, for many important problems we cannot devise algorithms that are nearly as good as quadratic algorithms! Why? The reason is that performance is not only a property of algorithms. As it turns out, it is also a property of the *problems* we attempt to solve with them.

Thus, when we think about searching algorithms, we can choose between various $O(\log N)$ and $O(N)$ algorithms. In addition, we have certain techniques (e.g., "hashing") that allow us to get closer to $O(1)$ performance. But, with sorting algorithms we cannot do as well. This is common sense, in sorting, we must deal with each value at least once. In fact, we must deal with each item somewhat more than once. We cannot achieve even a linear solution to the sorting problem. Fortunately, we can do better than $O(N^2)$, as the next example illustrates.

EXAMPLE 9.14 Recall the Mergesort algorithm discussed in Chapter 6. This algorithm repeatedly divides the list of numbers in half, first into two lists of $N/2$ numbers each, then into four lists of $N/4$ numbers each, then into eight lists of $N/8$ numbers each, and so on, until each list is of size 1. Let us call this "Phase 1" of the Mergesort algorithm. How many passes through the data would be required to accomplish this phase? Note that, each time, the collection of numbers is divided into twice as many lists as before, with each such list being half the size. Does this sound familiar? It should. This repeated pattern of "cutting in half" or "doubling the number" is generally a clue that we're facing an $O(\log N)$ phenomenon and, indeed, the first phase of Mergesort does indeed involve $O(\log N)$ passes through the data.

Once the list of N numbers has been decomposed into N lists of one number, what then? Mergesort proceeds to build sorted lists from the decomposed list. First it "merges" adjacent pairs of "one-item lists" to create $N/2$ sorted lists, each of size 2. Then, it merges pairs of these $N/2$ sorted "two-item lists" to create $N/4$ sorted lists of size 4 each. And so on, each time *doubling the size* of the sorted lists and *cutting the number of them in half*. Again, this sounds like $O(\log N)$, doesn't it?

In sum, Mergesort takes $O(\log N)$ steps to decompose the original list and $O(\log N)$ steps to reconstruct it into a properly sorted list. These two $O(\log N)$ steps occur in sequence, thus giving $2*\log N$ work, which is still $O(\log N)$. But this concerns only *the number of passes* through the data. How much work is involved in *each pass*? The answer is N regardless of the particulars of each pass because merging is an $O(N)$ operation. If the algorithm is merging N one-item lists into $N/2$ two-item lists, it is still dealing with each of N items, just as if it is merging $N/16$ 16-item lists into $N/32$ 32-item lists. Each of the N values is dealt with (compared, copied, etc.) during each of the $O(\log N)$ passes. Thus, we can see that Mergesort implies $O(\log N)*O(N)$ work, which is $O(N\log N)$. As it turns out, this is the best that can be accomplished with respect to sorting (except in very specialized circumstances).

As we can see from Table 9.3, while $O(N\log N)$ performance is not quite as good as simple linear performance, it is clearly preferable to $O(N^2)$ performance.

In the rest of this chapter, we will have more to say about two important issues:

- Categories of algorithmic performance.
- What is realistic performance and what is not.

Each of these topics can be readily mastered provided you have a foundation in understanding the basics of Big Oh. The material we have just covered is truly prerequisite to understanding the next section.

For now, concentrate on understanding what we mean by $O(1)$, $O(\log N)$, $O(N)$, $O(N\log N)$, and $O(N^2)$. Review the particular algorithms discussed here. Make sure that you understand how we arrived at our estimates for each one and what the performance implications are.

The following are four keys to finding Big Oh.

1. Look for *repetitive structures*. (Remember, iteration and recursion are equivalent to each other.) It's the repetitions that count. Judge how the amount of repetitive work will grow with respect to N.

2. When multiple repetitive structures are present, determine Big Oh for each and notice the relationship between them.

TABLE 9.3 $O(N \log N)$ performance is nearly as good as $O(N)$

N of no more than:	O(logN)	O(N)	O(NlogN)	O(N²)
16	4	16	64	256
64	6	64	384	4K
256	8	256	2,048	64K
1,024 (1K)	10	1K	10K	1M
16,384 (16K)	14	16K	224K	256M
131,072 (128K)	17	128K	2,176K	16G
262,144 (256K)	18	256K	4,608K	6.8719E+10
524,288 (512K)	19	512K	9,728K	2.7488E+11
1,048,576 (1M)	20	1M	20M	1.0995E+12
1,073,741,824 (1G)	30	1G	30G	1.1529E+18

3. If the repetitive structures are *nested,* then there is a *multiplicative* relationship with respect to Big Oh. For example, an $O(N)$ loop nested inside another $O(N)$ loop gives $O(N*N)$ which is $O(N^2)$.
4. If the repetitive structures are *sequential,* then there is an *additive* relationship with respect to Big Oh. For example, an $O(N)$ loop that is separate from and follows some other $O(N)$ loop gives $O(2N)$, which is $O(N)$.

The following example shows an $O(\log N)$ algorithm in a surprising place. It's what we might call "The $O(\log N)$ Basketball Championship."

EXAMPLE 9.15 We can see an example of an $O(\log N)$ algorithm at work each March in the NCAA Basketball Tournament. The tournament is "searching" for a champion. It begins with 64 teams and, with each round of games, half the teams are eliminated. This pattern of cutting work in half with each repetitive pass is the hallmark of $O(\log N)$ algorithms. As a $O(\log N)$ algorithm with an N of 64, we would expect the championship tournament to take log64 (or six) rounds of games to "locate" the champion. Indeed, both the champion and runner-up play exactly six games. Given its $O(\log N)$ nature, we can see that, by adding one more round of games, tournament participation could increase to 128 teams. Two more rounds (for a total of eight rounds) would accommodate 256 teams. With three more rounds, 512 teams could be accommodated, creating more slots than there are Division I college teams. Thus, with nine rounds of games (instead of the current six), *all* teams could be admitted to the tournament (thus making the college basketball season itself entirely superfluous!).

How many rounds would be required to allow participation by 300 colleges and 3000 high school teams?

9.9   Reasonable vs. Unreasonable Algorithms

It is often useful to categorize phenomena. So far, we have considered a few algorithms and classified them by their complexity, in other words, by $O(1)$, $O(\log N)$, $O(N)$, $O(N\log N)$, and $O(N^2)$. We have also looked at the performance implications of each category. We have seen how $O(N^2)$ (quadratic) algorithms imply far worse performance than $O(1)$ (constant), $O(\log N)$ (sublinear), $O(N)$ (linear), and $O(N\log N)$ (nearly linear) algorithms whenever N grows to a fairly large number.

From this, we can say that for large N, the performance of certain categories of algorithms is vastly superior to others. Based on what we've done so far, we can imagine that some algorithms might be $O(N^3)$, $O(N^4)$, $O(N^5)$, and so on. We can also reason that $O(N^5)$ algorithms would be worse than $O(N^4)$ algorithms, which in turn would be worse than $O(N^3)$, and so on. Simple calculation bears this out, as is shown in Table 9.4.

From this, we can see how much of an impact the performance of a given algorithm has. For an N of only 256 items, an $O(\log N)$ algorithm would require only about eight times the constant cost, while an $O(N^5)$ algorithm would require about a *trillion* times constant cost. If N grows to only 256K, an $O(\log N)$ algorithm can perform its job in only about 18 times constant cost, while an $O(N^5)$ algorithm would

TABLE 9.4 Performance can get worse than $O(N^2)$

N	$O(\log N)$	$O(N)$	$O(N^2)$	$O(N^3)$	$O(N^5)$
4	2	4	16	64	1024
16	4	16	256	4K	1M
64	6	64	4K	256K	1G
256	8	256	64K	16M	1.1E+12

require a "billion billion billion" times constant cost. As you can see, depending on the performance of the algorithm, things can quickly get out of hand, far worse than has the national debt.

Now, for the part that many people find hard to believe—things can get *far, far* worse. In fact, all of the categories of algorithms we have discussed so far are considered to be "good" or "reasonable" algorithms. You might well wonder, "If all of the above are "good," what in the world does it take to be "bad"?"

For an example of a "bad" or "unreasonable" algorithm, consider the solution to the standard Towers of Hanoi problem. First we'll describe the problem and show its solution in Example 9.16; then we'll discuss the cost of such a solution and generalize the results to other algorithms.

EXAMPLE 9.16 The Towers of Hanoi problem is quite simple: You are given three vertical pegs and some number of rings that are stacked up on one of the pegs. No two rings are of the same diameter, and they are stacked such that each ring has only larger rings below it and only smaller rings above it (like the shape of a traditional wedding cake), as shown in Fig. 9.6.

The problem simply requires that you move the stack of rings from one peg to another peg with only two constraints: (1) you cannot move more than one ring at a time, and (2) you may never place a larger ring on top of a smaller ring. (You may place any smaller ring on top of any larger ring.)

The solution is rather simple from a logical point of view. You can see that each peg works like a stack, and that the problem allows us to "pop" and "push" rings however we like, just so we never put a smaller one on top of a larger one. A rather simple recursive algorithm can solve this problem for any number of rings:

```
procedure Towers_Of_Hanoi (n, a, b, c isoftype in Num)

   if (n = 1) then
      print('Move' , a, ' to' , b)
   else
      Towers_Of_Hanoi (n - 1, a, c, b)
      print('Move ,' a, ' to ', b)
      Towers_Of_Hanoi (n - 1, c, b, a)
   endif

endprocedure //Towers_Of_Hanoi
```

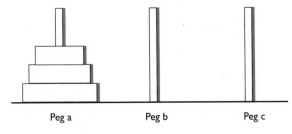

In the algorithm above, n initially refers to the total number of rings, and a, b, and c refer to the three pegs. The two print instructions are analogous to a combination of "Pop(from a to x)" and "Push(from x onto b)." Observe that each recursive call does two things:

1. It decrements n, ensuring that n will eventually reach 1, the terminating condition.

Peg a   Peg b   Peg c

FIGURE 9.6   The Towers of Hanoi problem involves three pegs and *N* rings

2. It passes the three "peg parameters" in a different order (e.g., the first recursive call sends the "peg identifiers" in the order a, c, b and the new clone of the procedure will receive them as a, b, c"). Thus, the various recursive calls deal with different combinations of the three pegs.

For example, given the situation as diagrammed in Fig. 9.6 with only three rings on peg a, the algorithm produces the following steps:

- Move the smallest ring to an empty b.
- Move the middle-sized ring to empty peg c.
- Move the smallest ring from b to c so that it rests on top of the middle size ring.
- Move the large ring from a to the now-empty b.
- Move the small ring from c to the now-empty a.
- Move the middle-size ring from c to b so that it rests on top of the large ring.
- Move the small ring from a to b so that it rests on the middle-size ring.
  The problem is now solved.

Warning: If you are a novice, make sure that you step through the execution of the recursive algorithm with diagrams of the pegs and a stack (to keep track of the recursive calls) on scratch paper until you understand it and can get the same results. Unless you can trace the execution accurately, you will likely have difficulty succeeding on similar homework and test problems.

Observe that it took seven operations to solve for three rings. What is the relationship between the N rings and the cost in operations? We might wish it the cost was $(2N+1)$, which would mean that we have an $O(N)$ algorithm. Unfortunately, this is not the case. Instead, we find that the cost is $(2^N - 1)$. For three rings, the cost is 7, for four rings the cost is 15, for five rings the cost is 31, for 10 rings the cost is 1023, for 20 rings the cost is more than a million, for 30 rings the cost is more than a billion, and so on.

Each time we increment the size of N by one, we *double* the amount of work required. This is similar to the relationship between N and work in $O(\log N)$ algorithms, but with the log factor going the other way (i.e., working against us, not for us). In $O(\log N)$ algorithms, incrementing work by one allows us to double N; here, incrementing N by one doubles the amount of work! This is the nature $O(2^N)$ algorithms, and the consequences are not pretty, as we see in Table 9.5.

For 64 rings, the cost is about 1.845E+19. How large is that? Well, if we could perform a million moves per second, it would take more than half a million years. A computer that can execute a million instructions per second (mip) would take a several times longer, since determining each move requires multiple instructions. Graphics modules that draw the movement of rings on the screen would take even longer still. So, perhaps we could use a 1-mip machine to do the job in only about 10 or 20 million years. (The exact factor by which we would have to multiply the "more than half a million years" is precisely the effect of the constants that are hidden by Big Oh.)

As N grows, things get worse in a hurry. For only 256 rings, the cost is a number so large that it features 77 zeros to the left of the decimal. As a point of comparison, consider that scientists believe that the number of microseconds since the Big Bang

TABLE 9.5 Comparing $O(2^N)$ performance to others

N	O (LogN)	O(N)	O(N²)	O(N⁵)	O(2^N)
4	2	4	16	1,024	16
16	4	16	256	1M	65K
64	6	64	4K	1G	1.845E+19
256	8	256	64K	1.1E+12	1.158E+77

has only 24 digits, and that the number of protons in the known universe has only 77 digits! We're already up to 78 digits and we are only considering 256 rings. What about a thousand rings? Certainly such an algorithm is far too costly.

In general, $O(2^N)$ algorithms are bad news. They are perfectly reasonable from a logical point of view, but are of no value from a practical point of view simply because we cannot use them for any significant value of N.

This fact will not change with continuing improvements of the speed of computers. In any $O(2^N)$ algorithm, each time we increment N by one, we double the amount of work required. Before we can increment N very far, we run into problems that cannot be solved by "fast computers." We encounter limitations imposed by the laws of physics. Even if it took no time to execute each instruction and we could move data between computer chips at the speed of light, the fact remains that the speed of light is only so fast and we would quickly encounter an N that made the amount of work unreasonable. Thus, while such algorithms may be acceptable for arbitrarily small values of N, as general algorithms their costs are unreasonable regardless of the kind of computer we might have or even imagine.

In fact, this is the terminology we use for the next level up the ladder of algorithm classification: "reasonable" vs. "unreasonable" algorithms.

- Algorithms that have N only as a *polynomial* factor in Big Oh are considered to be *reasonable*, including $O(\log N)$, $O(N)$, $O(N \log N)$, $O(N^K)$ where K is any constant value. There are two mostly interchangeable names for such algorithms: *reasonable* or *polynomial*.
- Algorithms that have N as an *exponential* factor in Big Oh are considered to be *unreasonable* and useful to theorists in various ways, but are useful to the rest of us only as points of comparison. There are two mostly interchangeable names for such algorithms: *unreasonable* or *exponential*.

Keep in mind that these are general categories of algorithms. In a given circumstance, a reasonable algorithm might take longer than an unreasonable one, provided that N is very small. However, as generalizable solutions to particular kinds of problems, the reasonable/unreasonable (or polynomial/exponential) dichotomy is valid and very useful. If an algorithm is reasonable, we might use it; if it's unreasonable, we don't even bother as there's no point in implementing it.

9.10 Categories of Unreasonable Algorithms

For a mundane example of another unreasonable algorithm, consider the bounded tiling problem. You've just bought a house that has an unfinished basement, and you want to put tile on the basement floor. You don't like linoleum, and instead want to spend a little extra and use ceramic tiles that were custom-made by an artist. Part of the appeal is that the tiles are not all identical, but instead feature four designs that cross the tile boundaries (i.e., each edge of each tile contains half of one of four designs). You must match the half of design 1 from one tile with the other half of design 1 from another tile by butting their edges together. There are only four such "overlapping images," but the tiles differ in terms of which half of which image appears at each of its four edges. In addition, the tiles are not perfectly square, and will fit together perfectly only if you don't rotate them (i.e., there is a specified top, a bottom, a left, and a right edge to each and every tile). The problem is one of determining whether or not you can arrange the tiles so that everything matches up correctly.

Observe that we are not concerned with trying to discover what pattern will work; we're only concerned with determining *whether or not you can* arrange the tiles so that all their various sides match up so that each half-image is adjacent to its other half. The output is a simple "yes, you can" or "no, you cannot." We will assume that you have N tiles (where N is the square of some positive integer, say M) and that you wish to tile a space that is square (i.e., each edge of the square requires the Square_Root(N) or M tiles).

EXAMPLE 9.17 As a particular example of the tiling problem, let's suppose that you have either very large tiles or a very small room, that is, you require only 25 tiles to cover a square space that is five-tiles by five-tiles in dimension. How much work will it take to provide an answer about whether or not you can do it?

There are 25 possibilities to consider for the first tile. With one of the 25 tiles in the first position, there are 24 remaining tiles that might go in the second position. With two tiles selected, there are 23 remaining tiles that might go in the third position, and so on. Of course, it might well happen that you'd get the first 24 tiles in place just fine, only to learn that the edges of 25th tile do not match up with edges of its neighbors. In the worst case, we might have to consider *all* the possibilities before being able to answer the question. How many possibilities is that? It's 25! ("25 factorial"), or 25*24*23*...*3*2*1.

Unfortunately, 25! contains 26 digits. As for a 1-mip computer, it would take 470 billion years to obtain an answer, much longer than the time elapsed since the Big Bang. Of course, if we had a machine that could run 1000 times faster, it would

TABLE 9.6 Polynomial vs. exponential performance

N	Polynomial				Exponential		
	O(logN)	O(N)	O(N²)	O(N³)	O(2ᴺ)	O(N!)	O(Nᴺ)
10	4	10	100	1,000	1,024	7 digits	11 digits
50	6	50	2,500	125,000	16 digits	65 digits	85 digits
100	7	100	10,000	7 digits	31 digits	161 digits	201 digits
1,000	10	1,000	7 digits	10 digits	302 digits	unimaginable	unimaginable

only take 470 million years. A machine that was a *million* times faster could give you an answer in only 470,000 years, and a machine that runs a *billion* times faster, could give you an answer in about 500 years. Unfortunately, you'd planned on doing the job next weekend. And, as it turns out, you measured wrong. You don't have a five-tile by five-tile area; your basement requires a 20-tile by 20-tile arrangement. Do you know what 400! is?

Just as there are various performance categories within the larger category of reasonable algorithms (e.g., $O(\log N)$, $O(N)$, $O(N^2)$, etc., there are various performance categories of unreasonable algorithms. So far, we've seen an $O(2^N)$ and an $O(N!)$ algorithm. We might also imagine a particular $O(N^N)$ algorithm. All are exponential, that is, unreasonable. The consequences for small N are summarized in Table 9.6.

What does all this mean? Quite obviously, it means that certain computational problems cannot be reasonably solved by general-solution algorithms. This, of course, goes against the current assumptions that most people make, namely, that computers are fast enough to crunch out solutions to any computational problem. Such is, quite simply, not the case; rather, it's a myth of the computer age.

This also explains why we're interested in approximate solutions to various problems such as the greedy-algorithm approach to optimization that we saw in Chapter 6. At first, one might think that approximate solutions are poor solutions. One might ask, "Why settle for an approximate solution that might not give the Right Answer, instead of computing the optimal solution?" By now, the answer should be obvious to you: An approximate solution that will give us an answer that's "not far off" is far better than a solution that takes several million years to obtain! For many problems, approximate solutions are the only ones we can really obtain.

FOOD FOR THOUGHT

How Well Do Your Ideas Perform?

Perhaps, while watching television, you have seen film footage from 100-year-old newsreels showing daring experimenters attempting to fly in absurd, ungainly contraptions. Such film is broadcast not as history but as humorous entertainment. Across America, thousands chuckle at "the fool" who would think that he could fly by creating a bicycle-like machine in which the "pilot" pedaled furiously to power the flapping of large floppy wings. In laughing, perhaps we show our own ignorance. In today's world, that man would be a fool. In today's world, we know his design doesn't stand a chance. But he is not a man of our world. He is a man from a time when the only way to know about your idea was to try it out. And so, he tried.

People have always had ideas. In eras gone by, the only way to evaluate whether or not ideas were useful was through direct trial-and-error experience. For most problems, there were no tools for modeling and simulation. Trial and error was the most advanced investigative technique.

Computing has changed that. It has given us the capability not only to implement our ideas in algorithms, but also to execute those algorithms and see what they do. Because of this capability, we are dealing with a fundamentally different kind of "object of our own creation" than did previous generations of people. Now, for the first time in history, we have the opportunity to routinely see how our ideas perform by implementing them algorithmically, by simulating their existence in data-based virtual worlds. We can build simulations about physical phenomena that will let us see, for example, whether a new bridge design will stand up to the various stresses upon it. We can also build simulations about intangible human phenomena such as emotions and opinions and behaviors that, by their very nature, cannot readily be constructed and tested.

Regardless of what our ideas are about, computing allows us to:

a. *Externalize our ideas* about how things work by expressing them as algorithms.
b. *Implement our ideas* in by writing our algorithms as computer programs.
c. *Try out our ideas* by running those programs.
d. *Evaluate the behavior of our ideas* by observing the results.

In short, we can using computing to allow us to do *virtual* trial-and-error experiments. Do our algorithms behave as anticipated? Do they satisfy what we want them to do? Do they show flaws in our ideas about the phenomena we're trying to model? If so, how can we learn from these flaws to create better models?

All these questions, and many more, inevitably arise because we are creating a new kind of human artifact: the specification, implementation, and empirical evaluation of the *behavior implied in our ideas* about various phenomena.

In Chapter 1, we saw that the alphabet gave humankind a means to externalize thoughts and observations into the written word via an abstract symbol system. Computing takes us to another level; it gives us a way to observe the *performance* of our ideas. To put it another way, the alphabet enables us to externalize our thoughts; computing gives us a way to externalize the *implications of our thoughts*. This capability is at the heart of the transformative power that computing provides: Via computer modeling and simulation, computing lets us evaluate if our ideas are *good enough*.

SUMMARY

The performance of algorithms is determined by the resources they consume, *time* (cpu cycles) and *space* (memory). While the speed of a given computer determines how many cycles can be performed in a given amount of time, the number of cycles required is primarily a property of the algorithm.

In general, the exact performance of an algorithm cannot be predicted. This is because algorithms make decisions, sometimes millions of them, and each particular decision can alter the number of subsequent instructions that are executed, as well as the amount of memory consumed. Thus, three measures of algorithm performance are considered: *best case, worst case,* and *average* (or *expected*) *case*. Generally, the best case measure is of little concern.

As a rule, we are concerned with worst case and expected case, but care must be taken with respect to the latter. The average or expected case is often difficult to ascertain, as it is often heavily influenced by properties of data that are difficult to know. In particular, one cannot simply assume that truly random data will present itself, so equating expected case with what one sees from random data is a dangerous assumption.

Frequently, the performance of an algorithm is tied to the size of the data: the greater the amount of data that is fed into an algorithm, the greater the amount of time and/or space resources that the algorithm will require. Because of this relationship between the size of the input and the cost of the algorithm, we are generally less concerned with absolute measures of performance and more concerned the *rate at which costs grow* as a function of the size of the input data.

We express this in "order notation," or *Big Oh*, where:

- $O(N)$ signifies a *linear* algorithm that has cost that grow in direct proportion to input size of N.
- $O(1)$ signifies an algorithm that has only *constant* costs (i.e., changes in input size N do not affect performance at all).
- $O(\log N)$ signifies a *sublinear* algorithm (i.e., one that has costs that grow only at a rate proportional to $\log_2$ of N).
- $O(N^2)$ signifies a *quadratic* algorithm, one whose costs grow proportionally to the square of the input size.

- $O(2^N)$ signifies an *exponential* algorithm, one that grows at a rate on the order of 2 raised to the size of the input.

and so on.

Such measures are *estimates* and are assessed by examining the points of repetition within the algorithm. That is, one assesses the relationship between input and the repetitive steps required by the algorithm. For example, for an input of size N, a given algorithm will, in the worst case, require $2N^2 - 2$ time. One then throws out numerical constants, leaving N^2, thus indicating an $O(N^2)$ algorithm.

The various kinds of data structures have certain performance implications. *Arrays* and *linked lists* are both linear structures and, thus, many operations on them, such as searches and traversals will be linear or $O(N)$. Arrays, however, allow *random access,* which is $O(1)$, while linked lists do not. Thus, access to a given location in an array is in constant time, while for a linked list it is $O(N)$ in the general case. Similarly, random access allows us to exploit a *sorted* array to locate a target value in $O(\log N)$ time via *binary search,* which linked lists can not support. *Binary search trees* are not linear and can, like sorted arrays, exploit binary search strategies to locate contents in $O(\log N)$, but only if the BSTs are full and balanced. If not full and balanced, BST search performance can deteriorate to that of a linked list: $O(N)$.

Algorithms that have performance estimates featuring N as a *polynomial* factor are considered *reasonable* algorithms. Those that feature N as an *exponential* factor are considered to be *unreasonable,* as their cost is sufficiently prohibitive that they have no practical utility.

EXERCISES

9.1 Consider the algorithm in Fig. 9.2. In light of data that shows 60 percent of operations to be multiplication, 25 percent to be addition, 10 percent to be division, and 5 percent to be subtraction, what is average (or expected) work for this algorithm?

9.2 Given the distribution of operations from problem 9.1, above, modify the algorithm of Fig. 9.2 to optimize expected performance. Do so by rearranging the order of operator tests. After optimization, what is expected performance for the modified algorithm?

9.3 The requirements for the algorithms in Figs. 9.1 and 9.2 specified that the divide-by-zero error need not be considered. Modify the algorithm from Fig. 9.2 so that it will respond effectively to such an error. You may assume that all other aspects of user input will be legal. In the case where division by zero is attempted, the algorithm shall print a brief error message to the user and prompt the user for a nonzero divisor. Then, evaluate best case, worst case, and average case work for the modified algorithm. For average work, assume a random distribution of operators and a random distribution of single-digit (0 to 9) operands.

9.4 You are given an array of 10 numbers. Your job is to create an algorithm that calculates the minimum, maximum, and average of these numbers. Your boss has informed you that processor time (i.e., the cost of instructions) is expensive while memory is cheap. Write an iterative algorithm that uses as much memory as desired while keeping the expected work down to a minimum. What is the expected work? How much data space is required?

9.5 You are given the same problem as 9.4, above, except that the economics have changed: processor time is now cheap while memory is very expensive. Write an algorithm that uses as many instructions as desired while using the fewest possible variables. How much data space is needed? What is the expected work?

9.6 The `exitif` statement is similar to the `if` statement in that it involves the test of a boolean condition to determine flow of control. Consider the algorithm in Example 9.5. Observe that the `exitif` test involves two conditions. Based on our discussion of work concerning our `Calculator` algorithm (the algorithms of Figs. 9.1 and 9.2), what are the performance costs for this compound test (i.e., how many instructions will it take to evaluate the `exitif` conditions and decide upon flow of control)?

9.7 Given your answer to problem 9.6, what are the actual time and space costs for the algorithm of Example 9.5 in terms of N. Be sure to assess the costs for best case, worst case, and average case. For the average case, you may assume that the target value will always be found and that it will randomly distributed throughout the list from one trial to another.

In the previous problems, you assessed actual performance costs. Our Big Oh estimates "throw away" much of this information. Since information is being thrown away, it is possible for our Big Oh estimates to be deceiving. Use this idea in problems 9.8 and 9.9.

9.8 Your manager shows you two algorithms: one is $O(N)$, the other is $O(1)$. He is confused because the $O(N)$ algorithm performs better than the $O(1)$ algorithm for his data set where $N = 16K$. Upon inspection, you determine that the $O(N)$ algorithm makes exactly N passes through the data and that each pass implies hidden constant costs of 17 instructions per pass. If the $O(1)$ algorithm makes exactly one pass through the data, estimate the hidden constant costs (i.e., instructions per pass) that you would expect to find in order to explain its slower performance.

9.9 Repeat problem 9.8, above, except that it's an $O(\log N)$ algorithm that's being outperformed by the same $O(N)$ algorithm. Upon inspection, you determine that the $O(\log N)$ algorithm makes $2\log N$ passes through the data. What must be the constant costs per pass to explain the algorithm's poorer performance?

For problems 9.10 to 9.14, give the estimate of worst case running time (Big Oh) of the algorithms described.

9.10 An algorithm searches for the `max` value in an array of numbers. The size of the array is `N` and the numbers in the array are arranged randomly.

9.11 An algorithm searches for both `max` and `min` values in an array of numbers. The size of the array is N, and the numbers in the array are arranged randomly.

9.12 An algorithm searches for both `max` and `min` values in an array of N numbers. The numbers in the array are arranged in sorted descending order.

9.13 An algorithm searches for the `max` value stored in a full and balanced BST that contains N nodes.

9.14 An algorithm inserts numbers into a linked list such that the linked list will store the numbers in sorted ascending order. Originally, the list is empty, and the algorithm inserts a total of N numbers into the list.

For problems 9.15 to 9.22, we have two separate data structures to build and use.

- In one case, N values must be stored in a balanced BST. For each value, the proper BST location for the new node must be determined. Once the location is found, a new node is allocated and that node and the new value are inserted into the tree. Then, a special algorithm (it's there, but we don't know the details of how it works) does whatever is required to guarantee that the tree will always be balanced. It does so at a constant cost of B work per insertion.
- In the other case, each value must be stored in sorted ascending order into a linked list.

Thus, we have three algorithms: one that builds an ordered linked list, the other that builds a balanced BST, and the "mystery algorithm" that is called by the BST algorithm to ensure tree balancing.

Give Big Oh for each of the following. Be sure to explain your answer.

9.15 Inserting each new value in the BST (finding location, insertion, balancing).

9.16 Inserting each new value in the linked list.

9.17 Inserting all N values into the BST.

9.18 Inserting all N values into the linked list.

9.19 Responding (via a single boolean result) to single query that asks if a given value is in the BST.

9.20 Responding (via a single boolean result per query) to N queries, each of which asks if a given value is in the linked list.

9.21 Determine the total work required to build the linked list, then identify the `min` value in the list.

9.22 Determine the total work required to build the BST, then identify the `max` value in the tree.

9.23 You are given an unsorted list of numbers and are told to find the *mode* (i.e., the number that occurs in the list with the greatest frequency). Create an algorithm that will work for any N. You may use an array type where constant max is N. What is Big Oh for your algorithm?

9.24 You are provided with a full and balanced BST containing T numbers and an unsorted list of L numbers. Your job is to examine each number in the unsorted list and determine if it is in the BST. What is Big Oh for the job?

9.25 You are provided the same data as given in problem 9.24. This time, you are to examine each value in the BST and determine if it is in the unsorted list of numbers. What is Big Oh for the job?

9.26 For reasons we can't fathom, a robot has been programmed to paint a batch of *N* used cars the same color. Furthermore, each car will be painted a *different* color than it was before. The robot will grab a bucket of paint and begin painting cars. As it approaches each car, it will first verify that the new color is different from the old color. If the robot discovers that it is using paint that matches the color of the current car, the robot discards its paint bucket, fetches a bucket with a different color, and begins painting all *N* cars again! What is Big Oh for the robot's algorithm?

9.27 The boss wants to snoop into his employee's private lives. You are provided with a database in which employee data records are stored in an array sorted by employee number. Your job is to identify any employees who live together. Imagine an algorithm to do the job. What is its Big Oh? How much memory will it require?

9.28 What is your opinion of the ethical implications of the job assigned in problem 9.27? If you were assigned this job, would you do it? If so, why? If not, why not?

9.29 In your opinion, how should society deal with the ethical issues in problem 9.27.

9.30 Imagine that a reasonable person disagrees with your position on problem 9.27. What rationale might that person have for disagreement?

The Limits of Computing

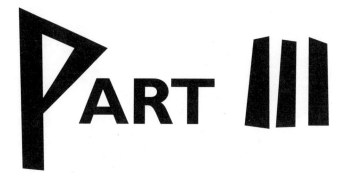

PART III

CHAPTER 10

Concurrency and Parallelism

So far, we have considered algorithms only as if there was a single processor devoted to the execution of a single algorithm. As a practical matter, many computers execute multiple algorithms at the same time. Other computers are designed so that they can devote more than one processor to the execution of a single algorithm. In this chapter, we will introduce the basic concepts that are relevant when we go beyond a simple "one algorithm, one processor" model. In addition, we will consider the implications for algorithmic performance, including the limits of the performance improvements that are possible.

10.1 Overview: Concurrency vs. Parallelism

Concurrency and *parallelism* are two terms that become relevant when we go beyond the "one algorithm, one processor" model. They mean quite different things, and it is not unusual to hear them being confused with one another in the general news media. Their respective meanings are explained below and the differences between the two are then described.

10.1.1　What Is Concurrency?

Definition: Concurrency refers to the execution of various different tasks at the same time.

EXAMPLE 10.1　At any given moment a time-shared (i.e., multiuser) computer may have a large number of users logged in. In a properly designed and appropriately loaded system, each of these users will have the illusion that the computer is devoted to his or her job only. In reality, the computer is busy juggling various jobs, giving only small "time slices" (small fractions of a second) to each of the many users. In other words, the computer is executing multiple different jobs, or processes, "at the same time."

Notice that we have put quotation marks around the phrase, "at the same time." This is because we need to be careful about the meaning we attach to this phrase.

- Perhaps there is a single processor that is rapidly taking turns among all the users' jobs.
- Perhaps there are several processors within a single machine and each processor gives its undivided attention to a single user.
- Perhaps each of several processors are rapidly taking turns among various users.

In the first case (one processor serving several users), the computer is, quite literally, doing only one thing at a time. Thus, strictly speaking, it is *not* doing several tasks "at the same time." However, by rotating its attention among the various users very rapidly, it can give the illusion of doing many things at once. As it rapidly gives service to the various users who are logged in, it spreads its resources (cpu cycles, memory, and so on) among the users. It does *not* begin and finish one user's job before going on to the next. Instead, it is "in the process" of many jobs at once. We say that such a system serves many users concurrently.

Concurrency refers to this kind of phenomena (regardless of how many processors are actually built into a given machine): more than one job is being executed at the same time.

EXAMPLE 10.2　Think of your grandmother cooking Thanksgiving dinner: She may have the turkey roasting, and the bread baking, and the beans boiling, all at the same time. Meanwhile, she is busy mashing the potatoes. The preparation of each item on her dinner menu is, logically speaking, a different task. Yet they are going on at the same time, with your grandmother spreading her attention around, monitoring each task as appropriate. In computer jargon, we might think of your grandmother as the "processor" who is "giving service" to multiple "concurrent processes."

10.1.2　What Is Parallelism?

Definition: Parallelism refers to the deployment of *multiple processors* on a *single task*.

EXAMPLE 10.3　Science researchers often have reason to analyze large quantities of data and it is sometimes important to analyze the data as quickly as possible. Imagine that a researcher has a huge two dimensional numerical array of C columns by R rows. Imagine further that he has need to find C averages, one for each column's R numbers.

With a single processor, an algorithm might sum the R values in the first column, divide that sum by R to find the average for that column, then repeat the same steps iteratively for each of the C columns. Thus, in the general case, the job would imply an $O(R*C)$ algorithm.

With adequate parallel processing capability, a different processor could be assigned to each column. Thus, given C processors, the entire job could be completed in $O(R)$ time, the same time required for a single processor to do $1/C$th of the job.

The crucial quality that defines parallelism is that multiple processors cooperate to collectively do a single job. There are various ways that such cooperation can occur. The number-crunching example above is just one such "architecture," in which each processor shares the same tasks as the others, with each processor focused upon a different subset of data.

EXAMPLE 10.4 A real-world analogy might occur if you want your grandmother to teach you how to bake cookies. As the entire clan is gathering for Thanksgiving, more than one batch of cookies is required. Your grandmother decides that she'll make one batch while instructing you, by both word and example, as you make the other batch. Thus, each of you first makes the cookie dough, each of you spoons it out onto cookie sheets, and so on. In computer jargon, we could say that two batches of cookies are being prepared "in parallel."

EXAMPLE 10.5 Another possible model for parallel processing might occur if, for example, your little brother has insisted on helping make the cookies and your grandmother has decided to keep the peace by giving everyone their own job.

1. During the first "chunk of time" she has you making a batch of the cookie dough.
2. During the second "chunk of time" (beginning when you say the dough is ready) your grandmother activates two processes:
   a. Your little brother spoons the first-batch dough onto a cookie sheet.
   b. You take a fresh bowl and make the dough for a second batch.
3. During the third "chunk of time" (i.e., when your brother finishes loading up the cookie sheet and you have the second batch of dough ready), three steps simultaneously occur:
   a. Your grandmother places the first batch in the oven for baking.
   b. Your brother spoons out the second batch onto another cookie sheet.
   c. You prepare a third batch of dough.

Thus, each "processor" (the three people involved) has a different task to complete, with one processor's "output" serving as the "input" to the next processor. We still have multiple processors cooperating on a single task, but this time the work is decomposed such that the various processors depend on one another's results, and such that their activities must be coordinated.

This "architecture" for parallelism is known as "pipeline parallelism," and is the implicit model of the traditional manufacturing assembly line: a job goes down a "pipeline" such that at various points along the way, different processors perform a specific task. Multiple jobs are in the pipeline at the same time, but each one is at a different stage of completion.

10.1.3   Confusion Between the Two

People who don't know much about computing often confuse the meanings of parallelism and concurrency. This is not surprising, given that the two concepts are each related to the phenomena of having more than one thing happening simultaneously. In fact, for practical purposes of everyday speech, the line between the two can easily become blurred. To see how, return to our example of concurrent processing (Example 10.5), your grandmother preparing Thanksgiving dinner.

Let's imagine that your grandfather doesn't have a clue about cooking and, instead of helping, he's "busy" using the remote control to flick between football games. During commercials, he wanders in to the kitchen to smell the food and find out how long until it's time to eat. Since he is oblivious to the particulars of the actual work that's required, dinner might mean "one thing" ("time to eat!") more than it means a variety of independent food-preparation "algorithms." Thus, from his point of view, he might perceive four different processors (two ovens and two burners) and one task ("make dinner"). From his point of view, we would have multiple processors sharing the work of one task. He would see "parallelism," not the multiple tasks of "concurrency."

It might be pointless to use this example to educate him about parallelism vs. concurrency, as his misunderstanding has to do with ignorance of the actual business of cooking, not with any particular terminology. On the other hand, he might easily grasp the distinction between the two if you explain that cable TV is bringing multiple football games into the house "concurrently," while each play of each game features 11 "parallel processors" per team.

10.2   Concurrency

As we have seen, concurrency refers to the processing of multiple different tasks "at the same time." With respect to computing systems, there are four kinds of concurrent systems. Of these, three have names that include the prefix *multi;* these three are commonly confused with one another. All four are described below.

10.2.1   Multiprogramming

Definition: Multiprogramming refers to a system in which a single processor shares its attention among various users.

The original time-shared computer systems found in universities and industry were examples of multiprogramming. In such systems, there is only a single processor and thus only one user's job can receive attention at any given moment. The illusion of simultaneous processing is achieved by the rapid swapping of processor attention amongst the various active jobs.

10.2.2 Multiprocessing

Definition: Multiprocessing is similar to multiprogramming, with the difference that the computer contains multiple processors, each of which shares its attention among multiple jobs.

The various processors share a common pool of memory and, since a given pool of memory can respond to only one processor at a time, the various processors access to memory must be coordinated; thus such systems are more complex than multiprogramming systems. Just as in multiprogramming systems, a processor's attention is distributed in small time slices to multiple concurrent user jobs. Since there are multiple processors, several jobs are being processed at any given moment.

10.2.3 Multitasking

Definition: Multitasking refers to the ability of a single user to have many jobs proceeding concurrently on a single machine.

Until recently, multitasking was found only in large, time-shared systems that would allow a single user to run multiple programs at the same time. In the last decade, however, this capability has migrated to PCs. A PC user can now have multiple "windows" open concurrently so that the machine is, for example, running a word processor in one window, a spreadsheet in another, a communications package in a third, and so on. The first generations of such systems provided only the illusion of multitasking via swapping the single processor's attention among the various jobs (similar to the idea behind multiprogramming). Modern generations of PC hardware and software allow one cpu to behave like multiple independent processors, each one giving its undivided attention to a single task.

10.2.4 Distributed Systems

Definition: A **distributed system** is a system that does not reside in a single box or at a single location. Instead, it consists of multiple computers, each with its own memory and each with one or more processors, that reside at different sites.

Each subsystem, or "node," of the system has its own set of tasks to do, which it does more-or-less independently from the other nodes of the system. However, the various nodes communicate with each other to ensure the appropriate functioning of the system as a whole. The first everyday example was the reservation systems used by airlines and travel agents for travel plans. Such systems do not exist in any particular place but instead are literally distributed across various sites. A more recent example of a distributed system is the network of the ATM banking machines that are now spread around the globe.

Distributed systems are *not* like a large time-shared system that allows multiple users to log on concurrently. Instead, many computers at different sites processes transactions and interact with a database of relevant information. Even the database itself is likely to be distributed across various sites. Such systems prevent many of the bottleneck problems of time-shared systems, but at the price of greater complexity. Instead of a single operating system governing a large, complex computer, a distributed system features many independent operating systems and other software that must interact with each other.

In a distributed system, there is no one program that is "in charge." Instead, control is distributed to many programs that must cooperate with one another. In human terms, a distributed system is less like a dictatorship with centralized control and more like a complex society with various constituents who coexist within the framework of standards of behavior. In distributed systems, the various processes interact according to "protocols" that specify standards of interprocess behavior.

10.3   Issues in Concurrency

Concurrent systems imply more complexity. Not only might multiple processors need to share a common pool of memory, but mechanisms must support the swapping of processor attention from one task to another. The governing of processor behavior, the swapping of processor attention among various jobs, and the swapping of the various jobs in and out of memory is handled by the computer's operating system. The operating system is, in effect, the first program that the computer runs, and it is this program that allows the computer to run other programs. In concurrent systems, the operating system must have capabilities for addressing each of three key issues: protection, fairness, and deadlock.

10.3.1   Protection

Definition: Protection refers to the steps that must be taken to ensure that, with many tasks being processed at once, one task does not contaminate the work of another task.

Memory must be partitioned appropriately so that each task's data resides in its own partition. Each task must be prevented from writing data to a memory location that belongs to another task. As various tasks begin and end, the partitioning of memory can become quite complicated. There are various "memory management" algorithms that govern how the operating system allocates memory to the various tasks.

Protection is an issue that applies as well to other resources such as printers, disk drives, and modems. For example, if one task has sent text to the printer, all other tasks must be prevented from sending their data to the printer until the task that "has" the printer is finished. In practice, the operating system manages a queue for each resource.

10.3.2 Fairness

Definition: In concurrent systems, **fairness** refers to the need to guarantee that each job gets its "fair share" of processor attention and other resources (such as memory, disk, and printer). It comes into play when the demands of one job affect the resources available to other jobs.

What is fair? For example, imagine that a given concurrent system can handle 10 jobs at a time. This would be a small system, but it will suffice for our example. At first, it would seem that normal queue behavior—"first come, first served" (FCFS)—would result in fairness. This approach certainly seems fair enough. But what if 10 different users happen to log on, each with their own extremely long job? Imagine that each of these long jobs is 100 times longer than the average job. Thus, under FCFS, these ten users will occupy the system for a time equal to the average load of 1000 users. Is it fair to allow a small number of users to monopolize a shared system? Is it fair that all other users be locked out of the system for a long period of time? What if this policy were applied to the time-shared system you use to submit your assignments? What if the system were tied up for 10 days straight by a small number of users with large jobs? Obviously, the great majority of users with average needs would perceive this situation as unfair.

So, what might be more fair? Perhaps we could give different priorities to each job based on how much time it has already used. Under such a scheme, new jobs would get a high priority and a big time slice of service. Since many jobs are short, we would hope that giving high priority to new jobs would move them through the system rapidly, allowing users to get done and get off, thus making way for new users to login. For a long job, the priority for that job would gradually fall as it stayed in the system. The longer the job was in the system, the smaller would be its time slice. In addition, we might "swap out" the large jobs to disk every so often, effectively making the long jobs take turns with one another instead of monopolizing the whole system.

This certainly seems fairer. We make the long jobs wait a bit, thus allowing fast jobs to get done quicker. In effect, we punish those with huge jobs and reward those with short jobs. We might do this in a way that would encourage those with large jobs to do them at nonpeak hours. In other words, we might let them run faster if they wait until the low-demand hours to run them. This approach would certainly please the largest number of users, and even those with large jobs would likely agree that it's more fair. But how do we ensure that the large jobs get enough time to finish in reasonable time?

In practice, there is a real danger of having the large (and thus "older") jobs get smaller and smaller amounts of processor attention. It might get to the point where a particularly large job *never* gets finished. This is neither fair to that user, nor is it desirable from the operating system's standpoint. We *want* to get rid of the old, big job. Furthermore, a basic tenet of fairness is that all jobs get to finish in "reasonable" time. There are various proven ways to address this problem, involving multiple priority levels and various queues that are based on priority, not just time of arrival.

10.3.3   Deadlock

 Definition: **Deadlock** refers to the phenomena of computer systems freezing up because each job is "on hold," waiting for something it cannot have.

For example, imagine that we have a concurrent system that can handle only three jobs at once.

- Job One wants to print data from disk to the printer. At the moment, it "has" the disk, but is waiting for the printer. It will not give up the disk until it gets the printer and prints its data because, if it were to give up the disk, then getting the printer would do it no good: It couldn't obtain the data it wants to print. However, Job Three has the printer.
- Job Two wants to receive data from another source over a modem and write that data to disk. It "has" the modem—that is, is connected to the other source—but is waiting for the disk. It will not give up the modem until it gets the disk because, if it were to give up the modem, then getting the disk would do it no good: It couldn't obtain the data it wants to write to the disk. However, Job One has the disk.
- Job Three wants to print data that it receives over the modem. It "has" the printer, but is waiting for the modem. It will not give up the printer until it gets the modem because, if it were to give up the printer, then getting the modem would do it no good: It couldn't obtain the data it wants to print. However, Job Two has the modem.

Thus, each job is occupying a resource while waiting for another resource to become free. Unfortunately, none of the needed resources will become free, as they are held by another job, which is in turn waiting for another resource. In effect, it is the same problem as rush-hour traffic "gridlock" when a car occupies a space and cannot move until another car moves, but the other cars can't move because they're waiting for other cars, and so on, in a circular fashion.

There are a few policies that can be implemented algorithmically that can prevent deadlock. We might prevent jobs from holding resources that they're not actually using. We might establish a hierarchy of resources and implement a rule that only allows a job to hold a "low" resource while waiting for a "high" one, but prevents a job from holding a "high" one while waiting for a "low" one. As with issues of fairness and protection, there are various strategies and permutations that can be used.

10.3.4   Summary of Concurrency Issues

The issues of protection, fairness, and deadlock each generate a host of problems. Any given solution usually contributes a further problem. The particulars of such algorithms are included in the subject matter of other courses, most usually a course in operating systems, and are beyond our focus here.

What is important is that you notice that we've got a host of algorithmic problems that are *created* by the fact that we're trying to handle multiple tasks concurrently. Such problems, and their solution algorithms, are *overhead costs;* that is, they take processor time, they take up memory, yet they don't accomplish any "real work"; instead, they are a cost of doing business, a price to be paid in order to make concurrency work.

We find many real-world analogies. In general, as a system becomes more complex, as it tries to do more and more things, the cost of complexity management rises rapidly, often exponentially. More and more resources are consumed by overhead costs, and fewer and fewer resources are available to do "real work." Everyday examples include generally large systems: large universities, large charities, "big government," large software development projects, extravagantly staged rock tours, and so on.

However, this analysis does not provide any compelling evidence against the usefulness of large systems; it only points out that their overhead costs will be high. The other side of the coin is that large systems often can do things that simply cannot be done by small systems.

Distributed systems are, in effect, an attempt to get the "best of both worlds" (the power of large systems with the benefits of small systems) via the connection of numerous small, simple systems. Each node is notably smaller and simpler than the comparable large system would be. The viability of distributed systems is dependent upon two factors:

(a) *Adequate bandwidth* (physical capacity for communication) to allow the nodes to communicate effectively.
(b) *Adequate protocols* (rules for communication and interaction) that concisely, yet effectively, govern the behavior of the various nodes with respect to one another and that guarantee that the whole job gets done.

It appears that distributed systems will play a larger and larger role in the future.

10.4   Parallelism

Parallelism refers to the use of multiple processors to reduce the time required to complete a single task. There are a few factors that come into play in determining how much parallelism is possible. The logical properties of the algorithm that is to be "parallelized" typically limit how much gain is possible. Just because we might have a machine with 256 processors, we cannot assume that we can achieve a speed-up by a factor of 256. We shall discuss these factors, show their impact on performance for given algorithms, and utilize a graphical method for representing the parallel potential for a given algorithm. We will also make clear the potential impact of parallelism.

EXAMPLE 10.6   Recall that the Bubblesort algorithm sorts a list of numbers by repeatedly comparing adjacent values and moving the larger value to the right. In general, it requires $N - 1$ comparisons-and-maybe-swaps on the first pass in order to move the largest value to its proper position. With the largest value in place, it then requires $N - 2$ comparisons-and-maybe-swaps to move the second-largest value into its proper position, and so on. We have seen that Bubblesort requires $O(N)$ passes of $O(N)$ work per pass, and is thus an $O(N^2)$ algorithm.

Let's now take the idea behind Bubblesort (i.e., repeatedly comparing adjacent values and reordering the pair if necessary) but imagine that we can use as many processors as we want. What kind of performance can we achieve? How might we go about achieving an increase in performance?

One approach would be to utilize multiple processors so that we can do multiple comparisons-and-maybe-swaps at once. For example we might compare the numbers in the first and second positions while simultaneously comparing those in the third and fourth, the fifth and sixth, the seventh and eighth, and so on. In effect, for any even N, we could use $N/2$ processors to allow us to do $N/2$ comparisons-and-maybe-swaps in one "time chunk."

To see what would happen, let's consider a "bad" scenario for sorting: We wish to sort the numbers into ascending order, but the original list has them sorted in descending order. This arrangement guarantees that we must move each and every number in the list. Below, we show what happens during the first time chunk. We indicate each of the various processors as lines beneath the pair of numbers that each processor is comparing-and-maybe-swapping, and we then show the resulting state of the list.

```
Original list of 8 numbers    93    87       74    65       57    45       33    27
          N/2 procs:       ├──────────┤   ├──────────┤   ├──────────┤   ├──────────┤
     List after 1 time chunk    87    93       65    74       45    57       27    33
```

Thus, in the first time chunk, we have compared-and-maybe-swapped four ($N/2$) pairs of numbers.

For the second time chunk, we might shift our processors over one position, for example, comparing the values in the second and third positions, the fourth and fifth positions, the sixth and seventh positions, all simultaneously.

```
     List after 1 time chunk    87    93       65    74       45    57       27    33
                                   ├──────────┤   ├──────────┤   ├──────────┤   ├──────────┤
    List after 2 time chunks    87    65       93    45       74    27       57    33
```

For the third time chunk we might shift our processors back (as the were in the first time chunk), and continue in this fashion, alternating which pairs of numbers are compared-and-maybe-swapped, until such time as the entire list is sorted.

In effect, we are having the various processors "vibrate" back an forth between odd/even and even/odd number positions. We show the results of the rest of this "vibrate sort" process, below.

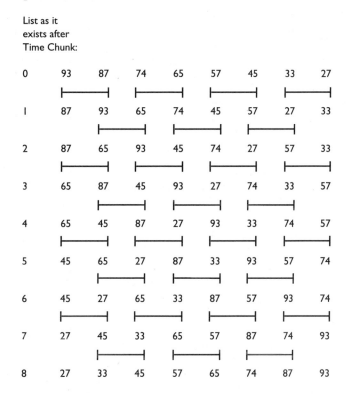

By the end of eight time chunks the entire list of eight numbers is in the correct sorted order. Thus, in this instance, we have exploited parallelism to reduce the time cost of the sorting algorithm from $O(N^2)$ to $O(N)$.

10.5 Limits of Parallelism

The example, above, illustrates the first limitation of parallelism. Observe that, while we have reduced time, we have not reduced the total work. True, we can get the job done in only $O(N)$ time. However, we do so at a cost of $O(N)$ work per each time chunk. $O(N)$ work for each of $O(N)$ time chunks still shows a total of $O(N^2)$ work.

A basic principle of parallelism: Parallelism cannot produce the same results with less work. All parallelism can do is transfer the required work to multiple processors so that more work can get done in any given chunk of time. Thus, an $O(N)$ algorithm is still (at best) $O(N)$, an $O(N^2)$ algorithm is still at least $O(N^2)$, and so on. Parallelism does not provide any magic by which total work is reduced; all parallelism can do is shift that work into fewer chunks of time by having multiple processors working at once.

In Chapter 9, when we considered algorithms and assumed that we had only one processor available, there was no real difference between time and work. Each time chunk allowed the processor to do one piece of work (i.e., we could equate time and work). When we introduce multiple processors, we break this one-to-one correspondence between time and work. Instead, we have what is known as *product complexity*.

 Definition: Product complexity is "the amount of work per time chunk" multiplied by the number of time chunks. For any given algorithmic approach to a problem, parallelism may change the required time, but cannot improve the product complexity.

This fact allows us to quickly estimate the ceiling of improvement that parallelism can provide. For example, imagine that we have an $O(N\log N)$ algorithm that we wish to parallelize. Further, imagine that we have $\log N$ processors available. These facts alone are sufficient to let us conclude that the "new, improved" parallel version of the algorithm will require *at least* $O(N)$ time. Similarly, having N processors available for an algorithmic approach that is $O(N^3)$ means that we will be able to do no better than $O(N^2)$ time, and so on.

Notice that we have said that the product complexity allows us to quickly gauge the ceiling of improvement, and that we have used phrases such as "no better than" or "at least" so much work. The product complexity tells us the *best that we can hope for*. How much of this desired gain can be actually achieved is determined by four particular factors, discussed below.

10.5.1 Fixed Number of Processors

Notice that we have casually referred to having N processors or $\log N$ processors. In actual fact, the number of processors available is a factor of hardware. Just because N might double, that doesn't mean that we can magically double the number of processors available.

As with many things in computing, the number of processors available in a parallel architecture is typically some power of 2. Thus, we might have a parallel machine that features an array of 16 processors or 256 or 1024. As time goes by, it is reasonable to expect that the number of processors built in to state-of-the-art parallel machines will grow. But it is absurd to think that this number will conveniently grow with whatever N might be for the problem at hand.

In practice, the number of processors is a constant. This means that order of magnitude improvements in processing time are limited to those N where N is no greater than the number of processors available. For all other "inconvenient" N, processing time can be improved by no more than a fixed factor, for example, "no more than twice as fast" or "no more than a thousand times as fast." Such improvements are sometimes quite valuable. In certain situations, they are necessary. But such improvement is something quite different than the order of magnitude improvements required to "revolutionize" computing or to "break the barrier" of problems that are, for practical purposes, too costly to be solvable. (We shall learn more about those in the next chapter.)

10.5.2 Overhead Costs

Parallelization is not free. There must be some way to relate the algorithmic problem at hand to the hardware so that each processor "knows" what to do. And, as we have stressed many times, processors have no sense whatsoever. Thus, there must be some mechanism that allocates the attention of various processors to the appropriate parts of the algorithm and/or subsets of data. So far, we have ignored this issue.

- For example, in Example 10.6 we simply assumed that the various processors would compare-and-maybe-swap the right pair of numbers, based simply upon what we imagined that we'd *want* them to do. However, we did nothing to make it happen that way.
- Similarly, early in the chapter, we briefly discussed the parallelization of an algorithm for averaging each of C columns of R rows of numbers in a two-dimensional array. In that case, we imagined that each processor would execute the inner loop of the sequential algorithm (i.e., sum a given column of numbers, then divide by R) for a different column. In effect, the outer loop of the sequential algorithm (do the inner loop for each column) was effectively replaced by the multiple processors. Yet, we discussed no means of *making* each processor deal with "its own" column.

In reality, we need some algorithmic way to govern which processor does what. And, like anything else, this ability does not come free. The costs associated with instructing the various processors to "do the right thing" depends on the particulars of the parallel processing environment (i.e., it is implementation specific). Thus, there are no general rules of thumb that we can apply across the board. Because the details are implementation specific, and because we are concerned with general principles, for the rest of this chapter we will continue to "wave our hands" at the overhead costs involved and we will ignore them.

Be advised, however, that they are there and that they can be quite significant. Often, they require that an algorithm be completely rewritten in a programming language designed for parallelism, often by an expensive programmer who specializes in such things. Often times the result will not generalize. A parallel version of an algorithm designed for one machine with X processors not work on another machine that has Y processors.

One way to think about the costs of parallelization is to imagine real-world, human situations in which things are done in parallel. Parallelization occurs whenever an organization has many people doing the same thing. Observe that the supervision of such tasks is a primary reason for the existence of management. Observe, too, that in large organizations (where, presumably, there is a greater deal of parallelization going on) the "management level" has typically grown to be many levels, and that the costs of management have often grown to dwarf those costs that can be rationalized.

10.5.3 Dependencies

Definition: A **dependency** is a relationship among various steps within an algorithm such that one step *depends upon* another step for data.

EXAMPLE 10.7 Consider the following algorithm:

```
(S1) read(a)
(S2) b <- a * 3
(S3) c <- b * a
```

This algorithm consists of three statements labeled S1 through S3. (The labels are not part of the algorithm; they simply provide a means for us to refer to particluar statements.) There are two dependencies in this algorithm.

- S2 assigns a new value to the variable b, based on computation applied to the value stored in variable a. The value of variable a is determined by the execution of S1. Thus, S2 depends on S1, that is, S2 cannot do its job until S1 has done its job.
- S3 (which assigns a new value to variable c) depends on both S1 (for the value of a) and S2 (for the value of b). Thus, S3 cannot be executed until both S1 and S2 have completed.

From this, we can see that this particular algorithm cannot benefit from parallelization. Regardless of how many processors are available, it will require three time chunks to execute: the first time chunk for S1, the second for S2, and the third for S3. Given an unlimited number of processors, the execution of this algorithm will require the same amount of time as is required given only a single processor.

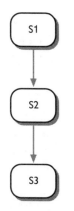

We represent dependencies via a *dependency graph* that shows the relationship among the various statements of an algorithm. Time is represented in the vertical dimension (rows) and the number of processors in the horizontal dimension (columns). Downward arrows represent the dependencies. A dependency graph for the code of Example 10.7 is shown in Fig. 10.1. It indicates that three time chunks (number of vertical rows) are required and that only a single processor (number of horizontal columns) can be utilized by the algorithm.

EXAMPLE 10.8 An algorithm of three steps that does not feature any dependencies, such as,

```
{S1} read(a)
{S2} b <- b + 3
{S3} c <- c * 4
```

FIGURE 10.1
Dependency graph for Example 10.7

would be represented as shown in the dependency graph of Fig. 10.2, indicating that it could be performed in one time chunk by three processors.

FIGURE 10.2 Dependency graph for Example 10.8

EXAMPLE 10.9   Consider the algorithm:

```
{S1} read(a)
{S2} read(b)
{S3} c <- a * 4
{S4} d <- b / 3
{S5} e <- c * d
{S6} f <- d + 8
```

Observe that there are various dependencies involved here: S3 depends on S1, S6 depends on S4, S5 depends on both S3 and S4, and so forth. How many processors can we make use of? And how much execution time can we save? Drawing a dependency graph, as shown in Fig. 10.3, gives us a way to answer these questions.

The first two statements feature no dependencies between themselves and thus can occur in parallel (one processor for S1, another for S2). S3 is dependent on S1 and may execute only after S1 is finished. Similarly, S4 is dependent upon S2 and must go after S2. S5 is dependent upon both S3 and S4 and must wait for both of them. S6 need only wait for S4. The graph indicates that we can utilize two processors to execute the algorithm in three time chunks (vs. six time chunks by using one processor). Several processors would do no good here: The dependencies of the algorithm determine that two processors is the most we can use.

EXAMPLE 10.10   Consider the following algorithm:

```
i <- 1
loop
      exitif (i > MAX_ARRAY)
{S1}  read(a[i])
{S2}  b[i] <- a[i] + 4
{S3}  c[i] <- a[i] / 3
{S4}  d[i] <- b[i] / c[i]
      i <- i + 1
endloop
```

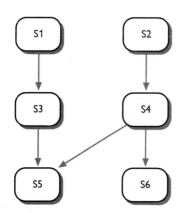

This algorithm accesses four different arrays (a, b, c, and d). Each pass through the loop accesses the *i*th element of each array. For *each pass*, S2 and S3 are dependent upon S1, while S4 is dependent upon both S2 and S3. Thus, the dependency graph for a single pass through the loop is as shown in Fig. 10.4. It shows that we can utilize two processors to get the job done in three time chunks. We do not fully utilize the second processor: It is busy only during the second time chunk. Thus, while we double the number of processors, we only reduce our time from four time chunks to three.

FIGURE 10.3   Dependency graph for Example 10.9

In Example 10.10, we know what dependencies exist for each pass through the loop. What can we conclude about the *various different* passes? Observe that each pass through the loop references a *different index* into each of the four arrays. Since each iteration deals with a different index, we can have a different processor deal with each array index.

FIGURE 10.4 Dependency graph for Example 10.10: one pass through

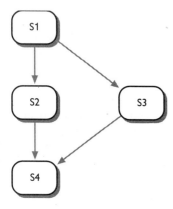

(All we are concerned with here is the logical problem of "how many processors can we use?" We ignore the overhead work of assigning each processor to its task, and the problem of *how* to do that. Such topics are addressed in courses on parallel computation. We are concerned here only with those statements that do "real work" (those labeled `S1..S4`). Thus, we also ignore the `exitif` and `i <- i + 1` statements. These statements are the overhead work of sequential execution. They don't do any "real work," but instead help us manage repetition. In essence they are overhead too, so we ignore them when identifying dependencies.)

Figure 10.5 shows the dependency graph for three passes through the loop. In it, we refer to the steps in the first loop pass as `S1..S4`, the steps of the second pass as `S1'..S4'` (verbally, "S1 prime"), the steps of the third pass as `S1"..S4"` (verbally, "S1 double-prime"), and so on. If `MAX_ARRAY` is 3, the dependency graph of Fig. 10.5 describes the excecution of the entire algorithm.

It indicates that we can complete the work of processing data for our various three-element arrays in three time chunks by utilizing six processors. We can generalize this for an array of size *N*: if we have $2N$ processors, we can finish the job in only three time chunks. This is tells us the limit of maximum parallelization, given unlimited resources.

EXAMPLE 10.11 Limited resources can change how we utilize processors. For example, conside the algorihm from Example 10.10 and assume that we are limited to those processors that we can keep fully utilized. By fully utilized we mean that the processors will not be sitting idly by once the algorithm is underway.

We can tolerate some idle cycles at the beginning and end, however. By observing the "holes" in the graph of Fig. 10.5, and by examining the pattern of the per-loop dependency graphs, we can arrive at the graph shown in Fig. 10.6. In it, we have created a repeating pattern that keeps both processors utilized.

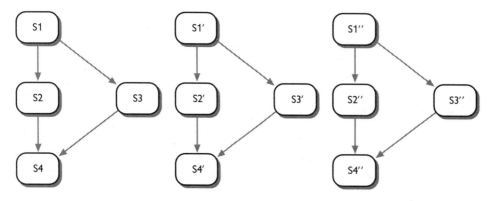

FIGURE 10.5 Dependency graph for Example 10.10: three passes through

How much time is required for arrays of size N? The first pass through the loop completes in three time chunks, the second pass completes after five time chunks, the third completes after seven time chunks, the fourth after nine, and so on. Thus, this graph indicates that we can fully utilize two processors in such a way that we can process arrays of N elements via the algorithm of Example 10.10 in $(2N + 1)$ time chunks for any N.

10.5.4 Precedences

Definition: A **precedence** is a relationship among various steps within an algorithm such that one step must be *prevented from contaminating* the data needed by another step.

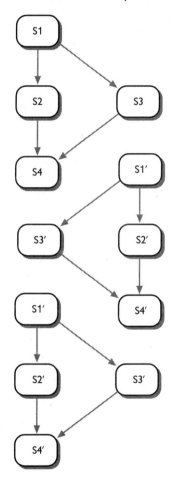

FIGURE 10.6 Dependency graph for Example 10.11

Precedence relationships are similar to dependencies, in that they refer to the need to prevent the execution of a subsequent statement until after a prior statement completes. The reason for this blockage is different however. In a dependency relationship, S2 would be blocked from executing until S1 has completed because S2 needs the data value produced by S1. In a precedence relationship the blockage occurs because the execution of S2 would contaminate the data value needed by S1. For example:

```
X <- 1
loop
        exitif (x > 3)
{S1}    read(a)
{S2}    print(a)
{S3}    a <- a * 7
{S4}    print(a)
        x <- x + 1
endloop
```

Observe that we cannot allow S3 to execute until after S2 has executed. Why? It is *not* because S3 needs a value from S2; it does not. Instead, S3 must be prevented from executing until after S2 is finished because S3 will alter a value that S2 must have unaltered. If S3 executes before S2, it will contaminate the data value that S2 is accessing. This is the essence of a precedence relationship: A later statement must be stopped from contaminating the data used by an earlier statement.

A precedence graph is used to show both dependency and precedence relationships. It is identical to a dependency graph except that precedences are also indicated graphically. A dependency is indicated (as before) by a downward pointing arrow; a precedence is indicated by a downward arrows featuring a horizontal bar, as shown in Fig. 10.7.

FIGURE 10.7 Notation for dependency and precedence relationships

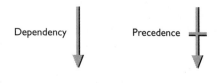

Dependency   Precedence

EXAMPLE 10.12 Consider the algorithm segment below:

```
i <- 1
loop
        exitif (i > n)
S1      read(a[i])
S2      a[i] <- a[i] * 7
S3      c <- a[i] / 3
S4      print(c)
        i <- i + 1
endloop
```

At first glance, this would appear to be readily parallelizable, that is, each pass through the loop deals with a different index into array a and, thus, we might be able to use as many processors as we have, one processor per index. However, each pass through the loop accesses (writes to and reads from) the atomic variable c. Thus, S3 from the second pass cannot execute until S4 from the first pass is done, or else the wrong value of c will be printed out.

As it stands (see Fig. 10.8), we can utilize no more than two processors; those two can be fully utilized. How much time will execution take for an array of N elements? The first pass is done after four time chunks, the second pass after six, the third pass after eight, and so on. Thus, the parallel version requires $(2N + 2)$ time chunks and can utilize no more than two processors.

Observe that a data structure optimization can make everything run faster. If we declared c to be an array of the same size as a rather than as an atomic variable, then the precedence would no longer exist. Each pass through the loop could calculate then print c[i] instead of c. Making this change would allow us to process an array of size N in only four time chunks given N processors.

EXAMPLE 10.13 Consider the following algorithm segment. This one accesses eight different arrays of size N.

```
    i <- 1
    loop
       exitif (i > n)
S1    a[i] <- a[i] * b[i]
S2    read(b[i])
S3    c[i] <- a[i] / 3
S4    d[i] <- b[i] * a[i+1]
S5    e[i] <- b[i] * c[i]
S6    f[i] <- e[i] * 7
S7    g[i] <- e[i] / 9
S8    h[i] <- c[i] mod 5
      i <- i + 1
    endloop
```

In light of the various dependencies and precedences, what degree of parallelization is possible? How many processors can be utilized? What time performance results? The

FIGURE 10.8 Precedence
graph for Example 10.12

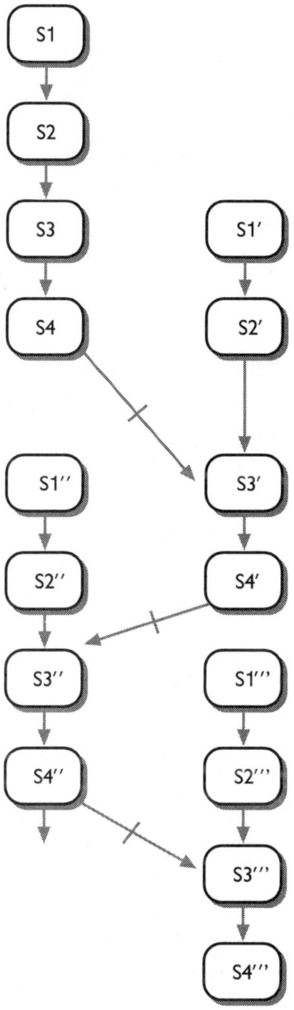

FIGURE 10.9 Precedence graph for
Example 10.13

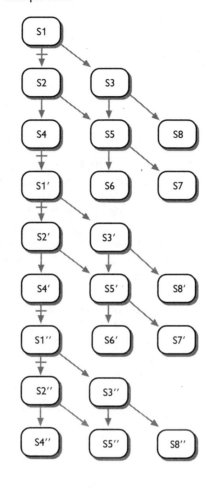

graph shown in Fig. 10.9 indicates that we have precedences such that each S1 blocks
the S2 of the same iteration (why?) and each S4 blocks the S1 of the subsequent iteration (why?). All other relationships are dependencies.

Given this graph, we observe that the first iteration completes in four time
chunks, the second iteration in seven, the third in 10, and so on. This repeating patterns translates in completion for an array of size N in $(3N+1)$ time chunks utilizing
a maximum of three processors.

FOOD FOR THOUGHT

Distributed Processing in a Free Society

In the recent past, there were considerable expectations that parallel processing would become a dominant force in computing via desktop computers that would feature arrays of parallel processors. In this scenario, the array of parallel processors would collectively execute algorithms. More recently, that expectation has changed. Except for certain specialized applications, the cost of creating algorithms for parallel processing architectures is too high for the benefits obtained. Instead, we can expect to see parallel processing impact us in two other ways, both of which are already well under way.

First, we will continue to see the deployment of multiple specialized processors in a computer so that each one has its own special task. There is still a single cpu, but it is supported by other processors that handle specific kinds of work so that the cpu is liberated from handling those tasks. For example, PCs frequently feature video boards that have their own processor so the cpu doesn't have to spend cycles managing the video display. Similarly, there is often another processor to manage data transfer between the hard disk and the computer's RAM. This trend of specialized device processors will continue.

Second, and more significantly, computation will occur concurrently via *distributed systems*. As mentioned earlier, distributed systems spread the work among various sites in such a way that there is no single centralized algorithm that coordinates and controls the others. Instead, multiple distributed processing sites cooperate to make the system work according to protocols that establish how each distributed process may affect the rest of the system.

Both of these approaches, increased specialization and increased deployment of distributed systems, mirror what we see in society at large. The former trend is evident in the increasing amount of education and training required for productive employment, and the need for periodic re-education as workers change careers with increasing frequency.

The latter trend can be seen more broadly in the evolution of the predominant national political structures. During much of the twentieth century, we saw the dominance of "super governments" devoted to centralized control of many aspects of society. Examples range from the Fascist governments of the 1930s and 1940s (Hitler's Germany, Mussolini's Italy, and Tojo's Japan) to the Russia-dominated Soviet bloc, to the humane Social-Democratic governments of northern Europe.

In recent years, the trend has been in a direction away from centralized government management of society. The widespread view is that such governments not only interfere with individual liberty, but are also notoriously inefficient and thus imply huge overhead costs to the societies which they govern. The recent trend has been to reduce government controls in order to allow efficient market forces to have the freedom to operate without government hindrance.

These market forces are, for all practical purposes, a distributed system. There is no single centralized algorithm at work to set prices or establish policies. Instead, a multitude of companies operate under the forces of free enterprise, and whatever happens happens: Successful companies prosper and create jobs, while inefficient companies fail and go away. Unlike centralized government control, it is dynamic self-correcting process.

As we saw in our discussion of *concurrent systems* (of which *distributed systems* are one example), there are always a few key issues to be tackled. Among these issues is *fairness*. Fairness implies the application of some policy of values. Is it fair to let high-priority users always get system resources first? Do we want a system that might keep a low-priority user waiting and effectively deny that user service? How do we define what fairness means? And, once we define it, how do we implement that definition of fairness in an algorithm?

In fact, we always face two fairness-related questions:

1. "What do we mean by fairness?"—a policy question.
2. "How do we guarantee that fairness happens?"—an algorithmic question.

These questions are implicit in *any* multiuser concurrent system.

One of many ways to think about the free enterprise system is as one example of a *multiuser concurrent system*. If we think of it in these terms, the two questions regarding fairness (policy and algorithm) are among the key issues that our society is forced to confront.

Many would say that free enterprise provides society with dynamic forces of creativity and growth, while government protects the citizenry from the excesses of an amoral market system. But even with this definition of roles, it is unclear exactly what the interface between them should be. What are the standards of fairness and responsibility that our society wants its dynamic business forces to honor? And how shall those policies be implemented? And who should be in charge of each?

As you listen to political debate, and as you participate in it, remember what the computing perspective tell us: There are two questions here, not one. There is a policy question ("What do we mean by *fair and responsible?*") and an *algorithmic* question ("How shall we *articulate and implement* our fairness policy?"). Who do you think is best responsible for fairness policy? And who should be held accountable for its implementation?

SUMMARY

Concurrency refers to one or more processors giving attention to multiple tasks at the same time or within the same chunk of time.

- There are four kinds of concurrent systems: *multiprogramming, multiprocessing, multitasking,* and *distributed* systems.
- Three key issues that must be addressed in making concurrent systems work are *protection, fairness,* and *deadlock.*

Parallelism refers to multiple processors working concurrently on the same task.

- *Product complexity* refers to an inherent limitation of parallel performance: Parallelism can reduce time, but it cannot reduce work. Product complexity is calculated as (*time* * *number of processors*) and is equal to *work*. For a given number of parallel processors, product complexity allows us to estimate the *ceiling of improvement* that parallel processing can provide. Actual improvement is generally less than this ceiling due to various overhead costs implied in managing parallelism.
- Due to the limitation implied by product complexity, parallelism does not allow us to make unreasonable algorithms perform reasonably, nor can it make intractable problems tractable. (Tractable vs. intractable problems are discussed in Chapter 11.)
- *Dependency* relationships limit the degree to which an algorithm may be parallelized based on the need of a given algorithmic statement to have data values that are produced by a previous algorithmic statement. For example, statement A must complete before statement B so that it can produce the data that statement B requires.
- *Precedence* relationships also limit the degree to which an algorithm may be parallelized based on the need for a given algorithmic statement to complete prior to the execution of a subsequent statement that may corrupt its data. For example, statement A must complete before statement B corrupts the data that statement A requires.

EXERCISES

For problems 10.1 through 10.6, draw the specified type of graph for the algorithms provided. The S numbers to the left of the individual statements are for statement identification purposes only. For a second occurrence of a given statement, use X′, where X is a statement number; for a third occurrence, use X″, and so on.

Note: Multiple read(some_var) operations that act on the same variable must be sequentialized. Thus, two read(b[3]) statements cannot execute in the same time chunk. Two statements that act on different variables, such as read(b[3]) and read(b[4]), may execute concurrently.

10.1 Consider the algorithm segment shown below. Draw a dependency graph that maps this algorithm to the utilziation of two processors. Indicate the percentage of time required as compared to single processor execution.

```
S1   read(a)
S2   read(b)
S3   read(c)
S4   d <- a + b
S5   d <- d + c
S6   average <- d/3
```

10.2 For the algorithm segment given in problem 10.1, draw a dependency graph that shows the greatest number of processors that can be utilized.

Indicate the percentage of time required as compared to single processor execution.

10.3 Consider the algorithm segment shown below. Draw a dependency graph, not a precedence graph. That is, you are to show only dependency relationships, not precedence relationships.

```
S1  read(a)
S2  read(b)
S3  read(c)
S4  c <- b + c
S5  a <- a + c
S6  c <- b + 4
```

10.4 For the algorithm segment given in problem 10.3, draw a precedence graph that shows both dependency and precedence relationships. Indicate the percentage of time required as compared to single processor execution.

10.5 Consider the algorithm segment. Draw a precedence graph that shows the greatest number of processors that may be utilized. Indicate the percentage of time required as compared to single processor execution.

```
    i <- 1
    loop
S1    a[i] <- 2 * i
S2    b[i] <- i + i
S3    c[i] <- a[i] * b[i]
S4    d[i] <- e[i] + (a[i] / 2) + (2 * b[i])
S5    e[i] <- c[i] * c[i]
      i <- i + 1
      exitif (i >= 2)
    endloop
```

10.6 Consider the algorithm segment. Draw a precedence graph that shows the greatest number of processors that may be utilized. Indicate the percentage of time required as compared to single processor execution.

```
    I <- 1
    loop
        exitif (i > 2)
S1    read(b[i])
S2    a[i] <- i * i + 3
S3    d[i] <- a[i] * b[i]
S4    c[i] <- a[i] / 2 + i - a[i+1]
S5    e[i] <- c[i] / d[i]
S6    read(c[i])
      i <- i + 1
    endloop
```

For problems 10.7 through 10.10, you are given an array of numbers of size m (assume m is very large). Your task is to find the average of the values in the array. Assume each mathematical operation takes one time chunk of processor time. Do not give Big Oh as your answer; report the actual number of time chunks *without* disregarding constant factors. Justify your answers.

10.7 How much time is required if one processor is used?

10.8   How much time is required if two processors are used ?
10.9   How much time is required if four processors are used ?
10.10 How much time is required if an unlimited number of processors are available? What is the maximum number of processors that can be utilized?

For problems 10.11 through 10.14, you are given a two dimensional array of numbers of size R rows by C columns. You may assume that $R <= C$. Your task is to find the average of all the values in the array. Assume each mathematical operation takes one time chunk of processor time. Do not give Big Oh as your answer; report the actual number of time chunks *without* disregarding constant factors. Justify your answers.

10.11 How much time is required if one processor is used?
10.12 How much time is required if two processors are used?
10.13 How much time is required if four processors are used?
10.14 How much time is required if an unlimited number of processors are available? What is the maximum number of processors that can be utilized?

For problems 10.15 through 10.18, you are given a large binary search tree containing n numbers. You may assume that the insertion and deletion routines employ some mechansim for keeping the tree full and balanaced. Your task is to find the average of all the values in the tree. Assume each mathematical operation takes one time chunk of processor time. Do not give Big Oh as your answer; report the actual number of time chunks *without* disregarding constant factors. Justify your answers.

10.15 How much time is required if one processor is used?
10.16 How much time is required if two processors are used?
10.17 How much time is required if four processors are used?
10.18 How much time is required if an unlimited number of processors are available? What is the maximum number of processors that can be utilized?

For problems 10.19 through 10.22, you are given a large linked list containing n unsorted numbers. Your task is to find the largest, second largest, smallest abd second smallest values in the list, as well as the average of all the values in the list. Assume each mathematical operation takes one time chunk of processor time. Do not give Big Oh as your answer; report the actual number of time chunks *without* disregarding constant factors. Justify your answers.

10.19 How much time is required if one processor is used?
10.20 How much time is required if two processors are used?
10.21 How much time is required if four processors are used?
10.22 How much time is required if an unlimited number of processors are available? What is the maximum number of processors that can be utilized?

CHAPTER 11

The Hierarchy of Problem Complexity

In Chapter 9, we considered various performance categories of algorithms, identified each as being reasonable or unreasonable, and considered the implications of performance in each category. Notice that all of this concerned particular algorithms, that is, particular solutions to problems.

We'd like to have this kind of information about *problems*, not just algorithms. If we only have information about algorithms, then we can't say very much about what is "do-able" and what isn't. Why? In a given instance, perhaps we're just looking at a poor algorithm and, with a better one, the "hard" problem would become easily solvable. After all, someone might invent a better algorithm tomorrow.

Fortunately, there is much we that do know about the limitations involved in solving various kinds of problems. In this chapter, we discuss the ways to characterize many kinds of problems in a way that's similar to the way in which we classify particular algorithms.

11.1 Problem Complexity

In Chapter 9, we considered three measures of algorithm performance: *best case, average case, and worst case.* Of these, we focus on worst case and average cases since they tell us the performance constraints that we'll have to tolerate. We pay rather little attention to best case, as we rarely worry about things "going right."

For problems, it would be useful to have measures analogous to best case and worst case. That is, we'd like to know the performance of the best kind of solution we can hope for (even if we don't know what that solution might be), and we'd also like to know the performance of the worst kind of solution we might have to tolerate. And, as it turns out, we do have such measures, measures that refer to the *complexity of problems.*

To understand the nature of problem complexity, it is necessary to understand the meaning of *upper bound* and *lower bound.* Each problem has both an upper and a lower bound.

Definition: A problem's **upper bound** refers to the best that we know how to do. It is determined by the best algorithmic solution that we have found for a given problem.

For example, we have seen examples of sorting algorithms that are $O(N^2)$ and $O(N\log N)$. While we might implement a sort that is $O(N^2)$ if N is small, we know that we *can* achieve $O(N\log N)$ if we only bother to do so. Thus, we say that sorting "admits a solution" that is $O(N\log N)$. We know of no solution better than $O(N\log N)$. For sorting problems, then, $O(N\log N)$ is the *upper bound:* We know that we don't have to settle for anything worse than $O(N\log N)$ if we don't want to.

Definition: A problem's **lower bound** refers to the best algorithmic solution that is theoretically possible. Lower bounds are determined by theoreticians who develop logical proofs about various kinds of problems and the amount of work necessary to solve them.

For example, a competent theoretician can prove that sorting an unsorted list *cannot* be done in less than $O(N\log N)$ work unless we make assumptions about the particular input data. This tells us that we cannot do any better than $O(N\log N)$. Thus $O(N\log N)$ is the *lower bound* for sorting problems.

Upper bounds tell us *the best we've been able to do so far.* Lower bounds tell us *the best we can hope to do.*

In the case of sorting, both the upper and lower bounds are the same: $O(N\log N)$. There is no gap between the two bounds, and we thus know that we shouldn't even bother to try to create sorting algorithms that are better than $O(N\log N)$.

Does this mean that there is no room for algorithmic improvement? No, it most certainly does not. Someone might well invent a better algorithm, but such algorithms will still be no better than $O(N\log N)$. Any improved algorithms can be better only in terms of improving (i.e., reducing) the costs that are hidden by Big Oh or in making the algorithm's performance more consistent. In other words, someone might invent a better $O(N\log N)$ algorithm for sorting, but no one will invent an algorithm that is better than $O(N\log N)$. As a result, we can say that the sorting problem "is an $O(N\log N)$ problem" or that it "has $O(N\log N)$ complexity."

Warning: Be sure that you understand the difference between the terms "upper bound" and "lower bound" and "worst case" and "best case":

- Best and worst case refer to the work implied by a given algorithm. They inform us about how much work that one algorithm will have to do.

- For a given algorithm, any differences between best and worst cases are due to *properties of the particular values and/or the ordering of the input data* that are fed into the algorithm. If there is no gap between best and worst cases, then the algorithm is not vulnerable to being affected by particular combinations or orderings of data values and thus will perform more or less the same each time it is used, depending on the number *N* of input values that it must process.

- Upper and lower bounds inform us about the amount of work required of a solution to a given problem.

- For a given kind of problem, any differences between *upper bound* and *lower bound* are due to *discrepancies between the best algorithm that we've been able to come up with so far and the best algorithm that we believe to be possible*. If there is a gap, then someone might invent a new algorithm that lowers the upper bound closer to the lower bound, or someone might invent a better proof that raises the lower bound closer to the upper bound. If there is no gap, then we *know* what the complexity of the problem is.

11.2 Open vs. Closed Problems

For a given problem, if the upper and lower bounds are the same, then we refer to that problem as a **closed problem**. For a closed problem, new algorithms may improve the factors hidden by Big Oh, but new algorithms will be not able to change Big Oh for that kind of problem.

If the upper and lower bounds are not the same, then we say that the problem is an **open problem**. For an open problem, we don't know what the future might bring. Perhaps a new, more efficient algorithm will lower the upper bound. Or, perhaps a new, more insightful proof will demonstrate that the lower bound is actually higher than we now think it is. Or, perhaps the upper and lower bounds will remain apart, and the truth about the problem will continue to be a mystery.

11.3 Tractable vs. Intractable Problems

Just as we divided algorithms into the categories of *reasonable* (or *polynomial*) and *unreasonable* (or *exponential*), we can do the same for problems. In fact, we do so using the same complexity thresholds:

Definition: Tractable problems are those that have both upper and lower bounds that feature N only as a *polynomial* factor in Big Oh, (i.e., $O(logN)$, $O(N)$, $O(NlogN)$, $O(N^K)$). Tractable problems are considered solvable via computation.

Definition: Intractable problems are those that have both upper and lower bounds that feature N as an *exponential* factor in Big Oh, (i.e., $O(2^N)$, $O(N!)$, $O(N^N)$). They are considered (for practical purposes) to be not solvable via computation.

Warning: Keep your terminology straight. We use the terms "reasonable" and "unreasonable" to label *specific algorithms*, not kinds of problems. We use the terms "tractable" and "intractable" to label *kinds of problems, not* particular algorithms. Notice how the terms are used in the following statements:

- Polynomial algorithms are reasonable; polynomial problems are tractable.
- Exponential algorithms are unreasonable; exponential problems are intractable.
- We use reasonable algorithms to solve tractable problems.
- We don't use unreasonable algorithms (except for very small *n*).
- We don't even bother to try to develop reasonable algorithms for intractable problems. (It's impossible!)
- We do try to find reasonable algorithms that provide approximate solutions to intractable problems.

11.4 Problems that Cross the Line

We have said that problems that have N as only a polynomial factor in *both* their upper and lower bounds are tractable, and that problems that have N as an exponential factor in *both* their upper and lower bounds are intractable. But what about problems that don't quite fit this dichotomy? What about a problem that has an *exponential upper bound* and a *polynomial lower bound*? Such a problem would be one for which:

- We have found only exponential solutions (i.e., from the standpoint of our algorithms, *it appears to be intractable*).
- We cannot prove the necessity of an exponential solution (i.e., from the standpoint of our proofs, we *cannot say that it is intractable*).

As you might guess, such problems are of great interest to algorithm and theory specialists within computer science. Not only is there a gap between the upper bound and the lower bound, those two bounds are in different categories. If we look only at the upper bound, we would think such problems intractable, but if we look only at the lower bound, we would think them tractable. Such problems cross the boundaries of our classification system in a way that confounds the experts.

For some such problems, it may be simply a matter of more hard work and/or creative insights by algorithm and theory specialists. Perhaps someone will develop a reasonable algorithm and thus show that the given problem is indeed tractable. Or, perhaps someone will develop a stronger proof, one that demonstrates that the given problem cannot be solved in reasonable time and thus show that it is intractable.

11.5 NP-Complete Problems

Among the problems that straddle the line between tractable and intractable, we find a very interesting phenomena: a group of many, many problems which share a set of peculiar traits. These problems are known as *NP-complete*. The traits they share are:

1. The upper bound suggests that the problem is intractable.
2. The lower bound suggest that the problem is tractable.

In addition to the fact that NP-complete problems straddle the line, they also share two additional traits:

3. The lower bounds suggest that most such problems can be done in linear time, that is, $O(N)$.
4. They are *all* reducible to one another.

This last attribute of NP-complete problems is a very powerful one. It means that if we had the ability to solve any *one* such problem in reasonable time, we would be able to solve all of them in reasonable time.

Thus, one way to become very famous very fast would be to go home this afternoon and develop a reasonable algorithm to solve any NP-complete problem. This would, in effect, lower the upper bound of all such problems down into the category of reasonable algorithms, indicating that all such problems are tractable. It would open the door to practical computational solutions to problems that currently defy such solutions.

Another route to fame would be to jot down a rigorous proof that shows that a single NP-complete problem is intractable. This would raise the lower bound up into the category of unreasonable algorithms, this demonstrating that all such problems are intractable.

Either development would resolve the question of whether such problems are tractable or intractable. As it is, we can only *suspect* that such problems are intractable.

There are hundreds of NP-complete problems. Examples include the following problems:

1. *Traveling salesman.* Given a weighted graph (e.g., cities with distances between them) and some distance k (e.g., the maximum distance you want to travel), is there some tour that visits all the points (e.g., cities) and returns home such that distance <= k?
2. *Three-coloring.* Given a graph, can it be colored with at most three colors such that each vertex gets one of three colors and the adjacent areas get a different color?
3. *Bin packing.* Given n items, each with a profit and a weight, and given some finite weight capacity, and given a desired profit of k, can you select items so that they fit and provide profit of at least k?
4. *Pert planning.* Given a list of actions with constraints as to which actions can/must precede others, can you minimize the total time required, as for example, building the space shuttle?
5. *Clique.* Given a graph that is not complete and a number k, is there a clique (a set of vertices each one of which is adjacent to the other) of size k?

NP-complete problems are important problems in computer science. They also present significant challenges to those in other fields who want to optimize planning or scheduling.

Certificates, Oracles, and Determinism

Oracles and *certificates* are useful concepts when it comes to understanding both NP-complete problems, as well as understanding a class of problems that are worse than intractable.

To understand the meaning of a certificate and an oracle, imagine that we are faced with some problem that requires us to make a series of decisions. Imagine further that to solve the problem we must consider a large number of possible actions. Thus, to know whether a given decision is correct, we must follow it through, perhaps making a series of additional decisions, before we can know whether we've made the right original decision or whether we've "gone down a dead end street."

For example, consider a scheduling problem that is *NP-complete*. Imagine that we have n teachers and a specification of the hours during which m classes can be scheduled; each teacher is available to teach a certain number of hours. We want to know whether it is possible to schedule the classes and the teachers so the following are true:

a. All the classes are scheduled.
b. No two teachers teach the same class at the same time.
c. No teacher is scheduled to teach two classes at once.

Some scheduling problems are tractable, but this one is NP-complete. It requires that we consider *all* the various scheduling possibilities before we can conclude "no working schedule can be found." If we find a working schedule, then we have shown that such a schedule can be found. We might be lucky and find a working schedule upon our first try, but one might just as well be found only when we consider the very last of all the various possibilities.

To solve the problem and answer the question, we must be prepared to try out all the various possibilities. This requires that we try out *partial* schedules, for example, schedule teacher A for a certain class at a certain time and teacher B for a certain class at a certain time. If teachers A and B are scheduled to teach the same class at the same time, then we know that this possibility won't work, that this particular schedule is a "dead end," and thus we don't have to take it further. However, if either the class or the time is different, then this partial schedule *might* work and we thus must continue to evaluate its viability by, for example, adding a particular course for teacher C at a particular time, seeing if that works or not, and so on.

We add more teachers and other classes, step-by-step, until we find that either "yes it will work" or "no it won't." Whenever we add a new element to the schedule, we must evaluate whether "it works so far" or not. If so, we continue with it. If not, then we "back out" of that solution path and try another possibility instead. Thus, for a given partial schedule, we might go all the way down the "tree of possibilities," finding an acceptable choice at each step, only to learn that the very last remaining possibility of class, teacher and time slot won't work. This process is very costly. The best of known solutions (i.e., the upper bound) suggest that the problem is intractable.

11.6.1   Certificates

Observe, however, that for a given input to the problem (teachers, classes, time slots), we don't need to find *all* the schedules that might work, we need find only one to demonstrate that a schedule *can* be found, thus answering the question. If we can come up with a single schedule that does work, then we can quite easily convince someone that a schedule can be found: We simply show them a schedule that does the job!

Such a piece of evidence is called a *certificate*. A certificate is nothing more or less than conclusive evidence that the answer to the question is yes. A yes answer requires only a simple example of a successful solution. Such an example "certifies" that there is a solution. There might be several possible certificates for a given input, but we require only one of them to certify the problem as solvable.

There is no such thing as a certificate that answers no. The only way to demonstrate a no answer is to show that *all* of the possibilities fail.

11.6.2   Oracles

Observe that a certificate is the result of a series of "good" decisions. Each certificate can be thought of as being a list of good decisions; in our example, each decision would be of the form, "schedule teacher X to teach course Y in time slot Z."

Each certificate for an NP-complete problem can be made to be reasonably short, with its size bounded by a polynomial n. Most often, certificates to NP-complete problems are *linear* (i.e., not just reasonable, but $O(N)$, which is *very* fast).

Thus, if we had some means to make the "right decision" at each decision point, then we could produce certificates in reasonable, usually linear, time. The problem is that we cannot do this, and often must follow a "bad decision path" for some considerable distance before we find out that it leads to a dead end. But, if we had some magical wisdom that allowed us to see down the path of a given decision and tell whether it was a good or bad path, then we could develop certificates quite quickly. Thus, if we had some process that had magical powers of foresight, these messy NP-complete problems would suddenly become tractable.

We call such a mythical process an *oracle*. As a practical matter, an oracle would be some omniscient process that can give us, in advance, the wisdom of hindsight with respect to a given decision path. In our example, we might ask, "Should we schedule teacher X for class Y in time slot Z?" An oracle would answer "yes" or "no" to each such question, providing us with the best possible answer.

To put it another way, when faced with a yes or no question and no basis for rational decision, we might flip a coin. Having an oracle would be like having a magic coin that, when flipped, always produced the correct answer. If both possibilities lead to complete solutions, or if neither of them did, then the magic coin would behave realistically (i.e., like a normal, random coin flip).

Thus, by examining the candidate solution provided by an oracle or magic coin, we can readily determine the answer to the problem. If the candidate solution is a successful solution, the answer is "yes, for the given input, there is a solution." If the candidate solution is not legal, then we know that the best possible solution does not satisfy the problem and, thus, that the answer is "no, for the given input, there is no solution."

Neither oracles nor magic coins exist. But we can imagine the effect of them if they did: They could tell us, in advance, whether a decision was good or bad, thus making NP-complete problems tractable.

11.6.3 Determinism vs. Nondeterminism

Algorithms that produce the correct answer via "proper guesses" are known as *nondeterministic* algorithms. They are called nondeterministic because there is no way to specify the basis upon which to determine the right decision. From a computational point of view, nondeterministic algorithms work "by magic."

In contrast, algorithms that produce answers by making information-based decisions at each step are known as *deterministic* algorithms. Any algorithm that can be executed by a computer or (reliably) by people is a deterministic algorithm.

For NP-complete problems, the best deterministic algorithms are exponential. If we had magical abilities to execute nondeterministic algorithms (e.g., oracles or magic coins), then they would be polynomial, often linear. This is where the category of NP-complete problems gets part of its name: "NP" stands for *"nondeterministic polynomial,"* that is, given magical nondeterminism, they can be solved in polynomial time. "Complete" is used to signify that all such problems are reducible to the others, that is, solve one of them and you solve the complete set of them.

11.7 NP-Complete vs. Intractable Problems

Both *NP-complete* problems and intractable problems feature upper bounds that are exponential. In other words, we are not able to solve either in reasonable time. Of such problems, relatively few have been proven to be intractable (i.e., have exponential lower bounds). There are more NP-complete problems than there are provably intractable ones.

One example of provably intractable problems is *generalized* chess or checkers (e.g., does Black have a guaranteed winning strategy?). Generalized means that we an algorithmic solution for each n where games are played on an n by n board; "normal" chess and checkers are not intractable, as n is always 8.

11.8 Undecidability

So far, we have three categories of problems:

- Tractable problems, those that can be solved in polynomial time.
- Problems, including NP-complete problems, for which we have only exponential solutions but for which we can establish only a polynomial lower bound. Our best guess is that these are intractable, but we cannot prove it.

■ Intractable problems, those that provably require exponential solutions.

Notice that all three share a common attribute: We *can* develop algorithmic solutions to them. The practical difference between them is that for the latter two categories, our solutions are of no practical value: We can solve these problems but it takes too much time for our solutions to do us any good.

In addition to these categories, we have categories of problems for which no algorithmic solution can be found. In other words, the solutions are not computable regardless of the cost.

As an example, consider again the tiling problem we discussed earlier. It was described as a *bounded* tiling problem: We specified that an areas of M by M must be tiled with N tiles, where $N = M^2$. Let us change the problem to ask: "For T kinds of tiles, and for a given set of restrictions on how these tiles can abut one another (e.g., make their patterns line up), can we arrive at an arrangement that we can use to tile *any* size area?" Thus, instead of asking about a fixed or bounded area as determined by the input, we are now asking about *all* possible areas. In other words, we have removed the bounds on the area. The problem now says, in effect,

```
if (the types of tiles in T can tile any area) then
    print("yes")
else
    print("no")
endif
```

This problem is *undecidable*. There is no way to program any algorithm that can evaluate the condition that determines whether the if or the else clause should be executed. No answer can be obtained in any finite time. This problem admits no algorithmic solution, period.

For another example of an undecidable problem, consider the "word correspondence" problem. In this problem, we are given two groups of words, say, X and Y. By words we mean only some string of characters in some alphabet; they do not have to be "real" words. For example, X and Y might consist of the following words from a limited alphabet that contains only two characters, a and b:

Group	1	2	3	4	5
X	abb	a	bab	baba	aba
Y	bbab	aa	ab	aa	a

Given these word groups, we want to know if we can concatenate the corresponding words from both X and Y to produce the same new word from each word group. Given the word groups above, we can accomplish this task, as can be seen by concatenating words 2, 1, 1, 4, 1, and 5. We produce the new word aabbabbbabaabbaba from both X and Y. However, if we remove the first letter from the first word of each group, as shown below, the goal cannot be accomplished.

Group	1	2	3	4	5
X	bb	a	bab	baba	aba
Y	bab	aa	ab	aa	a

The word correspondence problem is undecidable. There is no algorithm that can distinguish between our two examples of X and Y. The undecidability comes from the fact that there is no bound on the number of words that we might string together.

If we say that we must confine ourselves to choosing a string of 6 or 8 or 73 words to concatenate, then the problem can be decided (at a cost of what Big Oh?). Similarly, if we say that we can choose any number of words but do not have to choose the same words or the same number of words from each word group, then the problem becomes tractable (e.g., given our second example of X and Υ, we can choose 3, 2, 2 from X and 1, 2 from Υ and get babaa in either case).

A third example of an undecidable problem is the "halting problem." It states: Given some legal algorithm written in some programming language, and given some input to the algorithm, will the algorithm ever reach a stopping place? For example, if the algorithm is

```
read(x)
loop
    exitif (x = 1)
    x <- x - 2
endloop
```

and if the input can consist of any positive integer, we can see that the algorithm will halt if the input is odd and that it will never halt if the input is even. Thus, checking the input to see whether it is even or odd will tell us whether or not the algorithm will halt.

If the algorithm is:

```
read(x)
loop
    exitif(x=1)
    if (even(x)) then
        x <- x / 2
    else  // odd(x)
        x <- 3x +1
    endif
endloop
```

then it is more difficult to say. For example, given the input 3, X takes on the values 3, 10, 5, 16, 8, 4, 2, 1, respectively, and halts upon the next exitif test.

If we test this algorithm on any positive integer, then one of two things will happen. Either the algorithm will terminate or else it will produce an erratic sequence of values that shows no signs of either converging or diverging. To date, for any legal input, this algorithm has always terminated, given enough time. Yet no one has been able to prove that it will always terminate eventually.

In the general case, the halting problem is undecidable; that is, given any finite amount of time, there is no way to tell whether a given algorithm will terminate upon a given input. For any given input, it is easy to tell if it does terminate, if we observe the termination. The problem lies in trying to determine *when* we can conclude that the algorithm will not terminate. There is always the chance that, given a little more time, it might terminate.

11.8.1 Certificates for Undecidable Problems

Certificates demonstrate the "solvability" of a problem. In the case of NP-complete problems, it takes exponential time to produce a solution, yet the solution itself can be verified in polynomial, usually linear time. Thus, for NP-complete problems, we do not have reasonable solution algorithms but we do have reasonable-size or polynomial-time certificates.

There is an analogous relationship between undecidable problems and certificates. While an undecidable problem cannot be solved by algorithmic means, if we imagine having an oracle, we find that *some* (but not all) undecidable problems have *finite* certificates even though there are no finite-time algorithms. In fact, most undecidable problems admit finite certificates. We call such problems "partially undecidable."

Some undecidable problems do not admit finite certificates even in the face of magical oracles. Thus, not only are we unable to algorithmically solve them in finite time, we cannot even evaluate whether a given candidate solution is correct in finite time. We call these problems "highly undecidable."

FOOD FOR THOUGHT

HAL 9000, Where Are You?

How do we want our computers to behave? The answer is simple: We want them to act like they do in the movies. Unfortunately, anyone who as ever tried to actually use a computer can attest to the distinct lack of intelligence that our computers have. Why is this so?

In truth, it is because we understand ourselves so poorly. This simple fact ties our hands. Quite obviously, the computers in the movies do a remarkable job of communicating with us in our own natural language, and of thinking how we do, only better and faster. This is a widely accepted test of success for artificial intelligence (AI) applications: Can an AI program convince a human that its responses come from another human instead of a machine? To actually create computers that act like the ones in the movies, we must develop the ability to abstract our own communication and processing abilities into algorithms.

At present we cannot quite do this because we do not have an adequate conceptual model of how we communicate or of how we process our experience. For several decades now, researchers have attacked these problems without breakthrough success. Work is ongoing, but significant accomplishments remain very few and far between.

To date, there are two main approaches to AI: the *rule-based* approach and the *neural network* approach.

■ The rule-based approach is the older of the two, and strives to discern what processing rules people might be implicitly using when they perform acts of intelligence.

Once such rules are articulated, they are implemented in algorithms, which then mimic the "intelligent" behavior of people.

- The neural network approach is newer and strives to mirror the processing "hardware" of the human brain. Rather than try to construct explicit algorithmics, it instead tries to copy the "architecture" of the brain by creating networks of many processors. Each processor makes only the very simplest of decisions, filtering input and modifying it slightly, but collectively the mass of processors combine to form a response. The goal is to simulate the brain, wherein millions of biochemical synapses lead to an intelligent response.

To date, neither approach has demonstrated the achievement for which their proponents had hoped. In both cases, successful results tend to be limited to very narrowly defined problem domains, without much ability to transfer to other domains.

At present, the concerns of researchers in artificial intelligence and psychology overlap in the area of *cognitive science*. This relatively new field is attempting to bring the information-processing paradigm to bear on the problem of abstracting intelligence into algorithms.

There is debate about whether the information-processing paradigm is adequate to allow us to achieve what we're after. Is it adequate to say that human communication and human experience processing are reducible to "information processing"? Proponents assert that it is. They argue that any human experience can be seen as an occasion of information processing. Others disagree, arguing that cognitive scientists make the mistake of "confusing their model with reality" (the theme of Chapter 2's Food for Thought). Such critics charge that cognitive science makes the fundmental error of implicitly assuming that the human mind is a "special kind of computer." In their view, this assumption gets things backwards. Rather than seeing the mind as a kind of computer, they argue that the computer mimics only a very limited subset of the capabilities of the human mind. As you can see, these issues involve a complex mix of science and philosophy, and there is no clear road map to success.

While there is no scientific approach to understanding human phenomena that has truly proved itself, there are nevertheless signs of significant progress. For example, in the 1950s and 1960s, many psychological researchers refused to even consider as data the reports that people gave about their experiences. Such researchers were blinded by Mechanical Model ideas about science and thus they "couldn't see" anything that did not lend itself to tangible measurement and quantification. They assumed that all human subjects were to be distrusted, and they sought to learn about the human mind only by experiments that were designed to "fool" or "trick" human subjects. Many researchers then actually argued that subjective experience doesn't even exist. In recent years, human science researches have recognized that the research models they adopted from the natural sciences are not very useful for learning about people. In the last couple decades, we've seen increasing acknowledgment among scientists that descriptive reports of subjective experience can indeed be valid data if obtained and used properly. As a result, we are now seeing more and more research that identifies patterns and trends in subjective human experience. In short, we are beginning to learn about the structure and meaning of human experience in new ways.

At the present time, however, we find ourselves still very limited by our own lack of self-understanding. We don't know enough about the kinds of cognitive and emotional processing that people do to know whether such problems are tractable or even decidable. It is our lack of knowledge about our own human processes, not about computing, that prevents us from making computers act like they do in the movies.

SUMMARY

We have considered four major categories of problems: *highly undecidable, partially undecidable, intractable,* and *tractable*. In addition, *NP-complete* problems straddle the line between tractable and intractable problems. We suspect that they are intractable, but we cannot prove this to be so. If we *suppose* that NP-complete problems are intractable, we then have the hierarchy of problem complexity shown in Fig. 11.1.

We can return to the problem of arranging ceramic tiles to find examples of each of these four kinds of problem complexity.

- The "fixed width" tiling problem is tractable. You are given as inputs a set of kinds of tiles, T, and a number N. The task isto determine if a rectangle of size C (some fixed constant and is not part of the input) by N can be formed from T. This problem can be solved in polynomial time.
- The "bounded" tiling problem is NP-complete and assumed to be intractable. You are given as input a set of tiles, T, a square area of size $N = M * M$ and the task is as described earlier. This problem can be solved in exponential time and admits a polynomial certificate.
- The "unbounded" tiling problem is partially undecidable. You are given T as input and the task is to determine whether *any and all* (i.e., the integer grid) areas can be tiles within the constraints. There is no algorithm that can solve this problem, but it admits a finite-time certificate.
- The "recurring" tiling problem is highly undecidable. You are given T as input and the task is to determine whether T can tile the integer grid such that there is an infinite recurrence of a particular special tile. Not only is there no algorithm that can solve this problem, there is not even a finite-time certificate (i.e., we cannot even evaluate a candidate solution in finite time).

Much of this material is primarily of interest to theorists. The practical implications are summarized in the Fig. 11.1. From a practical point of

FIGURE 11.1

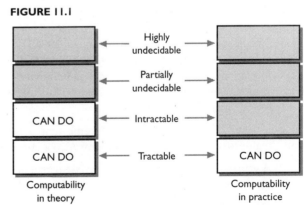

	Highly undecidable
	Partially undecidable
CAN DO	Intractable
CAN DO	Tractable	CAN DO

Computability in theory

Computability in practice

view, undecidable and intractable problems are equally "bad news." Often, people will refer to problems that are at least as bad as intractable (e.g., undecidable problems such as the halting problem) as intractable. Of course, from our point of view, undecidable problems are *worse* than intractable. When used in this way, the word "intractable" is being used to mean that (for all practical purposes) the problem is not solvable, that is, it is "exponential or worse."

EXERCISES

11.1 What is the difference between the complexity of an algorithm and the complexity of a problem?

11.2 Which do you find more interesting: open problems, which imply uncertainty about the truth, or closed problems, which imply clear certain knowledge?

For Exercises 11.3 through 11.8, refer to the table below.

Problem	Lower Bound of Work	Upper Bound of Work
A	$5\log N$	$147 + 16\log N$
B	$(N^2)/2$	$4N^3$
C	$3 * N^5$	$1{,}372 * N^5$
D	$12 * N\log N$	$(2^N)/512$
E	$17 * 2^N$	$17 * N^2$
F	$4 * 3^N$	$2 * 4^N$
G	$(3N^N) + 7N$	$(23N^N) - \log N$

11.3 Which problems appear to be open problems and which appear to be closed problems?

11.4 Which problems appear to be tractable?

11.5 Which problems appear to be intractable?

11.6 Which problems appear to be neither tractable nor intractable?

11.7 Do any of the table entries appear to be in error? If so, which one(s) and why?

11.8 Which problems appear to have the largest gap between their upper and lower bounds?

For questions 11.9 through 11.13, assume that Algorithms A and B are different solution algorithms for the same problem. Also assume that N is the size of input.

11.9 Algorithm A requires $(2N - \log N)$ instructions. Algorithm B requires 252 instructions of work regardless of N. What is the smallest value of N for which Algorithm B offers performance better than that of Algorithm A?

11.10 Algorithm A requires $(256N^2)$ work. Algorithm B requires (3^N) work. What is the smallest value of N for which Algorithm A offers better performance than does Algorithm B?

11.11 Algorithm A requires $(37N - 12\log N)$ work. Algorithm B requires (N^2) work. What is the smallest value of N for which Algorithm A offers better performance than does Algorithm B?

11.12 Algorithm A requires $(4\log N)$ work. Algorithm B requires $(N/2)$ work. What is the smallest value of N for which Algorithm A offers better performance than does Algorithm B?

11.13 Algorithm A requires $(3N^4)$ work. Algorithm B requires (N^5) work. What is the smallest value of N for which Algorithm A offers better performance than does Algorithm B?

11.14 Imagine an $O(\log N)$ algorithm that can do a given job in one hour on today's computer. If a computer 100 times faster were installed tomorrow, how many jobs could that computer do in the same hour using the same algorithm?

11.15 Imagine an $O(N)$ algorithm that can do a given job in one hour on today's computer. If a computer 100 times faster were installed tomorrow, how many jobs could that computer do in the same hour using the same algorithm?

11.16 Imagine an $O(N^2)$ algorithm that can do a given job in one hour on today's computer. If a computer 100 times faster were installed tomorrow, how many jobs could that computer do in the same hour using the same algorithm?

11.17 Imagine an $O(2^N)$ algorithm that can do a given job in one hour on today's computer. If a computer 100 times faster were installed tomorrow, how many jobs could that computer do in the same hour using the same algorithm?

11.18 Repeat Exercise 11.14, but this time imagine the new computer is 1000 times faster.

11.19 Repeat Exercise 11.15, but this time imagine the new computer is 1000 times faster.

11.20 Repeat Exercise 11.16, but this time imagine the new computer is 1000 times faster.

11.21 Repeat Exercise 11.17, but this time imagine the new computer is 1000 times faster.

11.22 What is the difference between an oracle and a certificate?

11.23 List three everyday situations in which you could serve as a perfectly adequate oracle but that you think would involve an intractable computing problem.

11.24 List three everyday situations in which computers serve you better than you could possible serve yourself.

CHAPTER 12

Epilogue: A History of Computing and Algorithms

In the Supplemental Chapter which follows this one, we consider a sketch of history. In that sketch, technology plays a key role in the evolution of how people understand the world. We see a repeating pattern. A paradigm dominates an era, then wanes shortly after a new technology of human communication is introduced into society. The introduction of the new communications technology is accompanied by breakthrough developments in knowledge and science. While initially controversial, such developments are soon widely accepted and, after a time, are recognized as having historical significance.

The new technologies themselves have key attributes that prove to be the very basis for the new paradigm that follows:

- The abstract quality of the alphabet prefigures the dominance of a world view rooted in absolute abstractions of Good and Evil.
- The mechanical quality of the printing press prefigures the dominance of a world view that enabled the scientific and industrial revolutions.
- Electronic media prefigures the emerging paradigm that sees the world as a complex network of interrelated processes fueling great strides in knowledge and science.

In this epilogue we summarize the history of computing and show how it features the same progression (through abstraction, mechanism, and interconnectivity) that we have seen in the longer story of Western history.

12.1 The Literal Paradigm

In our outline of Western history, the first paradigm is that of preliterate tribal societies who had no system for writing down their thoughts and observations. Their most advanced medium was the carving or painting of literal physical images.

In the history of computing, the analogous period is the 1930s to the mid-1940s. In the 1930s we had binary logic and the idea of algorithms. During this period, the theoretical foundations of computer science were established by key theoreticians such as Alan Turing, Kurt Godel, Alonzo Church, Andrei Markov, Emil Post, and Stephen Kleene. However, the modern digital computer did not yet exist, and we thus had no practical way to have a machine execute our algorithms for us.

The first modern digital computers were built in the 1940s. At first, we had no practical way to program them. The logic of an algorithm was literally "hardwired" by technicians who established physical connections by plugging in wires (much like the early telephone operators would route phone calls by plugging wires into a board of sockets). Thus, the logic of an algorithm was *physically* established.

12.2 The Advent of Abstraction

The introduction of the alphabet is a watershed event that signaled the beginnings of Western thought. The alphabet provided a way for people to share thoughts and observations via an abstract means of representing them. The ancient Greek culture that gave us the alphabet in its pure form also gave us those "early abstracters" who were the founders of virtually all our modern disciplines.

In computing, the analogous development occurred in the early 1950s with the use of symbolic names. For the first time, those who programmed a computer could refer to a variable by name rather than by the binary number that represented its exact location in memory. Similarly, the various operations that a computer could perform were given meaningful names (such as "Load", "Add," and "Store"). This provided the basis for programming a computer, not by physically establishing wired connections, but instead by referring to both data and operations *by name*. The result was the first computer programs in the modern sense of the term.

12.3 The Paradigm of Absolute Abstractions

The alphabet was followed by a paradigm that was based on powerful abstractions of Good and Evil. Worldly events in Europe were dominated by the Church. The most advanced media technology were handwritten documents that were written in Latin and that were thus not understandable to most people.

The use of symbolic names provided the basis for the comparable era of computing, the 1950s. Throughout this period, computer programs were written in an "assembly language" in which programmers use symbolic names. Assembly language programs are much harder for people to understand than is pseudocode. Each model of computer had its own assembly language and therefore the audience for a computer program was the particular model of computer on which it was to be run. During this era, computers were rare and computer memory was in short supply. As a result, programmers were forced to resort to all manner of clever tricks when writing their programs to make them run fast without using much memory. This made programs difficult, sometimes impossible, for other programmers to understand. During this era, programmers were almost like "technical priests" who wrote arcane documents indecipherable by others.

12.4 The Advent of Mechanism

The invention of the printing press signaled the beginning of the end for the age of absolute abstraction. Documents no longer had to be laboriously reproduced by hand. As printed documents became more accessible, they came to be written in the local language, not only in Latin. Shortly after the invention of the printing press, Copernicus announced the new view of the world that, like the printing press, was based in the model of a machine.

The analogous development in computing was the emergence of high-level languages that provided us with both data structures and procedures with parameters. This phase occurred in the late 1950s and 1960s with the programming languages Fortran (for scientists and engineers) and COBOL (for business and accounting). These languages featured a more natural and easier-to-understand syntax than did assembly language. With them, two important things became possible:

1. Within certain limitations, computer programs became transportable. That is, a Fortran program that could be compiled by one compiler to run on a certain model of computer could also be compiled by another compiler to run on another model of computer. (This advance worked in theory; it often didn't quite work in practice.) In effect, the audience for the computer program ceased to be a particular model of computer and instead became a programming language.
2. The advent of data structures (such as arrays) and procedures with parameters meant that the program itself could be viewed as a machine consisting of various interconnected parts. (This is what allows us to use the idea of a stack mechanism to trace the execution of an algorithm.)

Together, these developments meant that the programming language, including the data and control structures it provided, served as a "virtual machine" to which programmers could write programs. Writing programs "for the hardware" began to fade in importance as a general approach to programming, and programmers began to write "for a programming language."

12.5 The Paradigm of Mechanistic Thinking

The paradigm that followed the printing press was rooted in a view of the universe as a giant machine that operates according to predictable and knowable physical laws. This paradigm fueled great discovery throughout the natural sciences, and led to both the scientific and industrial revolutions.

In the evolution of computing, the analogous paradigm was "structured programming," which emerged as the dominant approach to programming in the 1970s. Structured programming relies upon appropriate interfaces between the different procedures and functions within a program, just as a complex machine requires appropriate interfaces between its various mechanical components. Programmers could not only give symbolic names to data, but could give such names to the procedural and data abstractions they created. Programmers could now create procedures such that each one was like a little machine with its own job to do.

The age of mechanistic thinking saw people begin to understand God as the "Engineer of the Universe." It also witnessed significant development in several engineering disciplines. Similarly, the era of the structured programming paradigm caused the redefinition of the talented programmer from "the clever hacker" to "the software engineer." Indeed, this era saw the invention of software engineering as a discipline within computer science. This discipline was created to arrive at principles and practices whereby programmers could create modular abstractions that could be assembled into computer programs. The goal was to make program development economical, manageable, and reliable.

During this era, the use of computing expanded greatly throughout science, engineering, business, and commerce. Programs were used to solve harder and more complex problems. As a result, the programs themselves became larger and more complex. The increase in the size and complexity of programs, coupled with the decrease in the "individuality" of programs caused by the use of standard programming languages, meant that computer programs became more like published books than handwritten documents. Indeed, the scope and detail of program documentation increased faster than did program size, to the point where documentation for any significant program began to consist of entire books.

During this era, languages such as Pascal and C achieved dominance. In programming language design, both recursion and dynamic memory became accepted as standard language features. The inclusion of recursion and dynamic memory set the stage for the next round of change. Recursion serves human logic more than efficient use of hardware, and dynamic memory introduces greater complexity in the interest of supporting solutions to complex dynamic problems.

12.6 The Advent of Instantaneous Connectivity

The telegraph and telephone signaled the beginning of the most recent paradigm shift. For the first time, we could send and receive sensory input instantaneously across great distances. Within 30 years of the telegraph, new disciplines were created (psychology, sociology, management, economics, and the other human sciences).

Less than 30 years after the telephone, major breakthroughs occurred in physics, psychology, medicine, and other areas. These developments implied a world view that seeks to understand intangible, interrelated, dynamic processes.

In computing, the comparable era was roughly the 1980s. By the late 1970s, computing had experienced the breakthrough combination of time-sharing operating systems and interactive programming environments. Until then, programs were input to the computer on punch cards, with each card containing one line of code. Simple "batch processing" meant that a given program could not be run unless all programs ahead of it in the input queue were first run. Thus, a programmer would write his program on paper, then use a card punch machine to create a punched card for each line of code, then hand the resulting deck of cards to the computer operator, and then wait (perhaps for hours) to see if the program worked. With time-sharing systems and interactive programming environments, the programmer no longer had to create and submit punch cards, then wait. Instead, the programmer could create, input, and debug the program online with nearly instantaneous feedback from the computer. This fact made program development potentially much faster and, together with falling computer prices, opened the door to even larger and more complex programs.

Also during this time, we see the development of a new set of priorities for computer software. The problems of reliability and program maintenance, which led to the creation of software engineering, continued to get worse. Because of this, coupled with falling computer prices, reliability and ease of maintenance became more important for most applications than fast execution or small memory requirements. Languages such as Smalltalk and C++ allowed separate development of autonomous program modules; the goal was to allow programmers to develop programs by assembling them from libraries of tested components. The result is the "object-oriented" view, which sees computer programs not so much as a machine but rather as a network of multiple separate, interconnected entities that communicate among themselves.

12.7 The Paradigm of Interdependent Processes

The current paradigm is rooted in a view of the world as a complex dynamic network of interrelated processes. Coupled with computing technology, this view has enabled tremendous progress in virtually every field, as computer modeling and simulation allow us to systematically study a range of phenomena to which we otherwise would not have access.

The current era of computing in the late-1990s is analogous to the emerging age of computational models. The object-oriented programming paradigm, itself a model of interdependent dynamic processes, is becoming dominant. Computer-independent OO languages such as Java, once fully developed, will mean that one will truly be able to write a program in a single language, then distribute translated versions of that program that will run on any computer. Because of these languages, and the explosive growth of the World Wide Web (WWW), we shall be seeing fundamental changes in how we go about the business of creating and distributing software. With

TABLE 12.1

Paradigms and paradigm shifts	Evolution in Western history	Evolution in computing history
Paradigm: Literal existence	Mythical belief systems embedded in nature	Binary logic embedded in hardwired connections
Paradigm shift: Advent of abstraction	Pure alphabet	Symbolic names
Paradigm: Absolute abstractions	Absolute belief system	Assembly language programs
Paradigm shift: Advent of mechanism	The printing press	Procedures/parameters and data structures
Paradigm: Mechanistic thinking	Mechanistic science	Structured programming
Paradigm shift: Advent of instantaneous connectivity	Electronic media	Interactive systems, separate compilation
Paradigm: Interdependent dynamic processes	Computational models	Hardware-independent object-oriented software

the WWW providing a universal shared network connecting people from around the globe, and with Java-like languages providing truly transportable software components, we appear to be on the horizon of being able to rapidly assemble and distribute programs from electronic libraries. Coupled with the ready availability of extremely sophisticated off-the-shelf software packages, this means that immensely powerful, sophisticated, and usable computing power is available to virtually anyone, and soon it will be tailored to particular needs and preferences.

12.8   What Happens Next?

Just as modern science is using computing to explore previously uncharted territory, so too has the evolution of computing itself brought us to a place where technical dreams of long standing are on the verge of realization. Yes, we finally can and do have immediate access to information resources around the globe. Yes, before long we finally will be able to write, distribute, and use powerful software that will be available everywhere to work on any computer.

So, what will we do with it all? We are at a curious point in time. History gives us a pattern from the past that perhaps can help us understand the present and the future. But what does it tell us? Will the age of computational models be long lived? Or will it be a brief period of stability until a new technology signals the crumbling of that paradigm and the birth of yet another one? Similarly, for computing itself, will the advent of hardware-independent object-oriented software, coupled with the WWW, provide a period of productive stability? Or will it be superseded by a new computing paradigm?

Because we are talking about the current paradigm, we can not fully understand what its contributions will be. We do know the limits of the algorithmic computing that enables the paradigm: We will not be able to generate practical algorithmic solutions for intractable or undecidable problems, and it appears unlikely that we will be able to do so for NP-complete problems. Beyond that, we cannot know what the ceiling of accomplishment might be. Based on what we've seen from history so far, what do you expect will happen?

Supplemental Chapter

A History of Technology, Science, and Culture

In this chapter, we present "the big picture" of what the contribution of computing is, how it fits in with important contributions of the past, and how it may be influencing human consciousness itself. Computing is no longer an arcane technical discipline understood by only a few experts. Instead, it is rapidly joining the more traditional subjects as a basic element of higher education. The reason for this change is the way in which computing has impacted virtually every profession and every field of study.

As we shall see, computing is a good deal more than pushing buttons and running programs. Computing provides an important contribution to how we think about the problems we face and how we go about solving them, and it changes how we experience the world. In short, computing appears to be a metaphor for the latest round of human evolution.

What is "computing"? Why does it mean different things to different people?

- For some, it is a complicated new technology that they do not like and do not understand.
- For consumers, it is the excuse used by a bank or retail company to explain that billing errors or inflexible policies are "not our fault," that is, they blame it on the computer.

- For writers and clerical staff, it is a word processor that allows them to create, edit, and reproduce documents with far less effort than was required when using mechanical typewriters.
- For architects and engineers, it is a computer aided design (CAD) tool that allows them to design and refine their creations.
- For the military, it is equipment that can detect enemy activities and control weapons precisely and from safe distances.
- For musicians, it is a synthesizer that creates digital representations that allow greater flexibility and power in creating and editing musical works.

We could easily go on to list hundreds of examples here, but making a list is not the point. What's important to note is that the impact of computing is more than just a collection of disparate impacts that save time. Perhaps its most powerful impact has more to do with the human mind and how we are learning to think about our world.

S.1 Technology and Human Evolution

There are countless obvious ways in which technology allows us to do the things we have always done in more convenient ways. In addition, technology allows us to do things we could never do before, like go to the moon. Beyond these obvious impacts, however, technology appears to be intimately related to the ways in which human consciousness changes and evolves.

The word "evolution" is often used to refer to gradual changes in the *physical* properties of species. Rarely do we think of the evolution of *mental* properties, e.g., our way of perceiving the world, solving problems, etc. Yet history tells us that the capabilities of human perception and thought *have* changed in significant and power-ful ways throughout Western history. Furthermore, technology seems to be inti-mately connected with the ways in which human consciousness evolves.

In the case of computing technology, it allows us to approach phenomena with new insights about the order and the behavior of things, to think of things in ways that we could not conceive of 50 years ago. Think about it: right now, you are taking an introductory course in computing and computer science. Sixty years ago, even the brightest college students would not have had a clue about what such a course would involve. The words "computer science" *would not make any sense to them.*

To understand what is new about the perspective that computing gives us, to understand how technology is changing the way that our society and the people in it understand reality, we must have some sense of history. We cannot fully appreciate the significance of what is going on now unless we can see how it differs from what came before. Looking at history allows us to notice certain patterns in the relationship between technology and consciousness, patterns that can perhaps help us understand the changes we are witnessing today.

S.1.1 A Historical Pattern

Throughout history, we find a reliable pattern: The introduction of a new technology for human communication in a society tends to trigger a paradigm shift in that society.

We have just used two words that require definition: *technology* and *paradigm*.

Technology is a way of externalizing human abilities into the things we make.[1]

According to this definition, any number of developments can qualify as a form of technology:

- A bowl is technology that externalizes our ability to hold things in our hands.
- A steamroller is technology that externalizes our ability to mash things down.
- An alphabet is technology that externalizes our ability to communicate words.
- An automobile is technology that externalizes our ability to walk from one place to another.

Of the four examples cited above, only the third is explicitly a technology for human communication.

A paradigm is a form or model evidencing a single theme or pattern. When we talk about *cultural paradigms* or *scientific paradigms*, we refer to the set of shared assumptions, the shared way of "making sense of the world" that a society holds to be true.

Ancient tribal peoples and modern scientists have radically different views of the world. Their beliefs about the nature of reality are different because the cultures from which they come have vastly different paradigms. If you are the product of a modern industrialized culture that produces modern scientists, your assumptions and beliefs about the world are probably more similar to that of the scientist than to the tribal person.

S.1.2 Paradigmatic Change in Science

Throughout history, we find a pattern in which advances in knowledge eventually cause the existing paradigm to crumble. A period of cultural chaos and confusion then ensues until a new paradigm emerges. Once a new paradigm is established, things settle down and stability returns until future knowledge shows the current paradigm to be inadequate, thus causing it to crumble, and the cycle repeats itself. This is the process by which human experience contributes to better and better models of reality, better theories, and new ways of understanding.[2]

Technology thus plays a powerful role in this cycle of paradigmatic stability and change. In particular, it seems that new technology for human communication, that

1. Many dictionaries provide a more narrow definition that refers to matters of science or engineering. We favor the broader definition that focuses on how a society goes about creating its material objects and effects.
2. Thomas Kuhn, *The Structure of Scientific Revolutions*, 2nd ed. (Chicago: University of Chicago Press, 1970).

is, *media*, is related to paradigmatic change in two ways:

1. New media tend to emerge just before an old paradigm starts to crumble.
2. New media tend to embody key attributes of the new, emerging paradigm.

We could debate whether new technology *causes* paradigmatic shifts or whether new technology is just one *expression* of human consciousness as it is evolving. Either way, the properties of a new media technology can tell us a lot about the cultural paradigmatic shift that comes with it.

S.1.3   Hallmarks of a Paradigm Shift

History tells us that certain kinds of phenomena tend to occur during the transitional period that follows the invention of a new communications medium. As we use technology to externalize new parts of ourselves, we see clusters of change. As we shall soon see, many paradigmatic changes follow the creation of new media:

- Fundamentally different models of reality emerge. What used to be accepted by a culture as "obvious fact" is first questioned and challenged. Those individuals who do the questioning and challenging are often treated harshly. But, after a period of time, some of them are seen as pioneers, perhaps geniuses, and their once-radical ideas are accepted.
- New bodies of knowledge emerge. Such developments are reflected in structural changes in our institutions of learning, as entire new disciplines come into being.
- Bursts of great chaos and strife occur. Periods of intense warfare occur, social norms are challenged, and the social institutions of society undergo major transformation.
- There is a fundamental shift in the nature and boundaries of power and influence. Not only does leadership change, but the very seats of power that govern a society are replaced by different structures.
- Fundamental changes occur in art, music, and other forms of human expression, and new communications technology relegates the previous media to the status of an art form.

S.2   An Outline of Paradigmatic History

Let's now look at the specifics of the cyclical pattern of paradigmatic stability and paradigmatic change as they have occurred in history. The two alternate, as periods of stability are separated by periods of paradigmatic change. We shall then discuss what this history tells us about the implications of computer technology for human evolution.

S.2.1   The Age of Tribal Consciousness

Our first paradigm is what we might call the "tribal consciousness" of preliterate societies. With respect to technology, such societies had no alphabet, no "technology" that allowed them to write down their observations. The only means such people had of "writing down" their stories, beliefs, and customs was drawing or painting on cave walls, in burial crypts, or on bowls and tools. This was not considered "art" but was instead their most advanced "communications technology."

Today we know only what anthropologists and archaeologists can tell us about preliterate cultures. What did they believe? What forces governed their world? How did they understand the nature of reality? As best we know, virtually all preliterate cultures shared similar beliefs about reality. They all had what we might call "mythological belief systems"—that is, they believed in multiple gods and goddesses closely related to aspects of nature such as the wind, the sun, and the moon. These deities often evidenced a mixture of human attributes: goodness and evil, strength and weakness, nobility and pettiness. Sometimes, they were capricious or angry, angry not necessarily in a moral sense, but because of a spat with another god or goddess, which might cause unfortunate consequences for the humans.

The fact that tribal societies understood the world this way affected what they did in their efforts to stay in the gods' favor. Their only "methods of science" were efforts that would honor and please their gods through ritual and sacrifice.

Such peoples lived in a very *literal* world of oral stories, songs, and primitive drawings. All knowledge came from direct first-hand experience. The ability to communicate over distances or over time did not exist, nor did the ability to think abstractly in terms of principles that we associate with science.

It is noteworthy that these characteristics seem to be consistent across preliterate cultures, irrespective of location or time. Whether the culture existed 6000 years ago near the Mediterranean or only 80 years ago in Micronesia, the absence of written communications technology—for example, an alphabet (or something like one)—appears to be the necessary and sufficient condition for these common traits. As we shall see, the arrival of "alphabet technology" in a culture signals a radical change.

S.2.2   The Alphabet and the Roots of Abstraction

The alphabet in its pure form evolved within the ancient Greek culture. Prior to that era, several Semite and Phoenician cultures had taken strides toward the alphabet. Other cultures had developed written language based on pictographs or ideographs, a system wherein each symbol has some literal meaning.[3] Such systems tend to include a very large number of symbols and are not nearly as flexible and adaptable as are alphabets.[4] Some cultures developed hybrid writing systems, featuring elements of pictographic, ideographic, and alphabetic symbology. With the Greeks, we find the emergence of an abstract alphabetic system based on pure abstraction, the expression of a quality apart from a particular object.

An alphabet is the most artificial and abstract form of written language because each letter in an alphabet has no literal meaning. The letter "s" does not refer to any

3. The traditional Chinese and Japanese writing systems are based on literally thousands of different pictographs. Some historians wonder if the difference between the alphabet in Western culture and the pictographs in Eastern culture might contribute to the dramatic differences in cultural consciousness. Modern derivatives of the traditional Asian written languages have evolved which function more like alphabets. These were developed largely to support the needs of business and commerce.

4. The large number of characters in the traditional Japanese symbol set is what led to the development of the Fax machine. How? Because it was more efficient to develop a technology to simply transmit a picture of the symbols than it was to transmit the long codes required by the large number of symbols.

tangible object. Instead, it symbolizes a particular *sound* that is combined with other letters or sounds to form words.

The letters thus take on meaning only when the sounds they signify correspond to a word. Thus, the string of letters "kllajh" has no meaning whatsoever in English, while the string of letters "textbook" has meaning. Even the letters "mayohnaiz" can convey meaning. It is not really a word, but you can use the letters to construct the sound of a meaningful word.

What is fascinating about this abstract quality of alphabets is that the very presence of an alphabet in a culture appears to signal the development of increasingly abstract thinking, problem-solving abilities, and models of reality.

The ancient Greeks provided the founders of virtually every field of human knowledge: philosophy, mathematics, geometry, engineering, astronomy, anatomy, and medicine, to name but a few. All of their accomplishments share a central quality. They were able to consider phenomena from a new perspective: *they were able to engage in abstraction.* Thus, while the Greeks made many different important contributions, it might be more fitting to say that they made exactly one crucial contribution and applied it to many particular phenomena. *They contributed the ability to engage in abstraction.* This represents a perceptual and cognitive watershed in Western history, before which things were seen in literal and mythological terms. It was a radical change in the "view of the world," the way in which people perceived themselves and their experiences. And, as with any radical change, the early "abstracters" were treated as heretics and traitors. Indeed, Plato's teacher, Socrates, was forced to commit suicide in order to stay true to his beliefs simply because what he was saying went "against the grain" of the then-established world view or *paradigm.*

While we cannot say that the alphabet *caused* such cultural changes, we can say that it gained dominance at the same period of history as did the human ability to engage in abstraction.

Some historians suspect that this relationship between the alphabet and abstraction explains many minor historical mysteries. For example, why, despite a variety of rich and very sophisticated cultures, did the original peoples of America never invent the wheel? Perhaps it is because they did not have an abstract symbol system and thus never developed the ability to look at a log and abstract the qualities of "a tool for moving things by rolling." While there may be a causal relationship here, we do not know that there is. We can only speculate and observe that the technology of abstract media and the cognitive and perceptual ability to engage in abstraction go hand in hand.

S.2.3   The Age of Absolute Abstraction

Over a period of a just a few hundred years (very fast relative to the pace of change in ancient times), the cognitive/perceptual ability to abstract transformed nothing less than the dominant view of reality. By the latter years of the Roman Empire, the mythological view of reality was effectively replaced by monotheism, the belief in one God. The difference here is more profound than simply the change from worshipping multiple gods to a single God. What we see here is the emergence of a belief system, a paradigm, a way of understanding reality, that *requires* the mental ability to abstract.

Most obviously, we find the abstractions of "good" and "evil" tied to particular divine forces. A single God represents all that is good, while Satan embodies all that is evil. The gods and goddesses no longer lived on the Earth among the people. Instead, as the abstractions of good and evil became understood as the work of God and Satan, respectively, they lived in unseen abstract places, in Heaven and Hell.

This is a dramatic shift from the locus of good and evil in the mythological belief systems of preliterate cultures, in which the divine forces of mythology embodied all that was human, both the higher and lower sides of human existence. Thus, *all* of humanity was reflected in the divinity of the gods and goddesses.

In contrast, the monotheistic view imposed dichotomy everywhere, even *inside* each person. No longer were all sides of human existence divine. Instead, the higher side of humanity, the good, was understood as divine and consistent with the wishes of God, while the lower side of human existence was understood as being satanic, sinful, and contrary to God's wishes. Thus the structure of the meaning of mundane life changed radically.

For many hundreds of years, this view of God and the world was dominant and virtually all phenomena came to be viewed as an expression of God's Plan, which meant there was no need for questioning or investigation about the nature of reality. This world view contributed to a stagnant period with respect to developments in science, mathematics, and philosophy. This was not because there were no "smart" people. Rather, during this time, smart people were engaged in the activity determined by their paradigm: they were searching for an understanding of God's Will, for therein lay truth and the secrets of the world.

There are two features about *absolute abstraction* that should be noted:

- It occurs only after the evolution of an abstract written language system. For example, the Judaic culture featured monotheism with absolute values for many generations prior to the rise in Europe of the dominant Christian view. The Judaic culture also featured an abstract symbol system quite early, from which the Greek alphabet derived, although the particulars are shrouded in the mysteries of prehistory.
- Educated people had the ability to think abstractly in the terms of principles and forces, but this ability was focused almost exclusively on trying to understand God's will, not on empirical investigation concerning phenomena in the world.

S.2.4 Mechanical Media Technology

The state of media technology in Western culture remained largely stagnant until the mid-fifteenth century when Johann Gutenberg developed the printing press. The idea of a printing press seems rather ordinary to us today, but its place in history is extremely significant. Let's consider what properties were embodied in the printing press.

First, the printing press is a *machine*. The workings of the simplest printing press involve the transfer of physical forces: the movement of a lever moves a gear, which in turn moves a plate, which in turn brings paper in contact with inked typefaces of alphabetic letters. This machine thus made it possible to produce writings in mass quantities, whereas before every copy of a document had to be written by hand. But more was changed than just the economics of producing multiple copies. For the first time, it was possible to produce things that were virtually identical.

The printing press, thus laid the foundation for the next round of radical change in the way people conceived of reality: the new ability to *mechanically reproduce precisely the same communication*. The development of the printing press appears to go hand in hand with the development of the human ability to engage in what we shall call "mechanistic thinking."

This relationship between media technology and consciousness was at the crux of the insight offered by historian Marshall McLuhan: "the medium is the message." By this he meant that the *technology of communication* is the "real" message of an era, much more so than the content of the various messages conveyed via the technology. The transformation that followed the printing press is a prime example.

Less than 100 years after the invention of the printing press, a radical "mechanistic model" of the universe was proposed, first by Copernicus who challenged the conventional belief that the sun and moon rotated around the earth, correctly claiming that the earth revolves around the sun in an annual orbit, and that the earth rotates on its axis every 24 hours. His view was taken up by Kepler who discovered that the orbits of the planets were elliptical, not circular, by Galileo who first used a telescope for observation and who formulated the mathematical law of falling bodies, and by Newton who applied the same law to both planetary motion and falling bodies.

While the views of reality proposed by these scientists proved correct, they were not readily accepted. Copernicus was ridiculed for lunacy and absurd notions. He was opposed both by the conservative Church and radical reformers alike. His views contradicted the Bible, went against common sense observations, and could not readily be proved. Yet he confined himself to technical papers and thus suffered only ridicule. Galileo openly opposed the authorities and eventually renounced what he knew to be true in order to avoid being put to death.

Of these men, only Galileo truly believed in a mechanistic model of the universe; yet the work of all four signals the beginning of a new way of thinking. By the end of the seventeenth century, mainstream Western thought had embraced the mechanistic model that had seemed so heretical less than 200 years before.

S.2.5 The Age of Mechanistic Thinking

Just as the ability to think in *abstract* terms led to a new conception of the workings of the universe and of the role of divinity in it, so too did the development in Renaissance Europe of the human ability to think in *mechanistic* terms. By the end of the 1600s, it was widely accepted that speculation and empirical investigation were proper science, not heresy.

Concurrent with these changes, God's role was redefined as being the "engineer of the universe." God created the "machine of the universe" and then "largely let it operate."[5] Before the paradigm shift triggered by the printing press, it was forbidden to question the nature of reality. After that shift, it became acceptable and expected that people would solve the puzzles and mysteries of the detailed workings of the machine that was created by God.

Once this view solidified, the great body of modern scientific knowledge was rapidly evolving as distinct from philosophy. Prior to this time, "philosophy" as defined by the ancient Greeks applied to all knowledge. Following the printing press, the "natural sciences"—for example, physics, chemistry, and biology—quickly became disciplines in their own right. Philosophy became increasingly focused on matters of religious, social, and psychological experience. Instead of philosophy being "the body of all knowledge," the sciences, mathematics, and philosophy were each a body of knowledge, and the concept of a *university* emerged to house them all together. In science, the "empirical method" (a set of rather mechanistic precepts) governed how scientific research should be conducted. Great strides were also made in mathematics, including geometry, trigonometry, and calculus.

During this time, the American and French Revolutions established major Western societies that defined matters of religion as private and separate from the matters of government. To modern Americans, this seems an obvious development aimed at protecting freedom. In the course of history, however, this was an extremely radical change. Only a few hundred years before the American Revolution, God, Church, and government were effectively *synonymous* with respect to both social governance and the "nature of reality."

Throughout the eighteenth and nineteenth centuries, and continuing through much of the twentieth century, the mechanistic model of reality became increasingly ingrained in Western consciousness. Developments in technology during this period focused almost exclusively on the development of machines that could amplify the human ability to manipulate physical forces. Knowledge of human anatomy evolved considerably, mainly as a result of conceiving of the human body as a machine with various functional components.

With the advent of farm machinery, workers moved from the farm to the factory, which was at its core itself a machine. Workers were components of the factory-machine as were the cogs and gears of plant equipment. Unlike machinery, workers did not cost very much and thus were "used up" and disposed of. For much of this time, child workers were viewed "just like adults, only better": they cost less and took up less space.

---

5. We say "largely let it operate" because there were and, according to some, still are, occasional divine interventions known as "miracles." This is effectively the operational definition of miracle for ecclesiastical purposes.

By the middle of the twentieth century, people increasingly modeled their life in a mechanical way, with a series of life stages, much as one part of a machine would transfer force to another part. Strife and sacrifice were accepted as elements of the early stages in the hope that later stages would provide happiness.

By the latter half of the current century, mechanistic science became for many people the *de facto* religion, the "true story" about the workings of the universe, and of life within it. Mechanistic Age societies came to expect their members to believe in scientific truth, and left religion to be a personal matter.

S.2.6   Electronic Media Technology

New technologies do not establish new dominant modes of human consciousness overnight. It takes generations. In the case of electronic media technology, the period of transition we are experiencing now, the watershed events began with the emergence of the telegraph in the 1830s (developed by Samuel Morse) and the telephone in the 1870s (developed by Alexander Graham Bell and Thomas Edison). Both inventions provided technology that allowed virtually instantaneous communication over great distances.

However, there is an important difference between the two. Morse code is an abstract binary aural system that is superimposed onto the abstract alphabetic symbols—that is, it *adds* a layer of abstraction. Telephonic communication transmits the sound, not only of the words but also of the speaker's actual voice, thus *removing* layers of abstraction.

Thomas Edison was at the same time refining the ability to record and replay sound. Taken together, these electronic media provided the ability to transmit *literal representations* of sensory stimuli across both time and space. In recent decades, communications technology has taken these new capabilities even further, from radio broadcasts to television and films to the VCR and the Internet.

Have you considered the implications of these developments on the evolution of the ways you think, the things in which you believe, the values which influence you?

S.3   The Significance of Recent Developments

Let's look again at two conclusions we might draw from our brief overview of history:

- The development of abstract media is a metaphor for (and perhaps a causal factor in) the transformation from literal tribal consciousness to an abstract, absolute religious consciousness.
- The development of mechanical media is a metaphor for (or causal factor in) the transformation from an abstract, absolute religious consciousness to a mechanistic scientific consciousness.

In light of these observations, the recent development of electronic media would suggest that perhaps a radical paradigmatic transformation is afoot. But how do we know? The major obstacle to gaining clarity about such things is that we seem to be *in the midst* of whatever the transformation is and thus can have no perspective on it. Only in hindsight do these things become clear. At the same time, what we know of history suggests a few things that we might look for if indeed a major transformation is underway.

S.3.1   Evidence of Paradigmatic Transformation

We said in Section S.1.3 that certain hallmarks typify the shift that follows the invention of new communications medium. Let's consider each in turn in a bit more depth.

NEW MODELS OF REALITY

If the impact of previous media technology is any guide, then we might expect that fundamentally *different models of reality* would emerge relatively early in the transformation. These would be conceptions of reality (analogous to Greek *abstraction* or Renaissance *mechanism*) that go beyond the established paradigm. We would expect these conceptions to be initially seen as foolishness or heresy, and to be later adopted as the basis for a new paradigm. Thus we might ask if we find evidence of *fundamentally new conceptions* of the nature of reality.

If we look at developments in science shortly after the advent of "instantaneous literal media" (the telephone), we see a number of such developments. Within the span of only 30 years, we find the development of Einstein's theory of relativity, Freud's theory of the unconscious, and various fundamental work on bacterial infection and physiology, all occurring at about the same time.

What is important about these developments is that they all went beyond the mechanistic model of reality, they all initially met with severe opposition, and they all have (in general, if not in particular) proved to be correct. In each case, the assumptions, beliefs, scientific work, and daily practice of our modern societies have been pervasively affected.

Observe that, in each case, we are not talking about perceivable physical forces acting on tangible matter. Instead, we're dealing with invisible forces and processes, phenomena that can not readily be observed and that do not readily lend themselves to study via the traditional "scientific method." The degree of conceptual innovation, and the degree of transformative effect, of these and similar developments did as much to "set the world on its ear" in recent times as did the work of Plato and Galileo in their times.

NEW ORGANIZATIONS OF KNOWLEDGE

As we saw with the creation of the natural sciences and the modern university, we see again new areas of knowledge gaining the status of independent disciplines: the birth of the human sciences (psychology, sociology, anthropology, economics, management, etc.).[6] Like the natural sciences before them, the human sciences split away from philosophy and became disciplines in their own right.[7] The new human sciences initially adopted the methodology of the natural sciences. After a century of producing much data and little information, there has been a search in recent years for new models and methodologies that are more useful than the mechanistic ones. While it is not clear to all what the new "knowledge paradigm" might be, the inadequacies of the old mechanistic paradigm are increasingly visible to scientists from all fields, including the natural sciences.

CHAOS AND STRIFE

Another hallmark of the transformative period that we might expect to see is a period of great uproar and strife in politics, war, and social structure. Clearly, the twentieth century has been filled with major, even cataclysmic wars (the First and Second World Wars), political upheavals (communism and fascism), and upheavals in social structure (civil rights and antiwar demonstrations, decolonization around the globe, the epidemic of family deconstruction and divorce in Western societies, etc.).

CHANGES IN POWER

Another transformative change we would expect to see is a fundamental shift in the nature of boundaries of power and influence. With the emergence of the alphabet, the tribe gave way to the city-state. During the establishment of a later paradigm, the city-state gave way to the church-state. During the period of upheaval near the time of the printing press, the church-state gave way to the "Divine Right" kingdom. With the emergence of the mechanistic paradigm, such kingdoms were replaced by the emergence of secular nations. Since the advent of electronic media, the character of national government changed with the emergence of what might be called "super-governments"—fascism, communism, socialism, and other philosophies of government that concerned themselves with more and more aspects of daily life.

CHANGES IN ART

Throughout history, new media technology has produced fundamental changes in the worlds of art, music, and other forms of human expression and relegates previous technologies to the status of an art form. Prior to the alphabet, painting and sculpture were not art; they were communications media. With the advent of the alphabet, they became obsolete as effective communications media, becoming artistic media instead.

---

6. The fact that the human sciences have not yet achieved the sort of fundamental breakthroughs that were evidenced by the natural sciences after they adopted the mechanistic model of reality can be attributed to the fact that the human sciences initially tried to adopt the mechanistic model from the natural sciences. This model appears to be not very useful for the phenomena that the human sciences are attempting to understand. The human sciences have not yet developed a model that is adequate to the study of their subject matter. Corrections are currently underway.

7. Unfortunately, the loss of both the natural sciences and the human sciences leaves philosophy with rather little to do. As a result, many academic "departments of philosophy" behave as if they were "museums of philosophy" with little subject matter of current interest except ethics.

Similarly, prior to the printing press, calligraphy was not an art form; it was media. After the printing press, calligraphy became art.

With the advent of electronic media, can we expect mechanical media to become art? Most certainly, in several ways. An interesting phenomenon is the "coffee table book," a large, heavily illustrated book whose purpose is one of providing an attractive visual presence regardless of particular content. Prior to electronic media, books were not art; they had a more utilitarian function. In recent years, they have become increasingly incapable of providing cutting edge information because the information they contain is "old news" by the time a book can be written, edited, published, and distributed. Thus the role of the book has shifted toward art.

We see other evidence of mechanical phenomena becoming art forms. In some styles of modern architecture, the mechanical systems of the building, the plumbing and ventilation systems, are accentuated as part of visual design. Old machines, previously seen as antiquated "junk," from old treadle sewing machines to antique farm implements, are now valued as decorative art objects. In sum, we do indeed seem to be in the midst of a major transformation in our culture's model of reality:

- Institutions and social structures that are based on established cultural assumptions are faltering.
- Scientific conceptions that transcend the established mechanistic paradigm are widely and increasingly accepted.
- A new electronic medium has replaced mechanical media as the source of most of our information and entertainment.

S.3.2 Attributes of the Emerging Paradigm

Given that a major transformation appears to be underway, what can we surmise about its nature and its outcome?

First, electronic media operate via *intangible* forces. (Whereas physical forces such as gravity, friction, and applied force can be perceived directly, the workings of electronic devices are hidden from us.) We cannot observe television signals or radio waves directly; we can only observe them indirectly via second-order observation through scopes, meters, etc. *Thus we might expect the emerging paradigm to be one that addresses intangibles, things that cannot be directly seen or measured.*

Second, electronic media operate via *instantaneous synergistic interaction*. There is thus a fundamental difference with mechanical devices, which operate via a causal chain of moving parts. Inside of a television set, there is no such chain of events. Instead, there is a synergistic process that produces a combined effect (picture and sound). *Thus, we might expect the emerging paradigm to be one that addresses synergistic instantaneous phenomena.*

Third, electronic media produce sensory stimuli. This is far different than the product of mechanical media, which is some material product (a printed page). The output of electronic media is not a material product or effect but instead a continuum of sensory stimuli, continuous sounds and moving images, *signals* not *things*. *Thus, we might expect the emerging paradigm to be one that focuses on a "currency" of signals (i.e., information), not on things.*

In contrast to the mechanistic paradigm's focus on the tangible, causal, time-ordered manipulation of physical matter via physical force, we might expect that the emerging paradigm will focus on the intangible, synergistic, instantaneous manipulation of sensory information. ▪

S.3.3 The Central Theme of the New Paradigm

Earlier we observed that one effect of new media technology is the transformation of the old medium into art. While the *media* of art incorporates old technology, the *vision* of art is something quite different. If we consider fundamental changes in the content and technique of artists, we find other fascinating correlations with the development of new technology and find clues to the emergent paradigm.

ARTISTIC VISION AND THE VARIOUS PARADIGMS

In the paintings and sculpture of preliterate cultures the human figure is not well formed or detailed and the artistic technique appears primitive, like the art work of a child in today's world.

When we look at the art of ancient Greek and Roman civilizations, we notice technique improvements of a particular kind. In sculpture, the transformation is dramatic. Human forms are not only well formed and detailed, they are also *ideal*—as if the ancients were able to consider the mass of humanity around them and "abstract out" the shape of the perfect eyes, the perfect arms, the perfect legs. This was, of course, consistent with the abstraction exemplified by the media technology of their culture, the alphabet. However, the ancients did not succeed as well in their drawing and painting technique, which remained flat and lifeless. Even as late as the pre-Renaissance, we see that artists did not know how to put foreground and background figures in perspective, how to create a dynamic sense of action, how to paint facial features in a "realistic" way.

Art took a momentous stride forward at just about the time that the printing press was invented. Suddenly, artists gained the ability to draw and paint in a way that we would call realistic, and they learned the technique of perspective. The "trick" of this technique can be taught to children (pick a point on an imaginary horizon, then draw lines to it from the various figures in the foreground; these lines can then be used to scale objects in between the foreground and the imaginary horizon). Notice that there is nothing very mysterious or difficult about this technique. In fact, it is a rather *mechanistic* trick. Yet it was not discovered until the beginning of the transformation that lead to the age of mechanistic thinking.

Thus, as with the ancients, the new artistic techniques of the Renaissance presented the same quality as did the new technology that was emerging at that time. In Renaissance Europe, the mechanical technique of drawing in perspective spread like wildfire, becoming a standard technique of artists far faster than mechanical thinking developed sufficiently to allow the scientific and industrial revolutions to occur.

This relationship between artistic technique and transformative technology was noticed by Marshall McLuhan. He began referring to artists as "probes from the future." To the extent that he is right, we might wonder what "message" we might get about the emerging paradigm from developments in artistic technique of the last 100 years.

THE MESSAGE OF MODERN ART

The most radical transformation in artistic technique after the Renaissance began to take root in the late nineteenth century. After several hundred years of mastering the techniques of realism, artists went in a radically new direction: They were using abstraction not as the *medium* of communication (*à la* the alphabet) but rather as the *content* of their work. The movement that resulted was called "abstract art." Painters thus moved dramatically away from realistic forms, instead creating art that was harder and harder for most people to understand. The subtle nuances of literal representations were abandoned, first in a movement to abstract angular shapes, then in a movement that abandoned the notion of representational shape altogether. The net effect was to take art away from the comprehension of "most people" into an increasingly abstract domain.

If artists are, as Marshall McLuhan has said, "probes from the future," what might we glean from this? We might conclude that they are inadvertently telling us that the essential quality contributed by electronic media is the ability to *externalize abstraction* into the things we create.

NEW TECHNOLOGY: ABSTRACTION DEVICES

As it turns out, devices for "externalizing abstraction" are precisely what computers are. Computers allow us to externalize our ability to create abstraction outside of ourselves. Before computers, only people could "abstract" (and only then if they had an alphabet). With computers, we are building little electronic boxes into which we *build* abstractions.

When we say this, what do we mean by abstraction? Go back to the basic definition: by abstraction we mean, "expression of a quality apart from any specific embodiment." This, as it turns out, is what computer scientists and software engineers attempt to do when they create algorithms. For example, we use computers to route phone calls to the proper places around the globe. We do not have a separate computer program for routing each phone call; we have instead created general algorithms that perform the logic necessary to solve "phone call routing problems."

As we shall see in later chapters, algorithms are the "logical recipes" that underlie computer programs. To put it another way, a given computer program expresses an algorithm in some particular programming language. The goal of an algorithm is to externalize some capability that has heretofore required a human mind. The goal is to allow an electronic box to perform what *used to require* a person's mental work such that the box does the work *for* the person. There is nothing new about trying to build our capabilities into the things we make: that is what all technology is about. What *is* new is what we're externalizing:

- With the alphabet, we learned to externalize our words into symbols that will tell our stories for us.
- With mechanical media, we learned to externalize the capabilities of our bodies into machines that would do physical work for us.
- With electronic media and modern digital computers, we are learning to externalize the capabilities of our mind and our central nervous system into electronic boxes so that they will do mental and sensory work for us.

S.4 The Emerging Paradigm

As recently as 30 years ago, many astute observers, fueled by the work of Thomas Kuhn and Marshall McLuhan, had noted the symptoms of a paradigm shift, but no one was particularly clear about the particulars of the new paradigm. It is only in the last decade that the shape of the new paradigm has started to become clear.

The various indications are clear. Researchers on the cutting edge of virtually every discipline rely on some form of algorithmic model. From economics to medical research, from social theory to financial analysis, from basic science to city planning, from weapons development to models of human psychology, virtually all cutting edge research relies on the computer in fundamental ways.

Just as the *machine* provided the defining metaphor for the previous paradigm, the *computer* is providing both the foundation for scientific development and the conceptual framework in which we understand a broad range of phenomena. In fact, in virtually all aspects of science, business, and industry, the "way of thinking" that is implied by computing is changing not only what we do, but how we think. We refer to this new way of seeing and thinking as the *computing perspective*.

The term **computing perspective** refers to a way of looking at the world, and at phenomena in it, as if reality were governed by a computer program. This does not mean that reality is governed by a computer. It does mean that it is useful to think of phenomena as if they were.

Why? Because doing so provides us with two crucial benefits:

■ An algorithmic conception of phenomena lets us notice things in a way that we otherwise could not.
■ It gives us a means of simulation and experimentation for dealing with phenomena that we otherwise could not empirically study.

We shall discuss each of these benefits in turn.

S.4.1 An Algorithmic Conception of Phenomena

The computing perspective allows us to see problems as a different kind of puzzle. Rather than defining problems as a puzzle of physical matter and physical forces, the computing perspective lets us see problems in terms of information and communication. For many kinds of problems, this is more useful.

For example, consider medical researchers who have been trying to solve the puzzle of treating and preventing cancer. Until recently, they applied a mechanistic conception and viewed the cancerous tumor itself as the problem, "attacking" it with surgery and potent chemotherapies. Their conception was mechanistic and, as a result, they treated cancer much like an auto repair shop might treat rust in a car: by cutting it out and hoping it doesn't return.

In the last decade, the thrust of cancer research has been replaced with an algorithmic approach. Researchers now believe that the cancer itself is not the problem but rather a symptom. Evidently, we all get cancer routinely and, in those of us who remain healthy, cancer is routinely destroyed by our immune system. Rather than attack the cancer (which likely may return), researchers study the immune system to learn how to strengthen or augment its ability to prevent cancer from prospering in the body. The computing perspective enables them to ask crucial questions:

- What process enables a person's immune system to recognize the presence of cancerous cells? What "information" is the immune system picking up?
- How is this process different than the process that causes another immune system to ignore those same kinds of cells? How does an immune system get fooled into "missing the important information?"
- If an immune system recognizes the presence of cancer, how does one part of this system "send instructions" to another part in order to destroy the cancer?
- How is this process different in a system in which cancer is recognized but not effectively killed? What interferes with one part of the immune system "communicating with" another part, thus allowing the cancer to survive?

In asking these kinds of questions, the researcher is thinking of the human body as if it were a computer governed by a computer program. In some people, the "program" (the immune system) processes "information" (biochemical "signals") about cancer more effectively than does the "program" of others. In effect, the researcher is trying to figure out how to "debug" the immune system, much like a computer programmer seeks to find and correct errors in a computer program.

Of course, this is not to say that the immune system *is* a computer program (it's not), nor that the cells *are* computers (they aren't). Instead, it means that it is useful to think of them "as if" they were. Nor does it mean that medical researchers are particularly knowledgeable about computing. Instead, we refer to a way of understanding phenomena in terms of the computing concepts of "processes," "algorithms," and "information." The medical researcher may not be *aware* that he is applying a computing model, and may not even know what the word "algorithm" means. But he is "thinking that way" nonetheless, just as Copernicus was thinking in mechanistic terms regardless of whether he realized it or not.

S.4.2   A Means of Simulation and Experimentation

The computing perspective also allows us to use computers to simulate and experiment with phenomena that we otherwise could not study. For example:

- When doctors are concerned about the state of a patient's brain or other critical organ, they cannot simply cut the patient open just to have a look. However, technicians can use computers that process ultrasound or magnetic resonance signals to create accurate visual images of what doctors cannot see.
- When engineers want to analyze the safety aspects of automobile design, they cannot strap people into car, then crash them into a wall at 50 miles per hour just to see what happens to them. However, they can and do crash cars occupied by inanimate dummies connected to computer sensors that gather data on the various forces and shocks.

Paradigm	Media Technology	Art	Religion
Preliterate literal existence	Spoken word, sculpture, drawing		Multiple gods and goddesses; divine forces incorporate both good and bad traits
Alphabet	Abstract symbol system	New art media: Sculpture — — — — — — — New technique: Ideal forms	Heresy: Postulating abstract principles (Socrates)
Absolute abstraction	Handwritten documents	Content: Divinity	One God, one Satan, good and bad separated; divine forces control events.
Printing press	Mechanical reproduction of physical objects	New art media: Calligraphy — — — — — — — New technique: 2D realism	Heresy: Positing laws of natural forces (Copernicus, Galileo)
Mechanistic thinking	Mechanically reproduced books, documents	Content: Real world (portraits, landscapes, still lifes, action scenes, etc.)	God as engineer of the universe; religion as part of family and community
Electronic media	Instantaneous transmission of sensory signals	New art media: Mechanicals — — — — — — — New technique: Abstract content	Heresy: Positing forces that cannot be directly measured, (Einstein, Freud, Curie)
Computational models	Literal audio/visual images	Content: Subjective meaning	God as source of elemental forces, for example, Big Bang; religion as personal matter.

Figure S.1   The evolution of media, science, and consciousness

World View	Knowledge, Science	Organization
Playground of the gods.	Appease the gods via ritual, homage, sacrifice, etc.	Tribe
Technology externalizes human expression, that is, the ability to convey thoughts, observations over time and space	Creation of philosophy as field of all knowledge	City-state
The Holy Battleground	Comprehend the Divine Plan	The Church
Technology externalizes the human body, that is, the ability to physically manipulate matter by applying physical force	Creation of the natural sciences and math, and their split from philosophy	"Divine Right" kingdoms
A physical machine governed by natural forces and laws	Master the manipulation of physical matter via application of physical forces	Secular nations
Technology externalizes the nervous system, for example, instantaneous information via real-time feedback system	Creation of the human sciences and their split from philosophy	Super-governments (facism, communism, socialism)
A network of complex processes	Master the manipulation of informational processes via algorithms	Complex network of global corporations and regulatory governments

Figure S.1   *(continued)*

- When economists seek to study the complexities of economic phenomena, they cannot arbitrarily implement a series of experimental economic policies just to see what happens. Doing so could wreck the economy, ruin businesses, and put millions out of work. However, by constructing algorithmic models of economic behavior, they can simulate the economy and use real-life scenarios to improve the adequacy of their model.

S.4.3   What It Means for You

In almost everything you will be doing, the computer will be one of your most basic and most powerful tools. Virtually every conceivable kind of professional (engineer, scientist, manager, writer, musician, executive, salesmanager, etc.) relies on computing tools for essentially the same reason: computing offers the state of the art with respect to communication, analysis, creation, decision, and management support tools. In short, there is no way out. If you want to be at the leading edge of your profession, *whatever that profession might be,* you will both be using computers and be influenced by computational models of whatever phenomena your work focuses on.

This does not mean that you will have to *program* computers in the traditional sense. It does mean that it is advisable for you to have a solid foundation in understanding computation and how "computer people" think and solve problems. Computing provides the model that is proving most useful for understanding complex phenomena of virtually any kind. Thus, irrespective of your career goals, you should understand that computing is increasingly providing the conceptual framework in our society. In order to be a well-educated citizen of the twenty first century, you will have to understand the basic foundations of computing, to view the world from the "computing perspective."

FOOD FOR THOUGHT

Is Consciousness Changing?

It is easy to assume that the human mind has stayed pretty much the same, and that we are mentally different from our ancestors only in terms of better education, more knowledge, etc. However, there is growing evidence that this is not the case, that there is an ongoing evolution of human consciousness, fundamental changes in how we perceive the world, how we think about things, how we go about solving problems, and how we respond and react to the meanings in our lives.

For example, psychiatry and clinical psychology had their beginnings near the turn of the century. There was a large "cast of characters" who were the founders of these fields. The most famous of them is Sigmund Freud. While there is much of Freud's work that has been criticized, there are many ways in which he laid the foundations for even those psychiatrists and psychologists who now disagree with much of what he said. Part of the criticism of Freud is due to an interesting phenomena: the kind of symptoms that Freud and others encountered around the turn of the century no longer present themselves. Thus, modern theorists and practitioners cannot reproduce some of his findings simply because they do not see the same kinds of patients.

The Case of "Anna O."

Freud was able to gain widespread recognition with the case of "Anna O.," a woman whose arm had become paralyzed for no apparent physiological reason. Freud figured out that there was indeed a cause, a psychological one. Here's the story:

Anna's father was ill and bedridden, and it fell to Anna to be responsible for his care. This responsibility dominated her life and, as a loving daughter, she was aware of no resentment or anger about this. She wanted to care for her father as best she could. Freud learned that Anna had terrifying nightmares in which she stabbed her father. With the onset of the nightmares, the arm that held the knife (in the dream) became suddenly paralyzed (in real life).

Freud was able to help her understand that, despite her genuine love for her father, she was nevertheless resentful that caring for him consumed her whole life. As Anna became able to understand and accept her emotions, and to see that she could be resentful about the consequences of her father's illness yet still be loving toward him, her paralysis ended. Rather than "block out" the emotion from her awareness, which led to unconscious symptoms, she learned to integrate it into her awareness, which led to a disappearance of the symptoms.

Freud called this kind of illness a "conversion reaction," an illness in which physical symptoms such as paralysis arise with no physical cause in order to safeguard the person from frightening unconscious urges. Numerous similar cases were documented in that era and became a mainstay of the early psychoanalytic literature.

There is no doubt that such cases did in fact occur. Yet today, such symptoms no longer seem to exist. In fact, the only place where such symptoms have been found in recent decades is in very isolated pockets of Appalachia, places where people live and work much as they did a hundred years ago, places having little contact with modern society. Can we thus conclude that contact with "modern society" serves to eliminate conversion reactions?

Psychological Wounds of War

Changes in psychological processes were noted by the medical staffs of the U.S. and British armies. For the last hundred years, there have been soldiers who suffered psychological wounds of war, sometimes so severe as to be disabling. The particular symptoms have been characterized differently over time. In World War I, the diagnosis was "shell shock"; in World War II and Korea, it was "battle fatigue"; in Vietnam it was "post-traumatic stress disorder."

These are *not* different labels for the same phenomena. Rather, the various labels apply to very *different* sets of symptoms. Shell-shocked soldiers were often catatonic (as if in a trance). Soldiers suffering from battle fatigue appeared as if their nervous system had "shorted out." Soldiers suffering from post-traumatic stress disorder appeared at first glance to function normally, yet they found themselves unable to deal with the stresses of relationships and responsibility, either withdrawing into passivity or lapsing into violent behavior when confronted with social demands.

More fascinating still, British Army doctors observed that the different symptoms of shell shock and battle fatigue during World War I corresponded to differences in social class. Officers, who at that time came only from the upper classes of British society, evidenced "battle fatigue," while the soldiers from the working class evidenced "shell shock." Why this difference? The trauma to which they had been subjected were the same. Could the difference be related to the fact that the upper classes had exposure to electronic media while the lower classes did not?

EXERCISES

S.1 The following quote is from the book *Mindstorms* by Seymour Pappert: "[Critics] fear that more communication via computers might lead to less human association and result in social fragmentation." Do you agree or disagree with this statement? Why?

S.2 In what ways do you see electronic media of any kind, including but not limited to interactive computing, contributing to "decay and deterioration in our social fabric"? How might these negative effects be countered?

S.3 In what ways do you expect to see high technology (of any form) make the strongest impact on our society in the next 20 years? In what ways will such changes be positive? In what ways will they be negative?

S.4 Given the power of modern technology (computer databases, electronic surveillance, blood/urine/DNA tests, etc.), it is now possible to monitor and investigate aspects of individual behavior in ways that could not have been imagined 200 years ago. In light of these technological developments, do you believe that the U.S. Constitution's Bill of Rights is sufficient to protect the citizenry from privacy intrusions by government and/or corporate entities? If you favor leaving the Bill of Rights alone, explain how/why you think it is adequate to modern society and why you don't want it modified. If you favor modifying it, in what ways do you think it should be updated and why?

S.5 Assume that "traditional values and ethics" evolved during a time when life was far different than today: when people had far less choice, when people had their "place in the world" determined for them, and when personal happiness was not a prime criteria for major life decisions. Let us further assume that we are today witnessing a weakening of such "traditional values and ethics" in our society, as individual choice and personal satisfaction play larger roles in life decisions. (You are not being asked whether you like or dislike such changes; just assume that they are occurring "for better or worse.") Finally, assume that there must be some shared system of values and ethics in order for our society to function and flourish. Given these assumptions, what do you think will be the central tenets of a new system of postindustrial values and ethics? In what ways will a new ethical system differ from the old?

S.6 Imagine that new political party has just been formed. Called the "Systems Party," it is based on the proposition that (1) society is a large and extremely complex "interactive system" much like an enormous computer system, and (2) it should be managed as such, with explicit decisions about costs, benefits, optimization targets, performance thresholds, etc. What do you expect the strengths and benefits of this party will be? What will its weaknesses and dangers be?

S.7 In recent years, there has been a sharp upturn in interest and funding for research and implementation in computer graphics, hypermedia, and data visualization. Scientists from across the board are increasingly interested in graphic representations of their data, and computer users are more and more "sold" on graphical user interfaces (such as the MacIntosh and Windows interfaces). This trend is compatible with Marshall McLuhan's 30-year-old claim that the alphabet is becoming an obsolete symbol system, outmoded for effective communication purposes. If McLuhan is right, then perhaps recent declines in reading skills and habits are signs of progress; if he is wrong, then such declines are signs of societal decay. Which do you think is the case?

S.8 Technology of various kinds has served to make many aspects of traditional gender roles obsolete. The stereotype of males as aggressive and females as nurturing is now considered sexist. Are there ways that traditional characterizations might be positive? Do you perceive any ways in which "equality" can in itself be a form of "oppression"?

S.9 List what you perceive as the top three threats to society. For each one, consider whether the issue might be related to a shift from "mechanical" to "electronic" consciousness.

S.10 Consult your own subjective experience of (a) reading books, (b) watching television, and (c) interacting with a computer. Describe the kind of subjective experience each media provides.

S.11 For each of the media listed in Exercise S.10, list three things about the experience of using each one that the others cannot quite provide in the same way. Can you imagine some medium that could indeed provide everything that those three provide without changing the nature of the experience?

S.12 Robert Frost once wrote, "Good fences make good neighbors." In light of the Internet, World Wide Web, and other forms of electronic connections, what kind of fences do you think we might need?

Index

ambiguity, 311
   and inheritance, resolving, 280
   definition of, 298
   errors, 298
analysis of work done, 322–323
AND operator, 77
anonymous data type, 147
arithmetic operators, 60
arrays, 214
   definition of, 197
   iterative traversal, 223
   of arrays, 211–212
   of records, 206–209
   recursive traversal, 222–223
   searching, 200
   searching efficiently, 201–203
   traversal of, 200
   vs. linked lists, 199
   wrap-around with stacks and queues,
      226–227
arrays, 197–203
art, 16
   changes in, 6, 14
   modern, 17
artificial intelligence
   neural networks, 388
   rule-based, 387
assignment
   operator, 58
   statement, definition of, 59
atomic data types, 63–65
   boolean, 65
   characters, 64
   numbers, 64
   pointers, 65, 148–151
atomic variable
   definition of, 57

B

balanced tree
   definition of, 188
Baltimore Orioles, 82
base case
   meaning of, 122
baseball, 82–83
basis of decision, 72
behavior
   conceiving of, 43
behavioral abstraction, 289, 253–291

Big Oh
   keys to finding, 337–338
   notation, 326–328
   polynomial vs. exponential, 342
   reasonable vs. unreasonable, 342
binary numbers, 37
binary search
   of arrays, 201–203
binary search tree
   adding nodes, 189
   definition of, 181
   deleting nodes, 189
   performance with random data, 330
   searching, 187–189
binary tree
   balanced, 188
   definition of, 178
   inorder traversal, 181–186
   postorder traversal, 186–187
   preorder traversal, 186–187
   trace of traversal, 181–186
   traversals, 179–187
binary trees, 177–190, 214
bodies of knowledge, 6, 13
boolean
   operators, 77–78
   data, 65
bounds
   definition of upper and lower, 378
breadth-first
   definition of, 224
breadth-first traversal, 229–231
   implementation of, 231–232
bubblesort, 332–334
   complexity of, 334–336
   parallel version, 362–363
bugs, 298

C

calculator
   vs. computer, 41
calling
   functions, 95
   procedures, 95
car racing, 81–82
certificates, 382–383
   for undecidable problems, 386–387
chaos and strife, 6, 14
characters, 64

incorrect results, 29
infinite loops
    see loop, infinite
information
    definition of, 39
    vs. data, 39
inheritance, 274–280, 291
    extending behavior, 275
    redefining behavior, 276–277
    resolving ambiguity, 280
    summary of, 279
initialization
    of objects, 265
    of variables, 67
inorder traversal
    trace of, 181–186
input
    parameters, 90, 104–106
    parameters, advantages of, 104
    random vs. actual, 323
input/output
    operators, 61
    parameters, 90, 110–111
insertion sort, 235
interface
    definition of, 90
    need for, 90
    of a function, 93
    of a procedure, 92
intractable
    definition of, 380
    vs. NP-complete, 384
    vs. unreasonable, 380
invariants, 305, 311
iteration, 192–197, 215
    definition of, 192
    vs. recursion, 195–197

K

Kepler, Johannes, 10
key field
    definition of, 233
keyword
    definition of, 57, 58
Kleene, Stephen, 394
knowledge
    scientific, 11
Kruskal's algorithm, 293
Kuhn, Thomas, 5, 18

L

language
    for algorithms, 55–84
    programming, 17, 36–37, 55, 56
Leland, Henry, 81
LeMans
    racing at, 82
less than operator, 72
less than or equal to operator, 72
level of abstraction
    algorithmic level, 38
    hardware level, 38
    human user, 37
    translation level, 38
levels of abstraction, 32, 33, 44
    in computers, 37
    using, 35
life span of data, 119
linear
    performance, 346
    structures, traversals of, 222–223
linked list
    building, 168–171
    definition of, 152
    iterative traversal, 222
    recursive search, 165–167
    recursive traversal, 163–165, 222
    structure of, 152
    summary of features, 172
    using pointers to delete values, 171
linked lists, 152–172, 214
    traversing, 162–163
    using pointers to access nodes, 154–158
    using pointers to add nodes, 159–161
    using pointers to delete nodes,
        160–162
    vs. arrays, 199
literals, 68
    definition of, 62
    inappropriate use of, 69
logic error, 311
    avoidance of, 302–304
    definition of, 301
loop, 192–197
    definition of, 192
    infinite see infinite loops
Lowenstein, John, 82
lower bound
    definition of, 378